An Arabian Diary

Introduced and Edited by Robert O. Collins

AN ARABIAN DIARY

Sir Gilbert Falkingham Clayton,

K.C.M.G., K.B.E., C.B., C.M.G.

UNIVERSITY OF CALIFORNIA PRESS
BERKELEY AND LOS ANGELES 1969

University of California
Berkeley and Los Angeles, California
University of California Press, Ltd.
London, England

Library of Congress Catalog Card Number: 73–83211
Designed by Dave Comstock
Printed in the United States of America

to Lady Clayton

Preface

In June 1962 I had the good fortune to return to England after an absence of some five years in order to spend ten months in research on British administration in the Southern Sudan. Having previously carried out historical investigations both in the Southern Sudan and in the archives of the Republic of the Sudan at Khartoum, I was eagerly anticipating examining documents in the various public repositories in Britain and seeking out former British administrators who had served in the Southern Sudan. At the suggestion of Richard Hill, at that time the Keeper and inspiration of the Sudan Archive at the School of Oriental Studies, Durham University, I wrote to Lady Clayton to inquire if her husband, the late Sir Gilbert Clayton, had left any papers relating to his sojourn in the Southern Sudan. Although I knew that Sir Gilbert had later served in important positions throughout the British Middle East, I was concerned at the time simply with his African experience in the Bahr al-Ghazal in 1902 and 1903. Lady Clayton graciously replied that indeed a collection of letters still existed from his tour of duty at Wau in the Southern Sudan, and that I was at liberty to peruse them.

During the ensuing months I returned many times to examine the Clayton papers, for to my astonishment, in addition to the letters from the Southern Sudan, there was a complete and carefully preserved collection of private letters, semiofficial correspondence, official correspondence and numerous government documents, memoranda, and official reports dealing with the Sudan, Egypt, Palestine, Arabia, Trans-Jordan, and 'Iraq. I was particularly attracted to the letters from Sir Reginald Wingate, Governor-General of the Sudan, in reply to Clayton's letters, which are found today among the Wingate collection deposited in the Sudan Archive at Durham. The remaining boxes were filled with an incredible assortment of materials dealing with the Middle East, including the two official reports written by Sir Gilbert concerning his missions to Ibn Sa'ud and the Imam of San'a' respectively which were printed by the Foreign Office for confidential circulation and without which the Diary could not have been adequately edited. Although as a historian of Africa I hesitate to judge, I am of the opinion that no history of Britain in the Middle East or the national questions in Egypt, Palestine, Arabia, or 'Iraq during the critical years between 1914 and 1928 can be adequately studied without reference to the Clayton Papers. I strongly encouraged Lady Clayton and her family to deposit Sir Gilbert's papers for safekeeping and future study in a public repository. I suggested the Sudan Archive at Durham, not only because of Clayton's long association with the Sudan, but because the Clayton Papers formed a perfect complement to those of Sir Reginald Wingate. Lady Clayton enthusiastically endorsed my suggestion, and the papers were duly transferred to Durham in 1963.

During my scrutiny of the Clayton Papers I became increasingly fascinated with Sir Gilbert's personality, character, and work. I was, moreover, encouraged by the warm welcome and interest of Lady Clayton and her sister-in-law, Miss E. M. Clayton. Toward the end of my stay in England Lady Clayton showed me a copy of Sir Gilbert's Diary of his negotiations with Ibn Sa'ud in 1925 and his subsequent visit to the Yemen. I offered to edit the manuscript. Lady Clayton and her family agreed, and upon my return to the United States in the spring of 1963, I set about the task of providing the proper notations and a suitable introduction. Like most scholarly projects, *An Arabian Diary* has taken longer than first anticipated, but after five years of intermittent work, it is finished. I am grateful for the patience of Lady Clayton and her family during these long years.

I have reproduced the Diary as it was written, neither altering Clayton's spelling of proper and place names nor changing or deleting words, phrases, or sentences. Occasionally, I have inserted a clarifying word in brackets or a mark of punctuation to avoid ambiguity.

The Diary remains today in the possession of Lady Clayton and consists of four Palestine government notebooks "manufactured with Glue specially prepared to withstand the ravages of insects." The writing is in Sir Gilbert's elegant hand in either indelible pencil or black ink. Each volume has a printed sticker on the cover labeled "Palestine Government" and a brief note as to its contents.

Sir Gilbert originally partitioned his Diary into four "volumes." For greater clarity and understanding I have reorganized the Diary into two parts consisting of nine chapters. Each part contains an introduction. At the end an epilogue and appendixes have been added. I have included in the biographies (Appendix IX) brief sketches of the participants appearing in the Diary. Those persons who do not have a biographical entry are regrettably those about whom I have been unable to find any further information. I have followed the system used by the United States Board on Geographic Names for the transliteration of Arabic place and personal names, except that I have deleted all diacritical marks except those representing the *ayn* and the *alif*.

I am deeply grateful for the very special help and encouragement of Lady Clayton, Miss E. M. Clayton, and S. W. Clayton without which this edition could not have been undertaken. I particularly wish to acknowledge those whose insights have improved the edition and whose knowledge has prevented egregious errors: D. W. R. Bahlman, Humphrey Bowman, C. E. Fouracres, Sir Laurence Grafftey-Smith, Richard Hill, Khalil G. Helou, J. C. Hurewitz, S. R. Jordan, Majid Khadduri, Sir George Rendel, George Rentz, Franz Rosenthal, Robert Tignor, and Shaykh Hafiz Wahba. Many others have contributed to the completion of this edition with valuable information that could only be supplied by their personal knowledge: Miss K. Acland, Ahmad Safwat Alawa, Mrs. George Antonius, Jean Baillou, Norman Bentwich, Mrs. J. Bolland, S. F. Broome, Campbell, Archbishop in Jerusalem, Giuseppe Cardillo, Sir Nicolas Cheetham, A. L. S. Coltman, C. J. Edmonds, A. J. Farrington, Safiyeh Firouz, Mrs. R. S. Flynn, Charles Gerrard, Mrs. P. L. Gerrard, Major F. S. Greenhouse, Rev. Canon, H. K. Das-Gupta, A. I. M. Hamo, D. K. Haskell, L. A. Halsall, V. J. Heath, Michael Hillary, C. J. H. Hunter, W. H. Ingrams, B. D. O. Jones, D. W.

King, Mrs. W. D. Kenney, J. Kerr, Charles A. Kfouri, Ganeshi Lall, J. F. Madden, Neil G. McNeill, Dr. Ahmad Minai, G. N. Morhig, Ahmad Mourad, J. J. Orchard, Colonel R. H. Penrose-Welsted, Lady Roberts, Fuad Sarruf, Sister Marie Ita of Sion, Mrs. M. M. Stiven, J. F. T. Thomson, Winifred K. Thorne, John Udal, Bertha Spafford Vester, Jonathan Weiss, and Miss Sims Williams. Michael Coray has been of invaluable assistance in the final editing of the manuscript.

I wish to acknowledge the financial grant from the Social Science Research Council of New York which made my sojourn in England possible, and the financial assistance from Williams College and the University of California which enabled me to prepare the Diary for publication.

Santa Barbara, California
September 1968

Contents

Abbreviations

A.D.C.	Aide-de-camp
A.H.Q.	Army Headquarters
B.G.G.S.	Brigadier General, General Staff
C.G.S.	Chief of the General Staff
C.P.	Clayton Papers, School of Oriental Studies, Durham
C.R.A.	Commander, Royal Artillery
D.A.A.	Deputy Assistant Adjutant
D.A.A.G.	Deputy Assistant Adjutant General
D.A.G.	Deputy Adjutant General
D.S.O.	Distinguished Service Order
E.E.F.	Egyptian Expeditionary Force
E.P.	European Personnel
G.O.C.	General Officer Commanding
G.S.O.	General Staff Officer
H.B.M.	His Britannic Majesty
H.M.G.	His Majesty's Government
H.Q.	Headquarters
I.M.S.	Indian Medical Service
M.I.	Military Intelligence
M.P.	Member of Parliament
N.C.O.	Non-commissioned Officer
O.C.	Officer Commanding
P. & O.	Peninsular and Oriental Steam Navigation Company
Q.V.O.	Queen Victoria's Own
R.A.F.	Royal Air Force

R.E.	Royal Engineers
R.I.M.	Royal Indian Marine
R.I.M.S.	Royal Indian Medical Service
R.M.S.	Royal Mail Service
R.N.R.	Royal Naval Reserve
R.N.V.R.	Royal Naval Volunteer Reserve

PART I

Mission to Ibn Sa'ud

Introduction

On a piercing sunlit morning in October 1925 Sir Gilbert Falkingham Clayton set out from the Arab city of Jiddah by car to drive to the camp of 'Abd al-'Aziz ibn Sa'ud, Sultan of Najd and its Dominions, situated in a shallow wadi near the ruined village of Bahra. Clayton was the official representative of the British government sent to negotiate with Ibn Sa'ud. His diplomatic task was to reach agreement with the Sultan of Najd, recognizing the position of the Wahhabis in Arabia, on the one hand, and British imperial interests in the Arabian Peninsula, on the other. Clayton's achievement secured these interests in Arabia which had been threatened by the dramatic rise of the Wahhabis. Ibn Sa'ud's accomplishment at Bahra permitted him to consolidate his dominant position in the peninsula unopposed by Britain. Given the strength of the Wahhabis and their leader, Clayton's concessions were no price at all—thus the significance of his negotiations. Continuity in British policy had been preserved by skillful diplomacy in Arabian politics without compromising British interests or resorting to British arms.

British interests in Arabia and those in the Middle East were fundamentally the same. Clayton himself realized that "the existence of an Arabian policy at all is, I imagine, chiefly due to the necessity of safeguarding imperial communications with the East, as represented by the Suez Canal and the Red Sea from Port Said to Perim."[1] Although referring mainly to the Sinai route to the East, Sir Gilbert might as well have included the more northern route through 'Iraq and the Persian Gulf.

[1] Sir Gilbert Clayton to Sir J. E. Shuckburgh, Assistant Undersecretary of State, Colonial Office, 21 April 1926, C.P.

Since the rise of her Indian and Far Eastern empires, the policy of Britain in the Middle East was primarily designed to control the lines of imperial communications between Europe and the East that were forced by the facts of geography to pass through the Arab corridor. Approximately a thousand miles wide, this corridor is confined in the east by the mountains of Turkey and Persia and closed on the west by the Sahara Desert. Open to the Mediterranean Sea at one end and the Arabian Sea at the other, the corridor includes Egypt, the Fertile Crescent, the Arabian Peninsula, and the two narrow bodies of water which form it, the Red Sea and the Persian Gulf. The special geographical position of the Middle East invested the Arab corridor with an importance out of all proportion to its actual value. This crossing was the vital link between the East and the West, the control of which sustained western domination over eastern principalities.

Once India had become the jewel of the British imperial crown, its defense became a preeminent factor in the minds of the strategists in London. In order to defend India, Great Britain required vital strategic points along all the routes of communication. The Cape Colony was acquired at the end of the Napoleonic wars to dominate the old sea lane to India, and in later years naval stations were established at Gibraltar, Malta, and Cyprus to assure the safety of British communications through the Mediterranean Sea to the East. The occupation of Egypt and later the Sudan combined with British protectorates in Somaliland and Aden to control the Red Sea, while varying degrees of indirect influence were exerted throughout the nineteenth century over Muslim potentates in southern Arabia, the Persian Gulf, and on the shores of the Indian Ocean.

So long as the Middle East routes remained in the hands of powerless states or technologically primitive tribes, there could be no threat from within the Middle East to Britain's imperial position. Prestige, influence, and the occasional gunboat were sufficient to protect it. But simply to be on friendly terms with petty rulers was not enough to prevent foreign powers from encroaching into the Arab corridor. Thus, when a rival power sought to challenge Britain's lifeline through the Middle East, the British employed numerous defensive devices ranging from diplomatic and military

ASIR
SAUDI ARABIA
Qizan
Sa'ada
Marib
Harib
YEMEN
Maidi
Bani Jami
Amran
Beihan Qasab
Kamaran I.
Yeman
Centre Peak
J. Shibam
Wasal
KAW KAB AN
J. Masar
San'a'
Obal
Bajil
Buhah
Manaha (Manakha)
Hodeida
Ma'Bar
MA'BAR PLAIN
W. Sihan
Jabal Dhamar
Muhla
Dhamar
Rada'
Beit Faqih
Sayan
Yerim
Salamah
Sumara Pass
Zabid
J Wa Lan
Al Makhadir
Safwan
Ras Zabid
Udain
Ibb
Sadda
Damt
Jiblah
Sabbe
J. Ba dan
Qa'Taba
Khaukhan
BAYAN
Taiz
Mawiya
Dhala
Mocha
Musaymir
ADEN
Habban
Riyan
Lodar
Lahej
Ahwar
Shaykh Othman
Aden
Perim I.
Ras Marshaq

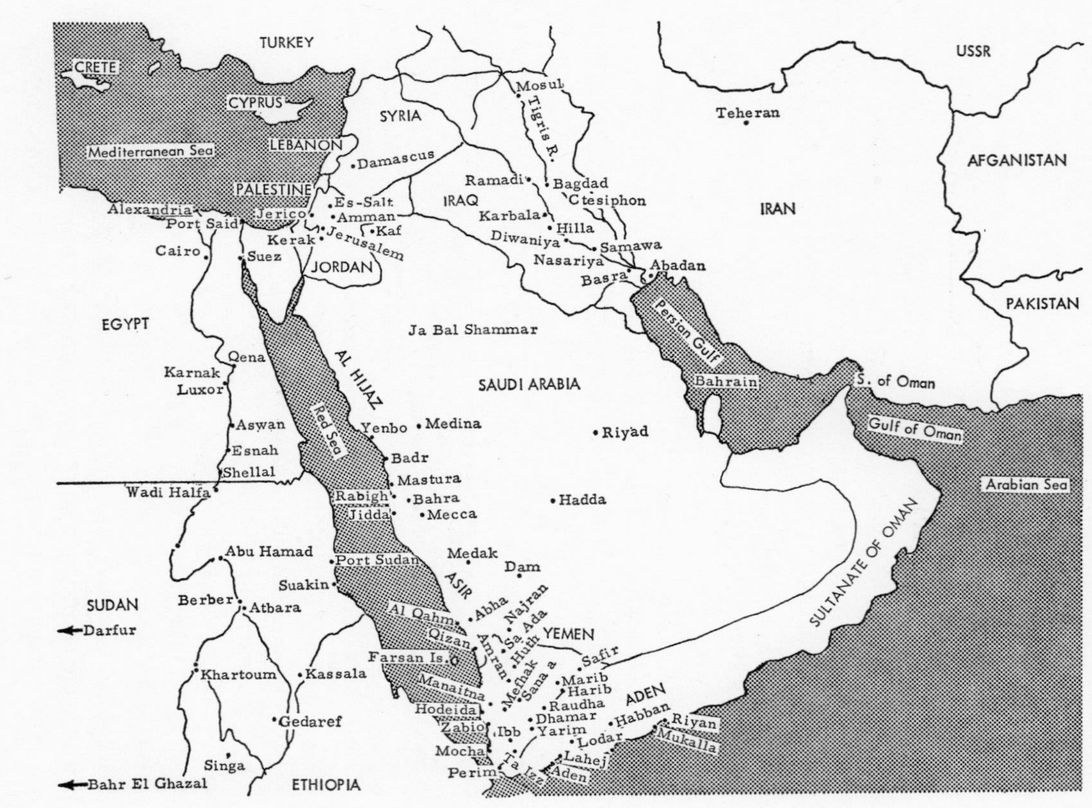
TURKEY
CRETE
CYPRUS
Mediterranean Sea
LEBANON
PALESTINE
SYRIA
Damascus
Alexandria
Port Said
Jerico
Es-Salt
Amman
Kaf
Kerak
Jerusalem
Cairo
Suez
JORDAN
Mosul
Tigris R.
Ramadi
Bagdad
Ctesiphon
IRAQ
Karbala
Hilla
Diwaniya
Samawa
Nasariya
Abadan
Basra
USSR
Teheran
AFGANISTAN
IRAN
PAKISTAN
EGYPT
Qena
Karnak
Luxor
Aswan
Esnah
Shellal
Wadi Halfa
Ja Bal Shammar
AL HIJAZ
Red Sea
Persian Gulf
Bahrain
S. of Oman
Gulf of Oman
Arabian Sea
SAUDI ARABIA
Yenbo
Medina
Riyad
Badr
Mastura
Rabigh
Bahra
Jidda
Mecca
Hadda
Abu Hamad
Port Sudan
Medak
Dam
ASIR
Suakin
SULTANATE OF OMAN
SUDAN
Berber
Atbara
Al Qahm
Abha
Najran
Sa Ada
YEMEN
Darfur
Qizan
Amran
Huth
Safir
Farsan Is.
Khartoum
Kassala
Menak
Sana a
Marib
Harib
ADEN
Manaitna
Raudha
Hodeida
Dhamar
Habban
Riyan
Gedaref
Zabio
Ibb
Yarim
Mukalla
Lodar
Mocha
Lahej
Singa
Ta Izz
Perim
Aden
Bahr El Ghazal
ETHIOPIA

action in Europe to veiled protectorates and outright occupation in the Middle East.

In the nineteenth century Britain had sought to exclude possible competitors by supporting the Ottoman Turks, who ruled many strategic regions throughout the Middle East over which the British had no wish to assume political control. So long as the Turks maintained the integrity of their own empire, there was no need for British intervention to protect the routes to India and the Far East. The friendly Turks did it for them. Even the alternative of an Arab state astride the Middle East heartland was repugnant to British statesmen who assumed that Arab rule was unavoidably marked by chaos, tyranny, and corruption. This view prevailed in Whitehall until Turkey's alliance with Germany in the First World War forced the British to seek alternative solutions. Clearly, if the Ottoman Empire collapsed, Britain would of necessity be the likely heir to her Middle East dominions. If Turkey could not control the land route to India, Great Britain was determined that no other European power should. And if the Arabs were to have self-rule, it would only be if Britain had sufficient influence to prevent corruption and anarchy among them so that the routes to her eastern empire would be secure.

The outbreak of war in 1914 created a major problem for Britain in the Middle East. The need to defend British interests and to gather allies was clearly the principal object at the outset of the war, but this fundamental requirement was hopelessly compromised once Turkey entered on the side of the Central Powers. Certainly, the Victorians had been right when they realized that the safety of the way East depended on the integrity of the Ottoman Empire. Once the Turks declared war, the security of British routes was threatened at innumerable points from Sinai to the Persian Gulf. The Ottoman Empire was no longer a friendly ramshackle buffer. Militarily weak, Turkey was geographically strong, and although the British were confident that the sick man of Europe would ultimately die, the contagion might first spread to weaken Britain's control of the routes to India. To win the war in Europe, Great Britain found it necessary to enter into a series of secret wartime agreements with her European allies by which each claimed what for it were the choice territories of the Ottomans. To win the war in the Middle East Great Britain also reached understandings with the Arabs. Frequently these two sets of arrangements were irreconcilable, creating a network of interlocking and conflicting agreements that resulted in so much contradiction and postwar squabbling that not even the diplomatic genius of its creator could reconcile them.

Shortly after the entrance of Turkey into the war in October 1914, the British began to seek Arab aid mainly for two reasons. First, Arab friendship would help to insure the security of the imperial routes even though the Ottoman government was an enemy. Second, the Arabs controlled the Islamic Holy Cities of Mecca and Medina, and with them as allies Britain could guarantee the safety of the yearly pilgrimage to her Muslim subjects and thereby help to counter the Ottoman Caliph's call to the jihad or holy war. The British had long been aware of discontent among the Ottoman-ruled Arabs and of their growing nationalist societies. These manifestations of an Arab nationalist movement encouraged the British to employ this nationalism to their own advantage, and they decided to channel their support for the Arabs through the Hashimite Sharif of Mecca, Husayn ibn 'Ali.

Since his appointment by the Ottomans in 1908 as the custodian of the Holy Cities, Husayn had displayed a will of his own and a desire for Arab independence. He had informed the British of his revolutionary feelings through his second son, 'Abd Allah, who had journeyed to Cairo in February 1914 to sound out British reaction toward an Arab separatist movement in the Hijaz. With the great prestige derived from his birth as well as his office, Husayn could be used as a counterpoise to the jihad, for the Caliph's call to holy war would be less effective without the endorsement of the Grand Sharif of Mecca. Moreover, Husayn appeared the natural leader to unite the small groups of Arab intellectuals in the cities, who thought of the Arab-speaking countries in terms of nationalist politics, and the virtually independent Arab princes and tribes of the hinterland, who wished to maintain their independence. Strategically, Husayn's position was in the center of Turkish power in the Arabian peninsula. With his tribal contingents he could strike at the heart of Ottoman authority in Arabia and isolate the Turkish garrisons that threatened the British from the Yemen and 'Asir by severing their communications with the north. The loss of the Hijaz would mean that the Turks could not threaten Egypt, the Suez, or the waterway to India.

While clearly recognizing the wartime advantage of an Arab alliance, British officials also foresaw its benefits after the conclusion of peace. They were aware that the defeat of Turkey would spell the collapse of the Ottoman Empire and mean that this traditional ruler would no longer exist to safeguard British imperial routes to the East. A possible alternative was to create a large Arab state or confederation of states friendly to Britain which would assure the safety of British communications and guard against the designs of any other European power. Certainly a friendly Muslim state would solve Britain's diplomatic problem. Both strategically and politically Husayn appeared to be the logical choice to construct such an Arab state, and when the importance of the eastern shore of the Red Sea was fully appreciated after the failure of the Dardanelles campaign, Great Britain was determined to obtain Husayn's cooperation by any means: subsidy, flattery, or visions of an Arab confederation with him at its head. The war had to be won.

On their part the Arab nationalists regarded Britain as their best potential ally in their struggle for independence against the Turks, and, fearful of French designs in Syria, they actively sought British assistance. Although British officials were unable to give any positive assurance at the time of 'Abd Allah's visit to Cairo, Sir Ronald Storrs continued to have a series of friendly conversations with the Hashimites. Meanwhile, Husayn had sent his third son, Faysal, to gain support of the Arab nationalist societies in Syria. In May 1915 Faysal returned with the price of cooperation, the Damascus Protocol. The Damascus Protocol proposed, in effect, an independent Arab state allied to Great Britain by a defense treaty and an economic agreement that gave Britain a privileged position. Having won the support of the Arab societies, Husayn began to dicker in earnest with the British, and in the famous correspondence that followed with the British High Commissioner in Egypt, Sir Henry McMahon, Britain agreed to recognize Arab nationalist territorial claims, guaranteed to protect the Holy Land of Islam against aggression, and promised to advise and assist the new Arab governments.

Although the wording of the arrangement was often vague and ambiguous, the Grand Sharif agreed to revolt on the strength of the McMahon Pledge. On 5 June 1916 he gave the signal for the Arabs to rise in arms against their Ottoman rulers. From that time until the end of the war Husayn's Arab army played an essential role in the Allied campaign in the Middle East. The Arabs conducted successful operations in the Hijaz, aided Allenby's forces in the capture of Damascus, and contributed indirect but equally important assistance to the Allied cause. According to British estimates, the Arab Revolt was responsible for containing 65,000 Turkish troops which would have otherwise been used against Allenby's army. Sharif Husayn had indeed upheld his part of the bargain. Unfortunately, the British equivocated. The McMahon Pledge had been motivated by British self-interest, and it soon proved impossible to reconcile that interest with the promises to the Arabs, let alone conflicting commitments made to others.

Before the end of the war the British had promised, not once but twice, the land already pledged to the Arabs. In May 1916 the Sykes-Picot Agreement divided the Middle East between Britain and France. In the following year the British sought to win the support of Jewish communities throughout the world by issuing the Balfour Declaration in which His Majesty's government viewed with favor the establishment in Palestine of a national home for the Jewish people. It would be possible to dwell endlessly on the subject of Britain's conflicting wartime commitments, but one thing upon which all are agreed is their imprecise and murky character. At best it could be argued that the letter of the agreements did not preclude partial satisfaction to all parties, but the interests that these pledges served were completely contradictory. The McMahon promises were addressed to Arab nationalism and expressed sympathy with the ideal of a nation that would embrace, with varying political ties, all the Arab peoples of the Middle East; while at the same time the Balfour Declaration was designed to court Hebrew nationalism, to pledge British support for the idea of a Jewish Palestine in which Arab rights would be recognized in the context of Hebraic culture. Overlaying these promises and in conflict with them was the Sykes-

Picot Agreement based on French and British imperial strategy. From the British point of view all three major agreements had been justified by imperial needs, but since the terms of the agreements were opposed and basically irreconcilable, the resulting problems encountered in the postwar settlement should have surprised no one. At the San Remo Conference of 1920 the Supreme Council of the League of Nations divided the Middle East into mandates that were assigned to Britain and France, corresponding in general to the terms of the Sykes-Picot Agreement. Britain's imperial interests were protected, and both mandatory powers moved quickly to assert their authority. As for the Arabs, only the Hijaz was given its independence with Husayn as its king, and the vision of a united independent Arab state vanished like a desert mirage.

The Arabs were disillusioned and bitter at the postwar settlement. Broken promises and empty pledges were all that remained of the heady hopes for a unified, independent Arab state. Sullen resentment followed betrayal, and reaction soon followed resentment. In 1920 unrest and rebellions erupted against the British in 'Iraq, Syria, and Palestine which were only put down after heavy loss of life and tremendous expenditure. With the assistance of France, Great Britain had succeeded in imposing the decisions of the Peace Conference on the Arabs by force. But force was a temporary expedient. It solved nothing, and independence appeared the only answer to halt insurrection. The time had come for Britain to formulate a long-range policy for her Middle East territories "which would be less costly and more subtle than military occupation and which, in the long run, would correspond to the vital requirements of British political strategy in the East."[2]

To devise just such a policy a Middle East Department was created within the Colonial Office to replace the previous cumbersome bureaucratic structure whereby different departments of the government had dealt with the different areas conquered and occupied during the war. Next a conference was called by the Colonial Secretary, Winston Churchill, to meet in Cairo in March 1921 to

[2] George Lenczowski, *The Middle East in World Affairs* (Ithaca, 1956), p. 96.

revise the previous arrangements for the Middle East "with a view to diminishing at the earliest possible moment the burden incurred by the British taxpayer, as well as to decide on broad issues of policy."[3] Presided over by Churchill and attended by a galaxy of Britain's foremost Arab experts and advisers, the Cairo Conference established a new order in the Middle East by creating nominally independent Arab territories without abandoning Britain's special interests. The settlement, perhaps to atone for broken promises, particularly rewarded the Hashimite family for its loyalty to Britain. The Amir Faysal was, in effect, offered the kingship of 'Iraq, which he accepted and for which he later received an overwhelming vote of confidence from the inhabitants. 'Abd Allah, Husayn's second son, was offered the Amirate of Trans-Jordan, largely as a bribe to keep him from carrying out his embarrassing threats to attack the French in Syria.

Territorially the British solutions at Cairo were exceedingly successful. Two Arab kingdoms had been created virtually dependent on British guidance and yet ostensibly independent. 'Iraq still controlled the Euphrates Valley and the Persian Gulf; Trans-Jordan dominated the road from the Mediterranean to Mesopotamia. "Thus, by 1921 the foundations for the new order in the Arab Middle East were laid. Despite the Wilsonian ideology of self-determination and despite American intervention in Paris, the new peace was imperialistic in character and corresponded in the main to the major wartime agreements."[4] New ways had been fashioned with which to control the way East. The British had first acted as a mandatory power over the strategic states; and then when direct administration failed to provide peace and stability, British officials sought by indirect means and the judicious use of "advisers" to maintain friendly influence over nominally independent kingdoms. As before the upheavals of the First World War, the Middle East was again peaceful and well disposed toward Britain. No other power, it seemed, could easily challenge such a predominant position or threaten the vital lifeline eastward.

[3] *Report on 'Iraq Administration, October 1920–March 1922* (London, 1923), p. 10.

[4] Lenczowski, *The Middle East in World Affairs*, p. 97.

Unknown to British diplomats at the Cairo Conference, however, only a few years were to pass before British imperial interests in the Middle East were once more in jeopardy. The threat did not come from without, as British statesmen had suspected and had taken steps to prevent, but from within. It was carried out by the fierce Wahhabi warriors of central Arabia and led by a man who had been hitherto regarded by British officials as little more than a petty tribal shaykh, 'Abd al-'Aziz ibn Sa'ud. Ibn Sa'ud was the head of the House of Sa'ud of Najd and a long-time bitter rival of Sharif Husayn of Mecca, head of the House of Hashime. When his troops shattered the army of Husayn in 1924, the British suddenly discovered that they must rapidly readjust their policy toward Ibn Sa'ud in order to preserve British influence in Arabia and to consolidate British power in the mandates on the Arabian frontier. This was the task of Sir Gilbert Clayton at Bahra.

In their attitudes toward Arabia British officials had been almost as divided as the Arabs, split into two opposing schools of imperial thought. On the one hand Anglo-Egyptian officials saw British interests in the Middle East best advanced through Husayn in western Arabia, while on the other the Anglo-Indian administrators saw the advantages of supporting Ibn Sa'ud in central Arabia. For a long time the two groups maneuvered for control of British policy in the Middle East under the paternal but frequently muddled guidance of the government at Westminister. This dichotomy in British policy had its origin in geography. The Ottoman Empire had been divided by the Great Syrian desert into two distinct regions: the western region stretching from Asia Minor through Syria, Palestine, the Hijaz, and the Yemen; and the eastern region extending from Kurdistan through Mesopotamia to Kuwait and the Persian Gulf. Ottoman sovereignty was uncertain farther south over the principalities of the Persian Gulf and the states of southern Arabia. These, within the British scheme of things, were the concern of the government of India, which possessed its own historic political and diplomatic ties with these shaykhdoms quite separate from the complex but equally traditional diplomatic establishment regulating general British relations with the Ottoman Empire. The government of India looked upon the Arabian Peninsula as its special province. Delhi, not London, managed the politics of Aden, its hinterland, and the area of the Persian Gulf, and its British officials pondered how to maintain good relations with the shaykhdoms of the Persian Gulf, prevent foreign encroachment into southern Mesopotamia, and defend the strategic overland route to the East.[5]

In contrast the Anglo-Egyptian school conducted operations from Cairo, the object of which was to turn the Red Sea into an Egyptian lake while at the same time extending Egyptian and British ascendancy northward through the Levant. In this way Islam's most sacred places–Mecca, Medina, and Jerusalem–would come under British influence. Certainly British officials in Egypt shared the concern of their Indian colleagues about imperial communications, but they placed higher priority on the maritime passage to the Indian Ocean than the overland route to the Persian Gulf. "It was hardly surprising," wrote Sir George Rendel, "that we should therefore find ourselves with one policy toward the Hashimite rulers of the Hijaz in Western Arabia, another toward the Saudis of Nejd in the east."[6] So long as the desert separated Hashimite from Sa'udi and the Gulf States from the Hijaz, the ambivalence of British policy was never contradictory but in fact logical and practical. Once, however, Ibn Sa'ud sought to add the Hijaz in the west to Najd and his possessions in the east, the Egyptian and Indian attitudes of British officials came into conflict, since their respective interests were linked to the irreconcilable pretensions of the two rival Arabian dynasties.

As Arab nationalism blossomed from the dismembered body of the Ottoman Empire, these two Arab leaders competed for the mastery of Arabia under the aegis of the British government. During the war the traditional hostility of the Hashimite and Sa'udi dynasties had been diverted by British gold and diplomacy toward the common cause against the Turk, but no sooner had the war ended than their mutual jealousy ripened into suspicion and hatred.

[5] Hans Kohn, *A History of Nationalism in the East* (New York, 1929), pp. 279–280, and Sir George Rendel, *The Sword and the Olive: Recollections of Diplomacy and the Foreign Service, 1913–1954* (London, 1957), p. 57.

[6] Rendel, p. 57.

> It is unfortunate that the rivals never met. At least King Hussein would have understood that here was a man not to be trifled with, and might have refrained from the provocation which caused his downfall. Hussein was small and dapper: he wore the garb of the Mecca townsman—a long black coat, and a fez-shaped headdress with a white turban wound round it. Like many Arab townsmen he looked down on tribal people. Ibn Saud, some thirty years younger, was a foot taller, and very broad and powerful; he dressed as a desert shaikh and bore the scars of many a desert battle. He had not lived in a capital, as Hussein had lived in Istanbul, but his manners were equal to any situation; and in talk he could have completely overthrown Hussein in politics and probably equalled him in theology, which occupied much of his reading and conversation.[7]

Since British policy, until the early twenties, was dominated by British officials in Egypt, British support was principally directed to Sharif Husayn of the Hijaz in western Arabia. Ibn Sa'ud in his lands to the east was considered a petty ruler to be dealt with like the shaykhs of Kuwait and Bahrain—not like the King of the Arabs who had sired the rulers of 'Iraq and Trans-Jordan and who controlled the Holy Cities of Islam. But by 1925 this fiction could no longer be maintained, and Britain was forced to come to terms with the man who had fashioned an Arabian kingdom from the sands and stones of the desert. He had defeated his rivals and had welded together the independent bedouin tribes of Arabia with himself as their absolute ruler. In 1925 he stood in the center of the Arabian Peninsula, threatening Britain's strategic interests on the periphery from Sinai to the Persian Gulf.

Known to the Arabs simply as 'Abd al-'Aziz, "Servant of the Mighty," Ibn Sa'ud was born probably in November or December 1880 in the palace at Riyadh. His father, 'Abd ar-Rahman, Sultan of Najd, was descended from Muhammad ibn Sa'ud, the founder of the dynasty, who as a petty baron had sheltered and supported the great Islamic reformer, Muhammad ibn 'Abd al-Wahhab. The rise of the House of Sa'ud in the eighteenth century coincided with

[7] Sir Reader Bullard, *The Camels Must Go, An Autobiography* (London, 1961), p. 137.

the emergence of Wahhabism, and the Sa'udis sustained it. The Wahhabi call for return to primitive, puritanical Islam captured the allegiance of many desert tribes. Although the Sa'udi armies were temporarily defeated by the Egyptian forces of Muhammad 'Ali in 1818, the second Sa'udi state was founded soon thereafter by Turki ibn Sa'ud, who led rebellions against the Turkish-Egyptian garrisons in Najd and established his capital at Riyadh. The Sa'udi state maintained its independence from Ottoman control under Turki's successor, Faysal, the most adroit of Ibn Sa'ud's forebears.

The British, of course, were little concerned with Muslim rivalries in the deserts of the Arabian Peninsula, but Wahhabi activities along the coast of the Persian Gulf and in the Trucial States, as well as in 'Uman and Muscat, soon involved British interests. In 1851 and again in 1859 a British naval force had to intervene at Bahrain to prevent its seizure by the Wahhabis, but not until 1865, when Colonel Lewis Pelly led a small mission to Riyadh, did the British government officially open relations with the House of Sa'ud. An Anglo-Arab treaty was subsequently concluded in which the Sa'udi ruler agreed not to oppose or to injure British subjects residing in his territories nor to attack the territories of those Arab tribes having treaty relations with the British government.[8] As Her Majesty's Political Resident in the Persian Gulf, Pelly was responsible for the conduct of British relations with Najd, but the Sa'udi regime with which he had dealt soon precipitously declined. After the death of Faysal, the House of Rashid at Ha'il rose to challenge Sa'udi supremacy in central Arabia. Moreover, Faysal's two sons 'Abd Allah and Sa'ud fought over the succession and in the struggle only managed to lose Najd to their Rashidi rivals from the north. Faysal's youngest son, 'Abd ar-Rahman, made some efforts to regain the family position and power after the death of his two brothers, but he was unsuccessful and ultimately went into exile with his family. His son 'Abd al-'Aziz went with him.

'Abd ar-Rahman's ambition was to reestablish the Sa'udi kingdom

[8] M. V. Seton-Watson, *Britain and the Arab States* (London, 1948), pp. 181–82. See also L. Pelly, *Report on a Journey to the Wahabee Capital of Riyadh in Central Arabia* (Bombay, 1866).

Sir Gilbert Falkingham Clayton

King ‘Abd al-‘Aziz ibn ‘Abd ar-Rahman ibn Faysal ibn Sa‘ud

and to spread the Wahhabi faith throughout Arabia. He lived first among the 'Ajman tribes and then among the Murrah before he was invited in 1891 to reside in Kuwait. While in the desert he taught his son fighting skills as well as the elements of his religious belief. In Kuwait young Ibn Sa'ud developed his intellectual faculties and learned more about the British from his political mentor Mubarak as-Sabah, Shaykh of Kuwait, who had accepted British protection in 1899. "It was undoubtedly at this period that the young Abdul-Aziz developed a boyish admiration for British imperialism, which accompanied him through life, modified only by the proviso that it should not impinge upon his own sphere of activity."[9]

In 1897 news reached Kuwait that Muhammad ibn Rashid had died. 'Abd ar-Rahman decided that his opportunity had come to overthrow Rashidi power in Najd and recover Riyadh. In 1900 the combined forces of the House of Sa'ud and Kuwait marched against the Rashids but were disastrously defeated on the battlefield at As-Sarif near Buraydah in February 1901. Ibn Sa'ud, who had been investing Riyadh, was bitterly disappointed after being compelled to withdraw to Kuwait so as not to be cut off by the victorious Rashidi forces. Encouraged by the Germans who wished to counter British influence, the Rashids responded by attacking Kuwait, but the campaign proved indecisive and Ibn Rashid withdrew to Ha'il. Neither 'Abd ar-Rahman nor Mubarak had any inclination to take the offensive again after their stunning defeat at As-Sarif, but they could not restrain the young Ibn Sa'ud. Gathering some forty family retainers, he rode into the desert to assault Riyadh. After a night of hiding in the walls of the city, Ibn Sa'ud and his men captured the fortress with startling precision on 15 January 1902. The inhabitants flocked to the victorious standard of the House of Sa'ud, and the first step in the reconquest of Najd was complete. Ibn Sa'ud proclaimed his father Imam of the Wahhabis but retained all political control in his own hands. During the following six years he proceeded to expand the sphere of Sa'udi control. They were wild times of intrigue, maneuver, and fighting in the oases of the desert

[9] H. St. John B. Philby, *Arabian Jubilee* (London, 1952), p. 6.

which Ibn Sa'ud always considered the finest of his life. Supported by a Turkish contingent and supplies, the Rashidi forces attempted to recapture Riyadh, but Ibn Sa'ud's warriors scattered them in a series of battles and the Turks withdrew. Left to themselves the Shammar forces of Ibn Rashid were no match for those of the House of Sa'ud. In April 1906 on the plains of Al-Muhannah the Rashidi leader, 'Abd al-'Aziz ibn Rashid, was killed and his army routed. Ibn Sa'ud was master of eastern Arabia.

During this same period Ibn Sa'ud sought to consolidate his state internally by associating himself with the Ikhwan, a religious movement which he adopted as public policy and of which he later assumed the spiritual leadership. Begun by a group of Harb and Mutayr bedouins who sought the way to God by establishing a religious fraternity centered around a hermit cantonment inhabited by true believers, the Ikhwan ("Brothers") were, in a way, a revival of Wahhabism in its purest sense. The movement channeled the warlike energies and divisive propensities of the Arabs into settled communities concerned with the search for the afterlife. Ibn Sa'ud, himself a devout Wahhabi, saw in the Ikhwan brotherhood not only the revival of Wahhabism, but also the means to increase his own authority by utilizing the Ikhwan to weld together many disruptive and hostile elements that had long existed in Najd. The settlement of the bedouin on the land and the agrarian revolution that it entailed created a new and different type of existence for the inhabitants of Najd which ran counter to their deepest traditions. Religion counteracted the individualism of clan and tribe, for tribal loyalty should only follow faith in God and obedience to the ruler. Ibn Sa'ud's intention was "to give a common direction to the warlike instinct of the Arabs and bring them to consider themselves as members of a single body. This will bring them possibilities of expansion which they do not even suspect."[10]

While consolidating his supremacy in Najd, Ibn Sa'ud began his long and bitter rivalry with Husayn ibn 'Ali. In 1908 he learned of the appointment of Husayn as Sharif of Mecca. Husayn immediately began to assert his authority throughout the Hijaz, including

[10] Jacques Benoist-Mechin, *Arabian Destiny* (London, 1957), p. 118.

the 'Utaybah tribes on its eastern fringe whom Ibn Sa'ud considered to be under his authority. But control of the 'Utaybah tribes involved more than just suzerainty over its wild inhabitants. The 'Utaybah highlands are the key to the eastern Hijaz, for they lie astride the caravan routes from Najd to Mecca. At the time the two Arab leaders succeeded in temporarily burying this explosive issue, but as with most disputes in central Arabia the settlement was regarded by neither side as permanent, and the 'Utaybah remained a bone of contention between them. At the same time Ibn Sa'ud's old enemies continued to scheme against him. The Young Turks sought to revitalize the Ottoman Empire and its influence in Arabia. The Rashidi family intrigued to reassert their former position. The Germans hoped for an opportunity to seize a Persian Gulf port. And even Mubarak, the Shaykh of Kuwait, was filled with envy over the success of his protégé.

Great Britain continued to remain aloof, ignoring events in eastern Arabia, and even the appearance in 1911 of Captain W. H. I. Shakespear of the Indian Civil Service in Najd and his subsequent discussions with Ibn Sa'ud did not alter British indifference to the interior of the Arabian Peninsula. Ibn Sa'ud pressed Shakespear to urge the British government to abandon its apathy toward his kingdom, and he frankly sought British support to offset Turkish encroachment in Al-Ahsa' Province which separated Najd from the Persian Gulf. In return Ibn Sa'ud offered to recognize a British resident at one of the gulf ports and to encourage British trade with the interior of Arabia. Shakespear and the British resident in the Persian Gulf, Sir Percy Cox, urged the Foreign Office to follow up Ibn Sa'ud's overtures, but Whitehall knew little of Arabia and cared less. The British government studiously continued to refrain from any involvement in activities irrelevant to its imperial interests.

Left to his own devices, Ibn Sa'ud continued to consolidate and expand his domain. In 1913 when the Turks were defeated in Tripoli, he seized the opportunity to drive them from Al-Ahsa' Province, thus gaining control of the eastern shore of the Persian Gulf to the frontier of Kuwait. He had thrown the Turks out of eastern Arabia, and he had done it without British aid or support while acquiring nearly 800 miles of shoreline and an outlet to the sea for his dominions. Although a remarkable triumph, the conquest of Al-Ahsa' now made him an important factor in British imperial calculations on the Persian Gulf littoral where the various Arab rulers had long ago allied themselves with Britain and accepted her protection. Moreover, Ibn Sa'ud was by no means confident that he could hold the province against a determined Turkish attempt to retake it, and he suspected that the Ottoman government was only waiting for a favorable opportunity to crush him as they had crushed his forebears a century before. He therefore turned once again to Great Britain but once again was rebuffed. Despite growing disenchantment with the Ottoman government, Britain remained sufficiently committed to Turkey that it did not wish to jeopardize Anglo-Turkish relations by supporting Ibn Sa'ud. Only a great war, not a desert shaykh, could break the traditional and historic ties between London and Constantinople.

Thus when Captain Shakespear passed through Riyadh at the end of 1913 on his way across Arabia, Ibn Sa'ud pressed him for an arrangement with Britain. "Shakespear was unable to commit himself," for at that very time the British government was claim-jumping in the dominions of Ibn Sa'ud.[11] In July 1913 Great Britain and the Turkish government had signed a convention settling the position of their respective spheres along the Persian Gulf littoral. The agreement was the result of negotiations begun in 1911 when Turkey was under pressure from the Italians in North Africa and had included discussions over the Baghdad Railway and Turkish customs duties, issues which were never brought to a satisfactory conclusion and ultimately prevented ratification of the Persian Gulf Convention. But the discussions did not end there. Both Britain and Turkey envisaged a much broader settlement to include the delimitation of the boundary between Aden and the Turkish province of Yemen to which was added a line running from Lakmat al-Shu'ub northeastward across the Empty Quarter to the 20° north latitude, and proceeding along the parallel to its juncture with the north-south line of demarcation agreed upon in the unratified Persian Gulf convention of 1913. The Anglo-Turkish convention of 1914

[11] Philby, *Arabian Jubilee*, pp. 35–36.

was signed in March and subsequently ratified in June; by it vast areas of southern Arabia were "gaily signed away to the British Empire by the envoy of a government which at no time had, nor ever would have, shown its nose in any part of the territory concerned."[12] All the territory west and north of the line was to be within the Turkish sphere. Soon after the signing of the second treaty, Colonel W. G. Grey, Shakespear's successor at Kuwait, informed Ibn Sa'ud that the British government could not assist him in his struggle with the Turks since it had already concluded a comprehensive treaty with the Turkish government dealing with Arabia.

Opportunism is a fickle master. Within a few short months the British government was soliciting not the Turk but Ibn Sa'ud. When the Ottoman Empire slipped into alliance with Germany, the British found themselves in an awkward relationship to the Sultan of Najd. Ibn Sa'ud and his Wahhabi warriors would be a great asset to either side should war between Britain and Turkey break out in the Middle East. As an ally Ibn Sa'ud could attack from central Arabia west toward the Hijaz and the Red Sea, or north into Syria across the Turkish line of advance into Egypt. As an enemy he could threaten the British position in the Persian Gulf and advance against the western flank of the British expeditionary force in Mesopotamia. Thus after the British landings at Al Faw, Sir Percy Cox, the Chief Political Officer to the Mesopotamian Expeditionary Force, sent Captain Shakespear again to Ibn Sa'ud to seek, at best, an alliance, at worst, friendly neutrality.

Shakespear had never lost the personal friendship of the Sultan of Najd, despite Britain's past lack of interest in his fate. He had military experience and a political flair for dealing with the Arabs that only a few, like Clayton and Cox, have ever equaled. Just before Turkey entered the war in October 1914, Shakespear and Ibn Sa'ud met at Khufaysah, the Wahhabi war camp. Even before Shakespear had arrived, the British government had offered Ibn

[12] Philby, *Arabian Jubilee*, p. 36; and "The Islamic World Since the Peace Settlement" in *Survey of International Affairs 1925*, ed. by Arnold J. Toynbee, Royal Institute of International Affairs (Oxford, 1927), vol. i, p. 282.

Sa'ud full British recognition of his position in Najd and Al-Ahsa' and a guarantee of protection against Turkish attack by land or sea if he would commit himself to the Allied cause. It was now the turn of Ibn Sa'ud to play the waiting game. Although he had rejected Turkish overtures in order to settle accounts with his old enemy, Ibn Rashid, who had declared himself with the Turks, Ibn Sa'ud did not immediately rush into the British camp. He wisely insisted that any assurances Great Britain might offer him must be embodied in a formal treaty, and Shakespear duly drafted provisional terms. Great Britain was to recognize and guarantee his complete independence while Ibn Sa'ud was to refrain from all dealings with other powers without reference to British authorities. Other clauses dealt with financial and military assistance that Great Britain would be expected to provide for operations against their mutual enemy, Ibn Rashid. Shakespear's report of these negotiations was sent to London, while he himself remained with Ibn Sa'ud to await a reply. Such were the first steps taken to bring the Sultan of Najd into the war on the side of the Allies. They were never brought to fruition —to the frustration of Ibn Sa'ud and the loss of his potential military support—for as events unfolded in 1915 and 1916 the efforts of the government of India to bring the Wahhabis into the war were steadily subordinated to the demands of the Egyptian government, which relegated Ibn Sa'ud to a minor role in any military or political operations against the Turkish forces.

Shakespear's discussions at Khufaysah were not confined merely to an Anglo-Arabian alliance. His most significant achievement was to urge Ibn Sa'ud to resist the call to the jihad which the Sublime Porte had issued to all Muslims after Turkey had entered the war. The Sultan of Najd himself had refused to proclaim the jihad in his dominions because of his hostility toward Ibn Rashid, but Sharif Husayn in the Hijaz was not so determined and consulted Ibn Sa'ud, who in turn discussed the matter with Shakespear on 17 January 1915. Shakespear's influence appears to have been decisive, and Ibn Sa'ud counseled the ruler of the Holy Cities against declaring holy war. A week later Shakespear was killed while participating in a Sa'udi attack against the Rashids at Jirab. Ibn Sa'ud deeply mourned the loss of this courageous soldier whom he regarded as a friend.

The death of Shakespear was indeed a misfortune—a disaster for Ibn Sa'ud and a defeat for Britain. No more influential liaison agent was ever found to replace Shakespear, not even H. St. John B. Philby, and Ibn Sa'ud quietly withdrew his army, confining himself during the rest of the war to occasional skirmishes and infrequent raids. Moreover, after Jirab he abandoned all attempts to support the Allied campaign against the Turks, virtually regarding the Great War at an end. His potential strength was written off in Cairo where plans for Arab cooperation shifted from eastern Arabia to the Hijaz, from the sphere of the Indian government to that of Egypt and the British officials who controlled it. Ibn Sa'ud missed his chance at Jirab to lead the Arabs in the vanguard of Allied victory. At the same time the government of India abandoned the Arabian adventure. The task of rallying the Arabs against the Turks passed from Delhi to Cairo, from Cox to Clayton and the Arab Bureau. "It was left to Lawrence and the army of the Hijaz to accomplish what in other circumstances—with a little better luck, and a little more imagination on the part of the authorities responsible for the conduct of the Mesopotamian campaign—might have been accomplished by Ibn Sa'ud and Shakespear."[13] The "Red Sea Slant" now pervaded Britain's Middle East policy. Husayn, not his rival, Ibn Sa'ud, was to drive the Turks out of Arabia. Although the support given Husayn during the war was certainly well directed and worth the expense, the British commitment to Husayn inexorably drew the British government into the dynastic struggle between these rival Arabian leaders. British aid to Husayn compromised British influence with Ibn Sa'ud while inflating Husayn's pretensions beyond the patience and toleration of the Sultan of Najd.

Although Ibn Sa'ud officially cast his lot with the British in a treaty of friendship signed at Darin near Al-Qatif in December 1915, his attitude was quickly cooled by Sharif Husayn's proclamation of the Arab Revolt in June 1916. Throughout the Al-Qatif negotiations Sir Percy Cox had remained studiously silent about any plans for an Arab revolt led by the Hashimites. The British now only hoped that if the Sultan of Najd could not be induced to

[13] H. St. John B. Philby, *The Heart of Arabia* (London, 1923), vol. i, p. 386.

launch his Wahhabi warriors against the Turk, perhaps he could at least be kept from sending them against Husayn. Ibn Sa'ud was to remain quiet in the east so that Husayn could wage war in the west. Or, if he became dissatisfied, his antipathy for Husayn was to be diverted by encouraging him to vent his anger on the Shammar forces of Ibn Rashid. Such was the basis of all further British conversations with Ibn Sa'ud during the remainder of the war. But to relegate the proud and forceful ruler of Najd to such a subordinate part in the struggle against the Turk was simply sowing the bad seed from which the bitter fruit of conflict would inevitably blossom. Britain's commitment to Husayn excited his aspirations while stimulating Ibn Sa'ud's resentment, until the hostility between the two Arab leaders could not be overcome without the elimination of one of them.

By the autumn of 1916 Ibn Sa'ud's irritation had soured to outright discontent. British preference for Husayn had deeply wounded his Arab pride. Moreover, not only were the two Arab leaders rivals but, ever since the proclamation of the Arab Revolt, the Sharif had used needlessly offensive and condescending language in his correspondence with Ibn Sa'ud. In October Husayn had declared himself "King of the Arabs," and this, despite assurances by the British, was interpreted by Ibn Sa'ud as a threat to his very independence. He was indignant that a man who had recently been but a Turkish lackey should now call himself "King of the Arabs." He was stung by the size of the British subsidy to Husayn compared to the mere pittance allotted to him. He expected to be treated by Great Britain with political and financial equality, but he found himself subordinated to Husayn in both. Nothing the British could say or do was enough to allay his fears, suspicions, and jealous, sullen rages as he watched the success of the Arab Revolt. As for Husayn, he made no attempt to smooth Ibn Sa'ud's ruffled feelings but rather returned bitterness with vituperation. Ibn Sa'ud was infuriated by the patronizing arrogance of Husayn, but he restrained himself from launching an attack against the Hijaz. Thus throughout the war Ibn Sa'ud remained on the sidelines, rejecting the call of the Arab Revolt, yet bitterly disappointed that he could not have led the Arabs like his rival Husayn.

Only a few British officials from the government of India, such as Sir Percy Cox and H. St. John B. Philby, ever sided with Ibn Sa'ud or appreciated the potential strength of his Wahhabi forces. On an official mission to the Sultan of Najd in November 1917 Philby seems to have been the first to become fully aware of Ibn Sa'ud's implacable hostility toward Sharif Husayn. Moreover, he became convinced that Ibn Sa'ud would win if the two rivals ever came to blows. When he left Riyadh, Philby set out on a personal campaign to obtain British support for the Sultan of Najd, obviously at the expense of the Sharif of Mecca. The only British agent who had firsthand experience with both sides of Arabia, he reported first to India and then to Cairo that Arabia's man of destiny was not Husayn but Ibn Sa'ud. In Cairo, Philby's arguments were opposed by T. E. Lawrence, Husayn's foremost advocate. Lawrence, who was highly respected as an expert on Arab affairs, succeeded in winning the overwhelming support of British officials in Egypt that he was right and Philby was wrong, and as Great Britain approached the task of postwar settlement, these officials still directed her Arab policy. They regarded Ibn Sa'ud as little more than a desert chieftain remotely situated in the center of Arabia far from the strategic peripheral areas where contradictory claims jeopardized British interests. At the Peace Conference the opinions of Philby and other British officials from India favoring Ibn Sa'ud counted for little. T. E. Lawrence was the acknowledged British authority on Arabia, and Lawrence argued persuasively on behalf of Husayn at the expense of the French, the Zionists, and Ibn Sa'ud. Even Lord Curzon, the former Viceroy of India and soon to be British Foreign Secretary, remained under the spell of the Arab Bureau in Cairo whose officials insisted that the spoils of victory should go to those Arabs who had fought successfully on the side of the Allies.

Neither reason nor sympathy prevailed against the Sharifian bias of the Cairo officials, and in the end only Husayn's own diplomatic and military bumbling dispelled the erroneous belief that the future of Arabia lay with him. The very first open clash between Husayn and Ibn Sa'ud became the one that eventually broke the Sharif and forced the British to reappraise their policy toward Arabia. Southeast of Mecca lies the resort town of At-Ta'if. Seventy-five miles to the east of At-Ta'if is Turabah situated at the southern tip of the highlands of Jabal Hadhan. Fifty miles farther north and east lies Al-Khurmah. This territory is the traditional home of the 'Utaybah tribes through which the Sharifian armies marched in 1911–12 in order to assert the authority of the Hijaz government. During this campaign Sa'd, the favorite brother of Ibn Sa'ud who was enlisting recruits in the 'Utaybah country, was taken hostage. In return for the release of Sa'd, Ibn Sa'ud reluctantly agreed to nominal Turkish sovereignty, but he never forgave the Hashimites. Later during the war Husayn raised the issue of control of the 'Utaybah by demanding that Ibn Sa'ud abandon all his claims to jurisdiction over the coveted area. The issue was never satisfactorily resolved from either the point of view of Husayn or of Ibn Sa'ud, but by 1917 the towns had accepted Wahhabism and become more firmly attached to the cause of the House of Sa'ud by the increase in the number of missionaries from Najd and the defection from the Sharifian cause of the amir of Al-Khurmah, Khalid ibn Lu'ayy. Soon both Al-Khurmah and Turabah were in arms against the Hashimites, and in spite of British efforts to discourage the Sharif, Husayn ordered a punitive expedition to restore his control. At first Ibn Lu'ayy successfully held off the Sharifian army, but Husayn was not easily repulsed. Two other attacks followed in 1918, each one larger than the preceding. Caught in a dilemma between rushing to aid his supporters in the 'Utaybah and honoring his pact of friendship with Great Britain not to attack Husayn's forces, Ibn Sa'ud warned Philby, who was then still at his side restraining him, that the next attack would mean war with the Hijaz. Philby was impressed with Ibn Sa'ud's threat, and the British successfully discouraged Husayn from taking further action against Al-Khurmah and Turabah, at least until the termination of the war.

Once the war had ended, however, Husayn announced his intention to reoccupy Al-Khurmah early in 1919 and sought British support for the undertaking. In March, the Foreign Office considered Husayn's request at a special meeting directed by Lord Curzon and attended by many high ranking British civil and military officials from the Middle East. The matter was decided on an assessment of the probable outcome of a conflict between Ibn Sa'ud and Husayn and not on the judicial merits of the case. The decision to support Husayn was concluded on the erroneous assumption that he could defeat Ibn Sa'ud without the involvement of British military forces in the desert. Lord Curzon summed up the prevailing opinion.

> The position is that we have promised both parties to settle this dispute between them. Husain is now pressing for a settlement, as he is entitled to do. The arguments on both sides have been fully considered. . . . There is indeed room for differences of opinion on the merits of the case, but the matter is pressing and it is a question rather of policy than of the merits of the case. Now in all these Arabian problems our policy is a Husain policy, and we need not argue the grounds on which that is based. But it is something more than a question of policy. It is a matter of expediency also. We must be satisfied that our man, if we decide in his favour as we would like to do, will win if it comes to a fight. Otherwise the consequences may be very serious indeed.[14]

The consequences were indeed very serious. Not only had British officials failed to recognize the changing situation in Arabia, but they refused to listen to anyone who had information that ran counter to their established policy. Everyone agreed that the well-trained, well-equipped armies of the Sharif could easily defeat the Wahhabi levies. Husayn was given moral support, and Ibn Sa'ud was advised to give way. Philby had been present at the Curzon conference and in vain had opposed the opinions and decisions of the group. He was right, but he was overruled. Ibn Sa'ud responded to British warnings by attacking Turabah. Advancing by night while the Sharifian army slept without sentries, the Ikhwan forces entered the town as Ibn Sa'ud himself approached with the main body of his army from the east. The army of the Sharif was annihilated. Many were murdered in their sleep, and out of five thousand men only about one hundred survived the dreadful slaughter. Husayn's prestige was shattered. Ibn Sa'ud had demonstrated his military superiority and awakened the British to the rising power of the House of Sa'ud throughout Arabia. The British could do little but recognize Sa'ud's victory and continue to pay his subsidy, relieved

[14] Quoted in H. St. John B. Philby, *Arabian Days* (London, 1948), p. 176.

that he had not moved deeper into the Hashimite Kingdom. On his part Ibn Sa'ud proved his statesmanship by his moderation. Although the Hijaz lay open to his army, he withdrew to Riyadh, leaving troops to protect the towns. He was content to wait and to see events unfold and to try to reach a better understanding with the British. As for Husayn, he now added diplomatic blundering to military defeat. Rather than seek peace with Ibn Sa'ud, he and his family sought to strengthen their ties with Ibn Rashid, a move calculated only to provoke the Sultan of Najd to even more aggressive activity.

While Ibn Sa'ud continued to smolder in the heart of Arabia, the British were diverted from the Sa'udi-Hashimite rivalry by uprisings on the periphery in 'Iraq, Palestine, and Syria. After the rebellions were suppressed in 1920, Sir Percy Cox was sent to 'Iraq as the British High Commissioner. On his way to Baghdad he stopped at Al-'Uqayr to visit Ibn Sa'ud. During the two-day conference Ibn Sa'ud expressed his concern over rumors that Husayn's son Faysal was going to be given the throne of 'Iraq. To extend Hashimite influence into Mesopotamia in the east was clearly not in his best interests. Cox assured the Sultan of Najd that such a move was not part of his program for 'Iraq and that he did not favor any such proposal at the time. Cox was of the Indian school of British Arabian policies, and he was unaware that British officials in Egypt were soon to intervene in Mesopotamia. At the same time Ibn Sa'ud learned from Philby, who had accompanied Cox, of Husayn's designs on the Shammar where the Sharif hoped to use the Rashids as a counterbalance to Wahhabi strength. Such a situation would threaten Najd from the north just as a Hashimite King in 'Iraq would menace Wahhabi lands from the east. To Ibn Sa'ud the intrigues of Husayn and the British manipulations in Mesopotamia appeared to create a crescent of actual or potential enemies from east to west along his northern frontier. After the 'Uquayr meeting he at once began to prepare his defenses, and a Wahhabi expedition was sent to secure the 'Asir highlands to the southwest and the strategic oases fringing them.

When the results of the Cairo Conference of March 1921 were made public and Ibn Sa'ud learned that the British had decided to install Husayn's sons 'Abd Allah and Faysal in Trans-Jordan and 'Iraq respectively, he at once sought to seize the initiative in Arabia by extending his control over Ha'il and the Shammar to prevent them from falling into the Sharifian-British sphere of influence. Again the British officials were surprised by Wahhabi strength, an obtuseness most likely attributed to the obstinacy of Lawrence and his circle who adamantly refused to recognize the power of the Sultan of Najd. "It was quite overlooked that the installation of Abdullah and Feisal as rulers of Trans-Jordan and Iraq would mean that the most powerful prince in Central Arabia, Ibn Saud, who regarded Sherifides as his deadly enemies, was surrounded on all sides by Sherifide kingdoms, and that this must inevitably lead to a life and death struggle."[15]

Although neglected by Britain and opposed to Husayn, Ibn Sa'ud decided that the situation in Arabia favored a Wahhabi attack on Ha'il. The Shammar had possessed no strong leader since the summer of 1920 when Sa'ud ibn Rashid had been assassinated by a cousin. Salim of Kuwait was no longer alive to threaten Ibn Sa'ud from that quarter, and Husayn, finding his resources fully committed in the Hijaz, was unable to send the promised troops to the Rashids. Britain was deeply involved in Palestine, Trans-Jordan, and 'Iraq and had no desire to fight Rashidi battles or to intervene on behalf of Hashimite diplomacy in the Shammar. Moreover, the Shammar tribesmen were already divided by Wahhabi religious propaganda so that many welcomed the arrival of Sa'udi forces. As the full impact of the Cairo Conference became increasingly apparent, Ibn Sa'ud pressed the campaign more vigorously and even assumed personal command of his forces. Ha'il was besieged, and on 2 November 1921 the city capitulated. Ibn Sa'ud himself led his triumphant army through the opened gates, extinguishing after ninety years the Rashidi amirate. The capture of this city was indeed a decisive victory, and British officials of all persuasions at once recognized its importance. Gertrude Bell warned that "Ibn Sa'ud has stepped therewith on to the Syrian and Palestine scene, not to speak of Transjordania and the whole L. of C. [Line of Communica-

[15] Kohn, p. 308.

tion] to the Hejaz."[16] The balance of power in Arabia was rapidly shifting in favor of the House of Sa'ud, which not only threatened the lines of imperial communication, but caused unrest and even fighting along the frontiers of Trans-Jordan and 'Iraq. "The Dhafir and some of the local tribes, profiting by the general unrest, engaged in raids and forays, sometimes on the Akhwan, sometimes on each other . . . while the Akhwan retaliated on their side. Secondly, it started a migration to the Iraq of Shammar tribes fleeing from the forces of Ibn Sa'ud."[17]

The British now recognized, somewhat belatedly, that the Sultan of Najd was the most powerful force in Arabian politics, and one with which it was desirable, if not necessary, to make arrangements for the security of their imperial interests. Four years were to pass, however, before Ibn Sa'ud and the British were even to begin to settle their differences, because the central issue, Sa'udi-Hashimite rivalry, remained unresolved, frustrating as well British attempts to settle the complex frontier questions between Najd on the one hand and 'Iraq, Trans-Jordan, and Kuwait on the other. As the High Commissioner in 'Iraq, Sir Percy Cox sought at once to arrange a treaty between Ibn Sa'ud and King Faysal which would settle the problems arising out of the conquest of Ha'il. Having instructed the Political Agent at Kuwait to congratulate the Sultan of Najd on his victory, Cox proposed an early meeting between the two rulers at which the whole problem of 'Iraqi-Najdi frontiers could be discussed. Ibn Sa'ud suggested that before drawing up a treaty it would be wise to settle the principles on which such an agreement would be based. He disliked, for instance, the European tendency to fix frontiers on geographical rather than tribal lines. In response, Cox suggested as a basis of negotiations that the tribes of the Muntafiq, 'Amarat 'Anazah, and Dhafir should be regarded as coming under 'Iraq's jurisdiction and that the 'Iraqi-Najdi frontier should be determined in accordance with the prescriptive rights to watering places. Ibn Sa'ud tentatively agreed to this proposal.

[16] Gertrude Bell to Colonel F. C. C. Balfour, 17 December 1921, *Gertrude Bell, From Her Personal Papers*, ed. by Elizabeth Burgoyne (London, 1961), vol. ii, p. 254.

[17] *Report on 'Iraq Administration, October 1920–March 1922*, pp. 118–119.

Although such principles appeared straightforward in theory, the whole frontier question in practice was enormously complex, mired by conflicting claims and tribal feuds. Among the 'Anazah tribal sections, for example, the 'Amarat appeared to prefer 'Iraqi jurisdiction, while the more westerly section, the Ruwala, wished to be part of the Wahhabi state. To complicate matters further a section of the Dhafir tribe considered to be in 'Iraq defected to Najd. "From the point of view of Iraq, this defection was serious; for just as the heart of the Hijaz lay open to the Wahhabis after the victory of Khurma in 1919, so the heart of Iraq now lay open to the Wahhabis, should they choose to enter."[18] And Ikhwan raiders did not wait long to choose. On 11 March 1922 they attacked the 'Iraq Camel Corps at Shaqrah, inflicting heavy losses both on the Corps itself and on the defenseless Muntafiq tribesmen camped nearby. Only the conciliatory efforts of both Sir Percy Cox and Ibn Sa'ud prevented this Ikhwan raid from developing into a serious rupture. Cox refrained from pressing Royal Air Force attacks against the Wahhabis and Ibn Sa'ud sought to punish the raiders who had acted without his authority. These conciliatory gestures cleared the way for a meeting between the representatives of Najd and 'Iraq to settle the frontier question.

The major obstacle to a delimitation between 'Iraq and Najd was the bedouin concept of a frontier. Not only was the idea of a fixed boundary alien to the bedouin, but the areas along the proposed frontier were inhabited by migrant tribes who thought in terms of communities in a general sense rather than well-defined territorial units.

> Since time immemorial tribesmen have wandered in the wastes of the [Arabian] peninsula in search of water and grazing grounds. Claims to ownership were usually limited to a coastal town, an oasis, or a water well. The desert in between could be likened to a high sea, to which no one could justify laying exclusive claims of control.[19]

[18] Kenneth Williams, *Ibn Sa'ud, the Puritan King of Arabia* (London, 1933), p. 145.

[19] Lenczowski, *Oil and State in the Middle East* (Ithaca, 1960), p. 137.

Consequently the representative of Najd at first refused to consent to a fixed frontier, but a treaty was agreed to and signed on 5 May 1922 at Al-Muhammarah in which tribal relations between 'Iraq and Najd were supposedly regulated. The Muntafiq, Dhafir, and 'Amarat 'Anazah were considered 'Iraqi tribes, and the Shammar tribes of Ibn Rashid's extinct principality were assigned to Najd. A joint 'Iraqi-Najdi Commission presided over by a British official would decide on wells and ranges used by each tribe. Certain wells and pasture grounds were enumerated as common to the tribes of both countries. On the basis of this information the commission was to determine a fixed frontier.[20] The treaty appeared at first to be a British diplomatic victory, for although no frontier had been fixed, the commission to determine such a frontier had been agreed upon. The British triumph was short-lived, however, for Ibn Sa'ud, reluctant to recognize a definite border in the desert, repudiated the work of his representatives. In the east the Ikhwan again raided into 'Iraq, while in the west Ibn Sa'ud's warriors penetrated northward up the Wadi as-Sirhan into Trans-Jordan.

The long valley of As-Sirhan is the key to communications between Arabia and Syria and an important outlet for Najdi trade. After the conquest of Ha'il, Ibn Sa'ud sought to seize the Wadi as-Sirhan districts that would extend his rule to the limits of the northern desert. The salt villages known as Qurayyat al-Milh and the villages of the Wadi as-Sirhan itself were all held by Nuri Sha'lan, Chief of the Ruwala tribe. He had held them before the war, relinquishing them to the Rashids, and had once again repossessed them after the fall of Ha'il. An old man who appreciated a comfortable, uncomplicated life, Nuri Sha'lan had come to terms with the French and lived in a town house in Damascus. He was willing to reach an agreement with the British as well, especially since his territory was threatened by the Wahhabis, whose propagandists were active there and who claimed the valley region as an integral part of the conquered dominions of the Rashids. The British were prepared to come to Nuri's support in order to keep

[20] For the Treaty of Al Muhammarah see *Report on 'Iraq Administration, April 1922–March 1923*, pp. 183–184.

Ibn Sa'ud out of the strategic valley. Direct relations with Nuri were managed by Philby, now working for the government of Trans-Jordan, where his official position inevitably conflicted with his sympathy for and friendship with Ibn Sa'ud.

> Transjordania implies Mr. Philby, who is now in authority there, so far as anyone is in authority. It's possible that he may espouse the cause of his princeling ['Abd Allah]–though I hear from T. E. Lawrence that he's a "real rotter"–or he may remain staunch to his old devotion to Ibn Sa'ud. Faisal takes a gloomy view; but on the whole I think that as our influence alone can keep Ibn Sa'ud from eating up the Hejaz or even Trans-jordania, it's on the whole an advantage that the British representative there should be on good terms with him.[21]

Nuri had agreed to accept the suzerainty of 'Abd Allah of Trans-Jordan if the latter would defend his outlying territories. The final decision was up to the British authorities and in particular Philby. In the spring of 1922 Philby set out to inspect the Wadi as-Sirhan, including Al-Jawf and Sakaka, with Major A. L. Holt of 'Iraq Railways. British interest in the territory was not completely confined to the support of 'Abd Allah. The prospect of a strategic railway linking Ma'an or 'Aqabah, both admittedly in Hijaz territory, with Baghdad or Al-Basrah, was of primary importance to Britain. Holt's presence on Philby's tour of inspection was justified by the need for a quick survey of the area. Neither a reconnaissance nor a survey were made, however, for just as Philby reached the Wadi as-Sirhan, Wahhabi levies arrived from Shammar. Flushed with the victory at Ha'il the Ikhwan marched up the Wadi and easily established themselves at Sakaka. By the early summer the important trade and caravan center of Al-Jawf had been occupied. At the same time the Ikhwan occupied the oases of Khaybar and Tayma' near the Hijaz border and attacked the Ruwala in the salt villages around Kaf. A reconnaissance expedition even swept north into Trans-Jordan proper in August, destroying Zuwayza and advancing within fifteen miles of 'Amman, the capital, before the raiders

[21] Gertrude Bell to Colonel F. C. C. Balfour, 17 December 1921; E. Burgoyne, *Gertrude Bell*, vol. ii, p. 254.

were cut down by British armored cars from the garrison and airplanes from the Royal Air Force station at Jerusalem. Only eight Ikhwan survived to return to Najd, and their welcome was anything but cordial. Realizing that the British could easily win if these raids into Trans-Jordan and 'Iraq erupted into open war between Britain and Najd, Ibn Sa'ud punished the returning raiders and agreed to resume the suspended negotiations over the 'Iraq frontier begun at Al-Muhammarah. His position was strong. He controlled all the desert oases of Arabia from the Fertile Crescent in the north to the Empty Quarter in the south, while from his position in the Wadi as-Sirhan he could threaten Trans-Jordan, Palestine, or Syria.

The conference assembled at Al-'Uqayr late in November 1922. With Cox was Sabih Bey and his staff representing 'Iraq, and Major J. C. More, the Political Agent at Kuwait, representing its ruler. Awaiting them was Ibn Sa'ud with a large entourage, including his personal bodyguard of 300 men. The negotiations soon developed into a contest between Sabih Bey and Ibn Sa'ud with Cox acting as referee. Although he was nominally on friendly terms with Great Britain, Ibn Sa'ud felt confined on all sides by hostile puppet states that Britain had created. His real sympathies were with his own people who wanted to drive Husayn from the Hijaz and overrun Trans-Jordan, 'Iraq, and Kuwait, but he was a realistic man with enormous sense who knew he could not in the end successfully defy Britain. Nevertheless at Al-'Uqayr he fought hard for a tribal boundary instead of the traditional fixed frontier. A hard line on a map was to him and his people unreal in the desert, and he felt that his tribesmen would not recognize it. Ibn Sa'ud further realized that to accept a fixed frontier would be tantamount to accepting the ring of new states ruled by his enemies. For the first few days no compromise was possible as each side put forth ridiculous demands obscured by Oriental rhetoric. On the sixth day Cox had a private meeting with Ibn Sa'ud.

> He [Cox] lost all patience over what he called the childish attitude of Ibn Sa'ud in his tribal-boundary idea. Sir Percy's Arabic was not too good, so I [H. R. P. Dickson] did the translating. It was astonishing to see the Sultan of Najd being reprimanded like a naughty schoolboy by H. M. High Commissioner, and being

> told sharply that he, Sir Percy Cox, would decide on the type and general line of the frontier. This ended the *impasse*. Ibn Sa'ud almost broke down, and pathetically remarked that Sir Percy was his father and mother, who had made him and raised him from nothing to the position which he held, and that he would surrender half his kingdom, nay the whole, if Sir Percy ordered.[22]

From that moment, Cox determined the frontiers, drawing the boundary on a map with a large red pencil. The territorial agreements which embodied his decisions were signed on 2 December 1922 and were known as the Protocols of Al-'Uqayr to be read with the Treaty of Al-Muhammarah. The first protocol defined the 'Iraqi-Najdi frontier, which started from the western edge of the Batin, at a point about 125 miles south-southwest of Al-Basrah as the crow flies, and ran in a northwesterly and westerly direction to the Jabal 'Unazah, the center point of the Shamiyah plateau, which was defined as the neighborhood of the intersection of latitude 32° north with longitude 39° east. A rhomboid territory at the southeastern extremity of the border which fell within the range of the Dhafir was declared neutral and common ground. In other articles, Najd tribes living near the border were given license to water at the neighboring 'Iraq wells, provided these were nearer to them than those within the Najd boundaries. The two governments mutually agreed not to fortify watering places adjoining the border and not to concentrate troops in their neighborhood. Special arrangements were made to ease the burden of customs and tolls in trade between the two states. As a result of these territorial arrangements, a good deal of territory claimed by Najd was handed to 'Iraq. Kuwait paid the bill.

The boundary between Najd and Kuwait began at the eastern edge of the Wadi al-Batin, at a point immediately opposite the starting point of the 'Iraqi-Najdi frontier, and ran in a direction slightly south of east until it struck latitude 29° north at a point about forty-five miles southwest of the town of Kuwait. From there the frontier was in the form of a circumference of a circle with its center in the town of Kuwait and a radius of about forty miles until it struck the

[22] H. R. P. Dickson, *Kuwait and Her Neighbours* (London, 1956), p. 274.

Persian Gulf just south of Ras al-Qulayah. This line constituted the indisputable southern frontier of the Shaykhdom of Kuwait, but to the south a second area was delimited, starting at the point where the southern frontier of Kuwait struck the 29° parallel and running first approximately south-southeast and then due east until it reached the coast, in its turn, at a point about eighty miles south of Kuwait town. This territory was to have a status similar to that of the rhomboid at the southeastern extremity of the 'Iraqi-Najdi frontier in which the two countries were to enjoy equal rights.[23] Shaykh Ahmad of Kuwait thus lost about two thirds of his tribal sphere, sacrificed to placate Ibn Sa'ud for the gains made by 'Iraq and necessitated by Britain's determination to strengthen her rule in Mesopotamia.

The Protocols of Al-'Uqayr were certainly a major diplomatic triumph for Sir Percy Cox. He had succeeded in forcing Ibn Sa'ud to accept a definitive frontier to which he had been strongly opposed. Cox apparently had an uncanny power over him which was decisive in concluding the treaty.

> Sir Percy was magnificent and . . . Ibn Sa'ud is convinced that the future of himself and his country depends on our goodwill. . . . It's really amazing that anyone should exercise influence such as his. . . . I don't think that any European in history has made a deeper impression on the Oriental mind.[24]

Although he was undeniably responsible for the establishment of frontiers that are still in existence today, perhaps Cox utilized his extraordinary influence too much. The Protocols of Al-'Uqayr were incomplete, the major political issue had been neglected. Cox had devoted his attention to Ibn Sa'ud's relations with Kuwait and 'Iraq. He had not attempted to solve the larger quarrel between Ibn Sa'ud and Husayn nor to consider Ibn Sa'ud's claims and interests in the Trans-Jordan marches. Moreover, once the Protocols limited the scope of Wahhabi activities in the east, Ibn Sa'ud was free to turn his attention to Trans-Jordan and the Hijaz in the west

[23] For the Protocols of Al-'Uqayr see *Report on 'Iraq Administration, April 1922–March 1923*, pp. 184–186.

[24] Gertrude Bell to Sir Hugh Bell, 16 and 18 December 1922, F. Bell, *The Letters of Gertrude Bell*, pp. 659–661.

where the questions arising from the Wahhabi occupation of Al-Jawf and the Wadi as-Sirhan, not to mention the victory at Turabah, had never been accepted as the final solution by either Ibn Sa'ud or the Hashimites.

To seal the Protocols of Al-'Uqayr, Sir Percy Cox had hoped to arrange a meeting between Ibn Sa'ud and King Faysal in the spring of 1923. When these plans failed, another conference was arranged by British officials to take place in the autumn to settle questions between Najd and the Hashimite kingdoms of Trans-Jordan and the Hijaz. British officials had sought to allay the deep-seated jealousy and suspicion among the Arab rulers by personal contact, but these hopes were crushed when Ibn Sa'ud refused to attend. Instead he sent a delegation of minor officials. Husayn was even more difficult. He declined to appoint any representatives until pledges were made to restore the House of Rashid at Ha'il—a ridiculous notion. Not willing to admit that the conference was doomed to failure before it even opened, the British put their hope in Lieutenant Colonel S. G. Knox, the former British Agent in the Persian Gulf. Under his chairmanship the conference finally convened at Kuwait on 17 December 1923.

While the British had sought to delimit the frontiers between Najd and Trans-Jordan and the Hijaz and to put a stop to the Ikhwan raids which had continued despite the Protocols of Al-'Uqayr, the major topics of discussion had little to do with fixing frontiers. The representatives of the Arab kingdoms were more concerned with the right of 'Iraq to give hospitality to nomadic tribesmen whose traditional home was in Najd, the obligation of the 'Iraq government to prevent such newcomers from using the country as a base for operations against the Ikhwan, and the "pretensions" of Ibn Sa'ud to continue to exercise authority and to collect revenue from tribes that had temporarily transferred their residence to 'Iraq. The most important issue was the Shammar tribesmen in 'Iraq whose extradition Ibn Sa'ud had requested after a series of raids into Najd in June 1923. He insisted that his authority over the Shammar transcended state boundaries, and he appealed for their immediate expulsion from 'Iraq. The 'Iraqi delegation refused to consider such a demand. Nor was this issue the only one over which the delegates quarreled. Disputes over the appointment of frontier inspectors, the calling up of armed forces from tribes in the territory of the other government, and the restitution of loot from past raids, all combined to frustrate any hope of agreement. Even the few points on which each side could compromise were threatened by the dubious status of the Sa'udi delegates whose authority remained unsure.

The conference adjourned twice, and the third session began in the first week of March 1924. The Najd delegation had returned with a note from Faysal ad-Dawish, the fanatical Ikhwan leader, threatening reprisals for recent raids by the Mutayr tribe into Najd territory. Despite the warning by Knox against such a threat the Ikhwan carried out a serious counterraid on 14 March. The British believed that Ibn Sa'ud was aware of the Ikhwan raid, unlike so many past instances when he could neither know nor control what the Ikhwan were up to, and Knox felt that the representatives of Najd should apologize to 'Iraq and make reparations before the conference continued. Ibn Sa'ud had no intention of apologizing, and the conference finally broke up. Knox left Kuwait in April.

Ibn Sa'ud was largely responsible for the failure of the conference to reach any substantial agreement. He never really seemed to desire a successful outcome. He rejected all compromises, even some of which Faysal approved. He seemed unwilling to listen to argument, and his failure to send one of his sons indicated that he did not regard as crucial British attempts to solve Arabian problems by conference at Kuwait. Perhaps his attitude was precipitated by the termination of the British subsidy on 31 March 1924. As a result of that untimely announcement "the Arab delegates assembled with the comfortable feeling that they had nothing to lose by intransigence."[25] Moreover, Knox had been expected to convince Ibn Sa'ud to cede Al-Khurmah and Turabah to King Husayn in return for the cession of the Wadi as-Sirhan and the salt villages which he already controlled since his occupation in the summer of 1922.[26] "More serious than the failure to reach a positive agreement was the evidence of growing intransigence and aggressiveness on the

[25] H. St. John B. Philby, *Sa'udi Arabia* (New York, 1955), p. 285.

[26] The Duke of Devonshire, Secretary of State for Colonies; to the Political Resident in the Persian Gulf, Lt. Col. F. B. Prideaux, Telegram No. 329, 8 November 1923, C.P.

Wahhabi side."[27] After years of incredible patience, Ibn Sa'ud made no attempt to hide his resentment at British policies, particularly support of the Hashimite Kings. A second raid by Faysal ad-Dawish and his Ikhwan was carried out on 31 May, and finally late in the summer of 1924 the Wahhabi forces attacked the Hijaz. When the Najdi-Hijazi war began, Ibn Sa'ud's boundaries with his northern neighbors were still unsettled, but events of the war were such that comprehensive settlements were reached with Trans-Jordan and 'Iraq before peace was made with the Hijaz.

For years the Sharif of Mecca had been saved from Wahhabi attack by Ibn Sa'ud's commitment to the terms of his wartime treaty with Great Britain which forbade him to assault Britain's allies. After numerous insults, limitations to his sovereignty, and even the risk of losing his leadership in Najd by restraining the Ikhwan, Ibn Sa'ud appears to have abandoned hope that a solution to his problem could be worked out around the conference table. His decision to invade the Hijaz was prompted by two critical events that occurred in March of that year, but the long-standing rivalry between himself and Husayn seems to have been the underlying cause of his implacable hostility. King Husayn was an active, shrewd old man who appealed personally to most of the British officials who made his acquaintance, but his exaggerated ambitions and consummate lack of statesmanship were destined to overshadow his personal appeal and his contribution to the Allied war effort.

> He was already about seventy-two years of age, but his energy was inexhaustible. Unfortunately much of it was misdirected. When an Italian pilot said there was not room in his aircraft for several sacks of grain the King wished him to carry, the King ordered him to stow them on the wings. The pilot was able to escape by resignation, but this course was not open to Hejazis. The King once ordered a policeman by telephone to bring a certain car from Jedda to Mecca and not to let the driver stop on the way. The driver was not allowed to stop to put water in the radiator and the engine was ruined. . . . Through old age, arrogance and petulance the King had become a figure of fun.[28]

[27] *Survey of International Affairs, 1925*, vol. i, p. 341.

[28] Sir Reader Bullard, *The Camels Must Go, An Autobiography* (London, 1961), pp. 124–125.

The Hashimite regime in the Hijaz was corrupt and inefficient and through its own follies verged, by 1924, on total collapse. Yet Husayn never realized his ridiculous position. "When . . . we reflected that 90 per cent of the Moslem World must call Husain a renegade and traitor to the Vicar of God, we could not conceal from ourselves (and with difficulty from him) that his pretensions bordered upon the tragi-comic."[29] Husayn was mistaken to think that he could speak for all Arabs, and his high-handed methods of managing affairs of state alienated his Muslim allies one by one. He became unpopular with his people, with whom he refused to deal directly, and he did not permit them the right to criticize or to complain. He had erred by breaking with the Turks before negotiating a definite treaty with Great Britain and had refused to sign the Treaty of Versailles. By 1924 he still had not signed a treaty with Britain, and his failure to become a member of the League of Nations deprived him of even the dubious benefits of collective security. "Old King Hussein who fortunately had never ratified the treaty which might have committed us to supporting him, had singularly failed to make good."[30] Any mention of the word "mandate" sent him into an understandable but irrational rage; and encouraged by T. E. Lawrence, he quarreled with the English and demanded that they recognize him as ruler of all Arabia at the expense of the Jews, the French, and Ibn Sa'ud. Having alienated the British and most of his neighbors, Husayn proceeded to make himself unpopular with the pilgrims, on whom the livelihood of the Hijaz depended. In the meantime Ibn Sa'ud busied himself by consolidating his position in Najd and by waiting. By the time the Wahhabis struck, Husayn had reduced himself to diplomatic isolation by his own mistakes and illusions.

On 7 March 1924 Husayn assumed the title of Caliph. On 31 March the British subsidy to Husayn ended. The first action precipitated his downfall, the second made it inevitable. Husayn's assumption of the caliphate provided the Wahhabis with the religious

[29] Sir Ronald Storrs, *The Memoirs of Sir Ronald Storrs* (New York, 1937), p. 168.

[30] Rendel, p. 58.

motive for a jihad or holy war, for no Wahhabi could accept Husayn as the Caliph of Islam. The Wahhabis sought to reform the Muslim religion and convert the Holy Land to a purer form of Islam. Unlike Husayn, Ibn Sa'ud had no religious ambitions, and he explained to Sir Gilbert Clayton that he had made up his mind to eliminate Husayn only when the pilgrimage became impossible to a great number of Muslims. His duty to his coreligionists defined and determined his actions.[31] No longer restrained by British gold, Ibn Sa'ud had nothing to lose by purifying the Holy Places while at the same time satisfying his territorial ambitions, expanding his kingdom, and breaking the ring of enemies which encircled him.

Having finally decided to resort to fire and sword, Ibn Sa'ud carefully prepared for war. He reorganized his military forces early in April, and in June he made a proclamation to the Islamic world, rejecting Husayn's claims to the caliphate and calling the Arabs to supplant Husayn as the leader of Arab nationalism. He not only had the support of his own people but that of the important Indian Khilafat Committee as well. Once the political arrangements were completed, the military campaign began on 29 August 1924 when the main body of the Sa'udi army crossed the Hijaz frontier. At the same time three expeditionary forces were dispatched to cut the Hijaz railway north of Medina and to raid Trans-Jordan and 'Iraq. Supporting columns were sent into the Wadi as-Sirhan and to Al-Jawf—all to act as diversions to prevent 'Abd Allah and Faysal from sending help to their father. On the Hijaz front the Amir 'Ali attempted to defend At-Ta'if, but the people of the town rallied to the Wahhabi banner and opened the gates to Ibn Sa'ud's forces on 5 September only to be slaughtered by the Ikhwan under the command of the ferocious Khalid ibn Lu'ayy. At this point the great exodus from Mecca began, and by late September 'Ali had retired on that city with the enemy at his heels.

At the last minute Husayn appealed to Great Britain for aid, but after four years of negotiations the Anglo-Hijazi treaty of alli-

[31] "Report by Sir Gilbert Clayton, K.B.E., C.B., C.M.G., on his Mission to negotiate certain Agreements with the Sultan of Nejd," February 1926, p. 15, C.P.

ance remained unsigned. Despite Husayn's desperate appeals to the memory of the Arab Revolt and his efforts on behalf of the Allies during the Great War, the British were not to be tempted and declared their official neutrality. Husayn abdicated on 3 October and was succeeded by his son 'Ali who took the throne as a constitutional sovereign on the following day only to find his dominions limited to the three beleaguered towns of Jiddah, Yanbu' al-Bahr, and Medina. Mecca fell on 16 October, and Ibn Sa'ud proclaimed that the Islamic community would henceforth determine the administration of the Holy Places, where however there could be no peace until all of the Hashimites had left the country.

Meanwhile the Wahhabi diversionary assaults on 'Iraq and Trans-Jordan ended in disaster. The raid into Trans-Jordan was much like the long distance Ikhwan raids of 1922. The invaders were located by British aircraft and armored cars and driven back with heavy losses. On the 'Iraq flank, Faysal ad-Dawish led a simultaneous Ikhwan raid against the Dhafir and the Muntafiq, but his momentary success in December 1924 was offset when the raiders were overtaken and shot up by British planes from Baghdad. The Najdi-Hijazi war dragged on through 1925 despite the efforts of several would-be peacemakers who tried to mediate between the two rivals. Ibn Sa'ud would accept nothing short of exile from Arabia for the Hashimites, and he did not have long to wait. The first Hashimite to flee was King Husayn himself who left Mecca in his fleet of cars loaded with the gold he had received as a British subsidy. He turned up at 'Aqabah on his private yacht where he continued to furnish the army of the Hijaz with men, arms, supplies, and money. In order to counter the King's influence, Ibn Sa'ud planned to attack the city, but the British intervened. Having no wish to see the Wahhabis at 'Aqabah they removed Husayn to Cyprus and occupied the area themselves with a contingent of armored cars. In July 1925 Britain annexed the northern province of the Hijaz to Trans-Jordan to secure a strategic outlet on the Red Sea for 'Abd Allah's emirate and a right of way for any future railway line from 'Aqabah to Baghdad. Ibn Sa'ud strongly objected to the annexation of this district, which unquestionably formed part of the Hijaz at the time, but the British refused to abandon 'Aqabah and until 1965 the frontier beyond was not officially recognized by the Sa'udi Arabian government. The alteration of British attitudes toward the Sa'udis in 1925 was predominantly influenced by imperial considerations. The British were taken by surprise at the unexpected but rapid demise of King Husayn. They had envisaged a long war ending in some sort of compromise that would have left both Husayn and Ibn Sa'ud weaker and more amenable. With Husayn gone so quickly, and with the inevitable extinction of 'Ali ibn Husayn's constitutional regime, the British hastened to come to terms with the Sultan of Najd before he became too strong, too arrogant, or both.

> It became an urgent matter for Great Britain to reach an agreement with Ibn Sa'ud in regard not only to the Najd-Transjordan frontier but to the tribal régime along the border between Ibn Sa'ud's dominions and both the areas under British mandate. If Jiddah and Medina were to fall before these issues between Ibn Sa'ud and Great Britain were settled, the Wahhabi ruler might be tempted. . . to settle the problems of his northern frontier by the sword—a development which would place Great Britain in an exceedingly difficult position.[32]

The danger of such a clash between Ibn Sa'ud and the protected rulers of the territories north of his growing dominions was a question that could not wait until the end of the war. During the war, Ibn Sa'ud had already demonstrated that his forces could threaten British imperial communications when his troops advanced north beyond the Wadi as-Sirhan up to the Syrian frontier, thereby separating Trans-Jordan from 'Iraq. If such an extension of Sa'udi territory were to remain permanent, the vital east-west line of communications between the Mediterranean and the Euphrates Valley would be severed. The plans for a transdesert pipeline as well as new automobile and air routes would have to be revised, for the old routes would no longer be controlled by Britain. In order to safeguard these imperial communications, Britain was determined to remain the master of the overland corridor. The postwar years were the time of a revival of interest in the overland route to India and the East as opposed to the sea route via Suez. Both the Chesney railway scheme and the Sykes-Picot railway project of earlier times had failed to reach fruition. To construct an unremunerative stra-

[32] *Survey of International Affairs, 1925*, vol. i, pp. 342–343.

tegic line 550 miles long would have required more money than Britain had at its disposal after the Great War.

"But the airman and chauffeur rushed in where the railway-engineer feared to tread."[33] The combination of the war's stimulating effect on the development of the airplane and the automobile as efficient means of transportation and the postwar economic revival in 'Iraq had resulted in an increased traffic of goods and passengers along the overland route. The new importance of this route made the northern extension of Ibn Sa'ud's domain even more of a future danger than it would have been in the past. As soon as this danger became a reality, British officials sought to work out a solution with Ibn Sa'ud which at the same time would protect British imperial interests. He had already expressed the need for such a conference when he wrote to the British Resident in the Persian Gulf in January 1925 concerning the problem of tribal raids along the 'Iraq frontier and the liberty of criminal Najd tribesmen to take refuge in 'Iraq. These were not new questions, but out of old problems Ibn Sa'ud appeared to seek new solutions. He now felt the need for special agreements for preventing raids and resolving the thorny question of extradition. He wrote to the Political Resident in the Persian Gulf, Lt. Colonel F. B. Prideaux. "I am still prepared to conclude special agreements with the 'Iraq Government or His Britannic Majesty's Government in their capacity as Mandatory Government for the purpose of establishing safety on the frontiers of the two countries, Najd and 'Iraq, and for the stemming up of raids by the tribes of the two countries."[34]

By the spring British officials were convinced of the necessity to seek a rapprochement with Ibn Sa'ud. In a letter to the Secretary of State for the Colonies, Cox recommended that a conference between 'Iraq and Najd might be very valuable to settle some of the outstanding points that remained unresolved at the breakup of the Kuwait conference.[35] These tentative plans for a meeting with Ibn

[33] *Ibid.*, pp. 328–329.

[34] Ibn Sa'ud to Political Resident in Persian Gulf (Prideaux), No. 125, 10 January 1925, C.P.

[35] B. H. Bourdillon for High Commissioner, 'Iraq, to L. C. M. S. Amery, Secretary of State for the Colonies, 12 March 1925, C.P.

Sa'ud to discuss 'Iraqi-Najdi raids were rapidly crystallized by the new strategic considerations raised by Wahhabi success in the west. Thus by the autumn of 1925, even before the conclusion of the Najdi-Hijazi war, a British mission set out for Arabia to settle with the Sultan of Najd. The head of the mission was one of Britain's most able and experienced Arab experts, Sir Gilbert Clayton.

* * * * *

Gilbert Falkingham Clayton was born on 6 July 1875 at the family home, Eastfield, at Ryde, Isle of Wight. At the time of Gilbert's birth the Clayton family had risen by common sense, prudent management, devoted naval and military service, and plain good luck from obscurity in early eighteenth-century England to a respected position among the gentry of the Isle of Wight in the nineteenth. Five generations before, Samuel Clayton (?–1735), described only as an Irish gentleman, emigrated to Barbadoes where in 1729 he married Thomasina Wittewronge, heiress of a well-to-do Dutch family that had settled in England during the sixteenth century, and granddaughter of Sir John Wittewronge, second Baronet. Their only child, Samuel Wittewronge Clayton (1730–1795), was sent to England at the age of eight in the care of the family chaplain to enter the Royal Navy as a midshipman. He served for sixty years in the navy. During the 1780 campaign against the French he commanded as Captain the *H.M.S. Victory*, at that time flagship of the Grand Fleet on which Nelson was killed twenty-five years later at Trafalgar. His eldest son, Thomas Wittewronge Whitewell Clayton (1766–1806), followed his father to sea and rose to the rank of Captain in the Royal Navy before he died at Dingle on the west coast of Ireland where he was in command of the "Fencibles," a local force organized to defend the Irish coast from invasion during the Napoleonic wars. Thomas Clayton had married Phoebe Falkingham, the only surviving daughter and sole heiress of a distinguished naval family.[36] In 1830 she and her son, Samuel Witte-

[36] Phoebe Falkingham's grandfather, John Falkingham (1707–1777), was a Captain in the Royal Navy; his brother, Edward Falkingham (1709–1783), was a Rear Admiral; and their uncle, Edward Falkingham (1697–1757), was an Admiral and Comptroller of the Navy.

wronge Clayton (1803–1875), Gilbert Clayton's grandfather, came to live at Ryde, Isle of Wight, where he built Eastfield in Dover Street as a family residence.

Although Samuel Clayton appears to have been content to manage the family estates rather than continue the naval tradition begun by his grandfather, the establishment of the family home at Ryde was the outgrowth of the attraction for naval families of the Isle of Wight. Located across the Spithead from the great harbor and dockyard of Portsmouth, the Isle of Wight had long been a refuge where the off-duty naval officer could enjoy a change from service conditions in the beauty of the island and the hospitality of its inhabitants. It was here in 1843 that Samuel Clayton married Anna Maria Nicholl of an old Welsh family whose father had come to Ryde in the same year as the Claytons and with whom he established close friendship. Their first son, William Lewis Nicholl Clayton (1845–1927), as was expected, remained at home to manage the family affairs, but his three younger brothers were sent off to Oxford and Cambridge and two were subsequently ordained in the Church of England.

Although he had wanted to join first the navy and then the army, William Clayton's ambitions appear to have been subordinated to the wishes of his father who required his eldest son at home to help oversee his affairs. Resigning himself to a quiet life on the Isle of Wight, William married Maria Martha Pilkington, herself from a family with military and naval traditions going back to the Crusades, and settled down to rear a family and manage his modest estate.[37] But his enthusiasm for the military life never waned, and he sought to satisfy his passion through his own activities in the Hampshire and Isle of Wight Artillery Militia and by watching with obvious satisfaction the military careers of his sons. The militia regiments were the successors to the old Train Bands, which were citizens instructed to bear arms in times of danger and to be ready in times of war or threat of invasion when they would be incorporated into

[37] Maria Martha Pilkington's father, Edward Williams Pilkington (1803–1867), was a Captain in the Royal Navy; and her two brothers, Edward (1840–1904) and Henry (1846–1930), were Captain in the Royal Navy and Major in the British Army respectively.

the standing army. The Militia Act of 1757 provided for annual training for service in the United Kingdom only, but later in the eighteenth century the sovereign was empowered to accept voluntary offers from militiamen to serve outside the British Isles. These militia regiments were generally attached to the county regiments and trained with them, and this applied specifically to the Royal Artillery units as well as the infantry. Thus the local Isle of Wight Artillery Militia, which some years later was joined by the Hampshire unit, provided just the soldiering at home to reconcile the military interests of William Clayton with the demands of his father and family. In July 1867 he joined the Isle of Wight Artillery Militia as a lieutenant and after twenty years service retired with the rank of Lieutenant-Colonel.[38] In the early 1880's the Isle of Wight Artillery Militia held its annual four-weeks training period in May when it marched daily from its headquarters in Newport to Carrisbrooke Castle where King Charles I was kept during his captivity. There on the bowling green of the castle the militia did its marching, musket drill, and artillery practice from several small field guns stationed on the ramparts. After his marriage William Clayton took rooms in Newport for the month of training, and as his family grew, the children would rush out onto the raised pathway beside the road and march beside the regiment to the next corner. Today, in an age of impersonal armaments manned by superbly trained technicians, the militiamen of Victorian England would perhaps appear an inefficient if not amateurish lot, but to the Clayton boys the bands and flags, muskets and marching men made a deep and lasting impression. From his earliest days Gilbert Clayton desired to be a "Gunner" as did his younger brother Iltyd (1886–1955), while John (1888–1953) took up again the naval traditions of the family and retired a Rear Admiral in the Royal Navy.

Gilbert Clayton received his education at the Isle of Wight College, and was later admitted to the Royal Military Academy at Woolwich where his quiet good nature soon gained the respect and friendship of his colleagues.

[38] William Lewis Nicholl Clayton was promoted to Captain in May 1871, Major in August 1885, and Lieutenant-Colonel in August 1887.

> He was essentially modest in manner and mode of life and would never put himself forward, though he was the best of good company, and ready for any fun that was going. He was keen on sport —good at cricket, golf, and polo. He was always interested in *people*, and when he met new acquaintances his mental approach was—"I am sure you are a good sort, and I am going to like you." This did not prevent a very keen perception of their characters. . . . And he did really seem to bring out the best in other people.[39]

A classmate recalled that his sense of humor and keen spirit frequently led him to organize "rags of the milder kind," such as an unsuccessful but fun-filled demonstration in nightshirts and top hats against "Lights-out" at ten o'clock. "As a student *Bertie* never 'mugged-up stuff, never burned the midnight oil. He had the mind that seizes facts, pigeonholes them, and brings them out at the opportune moments."[40] These two qualities, his perception of people, and his analytical skill in dealing with factual information, were to prove the essential reasons for his success as an administrator and diplomat.

Gilbert Clayton received his commission in November 1895 and entered the Royal Artillery as a subaltern. The pay of a junior officer was at that time hardly sufficient to make both ends meet, and so, like many of his colleagues without substantial private means, he chose to serve abroad rather than remain in England. Even then he required nearly £100 a year in addition to his pay, and this was only accomplished by a host of petty economies. He was stationed first in Egypt, where his interest in people and his natural curiosity for information soon equipped him with a rapidly increasing knowledge of the land and its inhabitants.

After two and a half years in Egypt during which he studied Arabic and absorbed the many new experiences of Egyptian life, Clayton was ordered up the Nile to join Kitchener's advancing army as an officer of the Maxim Battery of the 1st British Brigade. Here he met many of the men who were later to become prominent in the British administration of Egypt and the Sudan, describing

[39] Notes supplied to the editor by Sir Gilbert's sister, Miss Ellinor Maria Clayton.

[40] *The Evening Standard*, 12 September 1929, p. 10.

them and his life with the army in detailed letters to his family. He clearly enjoyed the hardships of the campaign and thrived on devising ways to overcome them. Beyond Aswan he entered the area officially designated as "active service," and although he was not immediately involved in action against the Mahdists he wrote in March 1898, "Tell Dad I am beginning to soldier now."[41] Traveling with a servant, pony, and groom (standard equipment for junior officers), Clayton looked up old friends from his Woolwich days who were posted in other regiments, made new friends among the junior officers, and met more senior ones.

On 8 April 1898 at Umm Dabbi near the 'Atbarah River Kitchener launched his Anglo-Egyptian troops against the entrenched camp of the Mahdist forces of Mahmud Ahmad. Stationed on the left flank with the four Maxim guns of his battery to cover the Cameron Highlanders, Clayton carried out his orders with cool efficiency in his first full-scale battle. The attack was overwhelmingly successful. "Presently they [the Mahdists] could stand it no longer and bolted out [of the stockade] across the open ground on the right to gain the bush–very few of them reached it however, as immediately they got out into the open we got on to them [with the Maxims] and shot nearly all."[42] The triumphant technology of Victorian England had proved decisive. Mahmud's army was destroyed without loss to the Maxim Battery and only 510 Anglo-Egyptian casualties. Kitchener then ordered his troops into summer quarters to prepare for the final advance on Umdurman.

The Maxim Battery was sent to Darmali on the Nile where the searing heat of the Sudan in summer added to the boredom of camp life that was "more than monotonous–in fact it is but an existence. . . . I fear that by the time our three months here is over we shall have degenerated into Sudanese vegetables."[43] Clayton's daily routine consisted of breakfast, riding, reading or writing in his mud hut, watering the mules, lunch, indoors until tea, bath and shave after a

[41] Clayton to his mother (Maria Martha Pilkington Clayton), 5 March 1898, C.P.

[42] Clayton to his mother, Easter Day, 10 April 1898, C.P.

[43] Clayton to his mother, 23 April 1898, C. P.

walk or ride, dinner, and early to bed. The men resorted to all sorts of entertainment to pass the time, including various sports events, watching the railway construction, or taking three-day trips down the Nile. Life was dull and he appeared more concerned with his father's position in the county at home than with the Mahdists in the Sudan.

By late August however the four idle months at Darmali were soon forgotten as the Battery moved with Kitchener's advancing army onto Umdurman. On 2 September 1898 Kitchener's troops met the forces of the Mahdist State in a climactic battle on the plains of Karari north of Umdurman. It was over by midday. Again the triumphant technology of the English had overwhelmed the matchless courage of the Sudanese, and as at Umm Dabbi the Maxim batteries proved decisive. On 4 September Clayton attended the Gordon Memorial Service at Khartoum, and by the 12th he was on a felucca traveling downstream to Cairo quite convinced that soldiering on the Nile was indeed an exciting and interesting profession. He had reason to be pleased. Mentioned in despatches and the recipient of the British and Egyptian medals, the latter with two clasps, for his actions at Umm Dabbi and Umdurman, his career was off to an auspicious start. A combination of ability and luck soon advanced it further. Captivated by the peoples of the Nile and charmed by their land, Clayton wanted to remain in Egypt and with his record during the river war managed to be seconded into the Egyptian Army. Service with the Egyptian Army was eagerly sought after by officers in the British Army; in addition to the increased pay, the chance for adventure and promotion were certainly greater on the Nile than on Salisbury Plain. The contracts for the Egyptian service were for ten years at the end of which the officer would return to his regiment in the British Army. The outbreak of the Boer War hastened the process of promotion, for numerous casualties in South Africa left vacancies in every regiment, and, although he was bitterly disappointed at not being ordered to the Cape, Clayton benefited by receiving promotion to captain in 1901, only six years after his first commission. Such good luck was to follow him throughout the rest of his career, but he was always sufficiently acute to recognize remarkable opportunities, and almost invariably well situated to take full advantage of them.

In the autumn of 1902 Gilbert Clayton left the artillery branch of the Egyptian Army to take service as a civil administrator in the Southern Sudan. At that time the Sudanese government was attempting to establish its authority among the Nilotic and Sudanic-speaking Africans inhabiting the valley of the Upper Nile. Only officers with military experience were recruited in those early days for service in the South, for although much of their work was concerned with civil affairs, these same officers were called upon for many years to lead punitive patrols, establish government control by military force, and command local police and troops amongst a population sullenly, if not openly, hostile to British administration. Just as he had joined the Egyptian Army to retain his military life in a land that fascinated him, he now saw an opportunity to acquire more experience in administration without jeopardizing his military career. His commander, Lieutenant-Colonel Malcolm Peake Pasha, had assured Clayton that he could reenter the artillery if there was a vacancy.[44] In his own words:

> This is quite a new move and entire change of life and work, and I don't know in the least how I shall like it, as of course it is quite an experiment. However it will be a great gain of experience and will much improve one and from all I hear I think I shall be very happy up there. . . . I am only taking up the oldest of things, which I shall throw away when I come down again—it is rather a good opportunity for wearing out disreputable old clothes, as they don't go in for fashions much, except in the matter of bead necklaces.[45]

Unsure of his ultimate destination, Clayton traveled up the White Nile and Bahr al-Ghazal Rivers by steamer to Mashra' ar-Raqq and then on up the Jur River to Wau, the British headquarters of the Bahr al-Ghazal Province. In spite of the long and difficult journey, he was in good health and charmed by Africa. "Wau is such a pretty place," he wrote his mother, "you would almost imagine yourself in England."[46] He plunged into the various tasks of a civil adminis-

[44] It was Peake Pasha who led the first *sadd*-cutting expedition to the Southern Sudan in 1899–1900 where he cleared much of the Bahr al-Jabal and found a passable channel to Gondokoro. He undoubtedly encouraged Clayton to gain experience on that frontier of British Africa.

[45] Clayton to his mother, 28 October 1902, C.P.

[46] Clayton to his mother, 6 February 1903, C.P.

trator in a land where the government was perpetually short of staff. He was often left alone in charge of Wau post, while his more senior colleagues trekked throughout the countryside, showing the flag and establishing administration in the outlying areas. Once after being alone for over a fortnight, he wrote "to tell you the truth I am getting a little 'fed-up' with my own society."[47] But he had much work to keep him occupied, and he wrote many letters filled with interesting comments on local flora and fauna punctuated by descriptions of the antics of the Sudanese soldiers and villagers. In his dealings with the local Africans he was "mayor, district council, and sanitary authority all in one," dispensing justice with impartial ignorance, while trying to concoct a budget for the province which would be intelligible to unimaginative treasury officials in Khartoum. He read *The Times*, always several months late, but daily and in the proper chronological order. He went shooting in the parklike grasslands surrounding Wau, and he kept a chimpanzee and a young lion for pets. All the time he observed and assimilated the new and strange environment of Africa, broadening his knowledge and experience.

Clayton clearly liked his life at Wau and probably would have remained in the obscurity of the Southern Sudan had not recurrent attacks of malaria required his transfer to Cairo in June 1903 as the Deputy Assistant Adjutant General on the Headquarters Staff of the Egyptian Army.[48] He considered himself extremely fortunate. And indeed he was, for to be plucked from the pestilential lands of the Upper Nile and assigned over numerous other captains to the Headquarters of the Egyptian Army, where expenses were high, pay less, but opportunities for advancement manifold, must be considered Clayton's luck, helped along by his susceptibility to malaria. As before, however, he made the most of his opportunities. In 1908 when Lee Stack, who had been private secretary to Sir Reginald Wingate, the Sirdar of the Egyptian Army and Governor-General of the Sudan, was promoted to the combined post of Sudan Agent in Cairo and the Director of Intelligence, Bertie Clayton was chosen

[47] *Ibid.*

[48] Diary of Captain Alfred Henry Sanders, 7 April 1903, Library of the Royal Commonwealth Society.

to succeed his friend and took up the post at the Governor-General's Palace at Khartoum.

Clayton remained six years with "Master," as Sir Reginald was sardonically known among his staff. As elsewhere, he made friends easily among the British community and became, like so many other British officials, deeply attached to the Sudanese and their land, so that in 1910 when he retired from the Egyptian Army as a captain, he transferred to the Sudan government service. At the Palace he ably carried out his duties with characteristic thoroughness and efficiency, and Sir Reginald was pleased with his private secretary. Wingate had established his reputation as an intelligence officer during the River War, but the qualities that had built a remarkably effective intelligence system were not necessarily those required of a governor-general. Overwhelmed with petty details, Wingate immersed himself in minutiae from which he would emerge only on occasion to provide guidelines and direction. His passion for detail was not a great handicap in the early days of the Anglo-Egyptian Condominium when the Political Service was small and its administration modest, but by the time Clayton became private secretary, Wingate's analytical failures were more apparent and particularly irritating beside Clayton's ability to assimilate and digest information from which general conclusions and sound decisions could be made. His awareness of Wingate's shortcomings did not, however, appear to have affected his loyalty, for his sense of duty was much too strong, and he served Sir Reginald faithfully and patiently, while at the same time absorbing knowledge and acquiring experience to qualify himself for higher positions beyond the direct influence of the Governor-General of the Sudan.

Clayton's loyalty was well repaid by Wingate's complete confidence in his private secretary. As the private secretary he was closely in touch with developments throughout the Sudan, ranging from questions of personnel to economic development, and encompassing hospitals, police forces, communications, and the delicate problem of religious rivalries. When Wingate fell ill in 1910, Clayton had to assume even greater responsibilities for Sudan affairs, and the Governor-General from his sick-bed in London would make no decisions until he had first learned Clayton's views. Theodore Roosevelt's visit to Khartoum in the spring of 1910 required extensive arrangements, the responsibility for which fell to Clayton. His effort as host, however, did not go without appropriate appreciation, and Wingate wrote from England, "Nothing could have exceeded Roosevelt's praise of the way he was treated in the Sudan; the whole party were loud in your praises."[49] During the summer of 1911 Clayton returned to England for a much-deserved leave. There he met Enid Caroline Thorowgood, the daughter of Frank Napier Thorowgood, a civil engineer living in South Kensington. When he once again returned to London late in the summer of the following year to sit on the Selection Board for the Sudan Political Service, he married Enid Thorowgood on 18 September 1912. Although he returned briefly to Khartoum, he did not remain long, for in the autumn of 1913 he was posted to Cairo with his wife and baby daughter, Patience. Following in the footsteps of Lee Stack, he succeeded Stack as the Sudan Agent and Director of Intelligence for the Egyptian Army in Cairo just as he had succeeded Stack as private secretary to Wingate in 1908. His wife was, of course, pleased to be in the more bustling and civilized city of Cairo, while Clayton himself was glad to be beyond the immediate reach of Sir Reginald Wingate.

As the Sudan Agent, Clayton acted as a liaison between the High Commissioner, Lord Kitchener, and the authorities in the Sudan. As the Director of Intelligence for the Egyptian Army, he was responsible for the gathering and analyzing of information. Ever since the conquest of the Mahdist State and the reduction of military activity in the Sudan to punitive patrols, the role of intelligence had been subordinated to the larger political problems dealt with by the Sudan Agent. Within a year however these positions were dramatically reversed by the outbreak of war; and by the historical accident that two positions, Sudan Agent and Director of Intelligence, were being filled by one man, Bertie Clayton found himself in one of the most important, demanding, and influential posts in the British Middle East. Clayton's luck had once again provided the opportunities; his abilities more than made the best of them.

[49] Wingate to Clayton, 29 March 1910, C.P.

At the outbreak of the First World War Clayton's talents were already beginning to receive recognition, for once he had broken from the orbit of the Governor-General's Palace at Khartoum, his faculties developed rapidly under the stimulus of official life in Cairo. As Sudan Agent he possessed a position in the hierarchy of Cairo officialdom, both European and Egyptian, which allowed him to know its complexities and understand the subtleties and influence of personal relationships.[50] At the same time Sudan problems had brought him into an ever-widening circle of British imperial and international affairs. In August 1913, for instance, he was back again in London to attend the conference at Whitehall concerning the Congo-Sudan-Uganda boundary question, keeping Wingate in Khartoum informed to the last detail—a practice that frequently drove Clayton to exhaustion and Wingate to amazement.

> I am so much obliged to you for your long letter of the 17th, giving me an account of your interview with Kelly, and his views on the establishment of the posts in the country we are about to take over from Uganda—you have boiled the whole thing down into thoroughly practical form and your letter is most useful to me, especially in view of my impending talk with Lord Kitchener at the end of this week.[51]

The rapid concentration of British forces in Egypt and the formulation of plans to defend the Suez Canal against the Turks required the expansion of the Department of Military Intelligence at British headquarters. Clayton was the logical choice to direct the expansion, since he had experience with the gathering and the analyzing of political information in his role as Director of Intelligence for the Egyptian Army at the Sudan Agency. He was now to combine his fund of political knowledge with British military requirements. Sir John Maxwell, the General Officer commanding in Egypt, promoted Clayton to the rank of Colonel and gave him a free hand to recruit officers with a knowledge of Arabic to work for the reorganized Military Intelligence Department that he set up at British headquarters.

[50] For example, see Clayton to Wingate, 12 January 1914, C.P.

[51] Wingate to Clayton, 19 August 1913, C.P.

Wingate was not altogether happy to see Clayton's role as Director of Military Intelligence suddenly rival or even overshadow his duties as Sudan Agent, but "I knew that by so doing I should be helping forward the good cause—though at some expense to our own [Sudan Agency] efficiency. . . . I hesitated considerably, though I did not say so."[52] Although he could hardly object, Wingate continued to bombard Clayton with numerous tasks, many unnecessary, others picayune, with which, as Sudan Agent, he was obliged to deal but which eventually became a serious distraction from his task at Military Intelligence. Although he was ably served by his staff at the Sudan Agency, it was Clayton himself who had to act as intermediary between the Governor-General's Palace at Khartoum and the British Residency at Cairo. The responsibilities were proportional to the work load, and since Wingate insisted in long, verbose letters that his views be known in Cairo, Clayton was required to reply in kind. Yet Wingate would not let Clayton leave the Sudan Agency or resign from the Sudan service, and jealously guarded his claim to Clayton with parental obstinacy. He wrote to Clayton in April 1916.

> On all hands I hear nothing but praise of what you have done in Egypt since the war began and this is a great credit not only to yourself but also to the Sudan Government and, as you know, I am very anxious that whatever military responsibilities you may have, you should never allow the idea to get about that you are in any way severing your connection with the latter [the Sudan Service].[53]

An unassuming and congenial man, devoted to duty and loyal to his superiors, Bertie Clayton was not prepared to break with "Master" and resigned himself to play his Sudan role. "I know how necessary it is in my present post to keep myself 'purely Sudan' and to try to look at every question from that point of view," he wrote to Wingate just before the war.[54] Clearly he could not continue to maintain a purely Sudan point of view when the centrifugal forces

[52] Wingate to Clayton, 20 August 1916, C.P.
[53] Wingate to Clayton, 9 April 1916, C.P.
[54] Clayton to Wingate, 2 February 1914, C.P.

of his more important offices created conflicts of interest, but he was able to diminish the force of such conflicts by integrating the Sudan into the larger war effort. He tactfully managed to reconcile Wingate's demands for troops, vehicles, and airplanes with the requirements of the armies in Egypt and Arabia. He spent considerable time on behalf of Wingate, who was determined to have the Sudan emerge from the war with a good active record. Clayton pressed for military support in the Southern Sudan and for the campaign against 'Ali Dinar, Sultan of Darfur. Not only did he draft an influential memorandum on the temporary administration for Darfur, but he helped to clear the political complications in Egypt so that the campaign could be brought to a conclusion.[55]

Although he was rarely seen in Khartoum, his influence was pervasive, since virtually every official and visitor to the Sudan made his acquaintance before proceeding up the Nile. It was during this period that Clayton gained the confidence of many of the most important British wartime officials, and as a result of the personal respect he won at Cairo he was able to provide for the Sudan. He helped to obtain naval forces to defend Port Sudan, expedited specie and supplies to Khartoum, and argued convincingly for the despatch of the Annuak-Gerjak patrol to establish control over those truculent Nilotes.[56] The more Clayton did, the more Wingate expected, and although he continually promised to send men to help the overworked staff at the Sudan Agency, few arrived, and those who came remained only for a short period during which their services were virtually useless. In fact Sir Reginald looked upon the Sudan Agency as a "convalescent depot for British officers in the Sudan who get seedy or who have had little or no leave."[57] By September 1915 Clayton was in the hospital, exhausted from overwork; but he continued to write, against doctors' orders, those long letters that Wingate expected. Sir Reginald perceived the problem, which he had helped to bring about, which he had done little to alleviate, and about which he would presumably continue to do nothing so long

[55] Wingate to Clayton, 10 April 1916, C.P.
[56] Wingate to Clayton, 30 September 1914, C.P.
[57] Wingate to Clayton, 8 October 1914, C.P.

as he regarded the Sudan first and Clayton its agent. He wrote to Clayton with misplaced sympathy and little understanding. "I am only afraid in your anxiety to do all you possibly could for your various 'Masters' you have brought about your unfortunate collapse."[58]

If his work at the Sudan Agency was taxing, his responsibilities as Director of Military Intelligence were overwhelming. There was no question that the problems of military intelligence were more important to the British war effort in the Middle East than the parochial difficulties of the Sudan. Wingate would certainly have agreed in theory but he did little in practice to make Clayton's duties at the Intelligence Department any easier and by 1916 was jealously complaining, "I sometimes wonder whether I was wise to hand you over so completely to Sir John Maxwell, for in this way you have had to take on more than any mortal man could do."[59] As usual Clayton made no complaint and dutifully tried to satisfy Wingate, and at the same time sit in his office at Military Intelligence, located in the Savoy Hotel, wrestling with a multiplicity of tasks assisted by a small but willing staff "to do the work of half a dozen non-existent or absent heads of departments."[60] First he had to convert the small existing Military Intelligence Department into the "I" branch of the General Staff, while at the same time constructing an organization for the systematic collection and analysis of military, geographical, and political information whose interests far transcended purely military matters. Unlike the chiefs of intelligence departments today, Clayton never surrounded himself with reports or secluded himself from people. He never lost his human touch, even in those harried days, and in his quiet and unassuming way maintained his friendly but frequently useful contacts with Arabs and Turks, shaykhs and pashas.

> Few men worked or could work as he did in those days, in conditions that often compelled him to combine the duties of a senior staff officer and a sub-lieutenant [subaltern]. Yet the files never

[58] Wingate to Clayton, 14 September 1915, C.P.
[59] Wingate to Clayton, 6 August 1916, C.P.
[60] Anonymous correspondent to *The Times*, 12 September 1929, p. 14.

> barricaded him against the world. He kept in touch with his friends, European and Oriental; again and again one could find him listening patiently to the news—often prolix—or the appreciations—often fantastic—of the situation brought by a refugee from Turkey, an old Sheikh from the Libyan desert, or a travelled merchant from a Red Sea port. For he understood the East; he knew that for an Intelligence officer 'haste is [of] the devil' and he never failed in courtesy as he never failed in understanding.[61]

He and his agents would gather information by any means, employing unconventional sources as well as prying facts from the more customary ones. When the Chancery neglected to send him information on Abyssinia ("they are not always very good about sending things over unless they actually want them dealt with"), he had "to go over there and forage."[62] One of his most valuable sources was Philip Graves, who had been correspondent for *The Times* in Constantinople before the war. Graves had watched the reorganization of the Turkish Army and was as knowledgeable about its actual capabilities as the War Office handbooks were not. Hitherto the British military authorities had ignored Graves. Clayton did not, and from him and Turkish refugees he was able to compile accurate information on the state of the railways and the quantities of artillery, ammunition, and men that the Turks could bring against the Suez Canal.[63]

Although they were delighted to receive such valuable information, paradoxically numerous officers did not approve of Clayton's methods. At that time the staff was encumbered with aging men who thought more about their personal records than carrying on the war. Among the officers in Egypt "ambitions, intrigues, and the pursuit of gold lace were unleashed, and behind too many desks were to be seen caricatures of colonels and majors, old fighting cocks with bloodshot eyes who lived with the *Army Almanac* and the *Aldershot Regulations* on their tables."[64] Scattered among them, however, were men who, like Clayton, saw the need for drastic

[61] *Ibid.*

[62] Clayton to Wingate, 29 April 1914, C.P.

[63] B. H. Liddell Hart, *Colonel Lawrence* (New York, 1934), p. 70.

[64] J. M. E. Béraud-Villars, *T. E. Lawrence . . .* (London, 1958), p. 70.

changes in the conduct of the war; and since Clayton's position at the Sudan Agency and at Military Intelligence placed him in immediate contact with the three most influential British officials in the Middle East, Maxwell, McMahon, and Wingate—all of whom shared his approach—he was able to bring about a change in the kind of warfare waged against the Turks. Early in the war Clayton perceived, as did others, that the Arabs must be separated from the Turks, and he set out to accomplish it.

First he sought to recruit men who knew the Arabs, for among them personality and knowledge of their language and customs inspires trust and confidence. Colonel Newcombe arrived from France as Clayton's assistant, bringing with him George Lloyd, Aubrey Herbert, Leonard Woolley, and T. E. Lawrence—the "five musketeers," more sinisterly known as the "Intrusives" because they ignored military procedure and sought to change the pattern of the conflict by advocating unorthodox methods.[65] Although they were scorned and boycotted by many officers, both high and low, their assignment by General Maxwell to work under Clayton at the Intelligence Department was recognition enough of their value. Clayton proved an excellent chief to this group of very individualistic and talented but often difficult men. He was "quiet, never fussy, never despondent in the blackest days, afraid of no responsibility, and ready to accept any suggestion from subordinates which his instructive good sense approved. He was an admirable judge of men, for he never allowed military formalism to blunt his appreciation of values."[66] To these men his broadminded outlook was his most winning characteristic, for without it their ideas and plans, which did not fit standard military practice, would certainly have been wasted. Because he himself was the most difficult and trying of all the Intrusives, T. E. Lawrence appears to have appreciated Clayton's leadership the most.

> We were not many; and nearly all of us rallied round Clayton. . . . Clayton made the perfect leader for such a band of wild men as we were. He was calm, detached, clear-sighted, of unconscious cour-

[65] Liddell Hart, p. 69; Béraud-Villars, p. 71.

[66] Anonymous correspondent to *The Times*, 12 September 1929, p. 14.

> age in assuming responsibility. He gave an open run to his subordinates. His own views were general, like his knowledge; and he worked by influence rather than by loud direction. It was not easy to descry his influence. He was like water, or permeating oil, creeping silently and insistently through everything. It was not possible to say where Clayton was and was not, and how much really belonged to him. He never visibly led; but his ideas were abreast of those who did: he impressed men by his sobriety, and by a certain quiet and stately moderation of hope. In practical matters he was loose, irregular, untidy, a man with whom independent men could bear.[67]

As British military fortunes declined in the Middle East, more and more officers were drawn to "Clayton's machine" for ideas, methods, and plans to replace the inflexible military procedures of the past, while even civilian administrators, like Ronald Storrs, cooperated closely with the Intrusives, drawing upon their knowledge and information of the Arabs as well as of the Turks. Clayton put his assistants into the Savoy Hotel and assigned to each particular tasks. Newcombe organized a spy service. Herbert concentrated on the secret police. Woolley specialized in propaganda. Lawrence, in many ways the least of this remarkable group of men, was in theory a cartographer, but in practice did almost everything but map work.[68] As their leader, Clayton wanted the truth, not myths, and his clarity of mind and expression defined the goals of the Department so that each of the experts knew the general context in which they were to fit their specialties. Possessing both the wisdom and the calm courage to take a broader view than some of his fellow officers, Clayton proved that he was indeed "a far bigger man than appeared at first sight."[69] In July 1915 he was awarded the C.M.G. for his services as the Director of Military Intelligence.

In 1916 Sir Archibald Murray, who had until then been Chief of the Imperial Staff in London, was appointed to the Command of the Suez Canal Forces. Almost at once he clashed with the less

67 T. E. Lawrence, *Seven Pillars of Wisdom* (Garden City, 1936), p. 57.

68 Béraud-Villars, pp. 71–72.

69 H. Charles Woods to *The Near East and India* (London, 1908–1935), 8 September 1929, p. 335.

conventional views of General Maxwell who shortly resigned, leaving Murray in sole command in Egypt. A firm believer in the strictest traditions of the British Army, without concern for Middle Eastern peoples or politics, Murray, not surprisingly, cared little for the methods of Clayton and his collaborators. Those officers who had hitherto regarded the Intrusives' methods with suspicion and distrust but had said little when Maxwell backed them, now openly criticized the Intelligence Department and those employed in it.[70] But the plans to separate the Arabs and to turn them against the Turks were too far advanced to be abruptly terminated, and the efforts of Storrs, Wingate, McMahon, and even Kitchener had laid the foundations for British support of the Arab Revolt which could not now be abandoned. Clayton, of course, had been working since he had organized the Intelligence Department to stir up discontent against the Turks. As early as November 1914 he had encouraged the Idrisi in 'Asir to declare against the Turks, cut their communications with Yemen, and relieve Turkish pressure on the incompetent British forces in Aden, and he was one of the first to listen seriously to the ideas of Storrs to counter Turkish influence in Arabia.[71] Even before the outbreak of war with Turkey, Storrs had discussed with Clayton in September the possibility of turning the Arabs against the Turks.

> I had recourse (like so many of my betters after me) to the calm, friendly wisdom of G. H. [sic] Clayton, the "Bertie" of Khartum, of Cairo, of Palestine and Mesopotamia. His balanced advice could no more be hustled by a crisis than could his beautiful deliberate handwriting: his character as an officer and a man was, when he left Jerusalem, to be well summed up by Sir Herbert Samuel in the last watchword of Marcus Aurelius, *Aequanimitas* . . . the time and the place and keys of necessary knowledge adding to his natural abilities that element of fortune without which none can achieve. Bertie approved my thesis. Further, he actively condoned my proposed irregularity of urging it upon Lord Kitchener in a private letter, which I accordingly dispatched.[72]

[70] Béraud-Villars, pp. 93–94.
[71] Richard Aldington, *Lawrence of Arabia* . . . (Chicago, 1955), p. 137.
[72] Storrs, p. 163.

Kitchener approved in less than a week, and from that point Clayton, Storrs, McMahon (who became High Commissioner in January 1915), and Wingate began to develop the idea of an Arab revolt. Storrs and Clayton discreetly opened conversations with Arab leaders living in Cairo. The conversations followed the same theme as the messages Kitchener was then sending to the Sharif of Mecca—alliance with Great Britain in opposition to the Turkish call to the jihad.[73] At the same time Clayton was using his influence to continue the trade in foodstuffs with the Hijaz, for even though the Turks would benefit, the Arabs would benefit more and would be grateful for the hand that feeds them. It was, as Wingate correctly pointed out, "a policy which is bound to tell in the long run."[74] In the end the Sharif was won over to the revolt, an achievement, as T. E. Lawrence observed, for which Clayton deserves much of the credit.

> The happy union of his [Storrs'] local knowledge, with the experience and acumen of Sir Henry [McMahon], and the sympathy of Clayton, so impressed the Sherif, that that very difficult person accepted their guarded undertakings as sufficient assurance for beginning his revolt against Turkey.[75]

Once the revolt began, Clayton had to ensure adequate support for the unorthodox operations in the desert. To facilitate such an enormous task, the Arab Bureau was created by Clayton as a branch of the Department of Military Intelligence, the core of which was composed of the remnants and spirit of the Intrusives. Established in February 1916, the Arab Bureau was regarded by its creators as a means not only to carry on the Arab Revolt and intelligence activities among the Arabs themselves, but also as an instrument to spread the unconventional methods of the revolt into the more orthodox circles of the Committee for Imperial Defence in London and the government of India at Delhi.[76] The Arab Bureau operated informally under the immediate direction of D. G. Hogarth, an archae-

[73] George Antonius, *The Arab Awakening* (New York, 1939), pp. 159–61.
[74] Wingate to Clayton, 23 January 1915, C.P.
[75] T. E. Lawrence, *Revolt in the Desert* (New York, 1927), p. 2.
[76] Wingate to Clayton, 18 February 1916, C.P.

ologist and Commander in the Royal Naval Volunteer Reserve, while Clayton remained in charge of the Intelligence Department itself but was ultimately responsible for the activities of the Bureau. Sir Henry McMahon was influential in the formation of this strange collection of travelers, archaeologists, and political officers and continued to work closely with it. The Bureau was composed of no more than fifteen officers at any one time, each with the most diverse activities. Behind the shield of Clayton's leadership, they "worked without interruption and bubbled over with ideas. In the common effort and celibate life these individuals rediscovered their student mentality."[77] Although the vague statement as to their functions theoretically restricted the Arab Bureau to "the study and development of British policy in Arab affairs and the collection of information," the Bureau's activities ranged far beyond that scope.[78] This was not unusual for its highly individualistic constituents. Lawrence prided himself as an Intrusive and a member of the Bureau who made no apologies for his colleagues' attempts

> to break into the accepted halls of English foreign policy, and build a new people in the East, despite the rails laid down for us by our ancestors. Therefore, from our hybrid Intelligence office in Cairo (a jangling place which for its incessant bells and running to and fro, was likened by Aubrey Herbert to an Oriental railway station) we began to work upon our chiefs, far and near.[79]

In some respects the Arab Bureau was more Arab than the Arabs. Its members regarded the Arab Revolt as more than simply a means to embarrass the Turks. It was for the Arabs themselves as much as for the British, and although the somewhat naïve idealism of those perennial students was drowned in the flood of postwar cynicism, in the end they succeeded in stimulating the nationalism of the Arabs far beyond their wildest daydreams. In other ways they were a boyish group, immature and irresponsible, but imaginative, appealing, and above all, successful. With the shallow but delightful sophistication of the Junior Common Room Hogarth summed up his colleagues in the doggerel:

[77] Béraud-Villars, p. 94.

[78] Quoted in Aldington, p. 148.

[79] Lawrence, *Seven Pillars of Wisdom*, pp. 58–59.

Do you know
The Arab Bureau?"
Asked Hogarth; and answered:
"Clayton stability,
Symes versatility
Cornwallis is practical
Dawnay syntactical,
Mackintosh havers,
And Fielding palavers,
Macindoe easy,
And Wordie not breezy:
Lawrence licentiate to dream and to dare
And Yours Very Faithfully, *bon à tout faire*.[80]

But the Arab Bureau, if the most exciting branch of his Department, was only one of Clayton's many responsibilities. He constituted, in effect, "a human link" between the several and rival authorities in Cairo. He not only played many parts but possessed the gifts to develop them. "Although seemingly casual, and even lazy, he had a knack of keeping touch with all relevant matters, together with a capacity to smile at troubles that often helped to allay them."[81] Lawrence admired his capacity for dealing with so many complex tasks with caution and imperturbability, remarking that he "habitually cut the lunch hour to cope with his thronging work."[82] His efforts did not go unnoticed, and in April 1916 he was promoted to the rank of Brigadier-General. In that same month he received further honors when, at a banquet given by the French agent, M. Defrance, on the occasion of Maxwell's departure, Clayton was awarded the order of Officier de la Légion d'Honneur.

In the summer of 1916 Clayton returned to London to seek further support for the Arab Revolt and to instill some enthusiasm into the Indian authorities for the idea. He had meetings at the Foreign Office, the India Office, the War Office, and the Admiralty, and concluded with an interview with the King. Everywhere he went he argued the case for the revolt with clarity and precision and

[80] Storrs, p. 169 n.
[81] Liddell Hart, p. 67.
[82] Lawrence, *Revolt in the Desert*, p. 121.

created a favorable impression not only of the Arab rebellion but of himself as well. Back in Cairo Clayton continued his work behind the scenes—subtle but effective. He succeeded in freeing General Ja'far al-'Askari, who later became King Faysal's representative in London, from a prison in Cairo. Exercising his discretion in the opposite direction, Clayton urged that a French military mission should be sent to the Hijaz to placate Britain's suspicious allies. Edouard Brémond led the French mission and, guided by Clayton, did much to prevent Anglo-French misunderstandings over the Hijaz operations.[83] It was Clayton who arranged and managed the visit of Sykes and Picot to the Hijaz to explain to Husayn and his son Faysal the broad provisions of their treaty and the intentions of the British government which helped to offset condemnatory German propaganda about it.[84] But his greatest contribution was the more mundane gathering, analysis, and dissemination of information. An "Arab Bulletin" was published between June 1916 and December 1918 for secret distribution among the highest officials. With his obsession for detail, Wingate was charmed.

> I am immensely struck with the excellence of the bulletins and the clear and concise way in which the matter is recorded—these bulletins alone are ample proof, if any is needed, of the valuable services that are being rendered by the Bureau in connection with the all important Arab question.[85]

In addition Clayton wrote long and detailed letters to his associates and friends all over the Middle East which served to inform and to coordinate their many activities. Stack, who in 1917 was the acting Sirdar and Governor-General when Wingate was elevated to the High Commissionership in Egypt, wrote of these letters: "Symes writes so diplomatically that he gives little real information. One letter of yours owing to its frankness gives me more of an insight into the 'heart of things' than a dozen from other sources."[86]

[83] Édouard Brémonde, *Le Hedjaz dans la Guerre Mondiale* (Paris, 1931), pp. 44–46.

[84] Liddell Hart, p. 49.

[85] Wingate to Clayton, 3 December 1916, C.P.

[86] Stack to Clayton, 19 May 1917, C.P.

With his staff at the Intelligence Department Clayton established a firm trust and understanding by his frank and straightforward manner devoid of bluster or bluff. His sense of humor made the failures of his subordinates more palatable and the differences with his superiors more tolerable, and "it was especially called upon to protect one of the former [Lawrence] from the frequent wrath of senior officers whose sense of dignity had quenched their sense of humour."[87] Without his defense, Lawrence's genius as a guerilla leader might well have foundered on his failures. He was rewarded by the ultimate success of the Arab Revolt. When Lawrence captured 'Aqabah in 1917 he did so contrary to Clayton's orders to concentrate on Medina, which the Bureau thought was soon to be evacuated by the Turks. When Lawrence returned to Cairo after his triumph, Clayton ignored his insubordination and agreed without hesitation to send gold and supplies to Arabia.

Clayton's flexibility, imagination, and disregard, when necessary, for military correctness, inevitably resulted in friction with the General Staff no matter how quietly and tactfully he went about his affairs. Consequently, in the summer of 1916 his Department was divided and several of his men were assigned to an officer in Murray's entourage, Colonel Holdich. Wingate was sympathetic but could do nothing. "Your effort to serve 2 (or 3?) masters was comparatively successful during the Maxwell regime owing to the personal relations existing between two at least of the masters—but with the disappearance of Maxwell and the arrival of Murray, you could hardly expect the latter to accept the anomalous situation, much less his GHQ staff."[88] But if Murray held Clayton's methods in low esteem and sought to restrict his influence, Sir Henry McMahon did not. He wrote a glowing tribute of Clayton's work during the first two years of the war, praising his knowledge, his imperturbable good nature, and especially his service "in the collection, formation, and supervision of the 'Arab bureau'. . . . The credit for his work has been claimed by some, and assigned, by the uninformed, to others. Such must ever be the lot of loyal and unself-

[87] Liddell Hart, p. 67.

[88] Wingate to Clayton, 13 September 1916, C.P., and Béraud-Villars, p. 95.

seeking men like Sir Gilbert Clayton."[89] Modesty kept him in the background, but it was precisely there that his incisive direction and unshakable courage enabled the Arab Revolt to be conducted successfully by the colorful but erratic T. E. Lawrence. Only one of several brilliant leaders of irregular troops in a long and hard-fought war, Lawrence owes his fame as much to the skillful promotion of Lowell Thomas as to his own deeds. Ironically, Gilbert Clayton, who was most responsible for Lawrence's opportunities, has been virtually forgotten.

Although Murray may not have approved of Clayton's views on the war in the Middle East, he was sensible enough not to let his talents go to waste. At the end of 1916 he was appointed Brigadier-General, General Staff for military operations in the Hijaz where Lawrence was rallying the bedouins for action against the long Turkish lines of communication. Although under Murray his influence at headquarters had diminished, Clayton was ideally suited to direct the Hijaz campaign. The ultimate responsibility, however, remained with Sir Reginald Wingate as Governor-General of the Sudan and Sirdar of the Egyptian Army, but Wingate's representative at Jiddah, Lieutenant-Colonel Cyril Wilson, preferred to work directly with Clayton. "I am so glad you are running the show in Cairo. . . . I was desperately afraid Master [Wingate] and Symes were going to do it all, now as you say you have a definite job."[90] Wilson's optimism was not unfounded, and after several Arab successes he wrote again that "ever since you took the job earlier this year, things have been infinitely better . . . for me."[91] But as the Arabs swept north, so too did Clayton.

In June 1917 General Allenby replaced Sir Archibald Murray. The new Commander-in-Chief set out to break the stalemate in southern Palestine, drive the Turks north, and capture Jerusalem by Christmas. Although he was being supplied with reinforcements of men and supplies, Allenby required a political officer with knowledge, experience, and the ability to reconcile the manifold conflicts

89 Sir Henry McMahon to *The Times*, 17 September 1929, p. 17.

90 Lt.-Col. Cyril Wilson to Clayton, January 1917, C.P.

91 Wilson to Clayton, 20 March 1917, C.P.

of a land where Muslim, Jew, and Christian combined their deep spiritual interests with suspicion, if not hostility, toward their religious rivals. He offered the position to Gilbert Clayton who accepted. The post, of course, meant a final break with the Sudan, and although all regretted his leaving the service, Lee Stack expressed the general opinion that "the work you would be doing there [in Palestine] is imperially more important than what you would be doing for the Soudan in Egypt."[92]

Jerusalem fell to the Egyptian Expeditionary Force on 9 December 1917 and two days later Allenby entered in triumph. The procession passed into the conquered city through the Jaffa Gate, Clayton walking behind his chief with M. Georges Picot, Lieutenant-Colonel W. H. Deedes, and T. E. Lawrence, whom Allenby had graciously made Clayton's Staff Officer for the day. Clayton's work really began after the capture of Jerusalem, for he had to combine the duties of a military governor of occupied Palestine (Occupied Enemy Territory Administration–South) with the supervision of Britain's relations with the Arab tribesmen beyond the Jordan. The work itself was overwhelming, and he requested that Ronald Storrs join him in Jerusalem. Storrs wrote in his journal: "After luncheon for a 2-hour talk with Clayton I find him still, outside and apart from his work, at which he is first class, a personality rich in common sense."[93] During the spring of 1918 Clayton worked feverishly to reestablish all the organization of government, which had broken down after the flight of Turkish officials, and to persuade the population of Palestine to accept the new administration, which in many ways was strikingly different from that of the Turks. He restored order to the chaotic finances, organized postal services, reopened schools, rehabilitated agriculture, and encouraged trade. From his camp attached to the G.H.Q. at Bir Salim, he dealt with all manner of people, many of whom were in a position to make endless trouble for the British administration if not handled properly. And the matters that had to be considered were not easily resolved.

[92] Lee Stack to Clayton, 31 December 1917, C.P.

[93] Storrs, p. 290.

It was Clayton who had to reconcile the people of Palestine to the introduction of Egyptian money and the demonetization of all their hoarded Turkish paper; to persuade the straining Army Transport to bear additional burdens, not only for the benefit of starving civilians, but even for the purpose of restarting local trade; to restrain over-enthusiastic Zionists from compromising their prospects by unwise speech-making; to maintain relations with semi-independent Arab tribes beyond the Jordan; to soothe the susceptibilities of multitudinous and querulous ecclesiastics of three faiths and a dozen churches; to maintain liaison with the Allied mission, and entertain Turkish deserters of high rank.[94]

Clayton managed the Palestinians as he had dealt with his subordinates in the Arab Bureau and the Sudan Agency, listening dispassionately, judging impartially, and inspiring confidence. One of the many disagreements of both caste and creed which were brought to him for settlement was the case of dirty windows in the Church of the Nativity. The windows belonged to two Christian communities who had long argued which should clean them. Clayton asked how long it was since the window was last cleaned. "Forty years," was the reply. "Well then, let it remain another year," was Clayton's answer. The subject was never heard of again.[95] But it was precisely these administrative matters, many of them petty, which began to interfere with his work as Chief Political Officer to the Egyptian Expeditionary Force that was advancing northward to Damascus, and on 16 April 1918 he handed over the Palestine administration to Sir Arthur Money. During his short tenure as Chief Administrator Clayton was known for his "power of being pleasantly but definitely final."[96] Storrs commented that under Clayton's "unruffled equanimity and sympathy no problem seemed insoluble. As Chief Political Officer to the Force he was far too busy (even if he desired) to interfere in detail. He expected, but never inflicted proposals. He was never in the way and never out of the way."[97] Sir Wyndham Deedes, who served under Clayton

[94] *The Times*, 12 September 1929, p. 14.
[95] Notes to the editor from Lady Clayton.
[96] *The Times*, 12 September 1929, p. 14.
[97] Storrs, p. 306.

during most of the war and for several years thereafter, appreciated the fact that he was always given a free hand, yet it was Clayton who assumed the responsibility for his subordinates' mistakes while giving them the credit for successes.

> If asked to name his most outstanding qualities, I should say wisdom and imperturbability . . . he was ever the same, cool and collected, and he had the capacity of communicating his calm to others. . . . Not a great talker, he was a tireless listener to the endless irrelevancies in which the Easterner delights to indulge. He had a singular understanding of the native mind . . . the Jews in Palestine looked upon him as their especial friend, but he equally claimed the affection of the Palestine Arabs. He was absolutely straight and impartial, and what counts for much in the East—he was known to be a strict follower of his own religion.[98]

Clayton's successes did not go unrecognized. He was mentioned in despatches seven times and was awarded the C.B. (1917), the K.B.E. (1919), and a host of foreign decorations, including the Grand Commandership of the Order of King George I of Greece, St. Anne of Russia, the Legion of Honor, and the Second Class Order of the Nahda. He had previously earned during his Sudan service the fourth class of Osmanieh and the third class of the Medjidie orders of Egypt.

In 1919 Lord Allenby was appointed High Commissioner for Egypt, and he selected Clayton for the crucial post of Adviser to the Egyptian Ministry of the Interior. This was one of the few positions for which Gilbert Clayton had ever openly expressed a desire, and with that goal in mind he had turned down several overtures from Sir Percy Cox to take the post of Deputy High Commissioner of 'Iraq.[99] At that time the British Adviser to the Egyptian Ministry of the Interior was the most critical post in the country because of the nationalist disorders and bitter anti-British feeling which had swept the country after the conclusion of the war. Britain had refused to withdraw the Protectorate and the Egyptians re-

[98] Sir Wyndham Deedes to *The Times*, 13 September 1929, p. 14.

[99] Arnold T. Wilson, *Loyalties, Mesopotamia, 1914–1917* (London, 1930), pp. 300–301; Stack to Clayton, 28 June 1917, C.P.

sented it. Aroused by the demands of the leading nationalist, Sa'd Zaghlul, and angered by his abrupt exile, the Egyptians reacted violently against the British community throughout March 1919. By the time Allenby had been appointed High Commissioner at the end of the month, a semblance of order, but neither peace nor confidence, had been restored by military force. Clayton's task was to establish peace where there was order, to regain confidence where there was none, and to repair, if possible, the damage to Anglo-Egyptian relations. To maintain order Clayton characteristically preferred the subtle methods of persuasion and influence to draconian repression. He urged that the censorship of the press be "tactful and sympathetic" and insisted that supplies of food and water be made more readily available. He advised the High Commissioner to remain aloof from religious questions and told British officials to carry on their functions without making official pronouncements that were usually distorted, creating more harm than good. He urged time and again that order is best maintained by personal contacts with the people and their leaders. He wrote:

> I am entirely of the opinion that nothing has so great an effect as the visible appearance in the provinces of high British officials. I have endeavoured to carry out this policy by visiting nearly every Mudiria and Markaz and I cannot but think that, from all I have heard the result has been good. I venture to think that this point might with good effect be impressed upon high officials of all Ministries. . . . A slight delay in or even neglect of routine work is amply compensated for by the effect produced in the Provinces by actual personal contact with responsible British officials.[100]

The results of such personal contact on the people were impressed upon a group of Members of Parliament in Egypt to study the Egyptian situation. When they halted at a railway crossing to wait for a passing train, an old man who kept a peanut stall by the roadside darted out to greet Sir Gilbert and exchange greetings about their respective families. As they drove on, a rather bewildered M.P. said, "But do you *know* that old man?" "Yes–known him for years," replied Clayton. "But do you know many like him?" queried

[100] Memorandum by Clayton, 29 May 1919, C.P.

the M.P. "Yes," answered Sir Gilbert, "I should think some hundreds."[101]

As the British Adviser to the Ministry of the Interior, Clayton was not only expected to keep the High Commissioner informed of Egyptian politics and public opinion but to suggest policies to reconcile Anglo-Egyptian relations. Gertrude Bell, who visited Cairo in September 1919, recounted his views at that time. His principal concern was that the nationalist movement might boycott the Milner Mission which was to ascertain the cause of the disorders. He feared that the Egyptians might ignore the Mission and instead entrust their views to their delegation at the Paris Peace Conference. Although he did not agree with all the details of the nationalist claims, in general he regarded the nationalist aspirations for independence as legitimate and that Britain should grant such independence but guard her imperial interests—the Suez Canal, the Nile waters, the army and the police, and the Sudan. He supposed that left to their own devices, the Egyptians would make mistakes and that departmental efficiency would diminish, but he insisted that they had the right, as they claimed, to a fair trial. If such concessions were made, he thought that the majority of the country would be won back to Britain.[102]

In 1919 this was indeed a courageous and, from the point of view of the British government, a most unpopular policy. Perhaps, however, more than any other example his support for Egyptian independence best demonstrates his flexibility and common sense that recognized that the realities of the past were but myths in the present; for in 1917, just two years before, he had advocated the annexation of Egypt to the British Empire. By 1919, however, he saw that this was no longer possible and was prepared to admit it. By 1921 he was determined to stake his career on that judgment.

His argument in 1917 for the abolition of the Protectorate and the annexation of Egypt to the British Empire was based primarily on imperial strategy.

> From what may be termed the Imperial strategical point of view, therefore, it does not seem possible under the existing regime

[101] Notes by Miss E. M. Clayton.

[102] E. Burgoyne, *Gertrude Bell*, vol. ii, pp. 111–13.

> to secure that complete and absolute control which is so necessary in Egypt where lies the keystone of our whole Near Eastern fabric.[103]

In March 1919, however, he accepted the Protectorate as the only means to restore order and helped to convince the nationalist leaders to use their influence to end the disturbances as the first step toward a new and presumably more liberal settlement.[104] As his work in the Ministry took him all over Egypt and placed him in contact with all classes of its people, he came more and more to appreciate the aspirations of the Egyptians, and by the early autumn of 1919 he was thinking in terms of political freedom for Egypt with, of course, adequate safeguards for imperial defense. His association with such a policy was undoubtedly the outstanding decision of his tenure at the Ministry, and in a memorandum dated 8 October 1921 he officially advocated the abolition of the Protectorate, which he had been urging privately, and the following January he made his recommendations public.

> A decision which does not admit the principle of Egyptian independence and which maintains the Protectorate must entail serious risk of revolution throughout the country, and in any case result in complete administrative chaos rendering Government impossible.[105]

Lord Allenby had come to the same conclusion as his counsellors and was clearly influenced by them, particularly Clayton. Negotiations had proved impossible in the anti-British atmosphere then existing in Egypt, and these men argued that only a unilateral declaration by Britain announcing Egypt's sovereign independence would provide the basis for discussions to secure Britain's imperial interests. In order to impress their views on the home government

103 "The Future Political Status of Egypt," by G. F. Clayton, 22 July 1917, C.P.

104 "Rough Notes Taken at the Meeting of the Nationalist Delegation with General Watson and a Subsequent Interview with General Clayton," by "Major G. S.," 16 March 1919; and "Memorandum on the Egyptian Situation," by G. F. Clayton, 17 March 1919, C.P.

105 "Memorandum by Dowson, Clayton, Patterson, and Hayter," January 1922, C.P.

Allenby, accompanied by Clayton and Maurice Amos, Adviser to the Ministry of Justice, left Alexandria for London in February 1922. During the critical talks that followed the three delegates succeeded in convincing the British government, where all others had failed, to abolish the Protectorate. The Declaration which followed on 28 February 1922 was in large measure attributable to the arguments of Allenby, Clayton, and Amos.[106]

In effect Clayton had talked himself out of a job, for with the publication of the Declaration the post of British Adviser to the Ministry of Interior was abolished. Clayton's work was done, and he left the Ministry in May 1922. His departure was regretted by all those Egyptians who had recognized his efforts on their behalf. A large farewell banquet was held at the Continental-Savoy Hotel in Clayton's honor, attended by the Prime Minister of Egypt, Sarwat Pasha, and all his Cabinet, three former prime ministers, notables, and all the governors from every province in Egypt. Sarwat Pasha spoke of Sir Gilbert's personal sacrifices for Egypt and his self-denial in laying the foundation of a new regime, knowing full well that the coming of that regime would lead to his own retirement. Although he was awarded the Grand Cordon of the Order of the Nile, the greatest tribute to Clayton and his work was that during these difficult years he had not only consolidated his friendship with the many Egyptians he had known in the prewar days, but established a large number of new ones among the local politicians. His perception and sympathy for the realities of the present had succeeded where insistence upon the traditions of the past would have surely failed.

Clayton was not long unemployed, and before the summer was out he had returned to Palestine to succeed Sir Wyndham Deedes as the Chief Secretary of the Government of Palestine, which at that time was under the High Commissioner, Sir Herbert Samuel. Once again in Jerusalem he exhibited the same impartial, painstaking, and patient qualities that he had demonstrated before and continued to win the respect of the rival races and religions. Perhaps his most important contribution during his three years in Palestine

[106] Lord Lloyd, *Egypt Since Cromer* (London, 1933), vol. ii, pp. 57–65.

was to negotiate an agreement between Britain and Trans-Jordan. The discussions opened on 16 October 1922 at the Carlton Hotel in London between Clayton, H. St. John B. Philby (the British Resident in Trans-Jordan whom Clayton had first met three and a half years before in Palestine), and 'Ali Rida' ar-Rikabi Pasha, the chief adviser to the Amir 'Abd Allah. The discussions ranged from customs dues to military assistance, and from the future political status of Trans-Jordan to the question of extradition for the assailants of General Gouraud. The problem of Trans-Jordan's relations with Najd was particularly acute, for the situation had been complicated on the one hand by the results of Philby's mission to Nuri Sha'lan and on the other by the encroachment of the Wahhabi faith into Trans-Jordan. These preliminary discussions and others that followed between Clayton and the Amir 'Abd Allah prepared the way for the conclusion of an agreement the following year which recognized the independence of Trans-Jordan.[107]

In Palestine itself Clayton's principal duty was to keep the peace between the rival religious and political factions, and during Lord Balfour's visit in 1923 Clayton's skill and tact were important factors in preventing disorder.

> I saw him repeatedly at that time; he was constantly pouring oil on troubled waters, and, when difficulties were overcome, one realized that this was largely the result of the work of a man who was trusted by Arabs and Jews alike.[108]

Another colleague in Palestine analyzed Clayton's ability to win the trust and confidence of the Palestinians.

> Clayton's outstanding characteristic was his sincerity; a sincerity firmly fixed on deep religious convictions, his honesty of purpose was so apparent that no man, Moslem, Jew, Agnostic, or Christian, could be long in his presence without being awed by it. I have known persons come in and begin to make the most scandalous statements to gain their own ends, but, after a few minutes with

[107] "Negotiations in London, October-December 1922 between G. F. Clayton and the Amir 'Abdullah," C.P.

[108] H. Charles Woods to *The Near East and India*, 18 September 1929, p. 335.

> Clayton, his quiet smile and steady gaze had quite disarmed them, and they left his presence abashed at their own baseness. During our two years of daily contact, I never knew him to lose his temper. He never let a colleague down. He never gave a promise that he did not keep.[109]

Clayton retired as Chief Secretary in 1925. In many ways his three years in Palestine were the happiest of his life. Not since the halcyon days in Cairo just before the war had he and his wife enjoyed the peace of Jerusalem, which had yet to see the bloody strife of later years. Tensions, ill-feeling, and even hatred existed in the land of peace, but none had yet reached the intensity that a little tact combined with forthright dealing could not prevent from erupting into disorder. Jerusalem society was friendly and congenial with all the warmth of a self-contained group and without the impersonal relations found in a larger city, and in his position as Chief Secretary Sir Gilbert extended his circle of friendship to all groups. Today he is still remembered as the best of Englishmen by the few who remain in Jerusalem from those quiet days.

Upon returning to England Sir Gilbert Clayton did not remain in retirement for long. The British Government was anxious to conclude a settlement with Ibn Sa'ud, whose rise to power in Arabia threatened British interests from the Persian Gulf to the Red Sea. The government required a negotiator experienced in dealing with the Arabs and yet one who could be relied upon to protect Britain's imperial interests, and Clayton appeared eminently qualified for the task. He had thirty years of experience in the Middle East both in civil and military positions, in which he had gained insights and knowledge of the Arabs. Moreover, he was known for his tact, firmness, and impartiality that had won the confidence, if not the friendship, of men of divergent interests and opinions from the Sudan to Syria. Perhaps "the essential point was his personality, in which (if a comparative stranger may venture to judge) the decisiveness of a man of action went hand in hand with a spontaneous kindliness towards his fellow men—of whatever race and whatever

[109] E. Keith-Roach to *The Times*, 4 October 1929, p. 10. E. Keith-Roach was Clayton's First Assistant Secretary in Palestine.

station."[110] He was asked to take charge of the mission on 6 August and two days later he agreed. He requested that George Antonius of the Education Department of the Palestine government be allowed to accompany the mission as its secretary. The request was granted and preparations begun for the journey and the negotiations.

In the autumn of 1925 the forces of Ibn Sa'ud were in effective occupation of the greater part of the Hijaz, including the Holy City of Mecca, and were investing Jiddah where the harried King 'Ali was maintaining a precarious hold. Neither combatant then occupied the northern districts of the Hijaz. In his discussions with Ibn Sa'ud Clayton was instructed to emphasize that the British government only wished to see a speedy termination of hostilities and the reestablishment of peace in the Hijaz. A British offer of mediation still stood, and Great Britain regretted Ibn Sa'ud's unwillingness to accept it, but despite Britain's past support of Husayn "while hostilities continue His Majesty's Government have no alternative but to maintain an attitude of strict neutrality."[111] The matter of Clayton's authority to negotiate agreements on behalf of Trans-Jordan and 'Iraq had to be precisely defined. The status of Trans-Jordan presented no problem, but the Organic Law of 'Iraq prevented that government from being bound to terms of any agreement Clayton, as a representative of the British government, might make with Ibn Sa'ud without ratification by the 'Iraqi Parliament.[112] This difficulty was gotten around by sending Tawfiq Bey as-Suwaydi, the Assistant Counsellor in the Ministry of Justice, with Clayton as the representative of that government; but Faysal, an old friend of Sir Gilbert, was satisfied to leave the actual task of negotiations in his hands. Even with Tawfiq Bey as-Suwaydi, however, the British High Commissioner in Baghdad could not absolutely guarantee ratification by the 'Iraqi Parliament but did not believe that there would be any real difficulties.

At the termination of the Kuwait Conference two main issues

[110] Arnold J. Toynbee, "Iraq, 'A Going Concern with one Proviso'," *Manchester Guardian*, 15 October 1929. Toynbee was the guest of Sir Gilbert at Baghdad at the time of his death in 1929.

[111] Vernon to Clayton, 10 September 1925, C.P.

[112] Colonial Office to Clayton, 8 September 1925, C.P.

remained unresolved between Britain and Ibn Sa'ud. According to the terms of the Second Protocol of Al-'Uqayr, Great Britain considered the 'Iraqi-Najdi border to be fixed. From Colonel Knox's experience at the Kuwait Conference, however, Clayton was warned to expect Ibn Sa'ud to advance a claim to the area north of Jabal 'Unazah. He was told, in his instructions from the Colonial Office, that

> such a frontier would involve the intersection of Nejd territory between Iraq and Trans-Jordan and would place Ibn Saud astride the Imperial Air Route to the East. *This cannot be permitted*, and in no circumstances should you assent to any extension of Nejd territory to the north which would have the effect of separating Iraq from Trans-Jordan.[113]

Imperial policy also determined the position that Clayton was to take in regard to the southern boundary of Trans-Jordan, which was not defined until the signing of a formal agreement between the kingdom of Jordan and Sa'udi Arabia in 1965. Britain had made a unilateral statement in July 1925 announcing the annexation of the Ma'an-'Aqabah province of the Hijaz to Trans-Jordan. Since this area had previously been part of the Hijaz, Ibn Sa'ud regarded that the British, on behalf of the Amir 'Abd Allah, had preempted what would rightfully fall to him as the conqueror of the Hijaz. This same area, however, was regarded as vital to imperial communications and could not be allowed to fall into the hands of a ruler over whom the British had little control or influence. Clayton was therefore instructed simply to inform Ibn Sa'ud, if the question arose, that:

> His Majesty's Government considers that it would be advisable in your conversations with him [Ibn Sa'ud] to treat this matter as a *chose jugée*, merely informing him, if he should raise the point, that the frontier of Trans-Jordan starts from the intersection of meridian 38° and parallel 29°35′, crosses the Hejaz Railway south of Mudawwara and joins the Gulf of Akaba at a point south of that town.[114]

This left then only the eastern border between Trans-Jordan and

[113] Vernon to Clayton, 10 September 1925, C.P.
[114] *Ibid.*

Najd to be determined. Having collected data from Colonel C. H. F. Cox, George Antonius composed a "Memorandum on the Eastern Frontier of Trans-Jordan" in which he listed the arguments in favor of keeping the boundary as far to the east as possible. Antonius urged that the town of Kaf together with the four smaller wadis leading eastward into the Wadi as-Sirhan and that valley's whole northern section should be included in Trans-Jordan. In support of this claim he listed three "weighty reasons." Strategically, Kaf was an excellent observation post for raids coming up the Wadi as-Sirhan toward 'Amman. British military advisers concurred in this view, and Colonel Cox added that "a further reason for denying him [Ibn Sa'ud] this area is that there is a good motor road running from Ma'an via Djafar (a fortified watering place) and Bair to Azrak."[115] If Ibn Sa'ud could control Kaf, he could also endanger 'Iraq's communications with Syria. Moreover, if the Trans-Jordan border were moved farther west, the Hijaz Railway, which the British had guaranteed to defend, would be within easy reach of raiders from Najd. Economic reasons were also used to include Kaf in Trans-Jordan. Both Cox and Antonius pointed out that the territory comprising the four wadis and the northern half of the Wadi as-Sirhan was the natural and customary grazing ground of two important tribes, the Ruwalah and the Bani Sakhr of Trans-Jordan, while the salt villages near Kaf provided for their residents an income of which it was felt it would be unfair to deprive them. The third "weighty reason" was political. Up to that date the Ruwalah and the Bani Sakhr had remained untouched by Wahhabi religious propaganda. If Ibn Sa'ud controlled Kaf it would provide an excellent base for the dissemination of Wahhabism among Trans-Jordan tribes.[116] Nevertheless, in spite of these rather important arguments for retaining Kaf, the Colonial Office did not wish to bind Clayton to an inflexible position during negotiations which, from past experience, would require give and take on both sides. He was thus left to his own discretion over the village and was instructed that he could, in the last resort, concede Kaf to Najd.

[115] Colonel C. H. F. Cox to Antonius, 9 September 1925, C.P.

[116] "Memorandum on the Eastern Frontier of Trans-Jordan" by George Antonius, C.P.

The outstanding issue between 'Iraq and Najd was the whole question of raiding across the frontier that had been established by the Protocols of Al-'Uqayr. The Kuwait Conference had made progress by defining the necessary steps that would be required to prevent transfrontier raids, but the delegates had failed to reach any accord on the important question of the restoration of loot and the payment of compensation for damages arising from past plundering. The raids of the refugee Shammar tribesmen in 'Iraq were as much a source of grievance to Ibn Sa'ud as the Wahhabi raids up the Wadi as–Sirhan were to Trans-Jordan. Clayton was instructed that a fixed boundary was required and that any agreement made to settle the question of raiding across that boundary should also apply to Trans-Jordan.[117] The Colonial Office hoped that an agreement on transfrontier raiding could be reached, particularly since the 'Iraq Government had removed the Shammar refugees inland to deny them easy access to the frontier. Other minor matters to be taken up between Clayton and Ibn Sa'ud included investigating means for the protection of Najd interests in Syria, the advisability of sending a permanent British representative to Najd, and the renegotiation of the Anglo-Sa'udi agreement of 1915, which had become outdated by the events of the postwar years. The manner in which Clayton achieved success in his negotiations with Ibn Sa'ud is recorded in his official report presented to the Colonial Office, but a more personal and readable account can be found in his diary.

[117] Vernon to Clayton, 10 September 1925, and Dobbs to Amery, 30 June 1925, C.P.

CHAPTER 1

From London to Bahra:
24 September–10 October 1925

24th September–Thursday.

I left Esher with Enid [Lady Clayton] by the 9:25 a.m. train for Waterloo, whence we drove to Victoria, calling at the Foreign Office on the way, where I picked up my passport and a special Courier's Bag (No. 35) for Jeddah. Left Victoria by the Continental train at 11:00 a.m. We had a calm crossing to Calais, and I had lunch on board the boat. At Calais I found some difficulty in securing a place in the through Wagon Lit coach to Marseilles as my sleeping berth had only been booked from Paris, but I eventually arranged matters by paying the supplementary fare as far as Paris. The only people travelling with me whom I knew were Mrs. Gerrard and Mrs. Shute of Sarafand and Miss Williams of Miss Warburton's school in Jerusalem.[1]

25th September–Friday.

We arrived at Marseilles at 10:40 a.m. after a comfortable journey as I had had a two-berth sleeping compartment to myself. I secured

---

24th September–Thursday.

[1] Located near Ramlah about four miles from Lyddah and almost eight miles from Jaffah, Sarafand was a British military cantonment where, in 1925, were stationed the 9th Lancers and the British Gendarmerie. Mrs. Gerrard occupied a large, two-story stone house about three miles from Sarafand which had been a German school before the war and was Lord Allenby's headquarters from January to September 1918. Sarafand is now known as Zerifin, Israel. Miss Warburton's School was the British High School at Jerusalem, later known as the Jerusalem Girls College. Begun by Miss Warburton

the services of the American Express Agency courier, collected my baggage, and drove down to the P. & O. which was already in dock. I found myself splendidly accommodated in a spacious, double-bedded cabine-de-luxe all to myself with private lobby and bathroom attached.

I lunched on board, unpacked, and then walked into the town, where I made a few small purchases, had tea at the Grand Hotel du Louvre, wrote to Enid, and sent postcards to the children. I walked back to the ship, dined, and spent the evening on board. The *Rawalpindi* is a very fine ship and quite new, this being her maiden voyage.[2]

26th September–Saturday.

We spent the day at sea, passing through the Straits of Bonifaccio in the afternoon. The weather was lovely–fine and calm, with a cool breeze.

On board I met General Godwin, now Inspector General of Cavalry in India, who was B.G.G.S. Desert Mounted Corps in E.E.F. during the war. Also Major Raymond, Indian Army, who was formerly at the Isle of Wight College. A dance was held after dinner.

27th September–Sunday.

16th Sunday after Trinity.

Still beautiful weather. We passed through the Straits of Messina in the late afternoon.

Matins were held at 10:30 a.m. in the dining saloon. They were conducted by Captain Redhead and were very well attended.

---

after the First World War under the auspices of various Anglican societies and the Church of Scotland, the school, formerly a German orphanage, continued to operate until 1948 when it was forced to close by hostilities between the Jews and the Arabs in Jerusalem. Miss Warburton left the school several years later. Miss Sims Williams was a teacher at the school.

25th September–Friday.

[2] R.M.S. *Rawalpindi* was built in 1925 by Harland & Wolff, Ltd., Greenock, for the Peninsular and Oriental Steam Navigation Company and for several

28th September—Monday.

Still at sea and the weather remains delightful. Passed Crete in the afternoon. The ship is quite full; practically all the passengers are for Bombay.

Preparations were made today for a deck-games tournament on a large scale, designed to last till arrival at Bombay.

A well patronized selling sweep on tomorrow's run was held after dinner followed by a dance.

29th September—Tuesday.

Still at sea and the weather perfect. I made the acquaintance of Sir Joseph and Lady Byrne who are on board. I knew him years ago in Cairo in the Inniskilling Fusiliers, and he is now Governor of the Seychelles. Lady Byrne is, I find, a daughter of the late [i.e. retired] Allan Joseph of the Egyptian Irrigation Service and spent her girlhood in Egypt, so we found many mutual friends and acquaintances. Their two girls, Clodagh and Ethne, were at school with Patience [Patience Elizabeth Clayton] at Barington Orange, Ryde.[3]

I am considerably impressed by the comfort and spacious accommodation on board the *Rawalpindi*, which is a considerable advance on that in any P. & O. in which I have previously travelled. The Captain, officers, and stewards are extremely solicitous of the passengers' comfort and study it in every possible way.

The weather remains lovely, and we have not even experienced what Ned Cecil [Lord Edward Cecil] used to call "the North African roll."

---

years ran on the Far East run. Her gross tonnage was 16,000 tons. She was sunk in the North Atlantic on 23 November 1939 by the German battleships *Scharnhorst* and *Gneisenau.*

29th September—Tuesday.

[3] Barington Orange was a small preparatory school in Ryde, Isle of Wight, where Patience Clayton was a boarder for two years before going to the Anglican Convent School.

30th September—Wednesday.

[4] Sir Gilbert undoubtedly means Sa'id Effendi, not Sayed Effendi.

[5] Prior to the Revolution of 1952 the seat of the Egyptian government moved each year from Cairo to Alexandria during the hot summer months,

30th September—Wednesday.

We reached Port Said at 7:00 a.m., and shortly after arrival the faithful Sayed Effendi appeared on board accompanied by my loyal friend Kamel Effendi Fahmy of the Egyptian State Railways and Mustapha in the uniform of a Corporal of Police.[4] A little later George Antonius and the British Consul at Port Said, Palmer, arrived, the latter very correct in top hat and tail coat. After breakfast I went ashore to the Consulate where we discussed future arrangements and where I met Harvey of the Palestine Government who is attached to the Mission as clerk and stenographer. George and I then paid a call on Dr. and Mrs. Stiven, the latter née Nellie Nimr. Left Port Said by the 12:30 p.m. train, lunching on route, and arriving at Alexandria (Sidi Gabir [Station]) in time for dinner at the Residency, Ramleh, where I had been invited to stay by Nevile Henderson who is acting as High Commissioner pending the arrival of George Lloyd.[5] Found Arthur Wiggin, Robin Furness, and Grafftey-Smith still there of those whom I had known of old. The others went off to a "pelota" match after dinner, and I had a long and interesting talk with Henderson on subjects ranging over Egypt, Turkey, and Arabia.[6] I found him a very charming fellow, exceedingly well-informed and, I should imagine, of very sound judgment. George Antonius stayed with his relatives in Alexandria. Harvey and Taufik Bey Suaidi (the Iraq representative who had joined us at Port Said) went straight to Cairo.

1st October—Thursday.

Had a long talk with Grafftey-Smith after breakfast. He had

---

and the diplomatic missions in Egypt followed the government. Consequently, the British constructed a Residence in both Cairo and Alexandria. The Residence in Alexandria was situated in Ramlah, a suburb of Alexandria, on property purchased in 1909 from the Alexandria Water Company. An adjoining building was bought in 1926 and used as Embassy offices so that the total properties, including the garden, comprised a total area of 7,265 square meters. When the government of the United Arab Republic decided in 1952 not to move to Alexandria in the summer, the British Embassy buildings at Ramlah were converted into a British Consulate-General.

[6] Pelota, more commonly known as jai alai, is the game played in a court with a ball and a wickerwork racket.

spent two years at Jeddah as British Agent and Consul, and we got much useful information from him regarding local conditions. Later went and spent an hour or so at the San Stefano Casino, which was the same as ever and very reminiscent of old times.[7] George Antonius came to lunch at the Residency, and after lunch we drove into Alexandria where we purchased our camp equipment. I then drove to the San Stefano Casino again and had tea. We left for Cairo by the 7:00 p.m. train, dining on board, and arriving shortly after 10:00 p.m. We were met by Sayed Effendi and also by Ryder, acting Sudan Agent, who drove us to the Continental Hotel where we stayed the night.

2nd October–Friday.

After breakfast we visited the Sudan Agency and fixed up all arrangements for our journey to Port Sudan. I then went to Davies Bryan's and bought some bedding, towels, and various other necessaries, while George Antonius ordered a reserve store of food and drink from Fleurent.[8] We lunched at the Hotel after which I went to the National Bank and fixed up about my letter of credit, arranging to draw funds as required at Port Sudan where the Bank has a branch. I then returned to the Hotel where I found Cherei Pasha, Rashwan Pasha Mahfouz, and various Egyptian friends waiting to see me. I then packed up (leaving some things in Cairo with Sayed Effendi), and we left for Luxor at 7:00 p.m. Said Shoucair and several old friends were there to see us off.

1st October–Thursday.

[7] The San Stefano Casino was one of Alexandria's leading hotels. It was not a gambling casino, as public gambling was not allowed in Egypt at that time for religious reasons.

2nd October–Friday.

[8] Davies Bryan was a men's general outfitters in Cairo which catered to English residents. Fleurent was a superior grocer's shop that stocked English and European brands.

3rd October–Saturday.

[9] The *Sudan*, sister ship to the *Britain*, was the first big ship to be built at Wadi Halfa' dockyard, having been moved from Aswan in 1907. She was

3rd October–Saturday.

We were accompanied on our journey by Kamel Effendi Fahmy who did everything possible for our comfort. We arrived at Luxor at 7:00 a.m. and were met by Mustafa el-Idrisi who carried us off to a sumptuous breakfast, which–needless to say–we could have done without on an extremely hot day. Still, he was as usual extremely cordial and hospitable. We left at 9:00 a.m. for Aswan in a special saloon which had been provided for us and which made all the difference to our comfort on a journey which is no less hot and dusty than of old. Kamel Effendi left us at Esnah as he had to get back to Cairo. We arrived at Shellal at 4:30 p.m. and embarked in the Sudan Government sternwheeler *Sudan,* sailing for Halfa at 6:00 p.m.[9]

At Qena before breakfast I received a visit from Ahmed Bey Saddik, formerly Inspector in the Interior and now the Mudir of Qena.[10]

4th October–Sunday.

Had an excellent view of Philae before leaving Shellal. The Nile being in flood and the dam-sluices open, the temple was fully uncovered and looked as beautiful as ever in the sunset light.[11]

It was like old times to be steaming once more up the swiftly flowing river, with rocky hills and banks of pure golden sand on either side, and a narrow strip of brilliant green or feathery date palms forming each bank of the Nile.

---

commissioned in 1908. She was 160 ft. in length, 26 ft. in width, and 6 ft. 4 in. draught. She was scrapped in 1964.

[10] *Mudīr* (Arabic): governor, manager, in general; governor of a province of the Sudan since 1833, replacing the term *ma'mūr* in this meaning; also used to designate the Commissioner of the Sudan Police.

4th October–Sunday.

[11] Situated just above the first cataract of the Nile, the islet of Philae, only a quarter of a mile long and some 160 yards in width, was a religious resort, not only for the ancient Egyptians, but for Greek and Roman visitors as well. With the completion of the Aswan Dam in 1902, all the ruins but the temple of Isis were completely submerged except for a few months of the year, and when the height of the dam was raised in 1907, even the temple of Isis became totally inundated but for the months from July to October.

"Old Lion" was still caterer and head steward on the *Sudan* and welcomed me with effusion as did the head suffragi who is also an old friend.[12]

It was extremely hot all day but George Antonius and I managed to get some useful preparatory work done, and there was an abundance of well-iced drinks on demand.

5th October–Monday.

There was no one on the boat whom I knew. Three or four young Englishmen, Bimbashi, Sudan Government Officials, and employees of the Sudan Plantation Syndicate, a sprinkling of Khartoum merchants, including young Kfouri and his wife and family, and various odds and ends.[13]

We arrived at Wadi Halfa and were met by the Acting Governor, Tom Leach (the Governor being on leave), and the local railway representative (F. E. Hills), both of whom were very helpful and saw to everything for us.[14]

George and I went for a stroll through the town and bazaar, and I found very little change–Halfa stands still, or even goes back,

---

[12] For "Old Lion" see Biographical Appendix, Lion. *Saffragi* (Sudan Colloquial Arabic): waiter.

5th October–Monday.

[13] *Bimbashi* is the colloquial Egyptian and Sudanese rendering of the Arabic *bikbashi*, which is derived from the Turkish *binbashi*, meaning literally commander of a thousand (men), and in the Egyptian Army of Muhammad 'Ali Pasha a battalion commander. In the Sudan Defence Force the rank was equivalent to a senior major in the British Army.

Founded in 1904 by the wealthy American businessman, Leigh Hunt, the Sudan Experimental Plantations Syndicate installed its first pump scheme at Az-Zaydab in 1906 for the cultivation of cotton. Proving at first unremunerative, the company was reorganized in 1907 and renamed the Sudan Plantations Syndicate Ltd. with Sir Frederick Eckstein, a pioneer of the South African Rand goldfields, as Chairman and Lord Lovat as one of the Directors. In 1911 the Syndicate took over the management of 600 acres of land rented from local landowners at Tayyibah, and this partnership between company and tenants proved enormously successful. Consequently in 1913 the Syndicate was brought into a larger, but limited partnership with the Sudan government to manage the development of Al-Jazirah. Thus was born the famous scheme between government, tenants, and private enterprise which laid the

since port Sudan was opened. We left at 5:00 p.m. in a very comfortable special saloon after I had shaken hands warmly with the Sudanese engine-driver, who had once been a servant of mine.

At 7:00 a.m. we had a splendid view of Abu Simbel with the rising sun shining full upon it.[15]

6th October—Tuesday.

On waking I found that we had passed Abu Hamed and left the absolute desert behind and were passing along the well-known route with the river on one side and the desert on the other along which the [Anglo-Egyptian] Army had marched to the Atbara [in the spring of 1898]: Abu Dis, Shulik, Berber, Es Sillim (where the Warwicks and Lincolns had their camp), Darmali (where we spent the summer of 1898 and where I spotted the little mud hut in which we had our mess still standing).[16]

Finally, at 11:00 a.m., to Atbara where we were met by Hunter, acting as General Manager, Harry Hawkins, who is just moving to Port Sudan, and Peter Lord, who is retiring in January next.[17]

We spent the day and lunched with Hunter, taking a stroll round

---

foundation for one of the world's great development projects, with the Sudan government utilizing the Syndicate's technical knowledge, managerial skill, and capital, in return for a share of the profits while keeping overall control.

14 F. E. Hills, was the District Traffic Manager of the Sudan Railways who joined the service in 1925 but left two years later.

15 The greatest of all the temples of Ramses II (1298–1232 B.C.) in which the Pharaoh combined worship of Egypt's great gods with his own deification. Since the Temple is oriented on an east-west axis, the rising sun sends its rays 180 feet back into the inner recesses of the temple from an entrance guarded by the four colossi of Ramses himself. The temple has now been cut from the rock and raised to the high ground above in order to preserve this stupendous structure from the flood waters of the High Dam at Aswan.

6th October—Tuesday.

16 Abu Dis, Shulik, Barbar, As-Sillim, Darmali are stations on the railway line from Wadi Halfa' to 'Atbarah Station at the junction of the Nile and the River 'Atbarah. Abu Dis is located 267 miles from Halfa', Shulik 291, As-Sillim 318, As-Sillim and Darmali were the sites of the British camp during the summer of 1898 where Clayton waited as a lieutenant in the Maxim Battery of the First British Brigade for the final advance up the Nile.

17 The civil engineer Harry Hawkins is otherwise unidentified.

the town, which has grown but is little changed, and going to the tennis club after tea. We left for Port Sudan at 7:00 p.m.

7th October—Wednesday.

We were still in our special saloon, and it became much less hot as we passed over the high ground between the Nile and the Red Sea. At Thamiam we saw a train waiting ready to steam off over the new line to Kassala. It recalled to mind my three journeys there—one by route march in June up the Atbara via Goz Regeb with the 2nd Battalion, Egyptian Army, one by the same route with a cavalry patrol under Bulkeley Johnson of the "Greys," and one by camel from Singa via Mafaza and Gredaret.[18]

We passed Summit and I saw the familiar road going off to Erkowit, which was full of life with all its summer residents from Port Sudan and Suakin.[19]

We arrived at Port Sudan at 4:50 p.m. and were met by the District Officer young Madden, son of Dr. Madden of Cairo, and Commander Woodward R.N. commanding H.M.S. *Clematis* and Senior Naval Officer, Red Sea.[20] The Governor, Tippetts, was on leave and the Acting Governor, R. K. Winter, had gone to Erkowit.

7th October—Wednesday.

[18] In June 1898 Clayton accompanied the 2nd Egyptian Battalion on a patrol to Qawz Rajab, 180 miles up the 'Atbarah from its junction with the Nile. Clayton later accompanied a second patrol up the 'Atbarah to Qawz Rajab and beyond to the Abyssinian frontier. The patrol was led by Major Bulkeley Johnson of the Scots Greys.

[19] Situated nearly 4,000 feet above sea level in the hills some thirty-five miles from Sawakin, Erkowit was a bracing refuge for British officials from the summer heat of the Sudan. The site was first discovered by Lieutenant H. H. Kelly in February 1906 and selected as a hill station the following year. The construction of the station was under the direction of Captain M. R. Kennedy, the Director of Public Works. Clayton had spent much time there when he accompanied Sir Reginald Wingate, the Governor-General of the Sudan, as his private secretary.

[20] H.M.S. *Clematis* was a sloop of 1200 tons commissioned in October 1915, and served on patrol and convoy-escort duty in the Mediterranean during the First World War. She later served in the Red Sea and Indian Ocean and was sold in February 1931.

We went to Madden's house for tea and a drink, and then to the Port Sudan hotel which we found very comfortable and where we stayed the night.

George and I dined that night with Woodward on the *Clematis* where we had a good dinner, a very enjoyable evening, and a couple of rubbers of bridge.

Port Sudan was extremely hot and unpleasant, the temperature being very well over 100° F. and the dampness terrific, but we spent quite a good night on the roof of the hotel where there was some breeze.

8th October–Thursday.

I did a little shopping in the forenoon, buying some stores (soda water, etc.) from Lorenzato's and a deck chair, I also had my hair cut. Visited the Bank and Messrs. Gellatly, Hankey and fixed up the question of supply of funds. We got £50 in English gold from Gellatly, Hankey–a most unusual sight.[21]

We went aboard *Clematis* at 1:00 p.m. to lunch, our kit having been taken on in the forenoon, and sailed for Jeddah at 2:00 p.m. The sea was beautifully calm, though it was very hot even when steaming.

8th October–Thursday.

[21] Lorenzato's was a well-known bar in Port Sudan, situated in the Lorenzato building opposite the Ottoman Bank and the old National Bank of Egypt, now the Bank of the Sudan. Here the European community would gather for a "sundowner" and to purchase supplies. The bar was closed in 1937 and Mr. Lorenzato himself retired to Greece in 1946, though the site was still known as "Lorenzato Corner" until a few years ago.

Established in 1862 from the shipping empire of Duncan Dunbar II, Gellatly, Hankey & Company (formerly Gellatly, Hankey & Sewell) specialized in marine underwriting, insurance, and acted as passenger and forwarding agents besides operating their own ships. The company began trading operations in the Red Sea at Sawakin and Jiddah in 1884–86 under the supervision of Algernon Alers Hankey, son of J. A. Hankey, one of the founders, and worked closely with the British authorities to facilitate the loading and unloading of supplies for the Sawakin Expeditionary Force. In 1905 the company opened an office under the direction of William Percival Cochrane at the new Port Sudan, and its business grew with the increasing volume of Sudan trade during the Condominium. The company is not only agent for the

The *Clematis* was built in 1915 for mine-sweeping and such-like work and has been converted for tropical service. Carries a complement of 8 officers and about 110 men of whom about 30 are Somalis.

The Commander kindly put me up in his cabin, and the others were fixed up by the wardroom.

9th October—Friday.

We arrived off Jeddah at 9:00 a.m. and being allowed to go up on the bridge we were able to appreciate some of the difficulties and dangers of navigation. There are two anchorages (an outer and an inner) and in both cases the channel is narrow and tortuous between wicked-looking, and none too well beaconed, coral reefs. In the inner anchorage where we dropped anchor were two French and one Italian sloops, an almost derelict Hejaz steamer, which is rapidly breaking up, and a very shabby old tug, called the *Rushdi*, which the Hejaz Government is still able to send to sea in case of great emergency.[22]

We had hardly come to our berth when a tug came off containing the Hejaz Government quarantine officer, an Egyptian doctor.[23] In addition to his normal duties, he was charged with a message of welcome for me from King Ali. I sent a suitable reply but did not see the Doctor, informing him through the Commander that I was not granting any interviews before going ashore. At noon we landed with the Commander and Mr. Jordan, the Acting British Agent and

---

many shipping lines that call at Port Sudan, but cotton agents, bankers, and merchants as well. The present Director of Gellatly, Hankey & Company at Port Sudan, J. Kerr, also represents Her Majesty's Government as the Honourable British Consul.

9th October—Friday.

[22]The harbor of Jiddah used to be one of the most difficult and dangerous on the Arabian coast, and only its proximity to Mecca accounted for its continued use. Between three main lines of north-south oriented reefs are spacious inner and outer anchorages linked by narrow and perilous channels. The outer anchorage is 2½ sea-miles offshore with 5–19 fathoms of water, while the inner anchorage is 1¼ sea-miles offshore with 4–6 fathoms of water. A shallow boat channel (less than three feet at low water) leads from

Consul who had come on board to see me. Jordan had, very rightly, discouraged King Ali, who was intending to give me an official reception with a guard and all honours and had informed him that, as my mission was not concerned with Hejaz-Najd hostilities in regard to which H.M.G. had declared neutrality, I was not desirous of any official or public recognition. Our landing was, therefore, quite quiet, and as we selected the hottest time of the day, we hardly saw a soul in the course of our very short drive to the [British] Agency. We lunched at the Agency where arrangements had been made for our accommodation, and after lunch Commander Woodward returned on board the *Clematis* with the intention of returning next day to Port Sudan where he is always at the end of a wireless message. The Consul had had some thoughts of asking him to stay at Jeddah, where the situation was not good and intrigues against King Ali's immediate advisors, Shaikh Fuad el Khatib and Mohammed Sagaf were threatening to lead to possible disturbances. He had decided, however, that the situation was not sufficiently critical to necessitate this precaution. In the afternoon I had a talk with Jordan, who struck me as sound and with a good grip of the situation. Unfortunately, he has no Arabic though he possesses a fair knowledge of Turkish. He gave me his impressions of the position, which certainly appeared a precarious one for King Ali whose Government and troops are badly paid, lacking in enthusiasm, discouraged, and riddled with petty intrigue.[24]

Jordan informed me that all arrangements had been made for us

---

the inner anchorage to the quarantine quay. In recent years a modern port has been built with berths for rather large ships.

[23] The Quarantine Officer was in fact a Turk, Nu'man Bey Thabit.

[24] Ibn Sa'ud's men were, in contrast "enthusiastic, to a large extent inspired by religious fervour and thoroughly under his control." They were, however, not so well armed as King 'Ali's men, but "although not highly trained according to [British] standards, they know their own methods thoroughly well." (Clayton to Wingate, 21 October 1925, C.P.). Both Jiddah and Medina were at the time besieged by the Wahhabi forces that could have carried the towns by assault at any moment. Ibn Sa'ud preferred, however, to play a waiting game. Until he could assess the impression his capture of Mecca had produced on the Muslim world, he rigorously forbade any attack on the slender defenses of Jiddah. He feared, moreover, that harm might come to

to proceed on the following morning to Bahra about 30 miles up the Mecca road, where Ibn Sa'ud had made all preparations for our reception.

During the afternoon after tea I went and paid a visit of courtesy to King Ali. The interview was quite informal and only Jordan, Antonius, and Shaikh Fuad el Khatib were present. The conversation was purely personal and did not touch on political matters. King Ali was very courteous and cordial, but he looked somewhat haggard and anxious and was evidently feeling the strain of his very precarious position. He is living in a large house quite close to the British Agency.

Jeddah is a fair sized town, very pictureque from the sea and like Suakin and other Red Sea ports in appearance. Tall, three or four storied houses, flanking narrow streets, with large carved wooden casements which have a very charming effect in the distance, although close inspection shows that the wood is common and the carving rough and in no way to be compared to the mushrabiya work of Egypt.[25] Various minarets break the line of house roofs, and the whole town is surrounded by a wall in a fair state of repair. On the northern side are signs of the bombardment which was carried out by the Wahhabis who were in occupation of the two adjacent villages some 3000 yards away, and the Agency which adjoins the town wall on that side bears several marks of shells, including one through the top of the sitting-room wall.[26] For the present, however, the Wahhabis have withdrawn their lines to the foothills some 5 or 6 miles away, whence they maintain a close investment on the land side. There are, therefore, but few outward signs of hostilities, though I detected several Hejazi guns in position and a hangar containing three aeroplanes, which are piloted by German mercenaries in King Ali's employ. They go up fairly frequently and drop a few

---

the foreign consuls at Jiddah if his forces were turned loose, and he clearly did not wish to compromise Clayton's mission. (Jordan to Clayton, 16 October 1925, and Clayton to Wingate 21 October 1925, C.P.). Nonetheless, only the foolishly optimistic thought that the Hijazi forces could successfully defend Jiddah indefinitely, and consequently numerous intrigues were plotted to topple King 'Ali's vacillating rule from within.

bombs but, as they usually keep up to 5000 or 6000 feet, their flights are short and targets very small or nonexistent. They do not appear greatly to inconvenience the Wahhabis.

I went for a short walk with Jordan and Antonius in the evening, and after dinner King Ali paid a return call. On this occasion I took occasion to impress upon him the fact that my mission was in no way concerned with the Hejaz-Najd struggle.

10th October–Saturday.

We left the Agency at 9:30 a.m. in King Ali's Mercedes car, which he had kindly lent, and drove to Nuzla, a suburb of the town lying a short distance outside the Mecca gate on the eastern side. Our kit and servants followed in the only vehicle which the Consul possesses, a Ford box-car of such antiquated and dilapidated appearance as to be a disgrace to H.M.G. and to excite the ridicule even of the inhabitants of Jeddah.

I left Taufik Bey Suaidi, the Iraq delegate, at Jeddah as I thought it better that he should not be present at our discussions or join us until matters had advanced somewhat.

At Nuzla we found two cars awaiting us (a 6-cylinder special Studebaker and a Ford) sent with some camels for our baggage to convey us to Bahra on the Jeddah-Mecca road where the discussions were to take place. One of Ibn Sa'ud's chief advisers, Shaikh Hafez Wahbeh, had come to meet us with a considerable escort of fully armed Arabs. We lost no time in transferring ourselves, and our belongings, myself, Antonius, and Shaikh Hafez travelled in the Studebaker and Harvey in the Ford. We set off over the coastal plain where the going was moderately good and after 6 or 7 miles when about to enter the foothills, we saw our first sight of Wahhabi military activity, being intercepted by two wild but very

---

[25] *Mushrabiya* (Arabic): a projecting window with a wooden latticework enclosure.

[26] In 1925 the British Consulate in Jiddah was a rather ramshackle, dilapidated, but picturesque building that had only been electrified the previous year. Situated on the edge of town with only the town wall between it and the desert, the Consulate was struck twice by Wahhabi shells, but the damage was more apparent than real.

determined-looking Arab horsemen who held us up at the business ends of two wicked-looking magazine rifles. Our conductors, however, gave the necessary password with commendable alacrity, and after the two scouts had kissed each of our escort on both cheeks, we were permitted to proceed.

Hereafter, the road became very bad—indeed it was practically non-existent—and we ploughed laboriously through deep sand, over boulders and stones, and through low but tenacious bush. Several times we became embedded in sand, but man-power to extricate us was at hand, as one of our escort was riding by the chauffeur (an Indian from Bombay, who spoke a little English) and three others were clinging like monkeys to the footboard throughout the journey. We continued up the course of a wide wadi following the pilgrim track until after a journey of about 22 miles we reached a well—and only just in time as the water in the radiator had been boiling merrily all the time and had by now almost evaporated.[27] After a pause for cooling the engine and filling us with water we went on and before long passed Bahra village, now abandoned and in ruins as a result of the Hejaz-Najd war. About 2 or 3 miles further on we descried Ibn Sa'ud's camp on the further or southern side of the wadi, which at this point is nearly 2 miles wide. We proceeded until opposite the camp and then the cars plunged into the wadi in an endeavor to cross. We got about three-quarters of the way over with much bumping and heaving and hauling, and then we alighted and eventually reached our destination on foot. I was not sorry to get out of the car, as our escort had insisted on placing their loaded rifles beside the chauffeur, and I therefore found myself

---

10th October—Saturday.

[27] *Wadi* (Arabic): depression or shallow valley.

[28] *E.P.* tent refers to tentage of Indian manufacture for the use of *European Personnel* as opposed to those intended for *Indian Personnel.* The description of tents and other stores as being *E.P.* or *I.P.* was in the days when the British and Indian armies served side by side. The tent that Sir Gilbert used was most probably a small, square, double-lined officers' tent as distinct from the single-lined bell tent used by enlisted men.

[29] The negotiations opened auspiciously. Clayton explained in his official report that "I emphasized the fact that I regarded my visit as an exceptional

most of the time gazing into the muzzles of no less than five loaded rifles which might have been exploded by any of the numerous and hearty bumps which our car indulged in. On arrival we were conducted to an excellent camp, consisting of a handsome conference or reception tent, an E.P. tent for me and numerous smaller tents for the staff and servants, all well carpeted with rugs, and my tent containing a good writing table, several cane-bottomed armchairs and a camp bed.[28] The reception tent was quite a gorgeous affair, the interior of which was highly decorated and equipped with a large table and a number of gilt armchairs upholstered in red satin.

Immediately after our arrival the Sultan Ibn Sa'ud (usually called by his people "The Shaikh es-Shiouk" or "Shaikh of the Shaikhs"—"Shiouk" for short) paid us a visit of welcome. He is a tall, fine-looking Arab, and every inch a ruler, but I will defer a full description of him until I know him better. He was very cordial and courteous and stayed about 20 minutes during which we exchanged compliments, greetings and small talk, after which he took his leave, saying that we must be tired and hungry after our journey.

We were then taken to a small marquee or awning, which had been provided as our eating tent, where we partook of quite a good lunch. After resting and settling down, at 5:00 p.m. I went and returned Ibn Sa'ud's call, and we had a talk on general subjects until the approach of sunset, when I took my leave so as not to intrude on the hour of sunset prayer (Arabic *maghrib*). At about 8:00 p.m. I had yet another talk with Ibn Sa'ud and told him in general terms what were the terms of my mission. Our interview lasted till 9:00 p.m. when he departed to his tent, and we went to our dinner.[29]

---

opportunity, which was unlikely to recur, of coming to a clear understanding in regard to outstanding questions, and of discussing any other matters which affected the interests of Great Britain and of Najd. Ibn Sa'ud replied with cordial protestations of welcome, and more than once during the interview reiterated his belief that the interests of Great Britain and Najd were not only closely connected but coincident. He made a great point of his sincere desire to stand well with H.M.G." "Report by Sir Gilbert Clayton, K.B.E., C.B., C.M.G., on his Mission to negotiate certain Agreements with the Sultan of Nejd, and Instructions issued to him in regard to his Mission," p. 14.)

The best Arab cook in Mecca has been provided to cook our meals, all of which are entirely at Ibn Sa'ud's expense. The dishes are of course all native, but they are very well cooked and served and are quite appetizing, and we are well provided with plates, knives, and forks and such civilised appurtenances. There is, of course, only water to drink and no cigarettes are provided, as alcohol and tobacco are strictly forbidden by the Wahhabi tenets, so any consumption of those luxuries has to take place in the seclusion of our tents.[30] We turned in about 10:30 p.m. pretty tired after a long day but feeling that we had now really got down to work.

---

[30] They were also provided with "quantities of servants and all the luxuries which an impoverished Mecca can provide." Clayton certainly appreciated Ibu Sa'ud's efforts to make his guests comfortable, but he could not help but complain mildly that "unfortunately Ibn Sa'ud has insisted that we should be his guests as regards food, and has provided a special cook and kitchen for our use. The result is . . . somewhat disturbing to the internal economy of the Average European after a time . . . and my whiskey and soda after sunset makes me feel rather like a schoolboy who is breaking the rules." (Clayton to Wingate, 21 October 1925, C.P.)

CHAPTER 2

At the Tents of Ibn Sa'ud:
11 October–2 November 1925

11th October–Sunday.

I had a long interview with Ibn Sa'ud, lasting from 9:00 a.m. till 11:30 a.m. This was our first official discussion, and I explained fully to him the objects of my mission, the general tenor of my instructions, and the nature of my credentials.[1] My actual credentials I was

---

11th October–Sunday.

[1] Ibn Sa'ud was not pleased to learn at this first official meeting that Great Britain insisted Kaf be included in Trans-Jordan and "he was visibly, and I believe, genuinely perturbed. . . . He also objected vehemently to the northern frontier being drawn so as to unite Trans-Jordan and 'Iraq and thus separate Najd from Syria:" "Report . . . ," p. 5. Ibn Sa'ud was deeply concerned with the attitude of the British government in regard to Kaf. He argued that the Wadi as-Sirhan was indivisible and that Kaf and the salt villages formed an integral part of the Wadi. He cited previous references by the British government that they were prepared to accept a line that included Kaf within his dominions. He referred in particular to the official statement of the British Agent at Bahrain of 23 October 1924 in which such a boundary was laid down as the basis for negotiations at the Kuwait Conference. Ibn Sa'ud asserted that since his government rested on his personal ascendancy over the tribes, he could not now abandon Kaf after once having told them it was his. Clayton rebutted by arguing that the situation in the autumn of 1925 was quite different from that in 1924, particularly since the Ikhwan attack of August 1924 had made it clear that Kaf must be included in Trans-Jordan for the proper defense of the mandate. In regard to the conflict between Britain's insistence on an east-west corridor against Ibn Sa'ud's desire for a north-south passage into Syria, Clayton flatly told the Sultan that on this question there could be no negotiations. The Colonial Office had warned

unable to present as they had not yet been signed by the King when I left London so are being sent after me. I hope they will arrive in time, as I am somewhat handicapped without them. Shaikhs Hafez Wahbeh and Yusuf Yasin, who are Ibn Sa'ud's assistants in the negotiations, are hardly likely to make things go more easily. They are the familiar type of "pinch-beck" oriental politician whose methods consist in arguing every small point, employing a certain amount of low cunning, and resorting at all times to a policy of consistent obstruction. Ibn Sa'ud, on his side, has the natural shrewdness of the Bedouin but is obstinate and devoid of all sense of logic as we know it.[2] I shall, therefore, have to go very warily and some days will have to be spent in establishing personal relations, creating the proper atmosphere, and, so to speak, maneuvering for position.[3]

In the afternoon George Antonius had a long talk with Shaikhs Hafez and Yusuf. I propose to encourage this procedure, as I can see that they have considerable influence over Ibn Sa'ud, and Antonius, who knows well how to deal with them, will do much in preparing the way for my talks with Ibn Sa'ud. Shaikh Hafez is an Egyptian ex-journalist who was expelled from Egypt to India at the beginning of the war. Soon after, he was expelled by the Indian Government in its turn and sent to the Persian Gulf. There he lived a precarious existence, indulging largely in politics, chiefly of an anti-British nature, succeeding for the third time in winning expulsion at the hands of the British Resident at Bahrein. Eventually he migrated to

---

Clayton in their instructions to him that Ibn Sa'ud would probably claim territory north of Jabal 'Unazah extending into Syria and placing Najd territory between 'Iraq and Trans-Jordan "astride the Imperial Air Route to the East. This cannot be permitted, and in no circumstances should you [Clayton] assent to any extension of Najd territory to the north, which would have the effect of separating 'Iraq from Trans-Jordan." (R. V. Vernon to Clayton, 10 September 1925 [C.O. 38484/25] and "Report . . . ," pp. 5, 16.)

[2] Clayton wrote to Wingate that the "disingenuous tricks" of Wahba and Yasin were "in reality foreign to the nature of Ibn Sa'ud, who—though obstinate and self-willed—is a fine type of the true desert Arab and possesses all his good points." (Clayton to Wingate, 21 October 1925, C.P.)

[3] Or as he described it to Wingate, he must demonstrate "a combination of firmness and 'spirit-breaking' patience." (Clayton to Wingate, 21 October 1925, C.P.)

Riad and offered his services to Ibn Sa'ud shortly before the Koweit Conference at which he was one of the Najd delegates.

In the evening after tea Antonius and I went for a walk in the wadi, and at 8:00 p.m. I had another long talk with Ibn Sa'ud after which came dinner and bed.

12th October—Monday.

The forenoon was again taken up by a long meeting with Ibn Sa'ud.[4] We have arranged a rough timetable for daily meetings at 9:00 a.m., 4:00 p.m., and 8:00 p.m. Our discussions have to be arranged to suit the hours of prayer, which are observed here with the utmost strictness. They are at dawn (the moment when the first glimpse of light appears), noon, 3:30 p.m. (or rather 9:30 Arab time), and sunset. Time here is somewhat confusing as the day starts at sunset and is reckoned from one sunset to the next. Consequently, as sunset gets later, or earlier, as the case may be every day, so the time alters slightly every day. Hence you have to set your watch afresh every day at sunset. Our morning meeting will, as a rule, be devoted to official discussions with Ibn Sa'ud. In the afternoon George Antonius will have informal meetings with Shaykhs Hafez and Yusuf, and the evening will usually be passed in private talk on general matters between me and Ibn Sa'ud.

In accordance with this plan, George Antonius had a long talk with the two Shaikhs in the afternoon after which we took our

---

12th October—Monday.

[4] This second official meeting was again devoted to the Trans-Jordan frontier. Ibn Sa'ud dwelt on his family's historic ties to Kaf and the Wadi as-Sirhan, and he insisted that it was only out of regard for Sir Percy Cox that he had refrained from occupying it. Clayton again stressed the fears of Trans-Jordan if such a stronghold was under Najd control, but Ibn Sa'ud insisted that although he wished to garrison the village his intentions were only defensive, not offensive. "Report . . . ," pp. 17–18. Acting on instructions from the Colonial Office, Lt.-Colonel Knox had proposed at the Kuwait Conference that the frontier between Trans-Jordan and Najd should "follow a line drawn from the intersection of meridian 39° with parallel 32° to the intersection of meridian 37° with parallel 31°30′. From this point, the line follows meridian 37° to parallel 31°, thence to the intersection of meridian 38° with parallel 30°, and thence along meridian 38° to parallel 29°35′ or a

evening walk. At 8:00 p.m. I had a long private talk with Ibn Sa'ud, in the course of which he gave a long, detailed, and most interesting account of his career and experiences. I only wish I could have taken it all down.

We had sent a messenger yesterday with our mails to the British Consul at Jeddah, and he returned this evening with local mails.

13th October–Tuesday.

Yesterday's mail only contained letters from the Consul [S. R. Jordan], and a few necessaries for which we had asked. Home mails only come in the Khedivial steamer from Suez which calls at Jeddah every ten days, and her next call will not be until the 25th or 26th of the month.

Our morning meeting was rather a strenuous one. Kaf is the crucial question, and it is practically the only card that I have up my sleeve, I must be very careful how I use it, otherwise no agreement would be possible, which will be a pity, especially, I am convinced, for Ibn Sa'ud's own interests.[5] In the afternoon George Antonius had another long conference with the Shaikhs, but they are difficult people. Shaikh Yusuf's methods are not dissimilar to those of Shaikh Hafez. He is a Syrian from Palestine, who left Palestine for political reasons. Both, therefore, have an engrained distrust of Great Britain and are persuaded of her Machiavellian policy of "grab."

At sunset George and I took our usual walk, after which at 8:00

---

point due west of the Nafud salient." [See Map] Ibn Sa'ud hoped to obtain a frontier considerably to the north and west of this line. (Vernon to Clayton, 10 September 1925, C.P.)

13th October–Tuesday.

[5] During this third official meeting with Ibn Sa'ud, Clayton switched his tactics from the narrow issue of Kaf to Arabia's position in the wider world. He stressed the need of Najd for British friendship in such a way as to apply subtle pressure on Ibn Sa'ud. Clayton reviewed the imperial interests of Great Britain in India, the Persian Gulf, the Red Sea, Sudan, Egypt, Trans-Jordan, and 'Iraq, tactfully pointing out that Ibn Sa'ud was encircled by spheres of British influence. In consideration of the larger scope of Arabian affairs Clayton emphasized the advantages of British friendship to Ibn Sa'ud in his

p.m. I had another interesting talk with Ibn Sa'ud, in the course of which he gave a long dissertation on the tenets of Wahhabism, urging that they were based on the purest principles of Islam and, far from being in any way heretical, were orthodox in the truest sense.

Our servants, to their great delight, set off in the evening on a visit to Mecca, kindly arranged by Shaikh Hafez.

14th October—Wednesday.

Discussions with Ibn Sa'ud were resumed at 9:00 a.m. and lasted until 11:00 a.m. It became evident that we were getting no nearer an agreement on the question of Kaf, so I suggested postponing discussions on this point and proceeding to consideration of other subjects, the settlement of which formed part of my mission.[6] George had a brief private talk with Ibn Sa'ud in the afternoon, and I saw him again at 8:00 p.m. when nothing definite transpired, though his attitude greatly improved and he showed signs of great reluctance to envisage any failure to come to an agreement.

We had our usual walk at sunset, when the temperature is pleasant after the severe heat of the middle day and early afternoon.

15th October—Thursday.

Our servants returned from Mecca soon after dawn greatly pleased with their trip. At our morning meeting we started discussions on Iraq questions. Things did not go very well as Ibn

---

present position and urged him to make small sacrifices to cement that friendship. "Report . . . ," pp. 20–21.

14th October—Wednesday.

[6] Although Clayton had been instructed to concede Kaf to Ibn Sa'ud if the latter insisted, Sir Gilbert wished to save its cession as a last resort. He had purposely opened the negotiations on the subject of Kaf to "test the genuineness of Ibn Sa'ud's professions and gauge the length to which he was prepared to carry resistance." Even after Ibn Sa'ud's deep concern for Kaf had been affirmed and asserted, Clayton continued to withhold the cession of Kaf at this fourth meeting despite Ibn Sa'ud's pressing insistence until the Sultan and his advisers "were in such a frame of mind as to consider it a concession which placed them under the obligation of furnishing adequate

Sa'ud and his two advisers started to "bluff" heavily. I therefore had to come down pretty heavily with both feet, which brought them to their senses. I closed the meeting by saying that I would draft my proposals and let Ibn Sa'ud have them for examination and consideration in a day or two.[7]

I had already said to Ibn Sa'ud that if he wished to go to Mecca for the Friday prayer, I hoped that he would not let my presence here stand in his way. An offer which he accepted with evident pleasure. He therefore left after the afternoon prayer in his car for Mecca, a journey which takes him just over an hour. We went out for our usual walk, which is becoming rather a monotonous performance and consists of tramping a mile or so over deep sand until we reach some rocky eminence which we climb and from which we can get some view. We usually start shortly before sunset, so as to get to some hill before the sun goes down. We then get a very delightful view, as the bare hills begin to take on a soft-purple light, and every night there is to the east over Mecca a great bank of cloud which reflects the setting sunlight and becomes a great welter of rosy flame. At the actual moment when the sun sets we always have to stop in order to allow our escort to say his prayers, which he does with great devotion and a lack of self-consciousness which Christians might well copy. He is a Sudanese slave, by name Idris, who has been made specially responsible for our safety and who never leaves us. He is always armed, sometimes with an Enfield rifle, sometimes with a curved sword in a heavily silver-mounted scabbard, sometimes with a heavy mace studded with nails, and oc-

---

guarantees in return." Thus rather than concede Kaf, Clayton preferred to discuss other questions while still insisting that Kaf be included in Trans-Jordan. "Report . . . ," p. 5.

15th October–Thursday.

[7] In reality Clayton had less trouble dealing with questions relating to 'Iraq than those pertaining to Trans-Jordan. The main obstacle was Ibn Sa'ud's urgent demand for the surrender of refugee tribes, the problem on which the Kuwait Conference had foundered. Since that conference the Shammar refugees who had fled to 'Iraq and then raided back into Najd had been moved back from the frontier, thus easing their temptations to raid across it. The Colonial Office hoped that this action would create the proper climate for Ibn Sa'ud to accept the British view that persons or tribes who

casionally with all three. He is a capital fellow. When I call "Ya Idris," he always replies "Ay wallah" (Yes, by God). Then I tell him to do something or ask for something, to which he always replies by one of three ejaculations: "Inshallah" (God willing) or "Marhabba" (Everything is open to you) or "Ma yekhalif" (There is no objection).

At 7:30 p.m. I received a visit from Amir Mohammed ibn Abdur Rahman ibn Faisal Al Sa'ud, who is a brother of Ibn Sa'ud. He had been in the camp all the time, but apparently it is contrary to etiquette that he should pay us a visit while his brother is here. He had, therefore, taken advantage of his brother's visit to Mecca to come and pay his respects to me. He is a fine-looking man, tall and well built, with rather a dark complexion and a slight black moustache and tuft of beard. He did not strike me as very intelligent, but his somewhat stupid air may have been the result of shyness at our first meeting. He stayed about half an hour during which we drank coffee and exchanged greetings, compliments, and small talk, and then he took his leave.

16th October—Friday.

Sent a mail to Jeddah and hope to get some news by return this evening. We spent a busy day drafting an agreement on the Iraq questions, so as to have it ready for Ibn Sa'ud's return from Mecca. George Antonius did sterling work with Shaikhs Hafez and Yusuf, who are at the back of most of Ibn Sa'ud's objections, and did a lot towards inducing them to be reasonable. George and I went for our

---

had fled from one territory to the other should not be automatically returned. Ibn Sa'ud insisted during this fifth meeting with Clayton that only if such tribes were returned could he "check the movements of tribes who raid and those who cross the border." Clearly Ibn Sa'ud's rule on the frontier would be much more effective "if the tribes knew they could not run away to another country with impunity." Neither the 'Iraq government nor Britain, argued Clayton, could agree to abandon the right and principle of political asylum, wherein Ibn Sa'ud "showed himself so insistent that I [Clayton] judged it necessary at that meeting to give him the choice between an abatement of his demands and a rupture." This threat succeeded in convincing Ibn Sa'ud to continue the discussion on a draft agreement that Clayton would present at their next official meeting. "Report . . . ," pp. 7, 24–28.

evening walk, and then I returned Amir Mohammed's call. We found him seated in his tent, surrounded by a throng of his Arab warriors, all fully armed. It was a most typical scene, and picturesque to a degree, especially as the sun had set and the light was dim, and supplemented only by a few lanterns, which served to show to excellent advantage the dark handsome faces of the Bedouin and their glittering accoutrements. We drank Arab coffee and tea, sweet of course and without milk, and chatted on various subjects, chiefly of horses on the subject of which Arabs always wax loquacious. There were two or three very jolly old Shaikhs present, and the Amir too was much more pleasant and chatty than at our first meeting, so we had quite an enjoyable half hour. Our mail arrived from Jeddah at 11:00 p.m. and, to our joy, contained home letters. I got one from Enid with news of the family, but it was written as long ago as the 30th September, only six days after I left home so long do letters take to reach this out-of-the-way spot.

17th October—Saturday.

Ibn Sa'ud sent a message to say that he was delayed by important business at Mecca and could not be back till Sunday morning. We, therefore, spent a quiet day completing our draft agreement and writing up our records. I heard from Jordan that Philby had turned up in Jeddah by the Khedivial boat. Jordan had no actual knowledge of his intentions, but he was reported to have set his chronometers on board ship and to be growing a beard, so it was thought that he contemplated a trip into the interior—probably for some newspaper. Anyway, he is not likely to do much good from the point of view of my mission, and he may try and be mischievous.[8]

17th October—Saturday.

[8] Philby had resigned as Chief British Representative, Trans-Jordan, in April 1924, and had returned to London where he subsequently planned an expedition to the Empty Quarter with Rosita Forbes. When the news reached Europe, however, of the Wahhabi invasion of the Hijaz, the defeat of Husayn's forces, and his abdication, Philby volunteered his services to Husayn's son and successor, King 'Ali, in his own words, to "help in the negotiations with Ibn Sa'ud." His offer was accepted by 'Ali, and Philby subsequently turned up at Jiddah late in the year 1924. His arrival caused a sensation among the Arabs and acute embarrassment to the British govern-

This place is infernally hot in the middle of the day. Between noon and 3:30 p.m. it is always about 112° F. in our tents, with a scorching west wind which carries with it quantities of fine sand. Today it was well over 114° F., indeed, nearly 115° F. Towards sunset, however, the temperature falls and the wind becomes cool and gradually drops altogether. The nights are quite bearable, and after midnight a cool *east* wind springs up, which quite often necessitates putting on a blanket. The worst pest is that of the flies, which are increasing day by day as the camp gets more fouled. George and I took our usual tramp in the evening and raised a thirst for our one, surreptitious whisky and soda which is one of the events of the day.

18th October—Sunday.

Ibn Sa'ud did not turn up as expected, being delayed until the evening, so we had another quiet day which enabled us to get well up to date. After our evening walk we found that he had returned, and at 8:00 p.m. I presented my official credentials which came the day before yesterday. I put on my uniform and did the thing with due ceremony, and I think Ibn Sa'ud was duly impressed by the appearance of the document, as also by the language in which it was couched which was ably translated into Arabic by George Antonius. As this ceremonious occasion was not a suitable one for talking on matters of business, we merely exchanged a little complimentary conversation, after which I withdrew.

19th October—Monday.

We had a long discussion in the morning over Iraq questions but were not able to come to any agreement. Ibn Sa'ud was insistent that

---

ment which was desperately trying to remain neutral in the Hijazi-Najdi war, yet no Arab would believe that Philby, who a few months before was the British representative in Trans-Jordan and was still a member of the Indian Civil Service, was not acting in some sort of official capacity. Not content with being a general nuisance, Philby was inconsiderate enough to fall ill and had to be kept going with food from the kitchen of the British Consulate. Moreover, Ibn Sa'ud had no intention of negotiating, and so in January 1925 Philby returned to London by way of Aden where the Governor officially warned him not to enter the interior of Arabia. In London Philby languished, restless and in despair over his prospects until he was

tribes, or portions of tribes, who moved their residence without leave from one territory to another should be sent back, by force if necessary, by the Government into whose territory they had migrated.[9] This principle I was quite unable to agree to. In the end I said I would submit my proposals in the form of a draft agreement for Ibn Sa'ud's examination and consideration.[10] We had no further official discussion during the day, but in the course of the afternoon I received Ibn Sa'ud's counter-proposals.[11]

In the evening after our usual walk I had a private interview and talk with Ibn Sa'ud, at which he presented to me his youngest brother, Amir Abdulla ibn Abdur Rahman Al Sa'ud, who is in actual command of the Wahhabi force which is invading Jeddah. He is a young man of not more than twenty five years of age, of middle height, slight and lean, and with very little hair on his face. He has a keen, intelligent, and very pleasant expression on his face and is evidently an ardent soldier whose one dominant interest is war and raiding. He is an especial favourite with Ibn Sa'ud, being practically the same age as the latter's son, Turki, who died early in the war during the struggle between Ibn Sa'ud and Ibn Rashid.

From what I have seen it seems to me that Ibn Sa'ud could take Jeddah, Medina, and Yambo whenever he chose. He is probably holding his hand for various reasons, among which may be the following: —

---

asked by R. E. Fisher to return to Jiddah to launch a trading company, Sharqieh Ltd. When Philby arrived in Jiddah in October, S. R. Jordan, the British Consul, repeated the prohibition against his proceeding into the interior. Perturbed by his previous visit, the Foreign Office was infuriated over the "disgraceful behavior" of a former official who had criticized the British government to the Arabs of the Hijaz and asked Jordan to warn Clayton of Philby's activities and to make sure that Clayton inform Ibn Sa'ud that Philby was in the Hijaz against the wishes of the British government and had no official status whatsoever. (Foreign Office to S. R. Jordan No. 68, 26 October 1925, C.P.) Philby was not the sort of man to be intimidated by thunderous pronouncements from Whitehall, and putting aside his business interests he set out at once to circumvent the prohibition. See Philby, *Arabian Days*, pp. 241–48, and Bullard, *The Camels Must Go*, pp. 142–43.

19th October–Monday.

[9] Ibn Sa'ud did not believe that the removal of the Shammar to the Mosul

A. He is anxious to gauge more fully the effect which his attack on the Holy Places and his capture of Mecca has had on the Moslem world in general and especially in India and Egypt. He is evidently anxious to impress the fact that Wahhabism is not really heretical and unorthodox but merely a return to the purest tenets of Islam.

B. He is apprehensive lest the Foreign Consuls at Jeddah may suffer harm in the course of any assault on the town, and even fears lest the Hejaz Government might secretly organise something of the kind with a view to attributing the blame to him. From what I hear, Tahsin Bey, the Military Commandant at Jeddah, is quite capable of formulating some such plan as the above.

C. He hopes that lack of funds and internal intrigue will cause the Hejaz Government to collapse and thus give him Jeddah without a fight, in which case the surrender of Medina and Yambo would follow.

D. He is impressed by the protests which the alleged damage done by his guns to holy spots at Medina has called forth, though I believe him when he declares that these reports are all false and fabricated by his enemies

E. He does not wish to commence any active hostilities while my mission is here.

Jordan reports that Jeddah rumour has it that Ibn Sa'ud will attack

---

District would make much difference and speculated that they were now raiding in the direction of Al Jawf. "Personally he [Ibn Sa'ud] had no wish for their [the Shammar] return to Najd . . . but they were a constant threat to peace and that was why he wanted them handed over." Clayton then assumed a more high-handed attitude, insisting that "if His Highness agreed to subscribe to an agreement designed to improve matters, well and good; if he was unable to accept any instrument that did not contain everything he wanted, both in practice and principle, then I was afraid I must admit that I had failed to attain my object." "Report . . . ," pp. 29–30.

[10] Clayton in his draft agreement made it clear to Ibn Sa'ud that the only extradition he could recognize was that of common criminals. Clayton stated to Ibn Sa'ud that the draft was designed "to meet the wishes of H.M.G. and the 'Iraq Government while going as far as possible in the directions required by Najd." "Report . . . ," pp. 29–30.

[11] Ibn Sa'ud and his officials in the counterproposal continued to argue for

as soon as I have left, and I think it not improbable, as I know that some thousands of reinforcements are expected daily from Riad at Mecca.

20th October–Tuesday.

We found that a mail had arrived from Jordan during the night. It bore no letters from home but contained 21 bottles of alleged soda, which, to our disappointment, turned out to be ginger beer and a welcome bottle of gin. We usually send a messenger from here with our mails and he brings back anything that the Consul may have for us. He departs on a donkey with a pass through the lines about 10:00 p.m. and usually gets back about the same time the following evening.

We had no meetings today as we were busy considering and framing a reply to Ibn Sa'ud's counter-proposals for an agreement on the Iraq questions.

Before taking our evening walk, I returned Amir Abdulla's visit informally in Shaikh Yusuf's tent. We had a pleasant chat about war and horses, and George seized the opportunity to photograph various groups.

21st October–Wednesday.

There was no meeting in the morning as Ibn Sa'ud and his advisers were considering my final draft of an Iraq agreement. Moreover, in

---

the extradition of refugee tribes who crossed the frontier, whether criminals or not.

21st October–Wednesday.

12 The Iranian mission to inquire into the extent of damages to Mecca by the forces of Ibn Sa'ud consisted of Mirza 'Ali Akbar Khan Bahman, the Minister of Iran to Egypt in 1925, and Mirza Habibolah Khan Hoveyda, the Consul General of Iran in Palestine (not at Damascus, as Sir Gilbert relates).

13 The *ihram* is the garment worn on the pilgrimage, consisting of one white cotton cloth thrown over the back leaving the right arm and shoulder exposed, and another wrapped around the loins from the waist to the knee.

14 This was, of course, a triumph for Clayton's persuasive diplomacy. He had written to Wingate, presumably before the four o'clock meeting: "I am endeavouring to use my not remarkably strong hand to the best advantage

the forenoon a Persian delegation arrived from Jeddah, and the Sultan was obliged to receive it. It was the Persian Government which accepted the reports of Wahhabi violence and damage to the Holy Places and which published an official announcement condemning them in exceedingly strong terms. They have now sent this delegation, headed by the Persian Minister in Egypt, to make enquiries at Mecca and are trying to arrange for other representatives (I hear that one of them is the Persian Consul at Damascus) to go to Medina.[12] Ibn Sa'ud declares that he fully welcomes any investigation into these false charges, so he received the delegation cordially and sent them on in his cars to Mecca in the afternoon. They were evidently going to combine their religious with their diplomatic duties, as when they arrived here they had already put on the *ihram*, or plain white robe in which pilgrims have to enter Mecca.[13]

In the afternoon at 4:00 p.m. I had a satisfactory meeting with Ibn Sa'ud, at which he gave way on all points in regard to the Iraq Agreement and accepted my draft.[14]

After our evening walk at 8:00 p.m. we had another meeting at which I raised again the Trans-Jordan question and was obliged to speak with a considerable measure of bluntness which I hope will help progress.[15]

22nd October—Thursday.

We had a meeting in the morning to discuss the Trans-Jordan

---

and, on the whole, things are not going badly. At any rate, the right atmosphere has been created . . . and the time is ripe for a definite push." (Clayton to Wingate, 21 October 1925, C.P.)

15 The calculated bluntness of Clayton's remarks can best be appreciated from his own account of comments to Ibn Sa'ud regarding the Trans-Jordan frontier. "On the other hand I regretted to have observed that in our discussion previous to our meeting that afternoon there had been but little evidence of willingness on His Highness' part to meet His Majesty's Government's wishes in such a manner as would bring home to them by practical proof the full value of his declarations of friendship. Every point of importance which I had raised had been hotly debated, and I had noticed a tendency to introduce into our discussions an atmosphere of contention and bargaining over every point, which would, I fear, have produced an unfavourable impression on His Majesty's Government had it not been counteracted to some extent by His Highness's attitude that afternoon, of

question once more, but I found the Sultan, egged on by his two advisers, still extremely obstinate and uncompromising.[16] I decided, therefore, that further discussion of a general nature would only be confusing, would bear no fruit, and would create a contentious atmosphere. With this in mind, I said that I must now put forward to Ibn Sa'ud final proposals to be considered by him as a whole.[17]

As Ibn Sa'ud wished to spend Friday at Mecca, both in order to perform the Friday prayers there and also to transact some business of State, he left in his motor car at 4:00 p.m. immediately after the afternoon prayer. George and I then took our daily constitutional. Taufik Bey Suaidi, who has now joined us from Jeddah, stoutly refuses to walk a yard further than is absolutely necessary in spite of all chaff and persuasion.

It may be of interest to record our daily routine which is one of monotonous regularity. About 5:00 a.m., before it is light, one of our temporary retainers steals into my tent with a large bowl of camel's milk, freshly milked. It is a favourite food of Ibn Sa'ud, and I am, therefore, expected to consume large quantities. I like it in moderation, and I usually drink a cupful when it is brought in fresh and warm. As the first glimmering of light appears the musical call to prayer goes up and the whole camp turns out to the morning

---

which I took this occasion to express my appreciation. My time was not unlimited, and I was unwilling to trespass indefinitely on His Highness' valuable time and generous hospitality; moreover, it was not in consonance with the dignity with which His Majesty's Government had invested my mission that it should prolong its stay indefinitely in the pursuit of fruitless discussions. I therefore earnestly begged him to give me, in regard to the remaining points for discussion, the same proof of willingness to meet the wishes of His Majesty's Government in a generous spirit as he had displayed at our meeting that afternoon, more especially as it was only by such a course of action that he would secure that confidence and sympathy which His Majesty's Government were only too anxious to offer and which I felt convinced it was in the truest interests of His Highness and the State of Najd to receive. Failure to reach a settlement and a consequent rupture of negotiations would have a truly lamentable effect on the relations between His Highness and His Majesty's Government." ("Report . . . ," p. 32.)

22nd October—Thursday.

[16] At the sixth official meeting (19 October) Ibn Sa'ud told Clayton that

prayer. At about 6:15 a.m. the flies appear, so I get up and have a cup of tea and a biscuit, after which I write or work until it is time to shave, bathe, and dress. At about 8:00 a.m. breakfast appears, consisting of three diminutive Hejaz eggs, lightly boiled, which I break into a cup, with some bread, followed by some native cheese and occasionally a preserved apple from Taif, the whole washed down with tea. At 9:00 a.m. we have a meeting with the Sultan and his two advisers, which usually lasts till 11:00 a.m., after which George and I talk over the results of the discussion and future arrangements until 12 noon. At this hour an important ceremony is performed which consists of drinking a split gin and tonic-water in the seclusion of my tent. About 12:30 p.m. we go to lunch, which is taken in the tent prepared for that purpose, at which assist Shaikh Hafez Wahbeh, Shaikh Yusuf Yasin, the Sultan's physician Dr. Mahmud Hamuda, a Syrian Muslim, who left Damascus for political reasons after the departure of Faisal and the entry of the French, and Shaikh Abdulla el-Fadl, a very pleasant Arab merchant who belongs to a fairly large firm with headquarters at Bombay and branches at Jeddah, Mecca, and various places on the Red Sea and Persian Gulf. We are waited on by a large retinue, many members of which have extremely light duties to perform. For example, the head man holds

---

his obstinacy was anything but destructive, arising rather "from his love of truth and from his earnest desire that when I left I should take with me a promise that would be honoured and fulfilled." ("Report . . . ," p. 30.) There is no doubt that Ibn Sa'ud was perfectly sincere in these protestations, and that Clayton in his diary slightly misrepresented Ibn Sa'ud's stubbornness while at the same time being too critical of his advisers who were, after all, working in the interests of Ibn Sa'ud and not the British. Such petulance was clearly the immediate reaction to the frustrations of diplomatic negotiations, but nevertheless it conveys an impression that Shaykhs Hafiz Wahba and Yusuf Yasin had a decisive influence over Ibn Sa'ud, which in reality never appears to have been the case.

[17] By this time Clayton was convinced that he must give up Kaf. "I had come to the conclusion that no form of persuasion would induce Ibn Sa'ud voluntarily to give up Kaf and that arbitrary dictation, even if successful in securing the desired object, would leave a sore which must neutralize to a great extent the benefits to accrue from the agreements which it was my mission to conclude." ("Report . . . ," pp. 5–6.) Clayton's handling of the Kaf Question is in startling contrast to the attitude of Sir Percy Cox at Al-

the towel for me only while I wash my hands, and also sees that my tumbler is kept filled with water. Another does the same for all the other guests. Another brushes the flies away from my head and endeavours to keep them out of my food. Another serves the coffee, and so on. The cook is rather a celebrity, having been many years in Mecca and cooked previously not only for King Hussein but for his predecessor as Sherif of Mecca. He is always present to serve the meals and acts as a sort of major-domo. Our food is very well cooked in Arab style and now the cook knows exactly what I like most and produces those dishes at every meal (lunch and dinner). This is satisfactory but has resulted in the monotony of a fixed menu, soup, chicken, a bamiya with small pieces of meat in it, onions and gherkins, rice, a sweet, bananas and pomegranates, unsweetened Arab coffee.[18] At dinner there is also ice for the water made in a tiny ice machine which Mecca has produced. Alcohol and tobacco are of course unobtainable, being strictly forbidden by the tenets of [Ibn] Abdul Wahhab, though if we do run short of cigarettes, as we did on one occasion, it is usually possible to get a box of Egyptian Matussians, though only in strict secrecy and by a species of conjuring tricks.[19] Talking of conjuring tricks, I find that our clerk and stenographer, Harvey, is no mean performer at sleight of hand, and several times he has done wonders with a 10 piastre piece after dinner to the amusement of our host and delighted amazement of our army of retainers.

After lunch we pass the time in working, reading or, if it is not too hot, a short nap until 3:30 p.m., the hour of afternoon prayer, when we have a cup of tea, after which George usually competes with Shaikhs Hafez and Yusuf in an attempt to pave the way to agreement at the official meetings with the Sultan. At 5:30 p.m. we go for a walk, duly escorted by the faithful slave, Idris, fully armed. We then return, hot and thirsty, to an important ceremony which is the consumption of our one daily whisky and soda–it is wonder-

---

'Uqayr when he arbitrarily demarcated the 'Iraqi-Najdi frontier (see Introduction pp. 34–36).

18 *Bamiya* (Arabic, also *bamiyah*): a gumbo or soup thickened with unripe okra pods.

19 Matossians were a brand of Egyptian cigarettes.

ful how good it tastes! At 7:30 p.m. we bathe and change and at 8:00 p.m. I usually have a private and informal talk with the Sultan which lasts an hour or so. After that comes what George calls "a committee meeting" which consists of mixing and consuming a concoction which we have dubbed "The Bahra Cocktail." Then dinner, which is a repetition of lunch, followed at a decent interval by bed and sleep, being well guarded by an Arab guard which mounts over our camp immediately after sunset and remains till dawn.

Taufik Bey Suaidi, the delegate from Iraq, is excellent value and an addition to our circle. He is a Professor of Law, studied in Paris, and is now in the Ministry of Justice at Baghdad. Red-haired, florid, short, rather fat, and full of talk, with a very keen sense of humour.

23rd October–Friday.

The Sultan being in Mecca, no meetings were possible, but we had plenty to do drawing up drafts and preparing my Trans-Jordan proposals. We were busy all day, therefore, until the evening when we took our usual walk. The flies are beginning to become pretty bad during the day, and also there is not the slightest sign of any drop in the temperature. We are becoming much attached to our chief retainers who are excellent fellows. The head of them placed in charge of us by Ibn Sa'ud, is a certain Ibrahim el Jumas'a. He accompanied Philby on his trip from Riad to Jeddah and again on his journey through Aflag and Wadi Dawasi.[20] Philby took a strong dislike to him, as appears from his book, but we have found him quite a good fellow. The second in command is an elderly Arab, who dyes the grey hairs in his beard with henna, by name Rashaid. He is always very chatty and cheery and is continually on the look out to do things for us. Harvey's conjuring tricks send him into convulsions of delight, and he spends much of his spare time squatting outside Harvey's tent in the hope that he will make something appear or disappear. The remaining members of the staff, who are of

---

23rd October–Friday.

[20] A cantankerous and difficult man himself, Philby seems to derive particular satisfaction in recording the perversities of Ibrahim el Jumai'ah (the correct spelling) in excruciating detail in *The Heart of Arabia*, 2 vols., London, 1923.

importance are Idris (to whom I have already referred), Almaz, and Faragalla, all of whom are black slaves brought over from the Sudan in early youth.

24th October—Saturday.

The Sultan was delayed in Mecca on business, chiefly I fancy in connection with the Persian delegation, so we had another free day in which to polish up our drafts and write up our records. George spent a long morning with Shaikhs Hafez and Yusuf. They are incredibly tiresome, combining equal measures of low cunning and obstinate stupidity, but George is quite marvellous in his way of dealing with them. In the afternoon George had a well-earned rest broken of course by Shaikh Yusuf, and we went for our usual walk in the evening. About 10:00 p.m. a messenger, whom we had sent to Jeddah on the previous evening, returned with a letter from Jordan, some cigarettes for me, and a bottle of gin. The last two items were very badly wanted.

25th October—Sunday.

Ibn Sa'ud returned from Mecca about 8:30 a.m. and at 9:30 a.m. we had a meeting at which I presented my draft proposals. The outlook was not very promising as Ibn Sa'ud was obdurate and very disinclined to give way. I eventually asked him to take away my proposals and examine them, bearing in mind that they represented practically the furthest limit to which I could go. We had no further interview on this day.[21]

25th October—Sunday.

[21] On 25 October Clayton made his final bid for settling the frontier between Trans-Jordan and Najd. He realized that the best course was to cede Kaf to Ibn Sa'ud in exchange for the main objectives, "the immunity of Trans-Jordan from aggression, the preservation of established rights, and the protection of tribes against disruptive propaganda." As for the northern frontier Clayton refused to yield, thereby securing the East-West corridor from the Mediterranean to Mesopotamia for British imperial communications. He did meet Ibn Sa'ud's requests for links with Syria, however, by offering certain restricted facilities for transit into and out of Syrian territory. On his part Ibn Sa'ud was not to establish a fortified post at Kaf and would do his utmost to prevent raiding. The draft agreement that Clayton presented was to be accepted or rejected as a whole, for clearly the cession of Kaf was

As we were starting on our afternoon walk, when about half a mile from our camp, we passed between two Arab tents about 100 yards apart and immediately out came two fanatical looking Arabs who began gesticulating and obviously cursing us roundly as dogs of Christians. We thought it best to take no notice so we walked straight on, leaving our escort, the faithful Idris, to deal with the situation. He was some time away and, looking back, we saw him surrounded by a small knot of people, all waving their arms and evidently talking. We were rather anxious lest there should be a real row, but presently Idris appeared again and explained that he had intended beating in the heads of the two men but that the knot of people who had gathered round had eventually succeeded in dissuading him. He was furiously angry, however, and said he should report the whole thing to the "Shioukh." When I got in, I thought it well to send a message to Sa'ud, saying that we were perhaps to blame for going, unwittingly, too near to the tents and hoping he would not punish the offenders too severely. To this he replied that he appreciated my action but that discipline must be maintained. Apparently, the two poor wretches had been brought straight before Ibn Sa'ud. They had greeted him in the usual way with "God greet you with prosperity, O Abdul Aziz," to which he had replied: "God greet you with dung in your faces, you curs." "Who are you who dare to insult my guests?" Whereupon they were each given 30 lashes in the Sultan's presence and then sent straight off to prison in Mecca that very night. Such are the drastic measures by which Ibn Sa'ud maintains his personal prestige and authority. But, on the

---

dependent on Ibn Sa'ud's commitment to cooperate with Trans-Jordan. "Report . . . ," pp. 6, 34–35.

In Clayton's draft agreement of 25 October the frontier was to start in "the northeast from the point of intersection of meridian 39° E. with parallel 32° N. which marks the termination of the frontier between Najd and 'Iraq, and proceeds in a straight line to the point of intersection of meridian 37° E. to its intersection with parallel 29°35′ N." With minor alterations this frontier was incorporated into the Hadda Agreement and remains the boundary between Jordan and Sa'udi Arabia to this day. This frontier was later confirmed by an agreement between Jordan and Sa'udi Arabia in August 1965. ("Draft Agreement concerning Trans-Jordan presented to the Sultan of Najd on 25 October 1925," Article 1, C.P.) See Map.

other hand, he is the father of his people, and some 2000 persons feed at his table daily while never a beggar goes away hungry.

26th October–Monday.

I had an interview with Ibn Sa'ud at which we discussed my draft proposals. He gave way on a few points but resisted strongly on several points of principle which I am unable to concede.[22] I was obliged to show quite clearly that my mind was made up on the questions of principle on which I could admit of no bargaining. I asked him to reconsider the whole matter in the light of my remarks. In the afternoon we had another meeting at which he gave way a little further but raised various tiresome points regarding the northern frontier and was evidently still struggling for an absolutely free corridor between Najd and Syria.[23] We were unable to come to any agreement, and shortly after the meeting Shaikh Hafez produced, informally but in writing, their observations and counter-proposals. The alterations, amendments, and additions to my draft were so obviously an attempt to undermine the principles that I had said clearly I must maintain that they were not susceptible of detailed dis-

---

26th October–Monday.

[22] Ibn Sa'ud first requested the boundary be drawn fifteen miles farther north of Kaf in order to prevent any difficulties arising out of grazing needs of the villagers. Although Clayton pointed out that tribes were free to cross the frontier for the purpose of grazing, he implied that this request could be met. Then Ibn Sa'ud requested the establishment of a neutral enclave, like the quadrilateral between Najd and 'Iraq on the eastern frontier, to be located along the southern sector of the frontier between Trans-Jordan and Najd. He also requested a similar neutral zone along the northern frontier to meet the requirements of Najd trade. The effect of these neutral zones would in fact have meant the extension of the limits of Najd some fifty miles to the west into Trans-Jordan to the Ardh as-Sawwan and an even more serious extension of territory northward, which in effect would have driven a wedge into the British East-West line of communications. To all of this Clayton replied that the boundary was fixed and "in view of this and of the Imperial interests involved, I was unable to consider or discuss such a proposal." He would, however, consider other proposals to safeguard Najd trade with Syria. "Report . . . ," pp. 36–37.

[23] In the afternoon Clayton agreed to redraw the northern frontier beginning at the intersection of meridian 39° E. with parallel 32° N. and thence proceeding in a straight line to the intersection of meridian 37° E. with

cussion, and, after discussion and consideration with George, I decided to reject them as a whole and say clearly that, if they could not meet me, I must break off negotiations and take my departure.[24]

We went for our usual walk at sunset and were amused to see that the incident of yesterday had caused our escort to be supplemented by Rashaid, carrying a loaded rifle. I am afraid that poor old Idris was rather crestfallen and felt that his reputation had suffered.

27th October–Tuesday.

We had a very strenuous day in the morning when I had to take a strong line and even threaten to break off the negotiations at once if these repeated attempts were made to haggle and to whittle down principles on which I was quite unable to give way. Ibn Sa'ud took up an air of injured surprise that I should adopt such a line and accused me of trying to carry matters through with a high hand and without discussion. He was on weak ground, however, and as I remained firm, he altered his tone and we parted in an atmosphere of friendliness. My remarks had, I think, gone home.[25]

During the rest of the day and far into the night, George tackled

---

parallel 31° 30′ N. rather than 31° 25′ N. as in the Clayton's draft agreement of 25 October. (See Map). Ibn Sa'ud then talked at length about the difficulties of Syrian-Najdi trade when a strip of territory belonging to Trans-Jordan and 'Iraq lay astride Ibn Sa'ud's line of communications with the north. His wishes were, of course, in direct conflict with British interests to maintain their East-West line of communications for which the corridor had been created in the first place. On this matter Clayton had no discretion.

[24] The counterproposals put forward by Shaykh Hafiz contained two changes. The first pushed the frontier north of the Wadi as-Sirhan another five hours' journey. The second provided for the inclusion of the two neutral zones in the frontier. Both of these proposals clearly eroded the principles on which Clayton had no discretion. He told Ibn Sa'ud that there were "certain Imperial interests which had nothing to do with Najd directly but which must be safeguarded. Trans-Jordan and 'Iraq are on the main air route, and there was Jerusalem–Baghdad car route, and I could not consider proposals which infringed on those Imperial interests." ("Report . . . ," p. 39.)

27th October–Tuesday.

[25] During the morning the negotiations were tense and heated. At one point Ibn Sa'ud bitterly burst out declaring "that the Wadi Sirhan was his property, and that he had made many concessions to Great Britain. He had

Shaikhs Hafez and Yusuf, doing the best of many splendid days' work. He is wonderful in the way he sees through them and defeats them by a combination of firmness and persuasion. By midnight he had almost won the battle and finally beaten down their resistance. If we get our agreements, it will be due in a very large measure to George Antonius, and I am quite convinced that I could not have succeeded without him.[26] The Persian delegation returned from Mecca during the day and after a brief stay here passed on to Jeddah, but I have not heard how they were impressed by their visit, though from all that I have heard Mecca is in a much better state under Ibn Sa'ud than ever it was in the time of King Hussein. A mail arrived bringing welcome letters from home and papers. I had a letter from Enid with excellent news of the family.

28th October—Wednesday.

We were busy all day preparing a final draft of a Trans-Jordan agreement, so no meetings were held though George at an early hour had another tussle with Shaikhs Hafez and Yusuf, whom we have nicknamed the "Vultures." They are struggling desperately to wriggle and squirm round all the points on which I have insisted, and they will take a lot of pinning down before we can get the final text agreed upon.

Taufik Bey Suaidi, the Iraq delegate, left for Jeddah at 3:30 p.m. in one of the Sultan's cars in order to catch the Khedivial steamer from Jeddah to Suez, whence he will proceed to Cairo, where he proposes resting from his labours (sic) for a fortnight or three weeks before returning to Baghdad. He was in high spirits, as he has, I think, hated every minute since he left Cairo. We shall miss him as

---

Faisal on one side and 'Abdullah on the other, both new creations fencing him in on either side and both hostile towards him. When he thought of the injustices to himself he was surprised at the moderation of his demands. He would prefer to have his throat cut with a sword rather than have anyone infringe upon his rights in his own dominions." ("Report . . . ," p. 40.) Clayton remained tenacious. Both agreed to turn over negotiations to their subordinates in order to discover the precise areas of disagreement and to allow both Ibn Sa'ud and Clayton a cooling-off period.

[26] Clayton both officially and unofficially gave Antonius the praise he richly deserved. Particularly during the afternoon of 27 October and through-

he is a good companion and always cheery though hardly a glutton for work which was perhaps just as well for the progress of business. At least, he never raised any difficulties. Indeed, at the end I think he would have put his name to anything rather than have his departure delayed.

George and I took our usual walk at sunset. There is some sameness about it as we do not think it tactful to walk through the camp and so are confined to a straight line there and back on one of three directions West, South-West, or North-West.

29th October—Thursday.

We had a meeting with Ibn Sa'ud at 4:30, having completed our final draft which during the morning George had at last induced the "Vultures" to agree to. Ibn Sa'ud, I am glad to say, also agreed, so I hope that we can now proceed to the drawing up of the final text, and its preparation by a skilled Arabic calligraphist who has been brought from Mecca for the purpose. We also fixed up the question of the restitution of loot for past raids between Najd and Iraq on lines which had previously been agreed upon between Taufik Bey and Hafez and Yusuf.[27] At the end of our interview I explained to Ibn Sa'ud Philby's position in respect of His Majesty's Government, pointing out that he held no Government post or position whatsoever, and that, moreover, he was in Jeddah contrary to the expressed wishes of H.M.G. Ibn Sa'ud thanked me for explaining the exact situation, and I hope that now Philby will be able to do as little harm as may be, though he will doubtless succeed sooner or later in penetrating to Ibn Sa'ud.

I have decided to leave here on Tuesday, 3rd November, and to

---

out the following day Antonius by his tact and firmness with Shaykhs Hafiz Wahba and Yusuf Yasin was able to bring them around to the British point of view by 29 October. In his report Clayton recommended that Antonius' services merited special recognition by the British government. "Report . . . ," p. 11.

29th October—Thursday.

[27] The position of the 'Iraq government was stated fully by Tawfiq Bey as-Suwaydi in a note to Clayton. The main point of conflict with Najd was the question of extradition of nonpolitical offenders. (Tawfiq Bey as-Suwaydi to Clayton, 25 October 1925, C.P., "Report . . . ," pp. 74–76.)

cross to Port Sudan on the 5th November. I shall go to Cairo, where I propose writing my report, by the Nile route, visiting Khartoum for two or three days. I hope that nothing will turn up to delay us, as we have all had enough of this place, where the flies and dirt are becoming unbearable.

30th October—Friday.

We had no meeting with Ibn Sa'ud in the morning, but George spent most of the day in a wrangle with the "Vultures," who are still struggling desperately to score small successes and whittle down the principles which I have laid down. I hope, however, that he has succeeded in defeating them and that tomorrow will see the final text of the Trans-Jordan Agreement settled.

We have decided to call the Iraq agreement, "the BAHRA Agreement," and the Trans-Jordan Agreement, "The UM-el-KARUN Agreement." Bahra is a ruined village about two or three miles from camp, down the Jeddah road, and Um-el-Karun is the name of a well quite close to camp.

The Persian Consul at Damascus has arrived from Jeddah, having been sent back with orders to proceed to Medina and report on the alleged damage to the Prophet's Tomb. He has a free pass into Medina, given by King Ali, and he is to make his way there under the auspices of Ibn Sa'ud. He is in a "blue" funk and hates the whole business.

After our evening walk and bath I had a long private talk with Ibn Sa'ud at which we discussed the questions (a) of establishing a more satisfactory channel of communication between him and His Majesty's Government, and (b) General arrangements for next year's pilgrimage. Ibn Sa'ud seemed pleased that I should have raised these questions and seemed anxious to discuss them. He said that he would give me his considered views at a later interview.

31st October—Saturday.

Ibn Sa'ud had to leave for Mecca early in the morning for the day on important business, so we were unable to have any meetings. George spent the day finishing off the text of the Trans-Jordan Agreement, which we have now agreed to call the "HADDA Agreement," with Shaikhs Hafez and Yusuf, so I had practically nothing to do.

There was a little rain last night and it looked thundery all the morning as if a storm was brewing. About 3:30 p.m. the storm burst with violent wind and heavy rain. At one time hailstones actually fell. The servants' tent collapsed early in the proceedings, quickly followed by mine and then by the reception tent. I had been lying down but luckily I got up and dressed directly the rain began, so I was able, just in time, to skip out of my tent at the very moment that it crashed to the ground. An army of slaves and dependents appeared immediately, apparently from nowhere, and extricated my belongings which were piled in George's tent which had fortunately held firm. My tent was rather torn, but the reception tent was soon re-erected, the storm only lasting an hour or so, and I moved into it. Two Arabs, however, appeared and quickly sewed up the rent in my tent which by nightfall was standing again. Luckily no damage was done to our belongings, or to our priceless official papers, and it is a high tribute to the complete honesty of these people that not so much as a pin was missing.

The Persian Consul from Damascus left about 4:30 p.m. in a Ford car for Mecca on his wearisome trip to Medina, looking very dejected and unhappy and accompanied by an even more miserable looking orderly in the garb of a Persian policeman but wearing white sand shoes. We enjoyed our evening walk as the air was cool after the storm, and the sand was firm and good walking after the drenching rain. It appears that the season is now beginning in which such heavy storms are to be expected, and there has already been rain on more than one recent occasion at Mecca and in the neighborhood although this is the first fall we have had here.

1st November–Sunday.

I had an interview with Ibn Sa'ud at 11:00 a.m. at which the "Bahra Agreement," regarding Iraq and Najd frontier affairs, was formally signed by the Sultan and myself.[28] We then had a talk in the course of which I told him that I was ready to hear any views or aspirations which he might wish communicated to His Majesty's Government. In the afternoon at 4:00 p.m. we had another meeting at which, after much circumlocution, he told me that he had several things to tell me, but that he wished first to be assured that his views and wishes would be considered fully by H.M.G. and a reply of some sort given to him. He had on previous occasions given these views and wishes to Sir Percy Cox, Mr. Philby and others, but there had never been any result, or even sign that they had reached H.M.G. I assured him that in this case his views would certainly be transmitted direct by me to H.M.G. by whom I felt sure that they would be considered carefully. I added that I was confident that he would receive a reply in due course, though I could not say what that reply would be, more especially as he had not yet expressed his views and wishes to me. Ibn Sa'ud thanked me and said that he would give me his views after dinner.

1st November–Sunday.

[28] The principal object of the Bahra Agreement was to arrive at some modus vivendi that would, as far as possible, prevent transfrontier raids and ensure peace on the border between 'Iraq and Najd. The provisions were based mainly on the instructions to Clayton from the Colonial Office (Vernon to Clayton, 10 September 1925) and the letter of Colonel C. H. F. Cox dated 12 March 1925. All the points agreed upon at the Kuwait Conference were embodied in the Bahra Agreement (Articles 1, 5, 6, 7), except for the proposal for the appointment of Inspectors of Boundaries which seemed of doubtful effectiveness. In this sense Clayton was completing the work of that abortive conference. The substance of the agreement, however, dealt with the three pressing questions of transfrontier raids, migration, and emigration. The question of tribal raids had been discussed at length at Kuwait, but no method had been arranged for the assessment of damage and the fixing of responsibility. Article 2 of the Bahra Agreement created a tribunal to accomplish those two important tasks. The decision of the tribunal was binding, and the government of the tribe held responsible was to execute the decision of the tribunal for restitution and redress. Both governments agreed to discourage tribal migration, which was to be controlled by requiring the consent of both governments before the frontier could be crossed, except for certain prescribed grazing rights (Article 3). The most difficult question was that of emigration. Both governments agreed not to accept the emigration of a tribe "unless its emigration takes place with the knowledge and consent of

At 7:00 p.m. we were entertained at a dinner in pure Bedouin style, at which the Sultan himself, Shaikhs Hafez and Yusuf, Dr. Mahmud, Antonius, Harvey, and myself were present. The meal consisted of three or four sheep, roasted whole and stuffed with rice, almonds, raisins, etc. This *pièce de résistance* was placed on a large, round, raised, metal dish, while on the floor round the centre dish were ranged bowls of broth and dishes of prepared bread and savoury vegetables. We all, having removed our slippers, sat round the feast on the floor and ate with our fingers, dipping into the dishes in turn, according to taste.

Ibn Sa'ud, being the host, was most hospitable in selecting savoury morsels and special tidbits from the centre dish and pressing them upon us. The meal only lasted about half an hour and was marked by an absence of the constant pressure to eat which is so embarrassing in Egypt and often in Palestine. Ibn Sa'ud was courtesy itself as host, and the food was appetizing and very well cooked. After the usual ablutions we retired to the reception tent for coffee and diges-

---

its Government." (Article 4). Such a provision, in effect, meant that 'Iraq would not receive Najd tribes unless Ibn Sa'ud had given them permission to settle in 'Iraq. This would presumably strengthen Ibn Sa'ud's precarious authority over his border tribes when they realized they could not seek asylum in 'Iraq without his consent. This was a victory for Ibn Sa'ud, but what was his gain was not necessarily 'Iraq's loss. The 'Iraq government wanted peace and stability on the frontier. Although compromising British ideas on the principle of political asylum, Article 4 would not only increase the stability of the border by strengthening the control of Ibn Sa'ud over his frontier tribes, but each government pledged not to encourage migration or emigration or offer bribes to do so. Since the mutual seduction of each other's tribes was a favorite sport of the Arab chieftains, this article, if carried out in good faith, would tend to stabilize the border. The question of extradition was significant by its omission. This was a victory for Clayton. Ibn Sa'ud had insisted that Najd tribes who fled to 'Iraq must be returned and in particular the Shammar. The position of the British and 'Iraq governments was that the right of political asylum must be upheld. Although Clayton agreed (Article 10) to negotiate in the future an extradition agreement to cover common criminals, he steadfastly refused to agree to the return of political refugees. To have resisted Ibn Sa'ud's insistent demands on this point was no mean accomplishment. See Appendix I for the complete text of the Bahra Agreement.

tion. We indulged in small talk for twenty minutes or so, and then Ibn Sa'ud expressed his wishes and views in regard to his future relations with H.M.G. In brief, they were that the existing treaty, made in 1916 between H.M.G. and himself, should be revised in order that its terms might be more in accord with his present position. He also alluded, rather diffidently, to his desire for a good supply of arms and his difficulty in making both ends meet.[29]

The weather is slightly cooler after the storm, but there is still rather a heavy, thundery feeling in the air, and it looked as if it might have rained again during the afternoon.

2nd November—Monday.

The morning was spent finishing off the Trans-Jordan agreement, the "Hadda Agreement," which was duly signed at noon.[30] After signing I had a short talk with Ibn Sa'ud on general subjects.[31]

Yesterday Ibn Sa'ud sent me some very handsome presents, which

---

[29] Clayton replied that the British government could hardly contemplate entering into negotiations with Ibn Sa'ud regarding the revision of the 1916 treaty while the Hijazi-Najdi war was in progress. The British government had declared its strict neutrality and any negotiations would violate that position, while at the same time a comprehensive treaty could hardly be arranged when the situation in Arabia was so "vague and undetermined." Ibn Sa'ud agreed that this was not the time, but at Sir Gilbert's request he outlined the main lines he wished to see any such revision take. They included proper international recognition for the status of Najd, the right to import arms, and financial assistance. (Clayton to L. C. M. S. Amery, Secretary of State for Colonies, 16 December 1925, C.P.)

2nd November—Monday.

[30] The substance of the Hadda Agreement was to fix the frontier between Najd and Trans-Jordan. Although Kaf and the Wadi as-Sirhan south of that village were ceded to Ibn Sa'ud, the northern and the southern frontiers were delineated in accordance with the wishes of the British government, preserving the important East-West corridor and the line of communications. Moreover, Clayton also preserved almost all the grazing ground west of Wadi as-Sirhan, including the four tributary valleys in dispute. Ibn Sa'ud also undertook not to establish a military center at Kaf. Articles 2, 4, and 8 secured, as far as possible, the immunity of Trans-Jordan from aggression, the preservation of established rights, and the protection of tribes against disruptive propa-

he delicately expressed as being for my sons who were "as his own sons." They consisted of three rugs, three camel's hair "abas," two white "abas" with "Kafias" and "ajal," two daggers and two beautiful Arab swords, richly mounted in gold.[32]

I thanked him suitably but I am afraid it means heavy expense in return. He also gave presents to Antonius and Harvey and to the servants. At 4:00 p.m. we went to Ibn Sa'ud's tent to see the striking of the camp, and the departure for Mecca of all but a small guard remaining to take care of us till tomorrow. The whole thing was done with wonderful precision and rapidity and within half an hour or so tents were struck and packed on camels, and the whole army was disappearing up the Wadi in the direction of Mecca.

I had a talk afterwards with Ibn Sa'ud and he brought up one or two matters on which he would like me to take action and express his views to H.M.G. I then took my leave as Ibn Sa'ud was leaving for Mecca that evening. Soon after we got back to our camp and

---

ganda. The prevention of raids was dealt with in Articles 7 and 8. Facilities for trade and pilgrimage were contained in the provisions of Articles 12 and 13, and in a separate undertaking Ibn Sa'ud agreed to grant reciprocal facilities to trading caravans crossing the Wadi as-Sirhan if established rights were proved to exist. Article 3 stipulated the maintenance of constant communication between the chief British representative in Trans-Jordan and the governor of the Wadi as-Sirhan, while Articles 9, 10, and 11 related to minor questions of frontier regulation. Articles 14, 15, and 16 were concerned with the language and name of the Agreement. See Appendix II for the complete text of the Hadda Agreement.

[31] The general subjects included Ibn Sa'ud's intercession on behalf of Sayyid Ahmad as-Sanusi who wished to retire to Egypt or Libya. He had entered the war against Britain after very heavy pressure from the Turks and was then living in exile in Mecca. Ibn Sa'ud also discussed the composition of the Najd delegation he was proposing to send to India, and the suitability of a new harbor at Ra's Tannurah on the Persian Gulf where Ibn Sa'ud hoped to arrange for the regular calling of British India line ships. He also asked Clayton for his opinion of the probable effect and reaction to a Wahhabi attack on Jiddah, but Sir Gilbert declined to comment because of the neutral position of the British government in the Hijazi-Najdi conflict.

[32] "Abas": *'aba'*, a loose, sleeveless cloaklike outer garment. "Kafias": *kaffiyah*, a square head-kerchief. "Ajal": *'uqul* (pl. of *'ipāl*), a headband made of camel's hair, worn over the head-kerchief.

just before the evening prayer began, my worst fears were realised and Shaikh Hafez appeared with an Arab mare sent to me as a present by Ibn Sa'ud. I could not refuse it but goodness knows what I am to do with it. Two camel men were ready to take it straight away to Jeddah with our baggage, but I begged Shaikh Hafez to keep it for me until I could make suitable arrangements for its transport. She is a jolly little beast and quite well made and bred. She would be topping for Pay [Patience Clayton] to ride if I could only get her home and keep her there. In the meantime, I must try and get her to Egypt, and find someone there who will keep her for me.[33]

After the evening prayer Ibn Sa'ud came and said his final good-byes, and went off in his car to Mecca. It has been a most interesting experience meeting him and getting to know him so well. He is quite a personality and, as long as he is alive, Najd will be a formidable power in Central Arabia. But his rule is entirely autocratic and based on his own personal prestige and authority, and I fancy that when he dies all will be once more confusion, unless one of his sons develops something of the father's capacity. He is a fine-looking man—very tall and strongly built, especially for an Arab—being well over six foot. He has a clean-cut handsome face, with a sallow, but not dark, complexion and slight beard and moustache. Dressed invariably in Bedouin costume, he is a striking and commanding figure. His expression in repose is rather sad, even at times slightly sulky, but his face lights up very attractively when he smiles. His Arabic is of the Central parts of Arabia and very difficult to understand by one used to the language of Egypt or Palestine, especially as he speaks fast and rather clips his words. I should say that he was a strong character, but the expansion of his dominions is bringing him up against problems and influences which are new and strange to him, and I fear lest, in his ignorance, he may fall into the hands of unscrupulous advisers. His health seemed good, but he has an infection of the left eye which requires careful attention and possibly an operation.

Our camels with servants and all but very light hand luggage left

---

[33] Unhappily, the horse never reached England.

for Jeddah about 6:30 p.m. and we hope to find them there when we arrive tomorrow.

After dinner Shaikh Hafez provided a short entertainment of singing and recitation for our amusement. The show consisted of a lengthy and very monotonous chorus sung in a curious minor key, and two almost interminable recitations by our henchman, Rashaid, dealing the one with travel through Central and Southern Arabia, and the other with war in Jebel Shammar.

During the afternoon a strong and sudden gust of wind brought my tent down again to the discomfort of a crowd of scorpions who have taken up their abode in the eaves.

CHAPTER 3

From Bahra to Cairo:

3–22 November 1925

3rd November—Tuesday.

At 8:00 a.m., after our usual light breakfast, we started off in the Studebaker and the Ford with Shaikhs Hafez and Yusuf accompanying us and the usual crowd of Arab warriors clinging to the footboards. We bade long and cordial farewells to our numerous retinue after distributing heavy largesse (£100, which I sincerely hope H.M.G. will not consider excessive).

We had a very good and quite uneventful run to Nuzla, the recent rain having much improved the road and arrived by 9:30 a.m. We found Jordan awaiting us with King Ali's car for our use and the Agency Ford for the baggage, which had duly arrived. We then drove into Jeddah, after saying good-bye to our Najd escort which we left fraternizing with their Hejaz enemies.

We put up at the Agency where Jordan was hospitable as ever. Before lunch we took a stroll through the town and bazaars, the style of which is almost exactly similar to that of Suakin, but everything was terribly poverty-stricken and comparatively deserted. There is evidently no business and no money. After tea I paid a visit to King Ali, but, being a visit of courtesy, nothing but general con-

---

4th November—Wednesday.

[1] Saleh was in February 1933 a deputy in the Ministry of Justice, Egypt.

[2] One of the leaders of the Young Turk Revolution of 1908–09, Jemal Pasha took command of the Ottoman army in Palestine and cautiously planned and

versation and small talk was indulged in, and I only stayed half an hour or so.

During the afternoon two planes went out on a bombing flight. They have refrained very scrupulously and honourably from any hostile action during the course of our negotiations.

4th November—Wednesday.

I received a return call from King Ali during the morning, and he asked me whether I would come and have a private talk with him in the evening, to which I assented. I also received a visit from the Egyptian Consul, Kaimakam Mohammed Bey Saleh, who was for many years an Inspector in the Sudan Government and who remembered me well.[1] He obviously hates Jeddah and is counting the days until he can get another job. Another visitor was Tahsin Pasha al-Kakir, the military Commander-in-Chief, a gaunt, nervous-looking Syrian who has seen service in the Turkish Army during the war at the attack by Jemal Pasha on the Suez Canal, the Caucasus, the Dardanelles, Bulgaria, Roumania, the Caspian, and Northern Syria.[2] He regaled us for about an hour with a lengthy account of his history bringing up to the time when he was Kaimakam of Salt and then served under Amir Abdulla, when he was brought by King Hussein to the Hejaz when the latter returned here from his visit to Trans-Jordan early in 1924.

After tea I returned Tahsin Pasha's call at the Ministry of War (sic) and got another good dose in the form of an incredibly bombastic and entirely inaccurate account of the recent operations here. You would have thought from Tahsin's version that he had personally led repeated attacks against Ibn Sa'ud in the course of which a series of crushing defeats had been inflicted on the Wahhabis with practically no loss to the Hejaz forces. It is, however, an established fact that this was not so. I then returned the Egyptian Consul's call, staying half an hour or so and chatting about Egypt and Egyptian

---

ably executed an offensive against the Suez Canal. In January 1915 his forces actually crossed the Sinai Desert and fought a sharp engagement with British defenders on the banks of the Canal before retiring. The Turks were never able seriously to threaten the Canal again.

personalities. Jordan and I then went for a walk around the lagoon which is his usual constitutional.

After dinner I went round to King Ali's palace as I had promised. It was rather a pathetic interview. Poor, kind, gentle Ali is at his wits' end and is pulled hither and thither by the rogues who surround him. He has no money, no men, and no kingdom. He begged me to ask H.M.G. to help him and was ready to make any promise in order to get help and money. I said I could do nothing whatsoever officially, but that I would repeat his requests to H.M.G. in a purely private capacity.

Very hot, sticky weather with little or no wind.

5th November—Thursday.

H.M.S. *Clematis* arrived at 9:00 a.m., and we sent off most of our baggage in the forenoon. I went round to Gellatly, Hankey & Co. during the morning and settled up their account for gold supplied to us at Bahra.[3] Jordan has promised to send the mare to Suez for me, possibly he may take her with him as he expects to leave for Port Said by the Khedivial boat of the 19th. I, therefore wrote to Shaikh Hafez asking him to send the mare to Jeddah, as soon as a convenient opportunity arose.

Lunch at the Agency and after lunch Philby came round and had

---

5th November—Thursday.

[3] Established in 1884, Gellatly, Hankey & Company's office at Jiddah was managed at this time by C. A. Mackinlay and was concerned with the transit of pilgrims to Mecca along with their more usual marine activities, banking, and general trading. The company extended loans to Ibn Sa'ud during the immediate years following the consolidation of his rule throughout the Hijaz. See 8 October.

[4] Determined to circumvent the prohibition of the British government against proceeding into the interior of Arabia, Philby made elaborate and secret preparations to disguise his intentions, though it was clear to all that he was determined to see Ibn Sa'ud. Both King 'Ali and more reluctantly Ibn Sa'ud made the necessary arrangements, and "at the dead of night on the date fixed, all the lights were left on in my rooms to create the impression that I was in residence as usual," while Philby stole away to a small sailing boat that took him to Rabigh. Here he was met by a Wahhabi escort that took him to Shumaysi where he met Ibn Sa'ud. Nothing came of the meeting,

a chat. I did not raise any contentious matters or ask him what his plans were, but he is growing a beard and evidently contemplates a trip into the interior, probably for the purpose of writing a book or newspaper articles.[4]

The Khedivial steamer arrived about 11:00 a.m. bringing the mails, so we were luckily able to get our letters and papers before we left. I had two lovely long letters from Enid, full of home news, all, I am thankful to say, good. Her last letter was dated 18th October and our latest *Times* the 22nd. We embarked at 3:00 p.m. from the Customs quay, seen off by various people, including Shaikh Fuad el-Khatib on behalf of King Ali, and went in the Agency launch to the *Clematis*. Jordan and his staff came on board with us to say good-bye, and we sailed for Port Sudan at 4:00 p.m.

6th November—Friday.

We arrived at Port Sudan at 10:00 a.m., having delayed for half an hour or so outside the harbour in order to let the P. & O. *Cathay* get clear. She had called at Port Sudan on her way home from Australia—a fine new ship of some 15,000 tons.[5]

On arrival, R. K. Winter, who is acting Governor of the Red Sea Province for Tippetts who is on leave, came off to see me, and soon afterwards Harry Hawkins arrived with an invitation to put up

---

as indeed nothing could. Philby consequently returned to Rabigh and embarked in a sailing vessel carrying "a stinking cargo of rotting shell-fish and half-cured hides" to Port Sudan where he remained until 1 January 1926 when he returned to Jiddah, then in Wahhabi hands, to attend to his neglected business interests. This was not one of Philby's more impressive exploits, and it remained one of his permanent regrets that he was on the other side of the Red Sea when S. R. Jordan very capably arranged for the abdication of King 'Ali, clearing the way for Ibn Sa'ud to complete his conquest of the Hijaz. The British authorities wisely ignored Philby's escapade. Philby, *Arabian Days*, pp. 248–254.

6th November—Friday.

[5] R.M.S. *Cathay*, 15,104 tons, was built in 1925 by Barclay, Curle & Company Ltd., Glasgow, for the Peninsular and Oriental Steam Navigation Company. She was commanded by Captain E. B. Bartlett and carried 300 first- and second-class passengers. She was sunk on 12 November 1942 by German aircraft off Bougie.

with them for meals. George Antonius stayed to look after the baggage and take it up to the station where we were accommodated in a saloon, while I drove off to the Hawkins' house. I found Mary Hawkins there, having arrived from home with Susette two days ago. After lunch and a rest the Hawkins took us out for a run in a launch all round the harbour which I found very interesting. The place has grown a good deal, and they have already found it necessary to start building a new quay on the south side.

We returned to tea and dined with the Hawkins—Major and Mrs. Stephens being the only other guests. He is an ex-Gunner, now employed by one of the coal companies.[6] Susette has grown into a beautiful girl of eighteen, very quiet, like her father, but with plenty in her when you get to know her, I should say.

Slept in the coach—temperature very hot, damp, and sticky.

7th November—Saturday.

Breakfasted at the Hawkins whose house is just opposite the station. During the morning visited the *mudiria* where we got our warrants for the journey, paid Lorensato's bill, and went to discuss the question of Ibn Sa'ud's wireless at Rabegh with the Manager of the Eastern Telegraph Company, who is a brother of Waterfield, formerly doctor in the Sudan Government service at Port Sudan.[7]

Lunched with the Hawkins and went to the Tennis Club in the afternoon where I met [Commander] Woodward and said goodbye to him. George and I dined with the Hawkins and left by the 9:00 p.m. train for Atbara where we branch off for Khartoum.

---

[6] Mitchell Cotts & Company Ltd. in Durban sent coal to the Sudan through their representative at Port Sudan, Contomichalos, Sons & Company Ltd. In 1925 Contomichalos had a deficiency in their stock of coal, and Major Stephens was sent by Mitchell Cotts to investigate.

7th November—Saturday.

[7] E. W. Waterfield, Assistant Superintendent, Eastern Telegraph Company, Port Sudan, and his brother Dr. N. E. Waterfield.

Mudiria, mudiriyah (Arabic): the headquarters building for the local administrative unit. Ibn Sa'ud wished to establish a radio station at Rabigh capable of reaching Port Sudan, from which communication could be made with more distant parts of the world through the wireless facilities there.

8th November—Sunday.

We spent the day in the train, feeling already the relief of a drier heat and some breeze, especially on the earlier part of the journey up to the Summit.

We arrived at Atbara soon after 5:00 p.m. and left again for Khartoum at 6:30 p.m. In the meantime Parker, successor to Midwinter as General Manager of Railways, came to see me, and we had a chat. Posted letters for home. Harvey and one of the servants, Abu Zaid, went direct on to Cairo with the bulk of the luggage and will await our arrival there.

The Governor-General, Sir Geoffrey Archer, is on his way up and wants to meet me on my way down, so arrangements are being made accordingly. Boyce of the [Sudan Government] Surveys dined with us in the saloon.

9th November—Monday.

We arrived at Khartoum Central at 5:45 a.m. and at 7:00 a.m. the A.D.C. arrived to meet us with cars which seemed strange to me in Khartoum. The Sterrys have asked me to stay, and George is being put up by Crowfoot, the Director of Education. It was quite thrilling driving through the town and seeing again all the familiar landmarks. Everything is the same as when I left, but the whole place has developed. It is like meeting a boy of eighteen whom one last saw at the age of twelve.

The Sterrys are living in the house built and formerly occupied by Harold Hall of the Sudan Development Company just behind

---

The Sudan government agreed on certain conditions concerning wavelengths, language, rates, and observance of international radio procedures, but the Directors of the Eastern Telegraph Company at that time turned down the proposal. (H. Wynne, Director of Posts and Telegraphs, Sudan Government, to Clayton, 10 November 1925, C.P.)

9th November—Monday.

[8] The Sudan Development and Exploration Company was registered in London in 1900. Four Directors were Egyptians and four were British. In 1902 the company extended its activities to river transport on the Nile under a Sudan government guarantee of 3 percent interest on its capital outlay. The company established its dockyard about a mile west of the present Sudan

the Grand Hotel.[8] I found the Sterrys very fit and evidently a very happy pair. After breakfast I went up to the Palace where I met George Antonius and the A.D.C., Captain Fouracres, and we had a great time going all over the house and garden. It was so very familiar and very little changed though the Archers are doing a good deal of refurnishing. The old *farrasheen*, who were there in Gordon's time, are still going strong, and they and some of the old Sudanese escort greeted me most effusively.[9]

We then visited the Cathedral, which I thought, as I have always done, was stunted, stuffy, and hardly worthy as a memorial to Gordon or as representative of the money it cost.[10] George and I then went to the Intelligence Office, where we saw one Davies, who struck me as alert and very keen and intelligent and gave him what information we could about Ibn Sa'ud, the Hejaz, and other matters which we had observed in the course of our mission.

We finished up the morning by a visit to and chat with Mr. George Morhig, one of the leading businessmen in Khartoum. He was delighted to see me, and we had a long talk, in the course of which

---

government dockyard at Khartoum North and launched steamers and barges. At that time the Sudan government wished to confine its fleet of steamers to maintain communications throughout the Sudan while that of the Sudan Development Company was to develop trade. In practice each did part of the tasks of the other. The company lost money and in 1912 went into voluntary liquidation with the Sudan government taking over the company's marine staff and fleet.

[9] *Farasheen, farrashin* (Arabic plural of *farrash*): house servants or attendants.

Charles George Gordon (1833–85) fought in the Crimean War and later became famous for taking a prominent part in the suppression of the Tai-ping Rebellion, 1863–64, during which he won many decorations and the sobriquet "Chinese" Gordon. In 1874 he was appointed governor of Equatoria in the Sudan and in 1877 was made governor-general of the whole country. He resigned in 1878, but in January 1884 the British government sent him to Khartoum to rescue the Egyptian garrisons in the Sudan beleaguered by the Mahdists who had risen in rebellion against Egyptian rule. Gordon defended Khartoum against the forces of the Mahdi until the city was overrun on 26 January 1885, and he was killed. His heroism and unorthodox personality made a powerful impression upon his time, and the deep feelings in Britain to avenge his death contributed to the reconquest of the Sudan in 1898 and

we recalled the time we had spent together in the Bahr el Ghazel in 1902 when Colonel W. S. Sparkes was *mudir* there.

I lunched with the Sterrys, and at 3:45 p.m. George and I with Fouracres started off in a launch for Omdurman. The rais of the launch greeted me warmly, and I found that she was the old *Katherine*, named after Lady Wingate, in which I had made many a trip.[11] It again brought back old times most vividly, indeed, the ghosts of Sir Reginald and Lady Wingate confronted me at every turn.

On arrival at the South Gate I found a Ford car waiting, placed at my disposal by El Sayid Abdur Rahman el Mahdi, the son of Mahdi—a curious development of history. We visited the Mahdi's tomb, the Khalifa's House, and the Mosque Square.[12] I then paid a call on old Saleh Gabril, formerly in the Intelligence [Department], but found him gone on a visit to Dongola. George Antonius was much interested in the bazaars to which we paid a visit and where we made a few small purchases. I found one or two old friends there, including Awad el-Kerim, the silversmith, who insisted on presenting me with a small keepsake. We had tea with Mrs. Nalder, wife of

---

to many memorials to his name.

[10] The first proposal to build an Anglican cathedral in the Sudan came from Lord Cromer in 1900 and was welcomed by Sir Reginald Wingate, the Governor-General, so long as the building of a church remained a private, nongovernment undertaking. Mr. Weir Schultz was retained to design a cathedral suitable, not only to the memory of Gordon, but to the future of Christianity in the Sudan as well. The cathedral was laid out in the shape of a Latin cross and constructed of red and yellow sandstone from Jabal Al-Awliya' south of Khartoum. The architecture is an eclectic combination of Gothic and Byzantine design with all the solidity of a fortress. The foundation stone was laid on 7 February 1904 and the cathedral consecrated on 26 February 1912 by the Bishop of London, but it was not until 25 January 1931 that the cathedral was completed by the consecration of the tower and bells in memory of Sir Lee Stack, the former Governor-General of the Sudan who had been assassinated in Cairo in 1924.

[11] Rais (Arabic *ra'is*): mate, or colloquially pilot of a Nile steamer. The *Katherine* was a small, six-seater launch for the use of the Chief Staff Officer of the Egyptian Army in Khartoum and later for the Qa'id al-'Amm of the Sudan Defence Force.

[12] The original tomb of the Mahdi was the traditional domed structure of Sudanese saints' burial-places. Known as the *qubbat al-Mahdi* (dome of the

the Inspector at Omdurman, but missed him as he was away on duty at Khartoum. He was in Iraq for some time and I think knew Iltyd [Clayton]. Returned from Omdurman in the *Katherine* just at sunset and saw ahead of us the familiar sight of the Governor-General's yacht, the *Elfin*, taking home the polo players. There is some activity at the Moghren point where the two Niles join as preparations are under way for the construction of a bridge across to Omdurman.[13]

In the evening the Sterrys and I dined with the Osbornes. He was a deputy inspector under me at Singa and is now a judge at Khartoum, having married in the meantime. There was no one else at dinner whom I knew except Udal, but the house was familiar, being that in which the Flemings used to live.

At dinner last night I had a long talk over old times, especially about poor old Pearson with whom Boyce was on the Darfur Boundary Commission.

10th November—Tuesday.

I had breakfast with Hugo Headlam who is commanding the British troops in Khartoum and lives with Huddleston in the house formerly occupied by the Assers. Huddleston is at present on leave in England. After breakfast Headlam had to go to Khartoum North to see some barrack rooms, so I went with him. I found Khartoum North rather changed in appearance, but the barrack rooms which we went to see were those which I had built with No. 5 Battery in 1901. On the way back I stopped at the Gordon College where I found George Antonius. I had a talk with Crowfoot and then went round the museum, the laboratories, and the geological section, all of which have expanded greatly since I was in Khartoum. I then went to the Government offices and had a chat with MacMichael, after which back to the Sterrys' to lunch.

Mahdi), the walls were constructed of stone brought from Khartoum and measured 30 feet high and 36 feet square. Above this a hexagonal wall fifteen feet high was built from which rose a forty-foot dome. On the orders of Kitchener, who did not want the tomb to become an object of pilgrimage, Major W. S. Gordon, R.E., demolished the dome and cupolas, leaving only four crumbling walls and a few arched openings. The bones of the Mahdi were scattered into the Nile. In 1927 a greatly enlarged but similar tomb and

Rested and wrote some letters until tea, which we had in the garden, after which they took me to the Zoo. It is very much improved under Brocklehurst, and the animals look very well and happy in nicely-laid out and well-kept grounds.

Dun, the Chief Justice, and Matthew, the Assistant Financial Secretary, came to dine as well as George Antonius. We left Khartoum at 8:45 p.m. in the saloon on a cattle train in order to get to Abu Hamed to meet the Governor-General at 8:00 p.m. on the following day.

11th November—Wednesday.

Armistice day which is being observed by Khartoum with various ceremonies and some festivities. We arrived at Atbara about breakfast time but did not stay long. Wilfrid Lord came to the coach to see me and we had a chat.

We proceeded slowly but surely and duly arrived at 4:30 p.m. at Abu Hamed, where we were able to get a good walk before dinner. I found the place quite unchanged.

The Governor-General's train arrived at 8:00 p.m., and I went on board and dined with him in his saloon—a party of four, which included George Schuster and Willie Kenny. We had a long talk, and I gave Archer as much information as I could about Ibn Sa'ud and the Hejaz. The remainder of the Governor-General's party had dined in a dining saloon attached to the train, and we joined them afterwards and all sat out on the platform in the cool breeze. There were—Lady Archer, Mrs. Schuster, Shoura Kenny, Sir Frederick and Lady Jackson (he is an uncle to Archer and was at one time Governor of Uganda), who are going to Khartoum to stay with the Archers, and a Colonel and Mrs. Ewart.

The Governor-General's train left at 11:30 p.m. for Khartoum, and we remained for the night at Abu Hamed Station.

---

dome was constructed by Sayyid 'Abd ar-Rahman, the posthumous son of the Mahdi, to replace that destroyed by the Anglo-Egyptian forces. The Khalifa's house was constructed by the Mahdi's Khalifa or successor, 'Abd Allahi. It was a rambling two-story building of brick construction with iron girders in places to support the roof. Both the dome of the Mahdi and the Khalifa's house are situated near the great open Mosque Square.

[13] The Moghren (*Muqran* from *qarn*, horn of an animal) was the port area

Received a wire asking me to stay at the Residency with the Lloyds.

12th November—Thursday.

We were picked up by the Express for [Wadi] Halfa at 10:00 a.m. and travelled all day across the desert, which brought back recollections of the Nile campaign of 1898. We reached Halfa at 9:30 p.m. and went straight on board the steamer *Sudan* where I found Old Lion still in charge as Commissary and Purser. Leach, the Governor, came down to see me and have a chat and Hills—the railway representative—did everything possible for us.

We started off at 10:30 p.m. on a nice cool night in the face of a delicious north breeze and should have a very pleasant trip after the heat and dust of Arabia.

13th November—Friday.

Spent a very cool and pleasant day going down the river and was able to start on working out the framework of our report on the Mission. A fairly empty boat—only a few missionaries and two elderly American female tourists. About 5:00 p.m. we passed the temple of Kalabsheh and the boat stopped to enable us to visit it. I was glad of the opportunity, which I had never had before, as it is a very well-preserved specimen and well worth a visit.[14]

Arrived at Shellal at 9:00 p.m. and stayed the night on board. Old Lion looked after us well. The dam sluices have now been shut, so the water is rising rapidly.

---

of Khartoum near the juncture of the White Nile and the Blue. The White Nile Bridge connects Khartoum to Umdurman and is constructed of nine 244-ft. spans of steel girders.

13th November—Friday.

[14] Located some fifty miles above Aswan, the temple of Kalabshah was built in the reign of the Emperor Augustus. It was the largest free-standing temple south of Philae but has now been permanently covered by the waters of the High Dam.

14th November—Saturday.

[15] A felluca (Arabic *falukah* from *fulk* "ship") is a narrow, lateen-rigged

14th November–Saturday.

George Antonius and some of the passengers got up early and went off in feluccas to see the Aswan Dam, but I did not go having often seen it before.[15]

We left for Luxor at 9:00 a.m. There was no special saloon for me this time nor was there any dining car, so we had to take a sandwich lunch with us.

About Esneh we ran into some quite heavy rain, which is rare in these parts.

The *mudir* of Assuan came to see me at the station, a certain Mohammed Zeki Saleh, who was sub-mudir of Menufia Province when I was Adviser [to the Egyptian Ministry of Interior]. Two Omdehs of the Khalifa family also came to see me at Daraw and travelled with us to Kom Ombo.[16]

Arrived Luxor at 4:45 p.m., the train being 45 minutes late, and left for Cairo at 6:00 p.m. It was pouring with rain at Luxor when we arrived–most inconvenient at a station where there is no sort of shelter. However, it did not last long and after some tea at the buffet, we packed ourselves into the Cairo train, which left at 6:00 p.m. Very few passengers on board, as everyone is moving south at this time of year. We were, therefore, lucky in getting a sleeping compartment each to ourselves from Luxor to Cairo. The rain at Luxor was tiresome, as we had intended to drive out and have another look at Karnak, but the place was a sea of mud and it was, therefore, out of the question. Howard Carter is at Luxor now, and I hear that he has opened up another chamber in the tomb contain-

---

vessel with low decks at the ends or from stern to foremast.

Situated 3½ miles above the town of Aswan, the dam was originally designed by Sir William Willcocks and completed in 1902 with a height of 130 feet. In 1912 the dam was raised 16½ feet, and in 1934 enlarged again to its present height of 175 feet and length of about a mile and a quarter. This dam will be superseded by the High Dam to be completed in 1970 and located several miles upstream.

16 *omdeh* or *omda* (Arabic, *'umdah*): village headman.

17 Located just to the north of Luxor on the east bank of the Nile, Karnak comprises the ruins of three great enclosures. During the period of Sir Gilbert's brief visit to Luxor in November 1925, Carter was at work across

ing some very wonderful finds.[17] I wish we had time to go and see them.

15th November—Sunday.

Arrived at Cairo at 8:00 a.m., half an hour late, and found Mohammed to meet me with the Residency car. Sayed Effendi was also there and several other old friends. Drove to the Residency and had breakfast and then spent the morning unpacking and settling down.[18] The Lloyds had to go off to Heliopolis for the dedication of a new church, so I did not meet them until lunch.

After lunch George Lloyd took me to the Zoo, where we had a walk. After tea at the Residency I went to evensong at St. Mary's, which is now being used as the church, All Saints being sold and dismantled.[19] Bishop Gwynne was there, and I looked in afterwards for a brief chat with him. I then called on Mrs. Frank Watson and

---

the Nile in the Valley of the Kings where he was raising the nest of coffins within the sarcophagus of Tutankhamen, examining them, and investigating the king's mummy—a task that was not completed until May 1926.

15th November—Sunday.

18 In 1889 the British government purchased 13,500 square meters on the east bank of the Nile in the Garden City for £2,580 on which to build the British Agency Residence. The Residence was built in 1890–94 at a cost of £39,894 in a mid-nineteenth century neo-Classical style. In 1891 the British government was given the right of user over the foreshore of the Nile bordering the site. In 1916 a further area of 9,500 square meters adjoining the southern edge of the Residence garden was purchased from the Egyptian government. This area contained a number of half-completed buildings which were finished in 1925 and used as Chancery offices. They were later demolished and in 1953–54 the present four-story Chancery was erected. In 1954 the Egyptian government built a corniche road along the Nile, requiring the surrender of a strip of land measuring 5,036 square meters along the western boundary of the Residence site.

19 All Saints Church, Cairo, was consecrated by Bishop Gobat, the Second Anglican Bishop in Jerusalem, and opened on 23 January 1876. The Duke of Sutherland had laid the foundation stone. Situated not far from the old Shepheard's Hotel on a busy corner, it was decided, particularly after some subsidence of the floor, to demolish the building, sell the site, and use the funds from so valuable a location to construct another church in a more suitable area. It was with these funds that the present cathedral was built and consecrated by Bishop William Temple on 25 April 1938. Situated near

found her in but Frank was out at [the] Gezira [Sporting Club].[20] Dined quietly at the Residency and had a long talk afterwards with George Lloyd. Everything is much the same at the Residency, but the Lloyds are contemplating considerable changes. The new Chancery is now completed and in occupation, which frees the ballroom for entertainment purposes. I have secured a room there in which to work while I am here, so that I can write my report comfortably, and George Antonius will have a quiet place for its preparation. There is somewhat of a ministerial crisis, owing to Ziwer Pasha having expressed openly his dislike of the interference of Nasha Pasha, King Fuad's *chef-de-Cabinet*.[21]

16th November—Monday.

Had breakfast and a chat with the Bishop. Arthur Bolland was there, but his wife and family are in England, where he has bought

---

the British Residency, St. Mary's Church was under construction in 1908 and consecrated the following year. During the First World War the bishop used it as his procathedral, and it became the church of the English community from 1925, when All Saints was pulled down, until the opening of the present cathedral in 1938, at which time St. Mary's Church was sold to the Greek Catholic Church that still maintains it.

[20] Founded in 1882 under the name of Khedivial Sporting Club, the club changed its name in 1904 to Gezira Sporting Club. In 1952 the name of the club was changed once again to Nadi Amir as-Sa'id ar-Riadi but reverted to the former name of the Gezira Sporting Club the following year. Until 1956 the club comprised 150 acres. Since then half of this acreage has been taken over by Egypt's Youth Organization, but the club still maintains a full complement of sporting and social activities.

[21] In 1924 Ziwar Pasha had become Prime Minister after the resignation of Zaghlul Pasha over the crisis following upon the assassination of Sir Lee Stack. Ziwar formed a moderate ministry that sought to cooperate with the British. He was unable to win support in parliament, however, and rather than turn over the government to the anti-British nationalist party, the Wafd, he convinced King Fu'ad to dissolve parliament in the spring of 1925. In the summer, Ziwar went to Europe on a holiday, and during his absence Hasan Nash'at Pasha, chef-de-cabinet to King Fu'ad and leader of a palace party, the Ittihad or party of union, sought to identify the Ziwar government with the Ittihad. Although Nash'at had no constitutional right to rule, he was able with the King's support to meddle in the government. Well-disposed toward Britain and possessing remarkable abilities and a charming

a small cottage. He tells me he has the intention of retiring shortly, and thinks he has secured a job at home. The Bishop was just as nice as ever and seems to get on famously with the Lloyds.

We started on the report in the morning, and I went to R.A.F. Headquarters to see about the possibility of flying from Amman to Baghdad. They had arranged to send me straight from Heliopolis on Thursday, but that is too soon, so I shall probably have to go by overland car-route and I am wiring to Jerusalem to reserve us places on Thursday the 26th November.

I lunched at the Residency and went for a walk afterwards with George Lloyd in the Grounds of the Gezira Sporting Club. George has been made a peer with the title of "Baron Lloyd of Dolabran in the County of Montgomeryshire."

I had tea with the Said Shoucairs and a long chat in the new house which they have built in conjunction and share with Dr. Sarruf in the Garden City. It is extremely nice and very quiet, but they are not yet settled down as they have only just moved in.

A quiet dinner at the Residency and a talk with George Lloyd afterwards.

17th November—Tuesday.

In the morning I called on Ziwer Pasha, the Prime Minister, and then went and saw Patterson, the Financial Adviser, more especially in regard to getting the same pension terms for my widow as were given to Amos and Dowson.

Lunched with the Dick Mores and played tennis at the Gezira [Sporting Club] with Dick and the Swanns (Air Vice-Marshal).

Had tea at the Gezira [Sporting Club], did some work on my report afterwards, and dined quietly at the Residency.

18th November—Wednesday.

George Antonius and I worked at our report in the morning.

---

personality, Nash'at Pasha's vigorous efforts to control government affairs led both the Wafd and even the moderate men who wished to uphold the constitution to oppose vigorously such interference from the palace. By early November their discontent could no longer be ignored. It is still a matter of controversy whether the King was using Nash'at and the Ittihad

I lunched at the Residency and walked to the Gezira [Sporting Club] in the afternoon, where I left cards on Sir Richard and Lady Haking (G.O.C. in Egypt).

Went to the Continental at 6:30 p.m. and had a talk with one of the Stamatopoulos regarding the Sudan Building and Agricultural Syndicate, of which Teddy Goschen is chairman and wants me to be a director. I have decided, after sounding George Schuster and others in the Sudan, to follow my own inclination and leave well alone.

Dined quietly with the Frank Watsons and had a pleasant chat.

19th November–Thursday.

I left for Alexandria by the 9:30 a.m. train with George Antonius, who was going to spend a couple of nights with his people. We arrived at 12:45 p.m., and I went and had some lunch at Claridge's Hotel. After lunch I took a car to the Montaza Palace, arriving in time for an audience with King Fuad, which had been fixed for 4:00 p.m. He was most cordial and friendly and kept me until nearly 6:00 p.m. talking of Ibn Sa'ud, the future of the Hejaz, and Egyptian politics. Two things were evident to me–

(a) that he wishes to take the predominant hand in the Govment of Egypt;

(b) that he is coquetting with the idea of becoming Caliph.

Either policy, if proceeded with, is likely to land him in serious trouble.

I caught the 7:00 p.m. train back to Cairo, arriving at 10:15 p.m. and drove straight to the Residency. I found George Lloyd still up and had a long talk with him on current Egyptian affairs. There is evidently a strong tendency on the part of many Egyptians to turn to England, probably because they are scared at the growth of the power of the Palace, but we must be very cautious about stepping in, or there is certain to be a violent reaction promoted by the popu-

---

to acquire greater powers than the constitution allowed, or whether the Ittihad was using the sympathies of the King to take over a government that they could not win at the ballot box. Probably both interpretations are correct, but many of the moderate men in Egypt turned to Lord Lloyd, the British Resident, to defend the constitution. The bitter opposition of the

lar leaders and the native press. The Egyptians must drink their own medicine to the dregs before we make any move, and we must be quite sure that they really want us before we attempt to step in.

20th November—Friday.

George Antonius, who returned from Alexandria at noon, and I worked on the report in the morning. I lunched with Cherei Pasha at Zeitoun, in company with K. B., Furness and Grafftey-Smith, and we had the usual gigantic meal.[22]

In the evening at 5:00 p.m. there was a private memorial service for Lee Stack at St. Mary's Church on the anniversary of his death. The Bishop conducted the service, which was very nice and peaceful, being attended only by his personal friends.

I dined quietly at the Residency. On Thursday on my return from Alexandria I found a cable from Mr. Amery approving my proposed visit to Baghdad and suggesting that I might go on and endeavour to conclude a long overdue treaty with Imam Yahya of the Yemen.[23] I wired today accepting, but it will mean my travelling via Basra, Bombay, Aden, and Hodeida to Sanaa and will entail my being away until well into February. On Tuesday I got a telegram of warm congratulation from the Secretaries of State for Colonies and Foreign Affairs.[24]

21st November—Saturday.

---

parties and the quiet intervention of Lord Lloyd convinced Fu'ad that Nash'at Pasha must be removed. He left Cairo shortly thereafter as the Egyptian Minister to Spain.

20th November—Friday.

[22] The "K. B." to whom Clayton refers is Sir Alexander W. Keown-Boyd, who was popularly known to everyone in Egypt as K. B.

[23] For the past three years the British government had been trying unsuccessfully to conclude an agreement with Imam Yahya of the Yemen. Negotiations had, however, reached the stage where personal contact between the Imam and a British representative was necessary to clarify the ambiguities and misrepresentations created during the long correspondence between the two governments and aggravated by encroachments into the Aden Protectorate of the Imam's forces. The Imam himself had asked for a representative, and the British government concurred, wishing to "proceed with the least possible delay in order that further complications on the Pro-

Did some work in the morning, and also did some shopping in the town. Lunched with Boulos Pasha on his dahabia, meeting Yousef Pasha Suleiman, Abdel Hamid Pasha Suleiman and Kamel Fahmy.[25]

After lunch I walked to the [Gezira] Sporting Club and had tea with the Dick Mores, after which I dropped cards on the Keown-Boyds and Graves at Gezira House—but both were out. I walked back to the Residency where I dined. All official entertainment is over for the present at the Residency, owing to the death of Queen Alexandra.[26]

The [Gezira] Sporting Club is much improved since we left. The new tea place, especially, is a great advance and much more roomy.

22nd November—Sunday.

I went to early celebration at St. Mary's at 8:00 a.m. The Bishop was away, but Steer was assisting. He is down from Jerusalem on account of the serious illness of one of his children who is now at Helouan.[27]

After breakfast, I drove to the cemetery and visited our little graves. They are beautifully kept and they look so sweet and child-like with their little shrubs and rose trees.[28] The cemetery is now practically finished and looks very nice.

---

tectorate frontier may be avoided." Sir Gilbert Clayton, fresh from his successful negotiations with Ibn Sa'ud, was the logical choice for the Mission to the Yemen. He not only possessed experience, knowledge, and judgment, but was within quick and easy reach of Aden. (See Amery to Clayton, Tel. 279, 18 November 1925, C. P.)

24 Leopold C. S. Amery and Sir J. Austen Chamberlain, respectively.

21st November—Saturday.

25 Dahabia (Arabic *dhahabiyah*, lit. "the golden one"), is a long, light-draft houseboat.

26 Alexandra, Dowager Queen of England, suffered a heart attack about noon on 20 November 1925 and died the following day.

22nd November—Sunday.

27 Helwan is a suburb of Cairo where two sanatoria were located for the convalescence and cures of the more affluent Europeans and Egyptians.

28 Sir Gilbert and Lady Clayton's eldest son, Thomas, died in infancy from

I went to the Sudan Agency and sorted our baggage, leaving some of mine to be picked up on my way home from Aden and then lunched at the Residency.

Called on the Hararis in the afternoon. They had only just returned from Alexandria but were delighted to see me, and we had a long chat. I went back to tea at the Residency, where I met Mrs. Wiggin, just returned from home.

At 6:00 p.m. we left Cairo for Kantara, en route for Jerusalem (George, Harvey, self and two servants). I was seen off, amongst others, by the usual crowd, including Abdul Hamid Pasha Suleiman, the General Manager of Railways, who very kindly placed his own private saloon at my disposal. We were, therefore, very comfortable as far as Kantara, but when we got there we found that no arrangements had been made, no saloon, not even any vacant sleeping berths (so like Palestine). Luckily, however, four people did not turn up, so we secured a compartment each in the sleeping-car.

---

an infected mosquito bite and their second daughter, Jane, aged 5½, died of the bubonic plague. They were both buried in the English cemetery in Cairo.

CHAPTER 4

From Cairo to Delhi:
23 November–17 December 1925

23rd November—Monday.

We arrived at Jerusalem at 9:30 a.m. after the familiar journey up through the hills. It all seemed so homelike, and I almost expected to see the children racing along the platform to meet the train, and Enid waiting to see me in the background.[1] I was met by Lord Plumer's A.D.C., Major Brooke, and we drove straight off to Government House for breakfast. There I met Mrs. Brooke (née Plumer), and shortly after breakfast Lady Plumer came in, having been down in the city. I then went off to the Government offices to see Lord Plumer, with whom I had a talk about my mission and its results.

All the offices were in a great state of excitement, and I had quite a time of it shaking hands with them all and renewing old acquaintanceship.

I drove back with Lord Plumer to lunch after which I walked down the hill to the City and called at the "Ecce Homo," where I saw the Mother Superior and Mother Irene, who were very pleased to see me and bombarded me with enquiries about and messages to

---

23rd November—Monday.

[1] Clayton had previously worked and lived in Jerusalem when in 1917–18 he was the Chief Political Officer of the Egyptian Expeditionary Force and charged with establishing the administration of occupied Palestine. Later in 1922 he returned to Jerusalem as the Chief Secretary to the government of Palestine under the then High Commissioner, Sir Herbert Samuel, where he remained until his retirement in 1925.

Enid and the children.[2] I went into the church for a few moments. It was just as beautiful and peaceful as ever. At 5:00 p.m. I went on to the School of Archaeology where the Professor [John Garstang] was giving a lecture. There, of course, I met countless friends, and it was quite difficult to tear myself away after the lecture. As it was, I am afraid I kept the Plumers waiting a few minutes for me.

Received a letter from Enid dated 8th November, the first since I left Jeddah, where my latest was dated 18th October.

We had an early dinner at 7:00 p.m. and went on to the opening night of the opera. They were playing *Carmen* and it was really very good. They have improved out of recognition since last year. There I met more friends, and my time was fully occupied between the acts. An embarrassing incident occurred at the end of the second act. Someone saw me and shouted my name and the whole house rose and cheered and clapped. I did not fully realize what it was all about until afterwards, but it was gratifying, although somewhat embarrassing. There is a wonderfully home-like and affectionate atmosphere here and I can hardly realize that we have really left and are not still living at Grant House.

24th November–Tuesday.

I spent the morning at the office finishing off our report and the

---

[2] In A.D. 135 the Emperor Hadrian had constructed a triple arch as the entrance to his new city, Colonia Aelia Capitolina, from which all Jews were debarred. For many centuries the center arch was all that was known, for the street (now known as the Via Dolorosa) passing through the arch was narrowed in time by Arabs and Turks building along the insides of the old Roman road. When large numbers of Christian pilgrims began to visit Jerusalem in the nineteenth century, they were told that this was the site where Pilate displayed Christ to the crowds with the words, "Ecce Homo," Behold the Man. In 1842 the Reverend Alphonse Marie Ratisbonne was converted from Judaism to Christianity in the Church of St. Andrea delle Fratte in Rome and resolved to found a congregation of Notre Dame de Sion (Our Lady of Zion) in the Holy Land. With the support of his elder brother, Theodore Ratisbonne, who had been ordained in Paris in 1831 and had founded the order of Notre Dame de Sion, Alphonse tried to purchase the arch over the Via Dolorosa in Jerusalem. As the Muslims were unwilling

various annexures and at 12:30 p.m. went and paid a visit to the Garstangs who were leaving for Kerak at 1:30 p.m. We had time for a bit of a chat but as usual did not have time to get through half of what we wanted to say. I lunched with the Storrs and in the afternoon they took me for a drive through Beitin to Tayiba which overlooks the Jordan Valley to the east of the Nablus road.[3] It is rather an interesting place, containing an old Roman fort from which one gets a magnificent view of the hills of Moab, from Ajlun to Kerak. The inhabitants are all Christians.

On my return to Jerusalem I went by special invitation and had a tea at the Manora Club, where I received a very hearty welcome.[4] I then paid a visit to Hum Bowman who kindly consented to let me have George Antonius for my mission to the Yemen. He is alone for the time being as Nora [Bowman] is not coming out until later.

There was a small dinner party to meet me at Government House in the evening, comprising Davis, Hum Bowman, the Mills, and Archer and Daisy Cust.

25th November—Wednesday.

In the morning at 9:30 a.m. I gave a brief lecture on the results of my mission and Ibn Sa'ud and Najd in general to Heads of Departments. I fear it was very sketchy, as I had no time to prepare it, but the audience seemed interested and were very appreciative. Symes

---

to sell, he bought land on the north side of the road where, in tearing down the ruins in 1856, he discovered the northern bay of the arch on which he built a chapel, known as the Basilica of the Ecce Homo, an orphanage, and a convent. Later a school was opened which was later merged with the orphanage. In 1925 the Reverend Mother Eleanor was the superior and the Reverend Marie Godeleine the assistant superior with whom Mother Irene worked from 1920 to 1926. Clayton wrongly identifies the assistant superior, the Reverend Marie Godeleine, as the superior; the Reverend Mother Eleanor, who at the time was bedridden, did not see Sir Gilbert.

24th November—Tuesday.

[3] At-Tayyibah has been identified with the Biblical Ephraim. Vespasian seized it during his campaign in A.D. 66 and fortified it, but the ruins to which Sir Gilbert refers are probably the medieval castle of St. Helyes (which was given to Boniface of Montferrat by Baudouin IV in 1185).

[4] The Manora Club was the Jewish ex-service men's club in Jerusalem.

returned from a short holiday in Cairo, and I had a talk with him.

I lunched at Government House and at 3:00 p.m. I went by invitation to the Haram esh Sherif where the Mufti showed me all the work of restoration.[5] They are getting on very well, the Aksa Mosque being now out of all danger, and they seem to be expending their funds wisely and economically. We finished up with tea at the office of the Supreme Moslem Council, the guests including Musa Kazim Pasha, Ismail Husseini Bey, Said Husseini Bey, Davis, Storrs, and George Antonius. An exceedingly pleasant afternoon and lots of enquiries after Enid, also *Sabria*, *Sami* and *Yahya*![6] After tea I walked up to the Church of the Holy Sepulchre for a few minutes and then went to the Austrian Hospice and had a drink and a long chat with Davis.[7] There was another small dinner party at Government House, comprising the Haycrafts and the MacInneses. After dinner the High Commissioner's Private Secretary, Captain Drummond, who lost his arm in the war, gave a quite marvellous display of one-handed conjuring.

25th November—Wednesday.

[5] The Haram ash-Sharif (august sanctuary), one of the most holy places of Islam, occupies the site of the Temple of Jerusalem and the surrounding enclosure. Within the enclosure are the Dome of the Rock (Qubbat as-Sakhra) and the mosque Al-Aqsa. At the time of Sir Gilbert's visit the Dome and the mosque were being refurbished with the help of the Pro-Jerusalem Society.

The Mufti is an Islamic religious official whose duty is to issue canonical rulings on points of Muslim religious law. All larger Muslim towns will have a Mufti, and although no political significance is usually attached to the office, the importance of Jerusalem made the office politically powerful as well as having religious prestige. At the time of the British occupation of Palestine the office of Mufti was held by Kamal Effendi al-Husayni of the important Husayni family of Jerusalem. The Husayni family came, according to tradition, from Persia to Palestine over two hundred years ago and consolidated its position in Palestine and Jerusalem by marrying into wealthy and powerful local families. Thus when Kamal al-Husayni died in 1921, the Husaynis put forward Hajj Muhammad Amin al-Husayni for the position of Mufti and with British support he was duly appointed.

[6] Sabria, Sami, and Yahya were the Arabic names of Patience, Samuel, and John, the Clayton children.

[7] Originally a group of small separate churches, the Church of the Holy Sepulchre received its present form from the Crusaders who erected one

I am glad to say that Lord Plumer is giving up the *official service* on 9th December and has also insisted on a proper observance of Armistice Day. Bishop MacInnes is of course furious but cannot do anything.[8]

26th November–Thursday.

The Plumers were out for the day, visiting Lydda, Ramla, and Rishon le Zion. I spent the morning in the Government offices. My report was finally signed yesterday but some of the annexures required completing.

I lunched with the Bentwiches, where I met a Mr. Ingpen, who is Deputy Judge Advocate General for the R.A.F. in Egypt, Palestine, and Iraq. I then went to the Symes and had a walk with him past Gethsemane to the wall of David, which has now been completely excavated and makes a fine monument.[9] We returned to tea with the Symes who have found a very nice Arab house overlooking the Men's Training College football ground and not far from where

---

large Romanesque church to embrace the various chapels. Since then the Church has been rebuilt and refurbished on numerous occasions, although the eastern dome is still part of the Crusaders' structure.

The Austrian Hospice was constructed in the mid-nineteenth century for the use of Austrian pilgrims.

[8] The *official service* was the annual service held on 9 December to commemorate the anniversary of the day on which Allenby entered Jerusalem in 1917. It was a service of thanksgiving to which the heads of all the various churches were invited. In 1925 Lord Plumer suggested that this service should be dropped, since many people were no longer thankful that the British had liberated Jerusalem. Despite Lord Plumer's objections the service was held in 1925, 1926, and 1927. It was attended in 1925 and 1926 by a large congregation and by both the Greek and Armenian Patriarchs. The High Commissioner himself was probably not present. Many people were disappointed to see the service discontinued, for it was an opportunity for the various Christian bodies to get together. In 1925 the proper observance of Armistice Day appears to have been confined to a military parade service.

26th November–Thursday.

[9] The Garden of Gethsemane, outside St. Stephen's Gate, is the supposed site where Jesus retired with his disciples and where Judas betrayed him.

David's Wall refers to the stone wall enclosing the City of David, the former stronghold of the Jebusites, which David captured. The wall began at the Millo, or embankment, followed the Kidron at some distance above

the Adam Kiewichs used to live.[10] It is very roomy and has been completely done up. I dined at the Plumers, after which we all went off to a pianoforte recital under the auspices of the Jerusalem Musical Society at the Y.M.C.A. hut. The performer was a Jewess. Her technique and execution were good, but I thought her playing hard and unsympathetic.

27th November—Friday.

Had a busy morning squaring things up for our departure tomorrow. The Colonial Office has sanctioned an advance of E. £. 1500, so I was able to liquidate the expenses of the Ibn Sa'ud mission and also get a letter of credit from the Anglo-Egyptian Bank for future disbursements.

I transmitted E. £. 120 to my own account with Lloyds Bank in London, being part reimbursement of my private money expended on account of the mission. I visited Vester and found that the account for dispatch of our baggage to England had been sent through their London agents to me in England, so Enid will doubtless pay it. I also saw Kenyon and found that he had sold about E. £. 31 worth of things, so I collected the cash from him, less his expenses and charges. There is still about E. £. 25 worth of stuff left to sell.[11]

I went back to lunch at Government House, after having paid a call at the French Consulate and had a chat with Maugras and Ballereau.

I went to the office for an hour or so after lunch and then walked to the Y.W.C.A. to meet Lady Plumer, who was attending a meeting there. They insisted on my going in, and at the end of the meeting I said a few words to them on Enid's behalf; they seemed very pleased and were full of all the help and support which Enid had given them, and they sent her every kind of message.

---

its bed, encircled the rocky cliff at the south end of the hill above the pool of Siloam, and then ran up the east side of the Tyropoeon Valley to the Millo.

[10] The Men's Training College, Jerusalem, was founded in 1919 by the British Military Administration with boarding facilities for fifty students and a teaching staff composed of both Muslims and Christians. An extension was added in 1921 to increase the number of boarding students to seventy-five.

My report was duly completed and left by mail today for the Colonial Office. I also sent a letter to Enid, I dined quietly with the Plumers at Government House.

28th November–Saturday.

George Antonius and I started at 10:00 a.m. by hired car from the government offices for Amman. It was sad leaving Jerusalem again, and I have been much affected by the genuine warmth of the welcome which I received on all sides. I do wish that Enid had been with me to share it, though the sight of Grant House, standing empty with a board up "To Let" was rather pathetic. As we drove down the hill towards Jericho, we passed a car coming up, and loud shrieks told us that it contained the Garstangs on their way back from Kerak, so we stopped and had a few last words. They were most grateful for what Enid is doing for Meroë in regard to her Christmas holidays.

We had a picnic lunch half way up the hill to Es-Salt, just above the road bridge over the stream, and we reached the Coxs' house at Amman at 2:15 p.m. I had a good chat with the Coxs, and at 4:00 p.m. I went and called on the Amir Abdulla. He was very friendly and cordial, as usual, but of course is not pleased with the terms of my agreement with Ibn Sa'ud which does not meet his very extravagant aspirations. However, he took it all in quite a good spirit. I returned to tea with the Coxs where I found MacEwen, Peake, and D'Albiac and had another chat with Cox. We all dined with the Amir–quite a party, including Rikabi Pasha, Hassan Khaled Pasha, and other Trans-Jordan ministers.

After dinner I had another long private talk with the Amir, in the course of which he urged the necessity and propriety of H.M.G. helping King Ali. I could not, of course, hold out any hope at all.[12]

27th November–Friday.

[11] Kenyon was a dealer in Jerusalem who disposed of the unwanted goods of the Claytons when Sir Gilbert retired as Chief Secretary in 1925.

28th November–Saturday.

[12] It would have been the grossest deception if Sir Gilbert Clayton had held out any hope that Britain would come to the aid of 'Ali after establishing a rapprochement with Ibn Sa'ud at Bahra.

29th November—Sunday.

We had an early breakfast at 6:15 a.m. and left at 6:45 a.m. by car for the aerodrome at Ziza.[13] We arrived at 8:00 a.m. and found a large Vernon machine waiting, with MacEwen to see us off.[14] We soon embarked and luckily they were able to take all our baggage. At 8:20 a.m. came the thrilling moment when, with a roar of engines, we taxied rapidly over the ground and then rose majestically into the air. It was most interesting, though the country over which the air route passed is dull and devoid of incident. Also the Vernon machines are enclosed so one's view out is somewhat restricted. At 2:15 p.m. after just on six hours' continuous flying, we had a forced landing at L.G. 1. [Landing Ground No. 1] the last station before reaching Ramadi on the Euphrates. A leaking radiator was the cause of the descent, but it was put right in about twenty minutes and we rose again. We managed to get into Ramadi (about twenty miles) but all the time one engine was misfiring badly, the water from the leaking radiator having got into it. At Ramadi we had a much-wanted meal of eggs and bacon at the small R.A.F. rest house after which our pilot broke the news to us that the engine was not working satisfactorily and he did not want to risk going on to Baghdad, as it was rapidly getting dark. We therefore had to spend the night at Ramadi. The Administrative Inspector, Major Wilson, was away, but Mrs. Wilson stepped nobly into the breach and put us both up, even improvising a small dinner-party in our honour, consisting of Major Meade, the local Commandant of Police and his wife, and Captain Loder, his second-in-command. Mrs. Wilson, it transpired, knew Norah [Clayton] with whom she had travelled from Bombay to Basra two years ago.[15] The Wilsons have only recently been transferred from Basra to Ramadi.

Ramadi is a town of some size—purely native—situated on the right bank of the Euphrates and surrounded by extensive groves of palms. It is the place where both the airroute and the overland car

---

29th November—Sunday.

[13] Known today as Zuwayza.

[14] The Vickers "Vernon" aircraft was a large biplane (wing span 87 ft. 4 in., length 57 ft. 9 in., height 17 ft. 9 in.) powered by two 450 horsepower Napier "Lion" engines and used by the R.A.F. in 'Iraq for troop carrying and transport service.

routes (from Damascus and from Amman) strike the river, so there is quite a stream of traffic through it, and the Air Force have a depot there at which their machines fill up with petrol in the course of the trans-desert flight.

30th November—Monday.

We left Ramadi at 8:00 a.m. in another plane, which had been sent out for us from Baghdad, and reached Hanaidi, the military cantonment and aerodrome, shortly before 9:00 a.m. It was an interesting flight as the route passes down the Euphrates for about half the distance and then cuts across to the Tigris.

Hanaidi is downstream from Baghdad, at about five miles distance, and to reach it one flies right over Baghdad itself. We therefore got a splendid view of the city spread out below us.

On landing we were taken to the R.A.F. mess and given a very good breakfast after which the High Commissioner's Private Secretary, Mr. Holt, who had come to meet us, drove us off in a car to the Residency. The British Residency being on the right, whereas the greater part of Baghdad is on the left bank of the Tigris, we passed up a large portion of the main (indeed the only) street in Baghdad and had to cross a pontoon bridge over the Tigris. We were thus able to get an impression of the city and also of the military and civil cantonments of Hanaidi through which we passed.

I should record that King Faisal sent his Chamberlain and his principal A.D.C. to meet us on the aerodrome.[16]

There are two bridges over the Tigris, named after General Maude, but both are pontoon bridges, too narrow to permit vehicles to pass one another, so one is reserved for passage east to west and the other for traffic in the opposite direction. It is not a convenient arrangement for the public, as the two bridges must be about a mile apart, but it is unavoidable in the circumstances.[17]

Just as we were approaching the bridge we happened to pass

---

[15] Norah Beryl Turner, Sir Gilbert's youngest sister.

30th November—Monday.

[16] Faysal's Chamberlain was Safwat Pasha al-Awa and his A.D.C. Tahsin al-Qadri.

[17] These two pontoon bridges were later replaced by two broad steel and concrete structures.

Gertrude Bell, so we took her into the car and I was able to have a few words with her. On arrival at the Residency I found Major and Mrs. Bourdillon, who are very kindly putting me up. They have unfortunately got workmen in the house, so have no room for George, who has gone to the Maude Hotel. Bourdillon is acting for Sir Henry Dobbs, whom I have unluckily missed, as he was called home by the Secretary of State [for Colonies, Amery] ten days before he had originally meant to go on leave.

I went up to my room on arrival and unpacked and wrote letters until lunch. My room is huge with a large bathroom attached and looks out over the river which is most attractive. The house itself is very nice, being built all around a large central hall which goes right up to the roof and has a fountain playing in the middle. At either side of the house, which is right on the river, are one-storied wings in which are the offices of the High Commissioner's staffs.[18]

We had a quiet lunch, at which the only guest was Iltyd.[19] It was jolly seeing him again. He was the same as ever and looked exceedingly fit and well. In the afternoon there was tennis in the Residency garden and I was quite glad of some mild exercise.

I dined with Gertrude Bell, who had the Joyces, Ken Cornwallis, and Iltyd to meet me, so we talked some. Gertrude has a Mrs. Henley staying with her. She lost her husband last summer, who fell down suddenly while playing cricket at Cologne—I remember seeing it in the paper. She is her cousin and came out for rest and change but

---

[18] The old British Residency is still in use today as the premises of the British Embassy. Situated in approximately eight acres of grounds in the center of Baghdad on the west bank of the Tigris, the central building is basically of Turkish construction dating from the first half of the nineteenth century when it was the Residence of the Wali of the Vilayet of Baghdad. Following the establishment of the British Mandate, the building was adapted for use as the offices of the British High Commission and a new Residence was constructed alongside it. During the revolution of 1958 the new Residence was gutted by fire, but the older structure was unharmed. Temporary offices have been erected on the site of the destroyed Residency, while the Ambassador's new house has been situated about one and a half miles down river on a new site.

[19] Brigadier Sir Iltyd Nicholl Clayton, younger brother of Sir Gilbert Clayton.

very soon developed serious eye trouble. She is now quite unable to use one eye and they are trying to get her out by air, as she cannot stand the car journey. I suggested that she should make her first stage as far as Jerusalem and there see Dr. Strathearn, and they seemed pleased with the idea.

Mrs. Joyce is very nice. She was a Miss Murray and was in Cairo with her brother, Alan Murray, who is very musical. It was there that she got engaged to Pierce Joyce.

1st December—Tuesday.

After breakfast I drove to King Faisal's palace, a modest building some distance outside the city on the up-stream side where I had an interview with him at 10:30 a.m. He was extremely cordial as usual, even affectionate, and we had a long talk in the course of which I explained the terms of the Bahra Agreement with which he seemed well pleased. George and I then went on and called on the Prime Minister, Abdul Mohsin Saadun, of the powerful Iraqi family of Saadun.[20] He is a dark-skinned, very intelligent man, with a pleasing personality, and I was very favourably impressed by him. We then went to the Ministry of War, where we met Iltyd, who took me in to see the Minister, my old friend Nuri Pasha Es Said, whom I knew so well during the war and afterwards at Damascus during Faisal's regime there.

I went back to lunch at the Residency where I met the Vernons.

1st December—Tuesday.

20 In the eighteenth and early nineteenth centuries the Sa'dun family had forged the large Muntafiq tribal confederation into a single princedom on the lower Euphrates. As the amirs of the Muntafiq, the Sa'dun remained virtually independent from the Turkish viceroy in Baghdad, frequently fighting amongst themselves if not against the viceroy himself. In the latter half of the nineteenth century the Ottoman government sought to administer the Muntafiq area, but lacking the resources to conquer and control the Sa'dun, Turkish officials relied on intrigue to reduce them to impotence. By supporting ambitious junior members in their pretensions to tribal leadership, the Turks soon divided the Sa'dun into two groups. One group, led first by Nasir Pasha as-Sa'dun and later by his son Falih, sought to turn the tribesmen into agricultural tenants on land near the Euphrates which could be easily administered by the Turks; Abdul Mohsin followed this policy.

He has come out from the Colonial Office to be Financial Adviser to the Government of Iraq. He will have a chance now of seeing the Colonial Office from the other end! At 2:30 p.m. Iltyd called for me with a car and after picking up George at the Maude Hotel, drove us out to Ctesiphon, about an hour's run down the river over a dead flat plain. There we saw the wonderful Ctesiphon arch which is the biggest span of *brick* arch in the world and is some 1500 years old.[21] It is well worth a visit, but it is grievous to think that some years ago the Turks should have blown half of it down with dynamite in order to get bricks with which to build a mosque!

We were also on the site of Townshends' battle of Ctesiphon, which Iltyd explained to us on the ground.[22] We drove back to Baghdad in time for tea at the Joyce's, after which Iltyd and I went back to the Residency.

In the evening there was a large dinner-party of Ministers, high

---

The rival group, led by Mansur Pasha as-Sa'dun and later his son, Sa'dun, hoped to maintain the old independence of the nomadic Muntafiq. Neither prevailed, and the intertribal warfare and rivalries continued unabated.

[21] Located about twenty miles south of Baghdad, the great Arch of Ctesiphon is the widest single-span vault of simple brickwork in the world, measuring eighty-two feet wide by twelve feet high. Built during the Sassanid empire, the Arch formed part of the King's palace.

[22] After their evacuation and retreat from Al-Kut at the end of September 1915, the Turks halted and manned an entrenched position at Ctesiphon. Here the Mesopotamian Expeditionary force under the command of Major-General C. V. Townshend prepared to assault the Turkish fortifications in spite of shortages of equipment, medical supplies, and general ignorance of the geography and climatic conditions of the Tigris Valley. The British attacked on 22 November 1915 with a wide-turning movement, but when the gunboats could not maneuver to support the assault because of low water, the Turkish forward position was carried only after heavy British losses. The Turkish Army then counterattacked with veteran Anatolian troops who had just arrived in Mesopotamia. Although their assault was thrown back with heavy losses, the British could not maintain their position on their already inadequate resources and so withdrew, eventually to Al-Kut. Here the British forces were besieged and despite attempts to relieve the garrison, General Townshend surrendered to the Turks on 29 April 1916, after a siege of 143 days.

[23] "The shop" was the Royal Military Academy, Woolwich, out of which both Sir Gilbert Clayton and Sir John Higgins passed into the army in 1895.

officials, both British and Iraqi, and notables, given by King Faisal in my honour. Among others were Sir John Higgins, who was at the shop with me and is now Air Vice-Marshal commanding the Air Force in Iraq.[23] Also General and Mrs. Daly, who is Inspector General of the Iraq Army. He is one of the Ryde Dalys and was at the Isle of Wight College as a small boy, while she is a sister of Eva Graves. The Amir Zaid was also present. He acted for Faisal while he was in Europe and returns to Oxford next week.

2nd December—Wednesday.

Mr. Greenhouse of the Turkish Petroleum Company came to see me after breakfast, being anxious to know whether I had secured a corridor of British mandated territory joining Iraq and Trans-Jordan with a view to a possible future pipeline. I was able to reassure him.[24]

2nd December—Wednesday.

[24] After the success of the Young Turk Revolution, the British government urged the formation of a National Bank in Turkey supported with British capital. One of the directors of the National Bank, C. S. Gulbenkian, persuaded the bank to interest itself in Turkish oil development and to join with the Germans for that purpose. By the end of 1910 Gulbenkian had succeeded in bringing the National Bank and the Deutsche Bank together to form a company to pursue oil operations throughout the Ottoman Empire. Consequently, in 1911 the African and Eastern Concessions Limited was organized and in the following year changed its name to the Turkish Petroleum Company. Through the intervention of the British government the Turkish Petroleum Company was reorganized in 1914. Half the share capital was taken by the all-British Anglo-Persian Oil Company, the shareholding of the National Bank disappeared, and the Deutsche Bank limited its shares to one-quarter of the total share capital. In June 1914 the Grand Vizier, Sa'id Halim Pasha, agreed to lease petroleum deposits in the Baghdad and Mosul areas to the Turkish Petroleum Company, and although the war prevented this concession from being fulfilled, it served as the basis for the Turkish Petroleum Company's claims after the war. The war, of course, broke up the syndicate, and the German shares were given to France in return for the French facilitating the passage of oil found in the Mosul area across Syria to the Mediterranean. The Turkish Petroleum Company's shares were thus redistributed so that Anglo-Saxon received 22½ percent, Anglo-Persian 47½ percent, the French 25 percent, and Gulbenkian 5 percent, and the whole arrangement was officially sanctioned by the San Remo Oil Agree-

At 10:30 a.m. King Faisal came to pay me a visit. He arrived quite privately in a car with only an A.D.C. and stayed nearly two hours. He spoke almost entirely on two subjects—Syria and the present disturbed conditions, the Hejaz, and King Ali's position in the face of Ibn Sa'ud's attacks. On both questions he asked my advice, as an old friend, as to the attitude which he should take up. In both cases my advice can be briefly summed up by "Leave well alone, for the present, and await events." It would be most dangerous, in my opinion, for Faisal being King of Iraq, to interfere in Syrian affairs, while as regards the Hejaz, I see no possibility of helping King Ali at this late stage. The military issue between him and Ibn Sa'ud must first be fought to a conclusion. Faisal seemed to see the logic of what I said, but whether he can refrain from putting his finger into the Syrian pie remains to be seen. It is a great temptation to him.[25]

As soon as Faisal had gone, I went to the Maude Hotel, picked up George Antonius, and we went to the Prime Minister's office, where we explained the Bahra Agreement at length to the Prime Minister, the Minister of Interior, and Ken Cornwallis. They all seemed perfectly satisfied.[26]

I then picked up Iltyd and we went to the Joyce's to lunch, where were also Amir Zaid and Nuri Pasha. After lunch we drove out to

---

ment of 24 April 1920. Negotiations were then begun for oil concessions in 'Iraq, the Turkish Petroleum Company basing its claim on the Turkish promise of 1914 for an oil concession in Mesopotamia. After prolonged negotiations a concession was granted in March 1925 to the Turkish Petroleum Company for the duration of seventy-five years, covering the whole of 'Iraq except Basra. In 1929 the Turkish Petroleum Company changed its name to the Iraq Petroleum Company. Once this rich concession had been granted, the Turkish Petroleum Company naturally wished to insure a corridor to the Mediterranean of British-secured territories through which to construct a pipeline.

[25] After the creation of the French mandate in Syria, conditions rapidly deteriorated. By the end of 1925 an insurrection against French control broke out in the Druze Mountains and, supported by a variety of nationalist groups, soon spread to Damascus and other parts of Syria. It is little wonder that Faysal, who had been expelled from Syria by the French only five years before, could hardly resist supporting the Syrian Arab nationalists against the French. Faysal felt that three political arrangements were open to the

the Iraq Army polo ground, which is on the way to Faisal's palace. Joyce, Iltyd, and Amir Zaid all played and also a number of British and native officers of the Iraq army.

We then drove back and Iltyd and I visited the famous Baghdad bookshop, where we were both enticed into buying books. Iltyd then took me to see the ruins of the old Governor's Palace of the time of Harun el-Rashid. There is quite a good deal still preserved, and some of the carving—all in brick—is quite wonderful in delicacy and design.[27] The Bourdillons gave a dinner party for me in the evening, comprising the Dalys, the Lindsay Burys (he is now installed as the Adviser for Public Works), Nuri Pasha Es Said, Iltyd, two other Iraqi Ministers and several others.

3rd December—Thursday.

After breakfast George and I went to the bank and to Cooks [Thomas Cook & Sons] to arrange for money and tickets for our voyage to Bombay, the Colonial Office having approved of my proposal to proceed by that route to Aden, staying a week at Bombay. At 10:30 a.m. we attended a special meeting of the Council of Ministers, to whom I again explained the Bahra Agreement. General satisfaction was expressed at the results achieved, and a special resolution was passed thanking me for my services. I then went and col-

Syrians: (1) the union of Syria and 'Iraq under one sovereign (Faysal), with the British and French mandates still in force; (2) a republic with an elected president; (3) a monarchy with a member of the Hashimite family on the throne. Clayton thought the first solution quite impractical, urged that the other choices were a matter for the Syrians, and advised Faysal not to get mixed up in the matter. This was sound, if painful advice, for the French bombarded Damascus the following spring and crushed the rebellion by the end of 1926. What aid Faysal could have rendered to the Syrians would have made little difference in the face of French determination and would surely have compromised his position in 'Iraq. As for the possibility of British support to King 'Ali, see Clayton's advice to Faysal's brother, 'Abd Allah, p. 155. (Clayton to Amery, Private, 10 December 1925, C.P.)

[26] The Prime Minister was 'Abd al-Muhsin as-Sa'dun; the Minister of the Interior, Hikmat Sulayman.

[27] The ruined palace of the Caliph al-Ma'mun (813–832), younger son of Harun ar-Rashid, is located in the citadel that rises above the north part of Baghdad.

lected and paid for my books and returned to the Residency to finish off some letters. At 1:30 p.m. I looked in at Gertrude Bell's house to say good-bye. I found that all arrangements had been made to fly Mrs. Henley to Amman that afternoon, staying the night at Ramadi, so I gave her a note to Dr. Strathearn and sent a wire to Cox about her. I picked up Ken Cornwallis at Gertrude's and went off to lunch with him at his house, which is at the extreme downstream end of Baghdad. After lunch we returned to the Residency for tennis, and I had three very good sets followed by tea before a roaring fire. It is quite chilly of an evening now here, and people have begun fires, although I fancy it gets much colder later on.

I went over the river by launch and dined with Sir John and Lady Higgins. The Dalys and several Air Force officers were there, also Colonel Dent of the Intelligence whom I remembered meeting at Jerusalem where I think he lunched with us. Mr. Monson, who has been staying at the Residency, left for Jerusalem today; he has been the Consul at Teheran and has been appointed Minister at Bogota.

4th December—Friday.

We left Baghdad by train for Basra at 10:00 a.m. There was quite a crowd to see us off—the Bourdillons, the Joyces, the Prime Minister, the Minister of War, the Minister of Public Works, and several others, including last—but by no means least—Iltyd.[28] It has been very jolly seeing old Tyd again. He is out at Artillery practice camp some way up the river, but he came into Baghdad for the few days of my visit. King Faisal has gone off to his country estate for a few days, and Gertrude Bell and Ken [Cornwallis] have also gone there to spend Friday, so were not there to see me off. We had quite a good saloon—though we had to pay five fares for it!—and we were able during the day to accommodate Miss Payne, who has been

---

4th December—Friday.

[28] The Prime Minister was 'Abd al-Muhsin as-Sa'dun; the Minister of War, Nuri Pasha as-Sa'id; the Minister of Public Works, Muhammad Amin Zaki.

[29] Buried in a number of mounds, the ruins have been pillaged for their fine kiln-burned bricks to construct buildings in Baghdad, Al Hillah, and Ctesiphon.

[30] Ur was originally a settlement and port at the mouth of one of the distributaries of the Euphrates delta but now lies 120 miles from the head of the Khawr az-Zubayr.

staying with the Bourdillons and is going to the Anglo-Persian oil fields to spend Christmas with friends.

We travelled all day down the Euphrates Valley—dead flat and very ugly and uninteresting, but it gave one some idea of the conditions in which the Mesopotamian campaign was fought, and one passed such familiar names as Hilla, Diwaniya, Nasariya, Zubeir. Not to speak also of Babylon, which is passed shortly before reaching Hilla. The train, unfortunately, does not stop to allow you to visit the ruins, but one can see the mounds of earth which mark the site of the ancient city.[29] Another tantalizing thing is that we pass quite close to Ur of the Chaldees, where Leonard Woolley is excavating, but unluckily at 2:00 a.m. in the morning, so a visit is out of the question.[30] It is a pity to be so very close and to have to hurry through on account of catching the boat.

5th December—Saturday.

We arrived at Makina (the town station of Basra) soon after 7:00 a.m. but stayed in the train and went right down to the docks where we drew up just opposite our ship, the British India [Steam Navigation] Company's S.S. *Varela.*[31] We embarked at once and settled into very roomy and comfortable deck cabins. We had breakfast on board and then took a taxi into Basra, some five miles, where we visited the Steamship Company's offices. I have some idea of getting off at Karachi and proceeding to Bombay by land via Delhi and Agra, and I wanted to find out if it was feasible. However, the Company was not able to give any useful information.

We then visited the Post Office, where I sent a cable to Enid, and then we paid calls on the Administrative Inspector, Major Bury, and the mutaserraf, Ahmad Pasha Sanaa.[32] The latter is a rich landowner of Basra, who appeared very intelligent and keen and who struck

---

5th December—Saturday.

[31] The S.S. *Varela* of 4,646 tons was built in 1914 by Swan, Hunter, and Wigham Richardson, Newcastle, for the British India Steam Navigation Company. At the outbreak of the First World War she was requisitioned as a supply and dispatch vessel for British forces. She was sold, for breaking up, in 1951.

[32] Mutaserraf (*mutasarrif*): governor of a *liwa* or province corresponding to the *mudir* of Egypt and the Anglo-Egyptian Sudan. In 'Iraq the *mudir* was the administrative officer of a much smaller unit, the *nahiyah* or parish.

me very favourably. We drove back to lunch on board and then wrote letters for posting before sailing.

Basra is not a very attractive place, being absolutely flat, intersected by many sluggish canals, and only redeemed by acres and acres of datepalms which it contains and by which it is surrounded. One gets the best impression of the place when steaming down the Shatt el Arab outward bound. The quays are some way upstream of the town just below the junction of the Euphrates and the Tigris, which form the Shatt el Arab. One therefore passes the whole length of the city as the steamer leaves the port.

We sailed at 4:00 p.m. and by 6:00 p.m. we were opposite Mohammera, on the left bank of the Shatt el Arab in Persian territory. We only stopped a few minutes in midstream and it was quite dark, so we unfortunately saw nothing of the place. After dinner we passed Abadan, also on the Persian bank where is the great distilling and loading centre of the Anglo-Persian Oil Company. It works night and day, and it was quite a wonderful sight to see the long line of flaring lights stretching for some miles along the left bank of the river with all the oil tankers waiting to take on their cargos for all parts of the world. The actual wells are some 200 miles up in the interior of Persia, and the oil is pumped down through a pipeline for distilling and subsequent loading at Abadan.[33]

6th December–Sunday.

We arrived off Bushire about 10:00 a.m. and anchored about eight miles from the shore. Bushire lies on a long, low island some fourteen miles in length and looks quite attractive from the sea, being comparatively well wooded.[34] We were not sure how long we

---

[33] Abadan Island was a mud flat belonging to the Shaykh of Muhammarah on which the Anglo-Persian Oil Company constructed their great refinery from 1910–13 in order to process the crude oil from the great field at Masjid-i-Sulayman (Shahrestan) where the first succesful well was drilled in January 1908.

6th December–Sunday.

[34] Bushire (Bushehr) is the principal seaport of Iran at the head of the mountain route into the interior, but it is an open roadstead so it is not as important as the river port of Khorramshahr (Al-Muhammarah). Bushire was the headquarters of the British Political Resident in the Persian Gulf

were staying, so it was not until lunch time that I sent a wireless to the [British] Political Resident, Colonel Prideaux, to inform him that we were on board. He answered that he would come on board and he duly arrived shortly before 5:00 p.m. We were able to have a chat about Najd affairs, which affect him closely, but it was, of course, too late for us to go ashore. It has been very unfortunate, as if we had wired him early we could have spent the day ashore and had a good look at Bushire. The Persian mail did not come aboard until 9:00 p.m. and we sailed at 10:00 p.m.

7th December–Monday.

We were at sea all day, steaming down the eastern coast of the Persian Gulf within full sight of the barren coastal hills of Persia, a most uninviting looking country as seen from the sea with hardly a sign of human habitation. The weather has been delightful, the sea like glass, and the temperature cool and balmy. This is a small ship but very comfortable and blessed with quite a good cook. There are only about twenty first-class passengers, but there are in the third-class a certain number of pilgrims, and a large draft of Bombay Sappers and Miners returning from Iraq to India. We sit at the Captain's table. He is a Scotsman, has been many years at sea, and is full of interesting information and experiences.[35] I have decided not to get out at Karachi but to go on to Bombay.

8th December–Tuesday.

At sea all day. Run at noon 292 miles. We passed through the Straits of Oman before breakfast, and were able to see the coast on both sides, Arabia to starboard and Persia to port.[36] We steamed all

---

from 1778 to 1946. The town is located at the west end of a ridged peninsula, not an island, of raised coral reef sixteen miles long and about five miles wide and connected to the mainland by a salt marsh. Since the roadstead is exposed to strong winds, large vessels must anchor seven miles out.

7th December–Monday.

[35] Captain Charles J. Halls.

8th December–Tuesday.

[36] The Straits of Oman ('Uman), also known as the Strait of Hormuz, lead from the Persian Gulf into the Gulf of Oman.

day within sight of the coast, which has now merged from Persia into Baluchistan. The weather continues perfect. George Antonius and I are busy trying to assimilate various books on the Yemen which we have brought with us.

9th December—Wednesday.

At sea all day, mostly out of sight of land. Run at noon again 292 miles, leaving 227 miles to Karachi. The weather is still delightful, and the sea perfectly calm, with a cool breeze.

10th December—Thursday.

We arrived at Karachi at 7:00 a.m. Both port and town are modern and built on the site of a small fishing village. There is, therefore, nothing of local interest to see, nor is there any Indian atmosphere to speak of. The port is roomy and commodious, and the town is reached along two or three miles of raised causeway between mud flats. The town is well laid out and very spacious, containing some handsome official and commercial buildings and some fairly good shops. George and I drove into the town about 10:00 a.m., and I called on the Commissioner in Sind, Cadell, whose headquarters are in Karachi. I had a short chat with him and sent off telegrams to the Governor of Bombay [Colonel Wilson] and the Resident, Aden [General Stewart], informing them of my movements and asking the latter for some idea of the proposed arrangements for my mission to Sanaa. We then went into the town, where George was inveigled into buying some embroideries and drove back to lunch on board through the native quarter of the city. In the afternoon went up to tea with the Commissioner and Mrs. Cadell, and on our way back we passed again by the shops, where George

---

12th December—Saturday.

[37] At the request of Ibn Sa'ud, Clayton wished to assure the Indian authorities that the Sultan of Najd wished to provide all possible facilities to pilgrims, particularly Indian Muslims. Clayton also inquired about the attitude of the Indian government to British India ships calling at Ibn Sa'ud's projected port on the Persian Gulf, Ra's Tannurah. The Indian officials had no objections provided the port was adequately equipped and the anchorage safe. Clayton also made arrangements to read the files of the Bombay govern-

fell again and bought a rug. We took on more passengers at Karachi for Bombay, and the ship is pretty full up. We sailed punctually at 9:00 p.m.

11th December—Friday.

At sea all day, within sight of land. Beautiful weather. Wrote to Enid and sent postcards to the chicks.

12th December—Saturday.

Arrived at Bombay at 7:00 a.m. I got up early and had a view of Bombay by dawn, a very beautiful sight, as the lights of the port were all alight and gradually faded as the dawn broke over the hills behind the city. Bombay is a wonderful sight as you approach it from the sea, especially at that time of day. There was no one to meet us (!) so we got our kit ashore and drove to the Grand Hotel which we had been told was the best. If our informants were correct, I can say very little in favour of Bombay hotels. We have two rooms with a private bathroom, certainly, but the general style of the place is quite miserable, almost squalid.

After settling down we went to the offices of the Bombay Government, where we saw the Political Secretary, Hotson, who was quite delightfully hospitable and kind. He immediately asked us to come to lunch and to go on with him and his wife and party to the races. We completed our business at the offices, wrote our names in the Governor's book and did some shopping.[37] We then returned to our hotel for a brush-up and repaired in a taxi—about five miles—to the Byculla Club where the Hotsons were giving their luncheon party.[38] There were about twelve at a very cheery and pleasant party. The Club is quite fascinating. It is the old Club of Bombay,

---

ment on the Yemen, which however had little information about relations between the Yemen and Aden.

[38] The Byculla Club was founded in 1833, and in the following year a race stand on the then outskirts of Bombay was made over to the club. Racing continued on the accompanying track until 1883 while the holdings of the club steadily increased. By 1905 the club owned twenty-seven acres of gardens and parklands as well as numerous residential and social buildings. After the Second World War the high cost of maintaining the old but

very exclusive, and they have retained all the old customs, manners, decorations, and furniture. For instance, we were kept cool all through lunch by gorgeously dressed servants wielding huge feather fans. One really might have been back in the days of the old Indian Nabobs. We then drove off to the races which are held on the most magnificient course. The stands are quite new and are said to be the largest in the world, with the possible exception of Buenos Ayres. The paddock and enclosure are beautifully spacious and are laid out with green lawns and gorgeous flower beds. Altogether, a most wonderful place. The racing was also very good and as I only lost 10 rupees I had a very good afternoon.[39] There was quite a crowd both of Europeans and Indians, and it was particularly interesting to see large numbers of handsome Parsee ladies, unveiled and wearing the loveliest Indian clothes.[40] After the races we went to the Willingdon Club for drinks. It is a mixed European and Indian Club founded by Lord Willingdon and is rather like the Cairo Gezira Sporting Club but fitted out in a much more lavish and luxurious scale, with drawing rooms, card rooms, and a dancing Hall.[41] After a pleasant hour there we took a taxi and drove to the topmost point of Malabar hill, whence you get an unrivalled view of Bombay across the "back bay," as they call it.[42] It was well worth the drive, as it was nearly dark and all the lights of the huge city and port were shining out. It was just like fairyland. We then drove home to a very late dinner and were glad to get to bed after a long day. I received a somewhat unsatisfactory telegram from Aden, saying that arrange-

---

spacious buildings was so great that the land and buildings were sold in 1947 and the club disbanded.

[39] 10 rupees were equivalent to 15 shillings in 1925.

[40] The Parsees are adherents of the Zoroastrian religion, descended from Persian refugees who settled in India, mostly in Bombay, whither they fled in the seventh and eighth centuries to escape Muslim persecution.

[41] The Willingdon Sports Club, Clerk Road, Bombay, was founded on 18 May 1917 by the first Marquess of Willingdon while Governor of Bombay. The membership of the club was open to all nationalities of the world, though it now excludes nationals of the Republic of South Africa of European extraction. The club is equipped with an eighteen hole golf course, swimming pool, and facilities for tennis, badminton, squash, bridge, billiards. There are no residential accommodations, but meals are provided for members and their guests.

ments for my mission were not yet completed, the dates were not yet fixed, and the matter was still under correspondence with the Imam. I am certainly not going to hang about Aden awaiting the Imam's convenience. It would be most undignified. I shall, therefore, postpone my departure from India for a week more, and utilize the time by making a trip to Delhi where I have some questions to discuss with the Government of India and possibly to Agra which I want to see. I don't feel very happy about this mission. I am afraid that the Colonial Office have rather rushed into it, and that the actual situation may be the reverse of favorable. If that is the case, I shall inform the Colonial Office and urge that negotiations be postponed indefinitely rather than court undignified failure.

13th December–Sunday.

I went to Choral celebration at St. Thomas' Cathedral, Bombay at 8:30 a.m. Quite a nice service and a large congregation of communicants. The Cathedral dates from the earlier days of Bombay and is not very beautiful from an architectural point of view, or very large, but it contains many interesting memorials of Englishmen who were famous in the city.[43]

After breakfast we did some reading up of files, of which we have been lent many by the Secretariat of the Bombay Government. At 1:30 p.m. I went off to lunch at Government House with Sir Leslie and Lady Wilson. They were very pleasant and said how sorry they were not to be able to have us to stay, but they are off tomorrow

---

42 Back Bay is a shallow roughly rectangular basin three miles long and two miles wide from northeast to southwest located at the southern end of Bombay Island and over-looked by Malabar Hill, approximately 200 feet high.

13th December–Sunday.

43 Built as a garrison church in 1718, consecrated in 1816, and made a cathedral on the establishment of the See of Bombay in 1835, the Cathedral of St. Thomas is simple in plan, composed of a mixture of the classical and Gothic styles. The chancel added in 1865 is modern early English in design. Among the many monuments to famous Englishmen of Bombay there are memorials to Jonathan Duncan, Governor of Bombay; Captain G. N. Hardinge, who died in 1808 in the capture of the French cruiser *Piedmontaise*; and Colonel Burr, who commanded at the battle of Kirkee, 5 November 1817.

to Sind on tour, and do not return till early in January. There was a muddle about George's invitation, which never turned up, so he was not able to come to lunch, but he came up afterwards.

Government House is a collection of very large and spacious bungalows in beautiful grounds, situated on the extreme end of the Malabar promonotory and overlooking the sea—a very pleasant situation.

We returned to the hotel after lunch and at 4:30 p.m. we drove up to Malabar Hill again and called on the Bishop of Bombay. The Bishop and his wife were in and we had tea and a long chat. He is a very nice man and was for many years at Balliol College, Oxford, where he was well known as Dr. Palmer.

After tea we walked back to the hotel, a distance of some five miles, arriving hot and tired and ready for bath, dinner, and bed.

The city of Bombay is well worth a visit, though it is of course European, or I should say rather cosmopolitan, and not in any way an example of Indian life. The public buildings are very fine and many of them rival those of London and the great European cities. The city also is very well laid out and planned with wide streets and large open spaces. The wealth is very apparent and the number of motorcars is prodigious. I went and looked at George Lloyd's pet reclamation scheme. It is an ambitious and costly affair, which most people seem to regard with considerable apprehension.[44]

14th December—Monday.

After breakfast went and fixed up our passages for Aden, in S.S. *Razmak* (P. & O.), sailing on the 26th December, then went to

---

[44] The great increase in Bombay trade at the end of the nineteenth and the beginning of the twentieth century brought a corresponding rise in the population of the city. In order to cope with overcrowding, the City Improvement Trust was set up to organize urban renewal in Bombay; and under the initiative of Sir George Lloyd, a development scheme was begun in 1918 in Back Bay to reclaim 1,300 acres for building sites by constructing a sea wall from Colaba point to Marine Lines. The project failed for technical reasons and was the subject of an inquiry in 1926. A drastically revised version of the plan was completed after World War II.

14th December—Monday.

[45] S.S. *Razmak* of 10,602 tons was built in 1925 by Harland and Wolff Ltd.,

the Government Secretariat and did various jobs, sending off dispatches and telegrams.[45] After lunch did some more reading up of files and then went to Thomas Cook & Sons to fix up our tickets for Delhi. We had tea at the "Taj" hotel, which is certainly a better class hotel than the one which we are in, and moreover is much better situated on the sea front facing the great "Gateway to India" which commemorates the visit of King George and Queen Mary to India.[46]

We dined with Hotsons at the Willingdon Club—a large party to meet Prince and Princess Firuz from Persia. An excellent dinner and a pleasant and interesting evening.

15th December—Tuesday.

After breakfast went to the P. & O. office and took our tickets for Aden. Spent the rest of the morning reading up files and did the same after lunch. At 4:30 p.m. Forbes Adam of the Bombay Secretariat called for us and took us to tea at his house on Malabar Hill, after which he and his wife took us for a drive round the island through the industrial and native quarters, showing us some of the housing and reclamation schemes which were initiated by George Lloyd. They are all on a large scale and should greatly benefit Bombay, which is much over-crowded, but the prices have risen and trade is depressed since they were started, and there seems a somewhat general opinion that as conditions are now, they will involve a heavy burden of capital expenditure which will be very difficult to meet and which will not give an adequate return. At 6:30 p.m. I attended, by invitation, a meeting of St. George's Lodge, Bombay.[47] A very interesting meeting with everything done ex-

---

Greenock for the Peninsular and Oriental Steam Navigation Company for use on the Aden-Bombay run. Commanded by Captain E. C. Miller, she was afterward sold to the Union Steam Ship Company under whose flag she broke the Pacific run record. She was sold for breaking up in 1953.

46 Located at the Bombay waterfront on the Apollo Bandar pier, the Gateway to India Arch was designed by George Wittet in the sixteenth century Gujarat style to commemorate the visit in 1911 of King George V and Queen Mary.

15th December—Tuesday.

47 St. George's Lodge, Bombay, was the Masonic Lodge of the city.

tremely well, after which I dined with the Lodge. I was asked to return thanks for the toast of the visitors and took the opportunity of telling them about Lodge "King Solomon's Temple" and assuring them of a very hearty welcome there should they ever visit Jerusalem.[48]

We have taken railway tickets for Delhi by the train leaving at 4:30 p.m. tomorrow, by the Bombay, Baroda and Central India Railway, and have also reserved accommodation at the Hotel Cecil, Delhi, and the Hotel Cecil, Agra.

16th December—Wednesday.

Did some final reading of files after breakfast and at 11:30 a.m. went to the Secretariat where we fixed up the engagement of a stenographer for our mission and also returned the files which had been lent us to read. We lunched at the Hotel, which I am not sorry to be leaving as it is a poor place, and they have selected the time of our visit to repaint the lounge and hall. The only merit is that the food is fairly good.

After lunch I wrote to Enid, and to the Resident at Aden [General Stewart], and also sent postcards to the children.

We caught the 4:30 p.m. train for Delhi from Colaba station. An excellent saloon carriage designed for four we had to ourselves, so we were quite comfortable. My woollen waistcoat was unfortunately lost at the station; I fear it must have been stolen.

17th December—Thursday.

---

[48] King Solomon's Temple Lodge, Jerusalem, was the Masonic Lodge of which Clayton had been a member during his tenure as Chief Secretary to the Palestine government.

17th December—Thursday.

[49] Multra, today called Mathura.

[50] On 11 May 1857 mutinous Indian cavalrymen of the 3rd Light Cavalry entered Delhi where they were joined by infantrymen from the Indian garrison and proceeded to the arsenal to seize the guns and ammunition. Under the command of Lieutenant Willoughby the British garrison of the arsenal, comprising eight artillery officers and N.C.O.'s, made ready to repel the mutineers or, failing that, to destroy the arsenal. Such a small force could

We spent the whole day travelling through India, passing through the provinces of Gujerat, Baroda, and Rajputana. Among other towns, we passed Baroda, Ratlam, Multra, and I was glued to the window most of the time watching the country and the people.[49] It was a novel sight to see monkeys in the trees and gorgeous peacocks in the fields from the windows of a train, and there were also many quaint little temples by the wayside. The people at the stations, also, were of the greatest interest to me. The country is for the most part flat but quite well wooded, with occasional groups of low, rocky, verdure-clad hills.

It was quite chilly during the night, and I was sorry not to have brought some blankets, but I made good shift with my leather-lined coat.

We reached Delhi punctually at 8:30 p.m. but were delayed for twenty minutes just outside the station. We then packed ourselves and our baggage into a quaint old-fashioned landau and drove to the Hotel Cecil, which is charmingly situated in a nice garden not far outside the walls. It was dark, of course, so one could not see much, but it gave one a thrill to find oneself driving out of the city through the famous Kashmir gate which was so gallantly blown in by the forlorn hope at the siege of Delhi during the Mutiny. We also passed the gates of the old magazine, which was blown up by its British garrison when they found that they could defend it no longer.[50]

We found very comfortable rooms awaiting us in the hotel each with a roaring fire which was cheerful.

---

hardly turn back the assault of the mutineers, who soon burst into the arsenal; Willoughby then gave the order to blow up the magazines. Hundreds of the mutineers were killed by the explosion and the falling masonry. Four of the British garrison survived, including Willoughby, who however was later killed during the retreat from Delhi.

The Kashmir Gate was blown up in broad daylight on 14 September 1857 by a demolition party under the command of Lieutenants Salkeld and Home, making a breach in the wall so that the Third Column of the attacking British force under Colonel Campbell could enter. There is today a slab on the Kashmir Gate recording the exploit of the demolition party.

CHAPTER 5

Interlude at Delhi:
18–26 December 1925

18th December—Friday.

After a fairly early breakfast, I went for a stroll in the neighbourhood of the hotel, visiting the Nicholson gardens in which is a fine statue of John Nicholson, and the cemetery in which he is buried. European Delhi is beautifully laid out with wide, well-watered roads, the houses and bungalows being in large well-kept gardens filled with fine shady trees.[1] At 10:30 a.m. we went to the Secretariat and had a long talk with Sir Denys Bray, the Foreign Secretary, from whom I got much useful information. He also very kindly asked us to lunch. We then went into the town after writing our names in the Commander-in-Chief's book. He is away in Calcutta for a council meeting and will not return until we have left.[2] We had a very pleasant lunch with the Brays, who were very cordial and kind, and then returned to the hotel where I rang up General Godwin, who travelled out with me in the *Rawalpindi.* I found him

---

18th December—Friday.

[1] The establishment of a new capital for India was first announced by King George V at the Durbar of 1911, and Lord Irwin formally inaugurated New Delhi in 1929 by moving his headquarters to the viceroy's house. Sir Edwin Luytens laid out the city on a series of hexagons with a wide, central road and great traffic circles where diagonal avenues met. The tree-lined roads are in three classes, 150 ft., 120 ft., and 76 ft., depending on their importance. John Nicholson (1821–57) was one of the heroes of the siege of Delhi. He was killed and buried outside the Kashmir Gate where a statue was later erected in his honor.

in and arranged to dine with him. George and I then spent a long afternoon in the famous Fort where is the Palace of the Moghuls. It is quite wonderful and beggars description in a brief diary such as this. Within a large area, surrounded by a great wall pierced with two mighty gates are many fine buildings of red sandstone situated in beautifully kept gardens. The Diwan-i-Am (public reception room) and Diwan-i-Khas (private reception hall) and also the Muti Masjid or Pearl Mosque are the gems.[3] On return to the hotel I went to Maidens Hotel and had a chat with Godwin. I also called on the Collins and found Mrs. Collins in. Jack was on tour but returns on Sunday. I had a very pleasant tête-à-tête dinner with Godwin.

19th December–Saturday.

After breakfast George Antonius and I went to see some of the treasures at the store of Imre Schwaiger, a famous dealer in Indian and Eastern *objets d'art*. He was very good and showed us some of his best pieces of Indian jewellery and metal work. It was quite wonderful and some of the things fairly took one's breath away, but of course the prices were far beyond any ordinary purse. We then went to the Secretariat and saw Sir D. Bray again, and I went on and had a long talk with the Military Intelligence people. We returned to the hotel where Mrs. Collins came to lunch with us and then took us on a delightful round in her car, acting herself as a most capable guide. Delhi district is covered with ruined cities of the Moghuls, who were continually building new capitals, with tombs, mosques, palaces, and other intensely interesting remains. It would take some days to do them all, but Mrs. Collins made an excellent selection. We started with one of the old Delhis which is called Farozabad.[4]

---

[2] Field Marshal William Riddell Birdwood, the Commander-in-Chief of the Army of India.

[3] The fort or Lal Kila, the Red Palace, was constructed between 1638–48 by Shah Jahan (1628–58). It is surprising that Shah Jahan did not provide a place of worship in his palace at Delhi, for the construction of the Muti Masjid or Pearl Mosque was left to his successor, Aurangzib (1658–1707).

19th December–Saturday.

[4] Farozabad (Firuzabad) was that extension of Delhi to the north constructed during the reign of Firuz Shah Tughluq (1351–88) and embracing

It is in rather a ruinous state, but it is all very well kept and the open spaces within the walls are all laid out as gardens and lawns, which makes it very peaceful and pleasing. We then drove through Raisina (or New Delhi) which fairly takes one's breath away by its size and the colossal expense that must be involved. The Secretariat is a vast building, rather recalling what Baalbek must have looked like—only more simple and less decorated. The Viceroy's Palace and the Legislative Assembly Hall are on a similar scale, and it will doubtless look very magnificent when it is finished.[5] But what an expense in these very hard times!

We went on to a most charming collection of old buildings, called the Haus Khas. It was a sort of country lodge of one of the Moghuls and consisted of a large tank, surrounded by the country house, a mosque, and one or two tombs of notable people.[6] Very peaceful and beautiful and I should have liked to spend many a quiet hour there. Again everything was in most beautiful order. It is due to Lord Curzon, who took a great interest in all the historical monuments, that ample funds are provided for repair, restoration, and upkeep of grounds and gardens. We then visited the tomb of Safjar Jang, Grand Vizier and Commander-in-Chief to one of the Moghuls. It is a mighty mausoleum built of red sandstone, picked out with marble, and is surmounted by a marble dome. Very imposing, but

---

a large part of modern Delhi. Among other edifices Firuzabad was traditionally to have contained eight public mosques and one private mosque in addition to three palaces and several royal hunting boxes. Few of the monuments have been preserved, the best and most considerable being the palace-fort or citadel of the emperor.

[5] In 1911 George V laid the foundation stone for New Delhi not far from the old Circuit House, the Viceroy's cold-weather residence, 1912–33. A commission charged with the responsibility to select a site preferred the tiny village of Raisina, five miles south of Shah Jahan's palace-fort because the original site was condemned as malarial. The foundation stone was subsequently moved.

The two great secretariat buildings were designed by Sir Herbert Baker as Italianate structures with four projecting blocks in pairs, each carrying a portico of columns with recessed courts between and facing on the processional way. Sir Herbert Baker also designed the circular building on the plain at the foot of the acropolis with its open colonnade, half a mile in circum-

not very beautiful, I thought.[7] Our last visit was to the famous Kutb Minar, a huge tower of ornamented and fluted red sandstone which can be seen for many miles round. It is very imposing and undoubtedly grows on one. It stands among a mass of quite beautiful old buildings, including the splendid mosque of Akbar and the tomb of the Emperor Altamash which is a marvel of delicate and beautiful carving.[8] Altogether, a very wonderful place which I only wish I could visit again and again. We drove back to Delhi, arriving at 5:30 p.m., and I went to tea with Lady Birdwood. The Field Marshal was unfortunately away in Calcutta so I did not see him, but I met there Katharine Acland, daughter of Alfred Acland whom I used to know well when I was at Khartoum. We had a very pleasant and interesting dinner at Maidens Hotel with Lt.-General Sir Andrew Skeen, C.G.S. in India.

20th December—Sunday.

I went to early Celebration at St. James' Church, just inside the famous Kashmir Gate, which was built at the expense of Colonel Robert Skinner, the founder of Skinner's Horse. It is not a particularly beautiful building, cruciform with a central dome, but it has interesting historic associations, and they have quite a nice service. In the churchyard are to be seen the original globe and cross which

---

ference, and containing the two houses of parliament, the central library, and what was formerly the chamber of princes but is now the supreme court. The Viceroy's Palace, now the residence of the president of the Republic of India, was designed by Sir Edwin Luytens.

[6] The Hauz-i-Khass is a group of monuments forming the College (not the country house) and Tomb of Firuz Shah Tughluq (1351–88), built on the remains of an older structure of 'Ala ad-Din Khalgi (1296–1316).

[7] Safdar Jang was a Persian Shiite and Viceroy of the Province of Oudh who in 1748 was appointed Wazir by the new emperor Ahmed Shah Bahadur (1748–54).

[8] The Qutb Minar was begun by Qutb ad-Din Aibak (1206–10) but was completed in 1231–32 by Shams ad-Din Iltutmish, a Turk, son-in-law and successor to Aibak.

The Akbar mosque to which Sir Gilbert refers is in reality the Jami' Quwwat al-Islam (Congregational Mosque of the Might of Islam) begun in 1191 by Qutb ad-Din Aibak after his capture of Delhi.

surmounted the church and which were riddled with bullet holes during the siege of Delhi.[9]

After breakfast George Antonius and I walked to the great mosque of Delhi (the Jama Masjid) and went all over it. It is a vast and imposing building, splendidly set on a lofty platform, and facing Delhi Fort. It is built of the usual red sandstone picked out with marble, the interior shrine being entirely of marble, and–like the Fort–was built by the Emperor Shah Jehan.[10] We drove back through the Chandi Chauk, the big bazaar of Delhi, after having paid a visit to a shop, called the Ivory Palace, where they produce the most wonderful work in carved ivory, brass, carved wood, and lacquer.[11] I made a few small purchases, but I could have spent hundreds of rupees. When we returned to the hotel there was still some time before lunch, so I took a tonga and drove along the Ridge, so famous at the siege of Delhi in the Mutiny days.[12] It was wonderful to see the whole scene of that gallant siege laid out before one, and it made it seem very real. On the top of the Ridge is a monument to those who fell in the siege, and the town is full of interesting memorials, such as the gateways of the old powder magazine, which was blown up by its defenders to keep it from falling into the hands of the mutineers.

I joined George at Schwaiger's, where he was being sorely

20th December–Sunday.

[9] In 1802 James Skinner joined the British forces under the command of Lord Lake and organized a troop of irregular cavalry known as the "Yellow Boys" because of their bright yellow uniforms, or more commonly as "Skinner's Horse." James Skinner retained command of his detachment until his death in 1841 at the age of 63.

The oldest extant church in Delhi, St. James's Church was consecrated on 21 November 1836, having been built by James Skinner in fulfillment of his vow made to his patron saint when wounded in January 1800. St. James's was constructed according to the plans of a church in Venice with exactly the same ground scheme by two officers of the Bengal Engineers, Colonel Robert Smith and Captain de Bude. James Skinner and several members of his family are buried in the church.

[10] The Jami' Masjid was an essential part of the capital of Shah Jahan (1628–58) and contemporary with the palace-fort. This largest and grandest mosque in India was begun in 1644 but not completed until fourteen years later.

tempted to buy expensive treasures. I bought two small things to take home with me.

After lunch the Collins—Jack having got back from his tour—came round for us with their car and took us for another delightful round. We started with the tomb of Nizam-ed-Din, a noted holy man in the early days of the Moghuls. It is rather an attractive place, with a curious tank attached to the mosque and tomb, but it is not well kept up and is somewhat encroached upon by a native village.[13] We then went on to the tomb of Humayon, the second of the Great Moghuls, which is a splendid building, close to the river Jamna—a square block of red sandstone with the usual small cupolas at intervals round the roof and at the corners, and a great white dome in the centre.[14] The whole building is very well set and stands in beautifully kept grounds.[15] Close by is a quaint little tomb and mosque in memory of Isa-ed-din, a quiet, peaceful spot standing in a circular lawn surrounded by a high wall.[16] We finished our round by visiting another of the old Delhis—that of Humayon—called Indrapat Parana Kila.[17] It is one of the most attractive places we have seen, as the whole of the enormous space enclosed within the city walls is quite free from buildings and covered with well-mown turf. The mosque, which overlooks the Jumna river, is extremely fine, and the three gates of the city—north, west and south, are very

---

11 The Chandni Chauk (silver street) is a long and imposing avenue that at one time claimed to be the richest street in the world.

12 A tonga (Hind. *tanga*) is a light two-wheeled vehicle usually for four persons drawn by ponies or bullocks.

The ridge was the site of the British base during the siege of Delhi in 1857. It is the last outcrop of the Aravalli hills and rises some sixty feet above the city.

13 Shaykh Nizam ad-Din was a Sufi mystic in the reign of Akbar (1556–1605).

14 The river Jamna is known today as Yamuna.

15 Begun in 1564 by Akbar, son of the listless Humayun (1530–38, 1555–56), the tomb was built by Humayun's widow Begam who lived with him in exile in Persia and who employed as architect Mirak Mirza Ghiyas of Persian extraction.

16 Situated close to Humayun's tomb is the octagonal mausoleum of 'Isa Khan ('Isa ad-Din), a grandee of the time of Sher Khan (1538–55).

17 Indrapat, also called Dinpanah or Parana Qil'a.

handsome and still well preserved.[18] We went back, feeling that we had been shown a very typical and good selection. We dined with the Collins in the evening at Maidens Hotel, and met at dinner the Air Vice-Marshal, Sir E. Ellington and Major-General Godwin.

After dinner Ellington took us up into his room, and showed us some of his very good collection of eastern rugs, some of them were exceedingly beautiful.

We have now finished a thrillingly interesting and very pleasant stay at Delhi. I have seldom visited a place with so many interests, and I only wish we could have stayed a little longer. The hotel is quite comfortable and I can warmly recommend it.

21st December—Monday.

We left at 9:20 a.m. by the Bombay Express for Agra, where we arrived well up to time at 1:20 p.m. We drove straight to our hotel—again the Hotel Cecil—and had lunch. After which we went straight off to see Agra Fort. It is a wonderful pile with a massive outer wall some forty feet in height and surrounded by a moat, which is now dry. The inner wall is about forty feet higher again and encloses a large area in which are the Palace of Akbar and many other buildings. The layout is very similar to that of the Fort at Delhi, but Agra Fort is considerably larger and more massive. It contains the usual Diwan-i-Am, Diwan-i-Khas, Royal Apartments,

---

[18] One of Humayun's earliest undertakings was to build a new city, Dinpanah (World-refuge), containing a magnificent palace and spacious gardens. When the Afghan usurper, Sher Khan (1538–55), seized the throne in 1538, one of his first acts was to raze to the ground Dinpanah and to build a new walled capital on the site, enclosing a citadel known as Parana Qil'a. Only two, not three, gates in the city wall have been preserved, but the massive ramparts of the Parana Qil'a have several well-preserved gateways.

21st December—Monday.

[19] Built by Akbar (1556–1605) under the supervision of Qasim Khan, the palace-fort at Agra is enclosed by massive walls of sandstone filled with rubble and concrete. Many of Akbar's structures were subsequently demolished to make room for the white marble pavilions of Shah Jahan (1628–57), such as the Diwan-i-'Amm (the public audience hall), the Diwan-i-Khass (the private audience hall), and the Muti Masjid (Pearl Mosque). The Zenana (Hind. *Zanana*) quarters were the secluded apartments of the

Zenana quarters, etc., but the gems are the Muti [Masjid] (or Pearl Mosque), the Diwan-i-Khas and the Jasmine Palace (a beautiful little suite of apartments with a balcony overlooking the Jumna river). All these buildings are of marble, carved and inlaid, in contradistinction to the rest of the Fort and buildings which are of red sandstone.[19] After seeing the Fort we drove to the glorious Taj Mahal, arriving as the sun was setting and flooding the building with golden light. As you enter the great arch of the main gate—a fine building of red sandstone inlaid with marble—the wonderful Taj bursts upon your view and literally strikes you speechless. You see it up a lovely vista of water with fountains playing down the centre and cypresses on either side. It is truly one of the great wonders of the world and the Moghul Emperor Shah Jehan has indeed perpetuated the memory of his beloved and beautiful wife, Mumtaz-i-Mahal.[20]

It is square in design, mounted on a great platform, flanked by four beautiful minarets and surmounted by a mighty dome. It is built entirely of pure white marble, relieved by inlay-work, and every square foot is perfect in design and execution. A truly marvellous and magnificent monument, perfectly sited and situated in a beautiful garden.

We stayed there until it was dark when we returned to the hotel for dinner after which we drove down and saw the glorious sight

---

women comparable to the harim of the Arabs.

The Jasmine Palace or Khass Mahall is situated on the east or river side of the palace of Agra and was constructed during the first three years of his reign by Shah Jahan (1628–57) for his consort.

[20] Arjumand Banu, the daughter of Asaf Khan, the richest and most powerful noble in the empire, was married in 1612 to Prince Khurram, the son of the Emperor Jahangiv (1605–27), and the future Emperor Shah Jahan, thus cementing an alliance between this powerful noble and the ruling family. Arjumand Banu was known, among other titles, as Mumtaz Mahall, or ornament of the palace, and the marriage with Shah Jahan was extraordinarily successful. She died on 17 June 1631 in childbirth and was buried first in a garden called Zainabad near Burhanpur but later her remains were removed to Agra to the beautiful tomb prepared for her by Shah Jahan. Seventeen years were required to construct the mausoleum under the supervision of Ustadh ‘Isa.

again by moonlight, when it was even more mysterious and lovely.

Our hotel is of the bungalow type and very pleasant and comfortable, though on the whole I prefer the Hotel Cecil at Delhi.

22nd December—Tuesday.

We hired a car for the day and, after breakfast, we drove off to Fultchpore Sikhri, a distance of twenty-three miles. It is one of the old Moghul capitals, which was built by the Emperor Akbar and was practically never inhabited. Now it stands almost perfect and practically as it was when built in the sixteenth century. The city walls are in existence, enclosing a vast area, but the principal interest centres in the Fort and Palace, which is of much the same character as those of Delhi and Agra, but somewhat more extensive and containing a magnificent mosque. All is built as usual of red sandstone.[21]

We spent the morning there and had an excellent lunch, after which we drove back to Sikandarah, which is about five miles up the Jumna [river] from Agra. There we visited the magnificent tomb of Sultan Akbar, a massive building of curious design, consisting of five decreasing stories one upon the other, the top story being of white marble while all the rest is red sandstone. It stands in a large enclosure, beautifully kept up, surrounded by a wall and entered by four fine gates.[22] We then drove over the Jumna Bridge and visited the Itmad-ed-Dowlah, the tomb of a famous Grand Vizier. It stands on the river bank in a lovely garden and is a perfect little gem in

---

22nd December—Tuesday.

[21] In 1570 the Emperor Akbar (1556–1605) resolved to found a city at Fathpur Sikri, and work was begun at once and pushed on with great rapidity. Fathpur Sikri was occupied as the capital of the empire for only about fifteen years when Akbar went north leaving his fantastic city forever, except for a passing visit in 1601.

[22] Completed in 1612–13 in the reign of Jahangir (1605–27), son and successor of Akbar, the tomb is located in a garden prepared by Akbar at Sikandrah.

[23] I'timad ad-Daula was the title given to Ghiyas Beg, a Persian, by the Emperor Jahangir (1605–27) when he appointed him revenue minister. Ghiyas Beg had previously served the Emperor Akbar, and his daughter married Jahangir in March 1611 while his granddaughter, Arjumand Banu,

white marble, richly carved, and inlaid. The top of the tomb consists of a beautiful little pavilion instead of the usual dome.[23] We then drove back to the hotel, after a brief and fruitless visit to the principal curio-dealer, arriving about 5:30 p.m.

Agra consists of a very squalid and ruinous native city and an extremely extensive European cantonment beautifully laid out with broad avenues, large compounds, and spacious public gardens. One cannot help thinking that a little more thought and money might have been expended on ameliorating conditions in the miserable poorer quarters in the native city. The money expended on unused public gardens would do much!

23rd December—Wednesday.

After breakfast, having packed our luggage and arranged for it to be taken up to the station, we drove to the Agra mosque. It is of the usual type—square courtyard surrounded by cloisters with the covered in shrine on the western side. It stands immediately facing the great fort of Agra and is chiefly remarkable for a magnificent lofty gateway on the south side and for the fine proportions of the shrine and western side of the mosque.[24] We then drove to the curio dealer, Ganeshi Lal, where we spent an hour or so. George in a vain endeavour tried to buy at a suitable price an old silver and Lucknow enamel box on which he has set his affections.[25] It was then time to go to the station where we caught the 1:20 p.m. express to Bombay. The route passes Gwalior, Jhansi, and over the Ghats

---

the future Mumtaz Mahall, married Prince Khurram, the future Shah Jahan, the following year. An able minister and wise friend to two emperors, I'timad ad-Daula died in 1621. His tomb was built near Agra under the direction of his daughter, the Empress Nur Mahall, and completed in 1628.

23rd December—Wednesday.

[24] Begun by Shah Jahan (1628–58) in 1644 but not completed until fourteen years later, the Jami' Masjid of Agra faces the Delhi gate of Agra Fort and stands on a raised platform eleven feet high, reached by flights of steps on the south and east sides.

[25] Ganeshi Lall & Son, The Emporium, Agra, is a well-known firm of jewellers, embroidery manufacturers, and curio dealers established in 1845 and still owned and operated by the family.

mountains and, though slightly longer than the Bombay, Baroda, and Central India route, is more interesting and picturesque especially where it passes over the Ghats. We had been repeatedly warned against train thieves, who are apparently prevalent, but fortunately no untoward incident has befallen us. The Commander-in-Chief's special coach was attached to our train as far as Gwalior where he is to spend Christmas and do a shoot, so we were able to witness his official reception at Gwalior with red carpets, guard of honour, and artillery salute. The Resident and young Maharajah were both at the station to meet him.[26] We reach Bombay (Victoria terminus) tomorrow at 4:30 p.m. so spent the remainder of the day in the train, which is not on the whole so well run as those of the Bombay, Baroda, and Central India Company.[27]

24th December—Thursday.

After an interesting journey, especially while passing over the Ghats (and also while passing Gwalior, where we got a good view of the fine old Fort) we reached Bombay fairly punctually.[28] We sent our luggage on to the Taj Mahal Hotel and did a little final shopping as the shops will be shut tomorrow and on Saturday. I had to buy a new woollen waistcoat to replace my old one, which was unfortunately lost when leaving for Delhi somewhere between the hotel and the station at Bombay. At the hotel I was overjoyed to find two letters from Enid—dated 25th October and 18th November, which caught me after devious wanderings.

---

[26] The Resident, Leslie Maurice Crump; the Maharajah of Gwalior, His Highness Jiwajirao Scindia; and the Commander-in-Chief, Field-Marshal William Riddell Birdwood.

[27] Victoria Station, Bombay, was designed by F. W. Stevens in the Italian Gothic style with certain Oriental modifications. Completed in 1888 at a cost of £300,000, it is an elaborate structure with a large central dome and prolific ornamentation.

24th December—Thursday.

[28] The great fortress of Gwalior is one of the most ancient and renowned strongholds in India. In 1777 the fort became the headquarters of the Scindia family, but in 1844 it was garrisoned by British troops. Restored to the Scindia family in 1853, it was seized by rebels during the mutiny but surrendered to British forces in 1858. In 1886 the fort was once again restored to the Scindia family in exchange for Jhansi.

We had a very pleasant dinner "à quatre" with the Adams, who have a nice flat on the western slopes of Malabar Hill. He was private secretary to George Lloyd, when he was Governor.

25th December–Friday. Christmas Day.

I went to Choral Eucharist at the Cathedral [of St. Thomas] at 8:30 a.m. There were crowds of communicants, and also at the 7:00 a.m. there were large numbers who I met coming out as I went in. It was a very nice service on good Catholic lines but without any very extreme ritual.

After breakfast George and I went for a stroll all round the native bazaars, which were very interesting, but not greatly different from the bazaars at Cairo, Damascus, or Baghdad except that the language was not Arabic.

We lunched at the very comfortable, even luxurious, Bombay Yacht Club with Mr. Percival–the Secretary, Legal Department, Bombay Government.[29] His wife is somewhat of an invalid and is in England, but his daughter is with him, and directly I saw her I saw her likeness to the Percival girl in Cairo. On enquiry I found that Percival of Bombay and Percival of Cairo are brothers.[30] We therefore had much in common. At 4:30 p.m. we drove up to Malabar Hill and had tea and a long chat with the Hotsons, who kindly sent us back to the hotel in their car. We dined at Malabar Hill with the Bishop of Bombay and Mrs. Palmer, driving up in Percival's car,

---

25th December–Friday.

29 Yachting and boat racing have been held at Bombay since the early nineteenth century. At first the Racing Committee met informally at the P. & O. offices in Bruce Street or the Apollo Bandar Refreshment Rooms, or even in the Sailors' Home. In 1876 Queen Victoria permitted the club to assume the title the "Royal Bombay Yacht Club" and in 1880 a clubhouse was designed by Mr. John Adams and was constructed on the site of the Wellington Reclamation leased from the Bombay Port Trust. A large addition was completed in 1883. In 1897 a block of residential chambers was added, located on the south side of the Apollo Bandar Road, the first two floors of which were converted into a clubhouse in 1948 after the lease on the Wellington Reclamation expired.

30 Philip Edward Percival of the Bombay Establishment; and his brother John Hope Percival, Judicial Adviser to the government of Egypt.

which they had very considerately placed at our disposal. We had a very pleasant evening dining with Bishop of Bombay and then called for the Percivals, who were dining near by. They were off that night to Poona, and thence to Mahableshwar, so we drove them to the station in their car and then returned to the hotel, where we found a rather rowdy dance in full swing—in which we did not participate. How I have missed Christmas with Enid and the Children!

26th December—Saturday.

After breakfast we packed in leisurely fashion and went on board the P. & O. *Razmak* at 11:00 a.m. We found that our cabins were quite excellent and the ship thoroughly comfortable. About noon the Hotsons arrived to see us off, and I gave him my copy of the Ibn Sa'ud report in order that he may take extracts and send it back to me by next mail. The native press have got hold of my mission and are trying to make capital out of it, publishing absolutely fake accounts of the results and making out that Ibn Sa'ud has sold himself and his country to the British. The Government of India, therefore, want to be in a position to publish the true facts.[31] We sailed at 1:00 p.m., and we had a wonderful view of Bombay as we steamed away from the shores of India.

26th December—Saturday.

[31] For instance the remarks of Mr. Syed Habib Shah, member of the Hijaz deputation of Jamiati Khuddam al-Haramain, who was reported in *The Bengalee* of Calcutta of Thursday, 31 December 1925, p. 5, col. 2, to have said in Bombay the day before the departure of the Clayton mission: "it is now proven beyond doubt that in 1914 Ibn Saud entered into an agreement with the British, a non-Moslem power which reduced him to the status of a mere puppet in his [sic] hands. Nejd is an inseparable part of Jaziratul Arab [the Arabian Peninsula] and this action of Ibn Saud is therefore against the last wish of the Holy Prophet. Further according to Reuter and Arabic papers, Ibn Saud after a conference with the British envoy Sir Gilbert Clayton has agreed to the delimitation of boundaries [for] Nejd, Mesopotamia, Hedjaz and Palestine. This means he has agreed to the non-Moslem control of these inseparable parts of the Jaziratul Arab and this cannot but perturb Moslems."

PART II

Mission to the Imam Yahya

Introduction

When Sir Gilbert Clayton set out for San'a' in January 1926, the Yemen was, as it remains today, a wild and remote upland country with precipitous mountains and deep valleys whose inhabitants had inherited all the separatism and independence traditionally associated with mountain people. Although Muslims, the Yemenis were divided between the Sunnis, who occupied the coastal lowlands (the Tihamah), and the Zaydis, a Shiite sect, who controlled the highlands of the interior. Although the Zaydi Imams had, on occasion, imposed their authority over much of the Yemen, their rule was continually challenged by family and tribal loyalties that cut across religious lines. Although preferring to be left alone, the Yemenis have long been subjected to invaders who played upon local rivalries and capitalized on religious and tribal animosities. Indeed the history of the Yemen is hardly ever free from alien overrule, let alone united against it, while the internal rule of the Imams appears designed to drive historians to despair and the passionate followers of oriental intrigue to delight.

At the end of the nineteenth century, affairs in the Yemen were like those at the end of the sixteenth. The Turks, who had captured San'a' for the second time in 1871 and had sought to reestablish their control throughout the country, had, as they had done before, alienated the tribes and estranged the townspeople. When the pious Imam Muhsin, whom the Turks had retained as a figurehead, died in 1891, the dissident elements in the Yemen rallied around his successor, Muhammad ibn Yahya Hamid ad-Din, known as Muhammad al-Mansur, and a general revolt erupted against Turkish rule. As had been characteristic of Yemeni history, neither the invaders nor the inhabitants were able to claim total victory. The Turks held the towns; the forces of the Imam, the countryside. But the Imam Muhammad was not solely concerned with the struggle against the Turks. Like other Imams before him he sought to regenerate the Imamate by making it hereditary and to strengthen it by marriage alliances with the powerful tribes. Thus when Muhammad al-Mansur died in 1904, his son, Yahya, succeeded him and was supported by the Bakil and Hashid tribal confederations, the latter of which he was tied to by marriage. Yahya took the title *Al Mutawakkil 'ala Allah*, "the Relier on God," quickly consolidated his control of the Imamate against the inevitable rival claimants, and then rejuvenated the revolt against the Turks.

The revolt was inconclusive. The Imamic forces besieged San'a' and, after much suffering on the part of the population, captured it only to lose the city again to the Turks in September 1905. Thereafter, the revolution degenerated into a weary, desultory affair consisting of raids and counterraids punctuated by periods of peaceful intrigue. The Sultan of Turkey made several attempts to come to agreement with the Imam but to no avail, for Yahya insisted on greater autonomy than the Turks were willing to concede. So the revolution continued, at least officially, for in practice the countryside which the Imam controlled was too exhausted to sustain the fighting, while in the towns the Turkish governor, Hasan Tahsin Pasha, unofficially conceded many of the Imam's terms and quietly sought to improve relations with him.

In 1910 Muhammad 'Ali Pasha replaced the more sensible and benevolent Hasan Tahsin. His harsh measures soon destroyed the fragile fabric of cooperation that his predecessor had woven with the Imam's supporters, and by 1911 active hostilities broke out once again. Yahya sallied forth from the traditional capital and stronghold of the Zaydi Imams, Sa'dah, with 150,000 tribesmen equipped with artillery. Once again San'a' was besieged. Once again it was rescued by a Turkish relief column which fought its way from the coast over the high passes to the capital. Once again the Turks reverted to a policy of cooperation with the Imam, and in 1911 an agreement was signed to last for ten years. The country was divided into two administrative regions, the Imam appointing the officials in the Zaydi districts, the Turks retaining control in the areas, mostly in the lowlands, inhabited by the more orthodox Sunnis of the Shafi'i and Hanafi rites.

Although the agreement was a sensible compromise to a hopeless situation and was in fact loyally observed by both parties, the peace did tend to undermine the Imam's authority among his own people. Not only had his position been weakened by the release of Sunni hostages, but many of his own tribal followers were clearly dissatisfied with anything less than total victory and were disgusted with the Imam for accepting a compromise solution. But Yahya remained faithful to the Turks, and at the outbreak of the First World War did not capitalize on Turkish involvement to seek gains in the Yemen. In fact the Imam was alarmed by the revolt of Sayyid Muhammad al-Idrisi in 'Asir against the Turks, whom he preferred to the Idrisi, and was prepared to make common cause with the Turks against the Idrisi and their British allies. The Turks themselves had some 14,000 troops in the Yemen, and in the summer of 1915 they crossed the Aden Protectorate frontier, occupied Lahij, and drove all the way to Shaykh 'Uthman before British Indian forces repulsed them. Both sides then settled down to await events, and a virtual stalemate lasted, with the Turks garrisoned at Lahij and the British entrenched at Aden, until the collapse of Turkey in 1918. After the armistice of Mudros, the Turks evacuated Yemen and the occupied parts of the Aden Protectorate, but they left behind in San'a' some 200 officials to facilitate the transfer of government to the Imam.

Under the guidance of Mahmud Bey Nadim and Raghib Bey, Yahya organized a government with Western institutions, including a prime minister, a cabinet, and a secretary. The Turks also modernized the army, providing uniforms and arms, and established a military college at San'a' to train officers. But beneath the facade of modernization the Imam Yahya himself was the real government.

> Yahya was a remarkable man, as was evidenced by his ability to rule such a country. His power was founded in Zeidi zeal, the native pride of the Yemeni mountaineer and in long isolation from outside influence.
>
> The Imam exemplified these things: he was pious and orthodox, secure in the prestige of two lineages, one ancient and native, that

from the Tubbas of Himyar, and one sacred, that from the Prophet. No ruler of importance could have so personified isolation. He had never been out of his country, nor seen the sea; he had always lived in the highlands. Nevertheless, he attracted much respect in the Arab world of the 1920's, not only for his ancient lineage and his reputation for piety and religious knowledge, but mainly because of his uncompromising stand for Arab independence.[1]

This then was the man with whom the British authorities in Aden had to establish relations, for after the Turkish withdrawal there was no one of comparable stature with whom to negotiate. British recognition would, of course, tend to strengthen the Imam's rule in areas where the Zaydis were traditionally weak, for although the Turks had handed over their administration to Yahya, that was no guarantee that his Sunni rivals would acknowledge his authority. Indeed, when Lieutenant-Colonel Harold F. Jacob, the First Assistant Resident at Aden, set out from Al-Hudaydah in August 1919 to negotiate an agreement with Yahya at San'a', he was detained for four months at Bajil by the Quhra tribe and then sent back to the coast. The Imam was powerless to intervene. Nevertheless, he gradually extended his control into the Tihamah by appointing Zaydi officials in the important towns; and when the British withdrew from Al-Hudaydah in 1921, leaving it in the hands of the Idrisi, Yahya took advantage of Idrisi weakness following the death of Sayyid Muhammad al-Idrisi to seize that strategic port and all the coastal region as far north as Maydi in 1925. Moreover, he sent officials and armed forces to take over certain parts of the Aden Protectorate that had previously been occupied by the Turks and refused to accept the Anglo-Turkish boundary, reasserting the historic but illusive claim of the Imams to all of southwest Arabia. Here indeed was a claim that the British authorities at Aden could not ignore and sought the Imam to disavow in subsequent negotiations.

Relations between Britain and the Yemen go back to 1609 when the East India Company's ship *Ascension* stopped at Aden and Mocha to establish trade relations. The ship's factor, John Jourdain, even reached San'a' but failed to open any commercial ties. Nor was

[1] William Harold Ingrams, *The Yemen* . . . (London, 1963), pp. 63–64.

a subsequent attempt any more successful, and it was not until 1612 when three English ships visited Mocha that the East India Company was permitted to trade freely. Cooperation between British and Yemeni merchants followed, and in 1618 Captain Shilling was allowed to erect a factory to facilitate the growing trade. The British merchants remained aloof from the political intrigue and struggles that dominated Yemeni history, dealt honestly with the local traders, and thereby prospered. By the mid-eighteenth century the East India Company controlled a preponderant share of the Mocha coffee trade, but the British government was indifferent, appearing to have had no imperial interest in southwest Arabia. In 1798 Napoleon destroyed the British government's detachment toward the lands bordering the Red and the Arabian seas. By invading Egypt, Napoleon directly threatened British overland and maritime communications with India and the East, and in 1799 British forces were rushed to the town of Aden and to the island of Perim in the Straits of Bab al-Mandab. Within a few months, when Napoleon's army became absorbed in Egypt and the larger danger passed, the troops were withdrawn, but British ships continued to call at southwest Arabian ports with increasing frequency. They were welcomed all along the coast, and the Imam even permitted the British naval authorities to establish a hospital at Mocha. Seeking to conclude even more formal arrangements, the East India Company sent Sir Home Popham to the Yemen in 1802, but he never reached San'a' and his mission failed.

British interests in Arabia shifted in the nineteenth century and with them British relations with the Yemen. Coffee, the principal export, was now more readily available from more accessible sources. Consequently, the British trade at Mocha, which had flourished for two centuries to the mutual benefit of British merchants and the Imam alike, declined and in later years all but disappeared. But while purely commercial interests decayed, the revolution in maritime transport revived the concern of the British government in southwest Arabia. The introduction of the steamship required the acquisition by the government, not just by trading companies, of coaling stations. Originally, Sirah Island, Mukalla, and even Socotra Island were considered as possible sites, but Aden was eventually accepted when Captain Haines of the Indian Navy seized the town in January 1839 as compensation for an attack made in 1837 on the crew and passengers of a British ship by the forces of the 'Abdali Sultan of Lahij. Between 1839 and 1857 the Sultan attempted to recapture the town on four occasions, but each time he was defeated. He remained implacably hostile, however, and it was not until his death in 1863 that his son, Fadl ibn Muhsin, succeeded to the Sultanate and sought to improve relations with his neighbors. On his part the Sultan of Lahij reconciled himself to the loss of Aden, while the British on theirs paid him a subsidy and supported him against Turkish encroachment.

Aden itself developed rapidly in the nineteenth century. As a principal coaling station and port of call the town expanded from a derelict village of a few hundred inhabitants to a prosperous city populated by Hindus, Somalis, Persians, and others in addition to the original Arabs. It soon replaced Mocha as the chief port of southwest Arabia, and the opening of the Suez Canal transformed Aden into a vital link in imperial communications. The ever-increasing maritime and mercantile activity required expansion. In 1869 Little Aden was purchased from the 'Aqrabi Sultan, and in 1882 the Sultan of Lahij sold the town of Shaykh 'Uthman to the British authorities. But as Aden increased in size and importance, her influence clashed with Turkish expansion south from the Yemen highlands, and throughout the last quarter of the nineteenth century Anglo-Turkish relations steadily deteriorated. The Turks, on the one hand, revived the claims of the Imam to those territories south of the highlands on the coast of the Arabian Sea, while the British, on the other, sought to check the Turkish advance by concluding a spate of treaties with the hinterland tribes. The more tribes to which Britain promised protection, however, the more she was drawn into the interior where incidents with the Turks became increasingly frequent. Finally, following an affair involving the Humar tribe in the Turkish sphere and the Haushabi tribe in the British, an Anglo-Turkish commission met at Ad-Dali' in 1902; and after many difficulties the boundary between the Yemen and the British sphere was

[2] Foreign Office to Lord Lloyd for Sir Gilbert Clayton, Tel. No. 279, 18 November 1925, C.P.

agreed upon in May 1904 and eventually ratified in 1914 by an Anglo-Turkish convention.

Following the Turkish withdrawal from the Yemen after the First World War, the British authorities hoped that the Imam would begin his relations with Aden where the Turks had left off. They were soon disillusioned. First, Lieutenant-Colonel Jacob was detained at Bajil in 1919 and never reached San'a'. Then the Resident at Aden sought to arrange an agreement with Yahya by an exchange of letters; but negotiations were not only dragged out by the sheer difficulty of communications, but for a long time interrupted by the Imam's indignation at the British leaving Al-Hudaydah in the hands of the Idrisi following their withdrawal in 1921.[2] By 1923 the negotiations were once more progressing and on 23 October Yahya sent a counterdraft to earlier British proposals. This was studied by the authorities at Aden and London and attempts were made to meet the Imam's complaints. They were embodied in a revised draft and sent to San'a' in August 1924. Yahya replied in October that the British revised draft was not entirely satisfactory and throughout the winter and spring of 1924–25 communications moved slowly back and forth between Aden and San'a' in an attempt to clarify the meaning of the British draft and to find a formula to meet the Imam's objections. This procedure soon proved utterly futile. The language difficulties, the problems of communication, and the military actions of the Imam's forces in the interim all combined to entangle the additional drafts and counterdrafts in ambiguity and misunderstanding. At last Yahya requested that the British send a suitable representative to San'a' for the purpose of "clearing up of a few outstanding points."[3]

The British government was delighted to send a plenipotentiary who would hopefully settle this interminable affair, for conditions on the Aden-Yemeni frontier had steadily deteriorated as the Imam's forces consolidated their control in areas south of the former Anglo-Turkish boundary. The Aden authorities had met military encroachments with air attacks, but "this action has not proved entirely successful and His Majesty's Government are anxious to use every

[3] *Ibid.*

effort to establish permanent conditions in the hinterland to Aden without recourse to armed force."[4] Sir Gilbert Clayton was at once asked if he would go to San'a'. He was an experienced and successful negotiator. He knew the Arabs, and he was already in the area within easy reach of Aden. Clayton accepted the mission and set out with George Antonius for San'a', traveling via Bombay, Delhi, and Aden.

Although the authorities in London felt that all Clayton had to do was clear up "a few outstanding points," the Resident at Aden, Major-General Sir John Henry Stewart, was not so sure, and he warned Clayton in December that the negotiations "will be far from an easy task."[5] Stewart was, of course, right and the authorities in London quite wrong. Upon studying the files at Aden and the Imam's letters to the Resident, it became abundantly clear to Clayton that the positions of Britain and the Imam Yahya regarding southwest Arabia were virtually irreconcilable. The Imam Yahya was determined that all the Yemen, including Aden, should be under Zaydi rule. This was a religious conviction more than a political policy, for since only the descendants of the Prophet through Fatima and 'Ali were his lawful successors, there could be no other suzerain except the Zaydi Imam. Moreover, history had confirmed this belief since the Imamate, established at Sa'dah in 885, had not only survived but a thousand years afterward had emerged triumphant. The invaders were gone, the rebels crushed, and the dissidents silenced. The final mission of the Imam Yahya was simply to insist that his position, his "thousand years' possession," be recognized throughout the Yemen; and to the Imam Yahya the historic Yemen embraced all of southwest Arabia, including Aden. Stretching from the shores of the Arabian Sea north to 'Asir and from the Tihamah to the Empty Quarter, the historic Yemen was not merely the high uplands, but the coastal regions as well. Given his sense of history and his deep religious convictions, the Imam could hardly recognize the Anglo-Turkish boundary of 1904 which to him and his followers had little meaning and even less validity. The British authorities, of course, could not accept this claim, but they misjudged the fervor

[4] *Ibid.*

[5] Stewart to Clayton, 5 December 1925, C.P.

with which it was held. They were prepared to recognize the independence of the Imam but insisted that in return Yahya recognize the Aden-Yemeni frontier demarcated in 1904, and the treaties Britain had made with the Protectorate chiefs who had freed themselves from Zaydi overlordship. This no Zaydi Imam would be likely to do.

Clayton understood the respective positions of Britain and the Imam while at Aden, but not even he really gauged the intensity of the historic claims until he reached San'a'. By that time it was too late. His instructions had been framed in ignorance of the realities at San'a', while subsequent events had robbed him of nearly all the bargaining powers he had hoped to employ to reconcile the conflicting views of the British government and the Imam. Clayton's instructions were drawn up on the basis of the draft of August 1924. Since that time, however, conditions in the Yemen had changed dramatically.

> A prominent factor in the situation was the proposal to induce the Idrisi, by means of persuasion and a grant of money, to relinquish Hodeida, which was then to be handed over to the Imam as a *quid pro quo* for his recognition of the Protectorate boundary and his withdrawal from the districts which he had occupied in the Aden Protectorate.[6]

The Imam had already frustrated this arrangement by capturing Al-Hudaydah and the Tihamah in 1925, thus eliminating one of the principal diplomatic weapons that Clayton was expected to use to reach agreement. Moreover, during the early stages of the negotiations the British authorities had held out hope of a subsidy to the Imam if an agreement was concluded, but the termination of the subsidies to the Arabs in 1924 robbed Clayton of the bait of British gold to tempt Yahya to come to terms. Even the Idrisi, whose prewar revolt had propelled Yahya into cooperation with the Turks, were no longer a sufficient threat to make the Imam want to seek an accommodation with Great Britain.

> I therefore found myself in the position, in the light of the in-

[6] "Report . . . San'a'," p. 7.

> structions contained in your telegram of the 24th December 1925, of having to face the Imam with what amounts to an ultimatum in regard to the Protectorate boundary, without being able to offer any compensating advantage which would incline him to accept a proposal to which he is strongly opposed as being a renunciation of what he considers his rightful claims and also a serious blow to his personal prestige.[7]

Clayton was thus left little with which to bargain. He could appeal to the advantage of British friendship, but such arguments were likely to be lost on Yahya who knew little of the outside world. Or he could quietly but firmly threaten the Imam with the dire consequences of armed hostilities against British might, but even this argument could hardly have moved him. During the First World War he had seen the contemptible Turks easily besiege Aden for three years, while he himself had led a successful revolt against the Turks and had even occupied some of the territory they had seized in the Aden Protectorate from which the British forces had failed to turn him out. Of even greater importance, however, the influential chiefs and religious leaders were equally ignorant of the world beyond Arabia and were even more militant against British claims in the Aden than the Imam, without possessing any of his instinctive political sense. Even if the Imam could accept an agreement if appropriate solutions were found to his objections, there was no guarantee that he would be able to override the bias and xenophobia of his followers.

Possessing no diplomatic advantage and armed with but a few weak arguments to counter the Imam's claims, Sir Gilbert Clayton set out for San'a' with little confidence that his instructions would meet the realities of the situation and even less hope for the success of his mission.

[7] *Ibid*.

CHAPTER 6

From Bombay to Hodeida:
27 December 1925–17 January 1926

27th December–Sunday.

We were at sea all day. The weather is perfect and the passengers are few but just sufficient not to make it lonely. I am sitting at the captain's table, but he is in bed, unfortunately, with a bad bronchial cold.[1] A nice old Scotch couple, by name Tannahill, are also at the table. He is a Calcutta merchant and a native of Ayrshire. There is also a nice fellow called [Sir Ernest] Miller, who is the representative of the Asiatic Petroleum Company in Bombay and who served through the war in the Scots Guards. The beauty of the ship is a Mrs. Sampson–pretty and extremely smart. She is going home to be operated on for appendicitis, but the journey to Bombay has upset her and she seems in rather a serious way. No service today as the Captain is ill.

28th December–Monday.

At sea all day. No incidents. The ship is first-rate. Attendance and cooking both excellent. There is a Mrs. Fell on board. Her husband was on the Staff at Alexandria in 1919 and 1920. He came to see her off and introduced me, but I remember meeting her in Khartoum in 1912. She was there as a tourist and was a friend of Lady Asser, of whom she is also a fellow countrywoman. There is no one else on board of any particular interest as far as I can tell.

27th December–Sunday.

[1] Captain E. C. Miller.

29th December—Tuesday.

At sea all day. Run both today and yesterday was 422 miles, so we are doing well. Weather still lovely, though a bit hot and sticky. Wrote Enid and chicks, Dad, George Lloyd.[2]

30th December—Wednesday.

We arrived at Aden at 1:00 p.m. after a very comfortable journey. I cannot speak too highly of the attendance, food, accommodation, and general comfort on board the *Razmak*. The Commander, Captain Miller, at whose table I sat, was confined to his quarters most of the voyage with a bad bronchial cold, but he was down the last day. I found him very nice and he took me up to his quarters on the last morning and showed me round. We lunched on board, after which the Resident's launch, with one of the Assistant Political Officers, came off to take us ashore. We landed (myself, George Antonius, and Mr. Kaikini—the Indian stenographer whom we secured at Bombay) and drove up to the Residency. The Resident and his wife, General and Mrs. Stewart, are very kindly putting up George and myself, and Kaikini is accommodated at the hotel. I have a charming little bungalow to myself with a roomy verandah all round and a shelter for sleeping on the roof, so I am very comfortable and have every privacy and facility for my work. After tea the Stewarts took us for a motor drive to the Crater, some 6 or 7 miles, where is the principal native residential town and showed us the famous tanks. They are wonderfully constructed to catch every drop of water which may fall and are of very considerable antiquity.[3] We then returned by the back of the peninsula, the road passing at

---

29th December—Tuesday.

[2] Sir Gilbert Clayton's father was Lieutenant-Colonel William Lewis Nicholl Clayton.

30th December—Wednesday.

[3] Although called the old town, the settlement known as the Crater has been largely constructed during the British occupation. Laid out with military regularity, the barracks, bazaars, mosques, and churches are placed in square patterns. At the upper end of the town are the ancient water tanks of pre-Islamic origin. Repaired in 1856, thirteen of them could hold eight million gallons of water obtained after careful damming of the gullies of Jabal Sham-

one point through a long tunnel in the rock to Steamer Point where are the Residency, the port, and the Government offices.[4] Dined at the Residency.

31st December–Thursday.

After breakfast we went down with General Stewart to his office where we had some preliminary discussions and collected various correspondence and files, which it is necessary for us to study before we start on our mission. We also did a little very mild shopping and visited rather an interesting little museum belonging to a Parsee, by name Muncherjee. His exhibits are most from the Aden hinterland, which of course has historical associations going back as far as the Queen of Sheba. After lunch I did some reading up of files and after tea Stewart took us to see a small museum at the Crater, which is run by the Aden Historical Society and contains some quite interesting pieces of old alabaster sculpture, as well as several curious old prints of Aden and maps of Arabia. I then called on the officers' messes of the Royal Scots and the Queen Victoria's Own Corps of Guides both of whom are quartered at the Crater, with small detachments at Steamer Point; after which we drove across the isthmus to the mainland, past the aerodrome of the R.A.F., the golf club, the race course and polo ground, and the extensive Aden Salt Works. The Salt Works are run by an Italian Company who have been in possession for many years and who make a good thing of it, as the percentage of salt is high and conditions are very favourable for evaporation. The water is pumped from pan to pan by means of windmills, a further economy.[5] We drove on as far as Shaikh Oth-

---

san, but the present water supply is drawn by pipe from wells at Shaykh 'Uthman.

[4] The tunnel passes through the Mansuri Hills connecting Crater with the isthmus to Shaykh 'Uthman. Steamer Point is situated in the settlement of At-Tawahi which also contains the business quarter, the offices of the Port of Aden, the Aden Secretariat and the Residency on the southwestern outskirts near Ras Tarshayn.

31st December–Thursday.

[5] The climate and geography of Aden are ideal for the production of salt from evaporated seawater. High, uniform temperature, low rainfall, and strong winds make for rapid evaporation, while the shallow lagoons of Aden

man, the first village outside Aden, and the furthest point of occupation by the Turks during the War. It possesses some gardens and palm groves which are a welcome relief to the general barren view.

1st January, 1926—Friday, New Year's Day.

The offices are shut today, which is kept as a holiday, so I spent the morning reading up files in my room. After tea the Stewarts drove us along the coast to the eastward to a bay where we got out and had a walk along the sands and a pleasant scramble over the rocks. Aden is just a confused mass of tumbled rock thrown up by volcanic action, the highest point being nearly 1800 feet above sea level. The coast is very rocky and indented by bays and reminds one rather of Cornwall or the Channel Islands. I have decided to leave here in the Aden Protectorate steamer, the *Cornwallis*, on the 12th instant, to cruise up the coast as far as Kameran Island and to arrive at Hodeida on the 18th, leaving at once if the Imam has got all arrangements for transport and escort ready for Sanaa.[6]

2nd January—Saturday.

We went to the office in the morning and continued the preparation for our journey, including a visit to the bank to get some more money. An Italian ship arrived, containing a Vice-Admiral so the usual exchange of artillery salutes took place. In the afternoon I went for a walk with Stewart to the Club, after which we watched a football match. The A.D.C., Lieutenant Goble, is married to a very nice young girl—about 19 I should think—and they both live with the Stewarts, so it is quite a nice little family party. The American Consul, Loder Park, called in the afternoon, bringing with him an

---

have a higher salt content than the open sea, and their clay bottoms are impervious. Brine is admitted from the lagoons into large pans where after two months the salt crust is broken up, piled, and left to dry and later stacked or removed to the crushing mill. The first salt works was constructed at Shaykh 'Uthman in 1885 by an Italian firm now called the Aden Salt Works. In 1909 and 1923 two Indian firms began the manufacture of salt, and in 1927 the Little Aden Salt Industrial Company began operations.

1st January, 1926—Friday.

[6] R.I.M.S. *Cornwallis* (ex *Lychnis*) was a convoy sloop of 1290 tons built by Armstrong-Whitworth in June 1917 and presented to the Indian govern-

itinerant inspecting Consul, by name Wilson, who is paying an inspection visit here. The latter struck me as a very nice fellow—quiet, cultured and well-informed.[7] Called on the Royal Artillery Mess.

3rd January—Sunday.

We all went to quite a nice parade service—Matins—at the Garrison Church at 9:30 a.m., after which I did some reading. The home mail arrived in the early afternoon, bringing a welcome batch of letters from Enid, Lenore, Hum Bowman, and a very nicely done Christmas card from dear old Sam.[8] Mr. Ramsay Macdonald was in the P. & O. on a trip to Ceylon.[9] I was told afterwards that when he heard I was here he tried to see me, but unfortunately I was out and it was then too late as the boat was about to leave. I am sorry to have missed him as I should much have liked to meet him. After tea we drove to another bay and had a walk over the sands and rocks, hunting up the various queer shellfish and other marine beasts that abound here.

4th January—Monday.

We went to the office again in the morning for a short time. I have plenty to do reading up all the very voluminous files and making preparations for our trip. We are taking an Indian doctor with us, Lieut. Colonel Irani, I.M.S. I met him this morning and took quite a fancy to him. I think he will do very well. H.M.S. *Calliope*, Captain Brock Birkett, R.N., and *Yarmouth*, Captain Isaacson, R.N., came in during the forenoon and the two Captains came to lunch.[10] They are trooping to China. I remember Brock Birkett in 1919 in Egypt when he took an armed sternwheeler up the Nile to Assuit

---

ment in September 1921 where she served as a R.I.M. training ship.

2nd January—Saturday.

[7] Thomas Murray Wilson.

3rd January—Sunday.

[8] Enid Clayton, Lenore (Ellinor Maria Clayton), Humphrey Bowman, and Sir Gilbert's son Samuel Wittewronge Clayton.

[9] Ramsay MacDonald was traveling to Ceylon for a holiday. He left England on 21 December 1925 and returned on 6 February 1926.

4th January—Monday.

[10] H.M.S. *Calliope* was a light cruiser of 3,750 tons launched at Chatham

during the riots.[11] In the afternoon I walked into the town and called on the American Consuls. There was a large dinner party at the Residency in the evening, followed by a very pleasant dance at which I had a chance of seeing Aden society.

5th January—Tuesday.

I had a bathe before breakfast. They have a nice little sandy cove below the Residency, where a net is put out daily to keep away the sharks which affords excellent bathing. The temperature of the water is perfect at this season. I read up files on the Yemen and Asir all the morning and after lunch. After tea I went for a walk along the beach under the cliffs.

6th January—Wednesday.

I bathed before breakfast. I read up files for a bit after breakfast and then went to the Resident's office. Read after lunch, and after tea went for a walk and watched quite a good local football match. In the evening went to a Fancy Dress dance given by the Staff of the Eastern Telegraph Company, who have a very large station here.

7th January—Thursday.

Read up files after breakfast and then went to the Resident's office where I was vaccinated. Did some reading as usual after lunch and after tea went and watched a football match, after which I went for a stroll and looked in at the service of Benediction at the Roman Catholic Church here. It was extremely well attended. Captain Gordon, R.I.M., Commanding the *Cornwallis*, and Lieut. Col. Lake, formerly commanding the Yemen Infantry, and Lieut. Col. Irani, I.M.S., came to lunch. Dined quietly at the Residency.

Yesterday was mail day for England. I wrote Enid and to mother-in-law.[12] Also to Lenore in answer to her letter to me. It is suggested

---

in 1914 which took part in the Battle of Jutland, 1916. In 1918–19 she was the flagship of Rear-Admiral A. F. Everett and was sold in 1931.

H.M.S. *Yarmouth* was a light cruiser of 5,250 tons built by the London & Glasgow Shipbuilding Co. and launched in April 1911. She served on the China Station in 1914 and took part in the Battle of Jutland 1916. She was sold in July 1929.

[11] During March 1919 nationalist disturbances erupted in Lower Egypt

that Colonel Lake should accompany our mission. He seems an excellent fellow and has a good deal of local experience, so I think I shall take him.

8th January—Friday.

Dear Sammy is eight years old today. I climbed Jebel ShamSham, 1760 feet high and the highest peak in Aden in company with Mrs. Clauder, Mrs. Goble, Mr. Loder Park, the American Consul, Mr. Wilson, the travelling American Consul, and George Antonius. We left the Residency at 5:30 a.m. and drove to the Crater, whence we started our walk at 6:00 a.m. arriving at the summit at 7:50 a.m. Here we remained an hour looking at a glorious view and consuming sandwiches and hard-boiled eggs. The caretaker of the signal station which is on the summit produced an excellent pot of tea. We took 55 minutes to come down and arrived back at the Residency to a late breakfast about 9:30 a.m. Did some reading in the forenoon and after lunch. After tea walked down the town and did some shopping of necessaries for our trip to Sanaa. Dined and had a long chat with Major Reilly, the First Assistant Resident.

9th January—Saturday.

Did some reading after breakfast and then went to the Resident's office, where we had a conference with General Stewart and Major Reilly on general questions connected with our mission. Did some reading and writing after lunch, the Stewarts drove me after tea to Khor Maksar, on the isthmus which joins Aden to the mainland where we had a pleasant walk on the beach. On the way back I had a long talk at the office with Sayed Arabi el Idrisi, the agent of the Idrisi now in Aden. He begged for reconsideration of Government's decision not to give the Idrisi help against the Imam Yahya, basing his arguments on the treaty engagements between H.M.G. and the

---

and quickly spread up the Nile to Asyut where British and other foreign residents were threatened. They all sought refuge in one building where they were defended by a small detachment of Punjabis. They were relieved on the 25th by a column of British forces accompanied up the Nile by an armed gunboat under the command of the then Commander Birkett.

7th January—Thursday.

[12] Elizabeth Montgomery Thorowgood.

Idrisi. It was not easy to answer him, as there is very little doubt that the Idrisi has been to some extent, though perhaps unavoidably, let down.[13] Dined quietly at the Residency.

10th January—Sunday.

Went to Holy Communion at the Aden Garrison Church at 8:00 a.m. A nice service properly done with vestments. We went with the Stewarts to the Parade service at 9:30 a.m. The P. & O. from home came in at 10:00 a.m. and a party of M.P.s visiting India to see the country and stay with various rajahs came up to call at the Residency in the morning. The party consisted of Sir John Bull, Sir Warden Chilcott, Sir John Power and Sir Edward Worthington—under the guidance of Major Barber as Secretary who was formerly in the M.I. and Camel Corps School at Abbassia, and whom I know well as a prominent member of the "Lord Kitchener" Lodge, Cairo.[14] I did some writing and packing after lunch, and after tea walked down to the town and made a few final purchases. The padre (Wormald) came to dine.

11th January—Monday.

We did a little work at the Resident's office after breakfast and at 11:20 a.m. started off to pay a visit to the Sultan of Lahej.[15] The

---

9th January—Saturday.

[13] Under the energetic leadership of Sayyid Muhammad ibn 'Ali al-Idrisi a rebellion broke out against the Turks in 'Asir in 1911. With arms and ammunition supplied by the Italians, who were then fighting the Turks in Libya, the Idrisi managed to gain control of most of 'Asir. At the outbreak of the First World War the British sought to win Idrisi to the side of the Allies and consequently concluded an alliance with him in May 1915. He then launched an offensive against the Turks in the Tihamah in which his forces overran the northern region but failed to capture Al-Luhayyah. Following the war the Wahhabi forces of Ibn Sa'ud conquered 'Asir in 1920 as part of the Hijaz campaign, but Idrisi still controlled the northern Tihamah and the port of Al-Hudaydah which the British had handed over to him after his withdrawal in 1921. The following year Sayyid Muhammad al-Idrisi died, and a civil war ensued between his son, 'Ali al-Idrisi, and his brother, Husayn, for control. In 1925 the Imam Yahya seized the opportunity of this rivalry to seize the Tihamah and Al-Hudaydah, while Ibn Sa'ud capitalized on it to establish a virtual protectorate in 'Asir by recognizing Husayn as a Wahhabi puppet. The British, of course, had no intention of supporting the rival

(narrow gauge) railway line runs to Lahej, a distance of 23 miles, and we set out in a Ford motor trolley. We had a very pleasant ride, past the aerodrome, the R.A.F. cantonments, the barracks of the Aden troop, the golf course and the polo ground, all of which are on the isthmus, then through the salt pans and the village of Shaikh Othman 8 miles from Aden. We arrived at Lahej, a small native town situated in the fork of two wadis, punctually at 12:30 p.m. and were met by a guard of honour, one of the Sultan's myrmidons, and two motor cars. After a drive of only about a quarter of a mile, we reached the Palace, which is quite a handsome stone building built since the war. The Sultan met us at the gateway after we had passed two more guards of honour in rapid succession and were conducted to his reception. The Sultan is an intelligent man with a rather shy but pleasing manner. He would be good looking were it not that his face is badly pitted by smallpox. We had an interesting talk at which assisted the Sultan's brother, an Arab poet and historian of some merit; the Prime Minister, Shaikh Alawi; and the Amir of Dhala, who has now been resident for some years in Aden having been turned out of his dominion by the Imam Yahya.[16] He is one of our hard cases as he was promised protection and support of Government. At 1:30 p.m. lunch was announced, a very good meal

---

claimants against either each other, or Ibn Sa'ud, or the Imam Yahya, and despite past support and treaty arrangements refused the pleas of all claimants for assistance.

10th January—Sunday.

[14] During his service in Khartoum as Wingate's secretary and later as Sudan Agent, Cairo, Clayton was an active and enthusiastic Mason. While a member of the Lord Kitchener Lodge, Cairo, he served as District Grand Standard Bearer and District Grand Director of Ceremonies between 1910 and 1913. He was elected an honorary member of the Lord Kitchener Lodge in 1923 and an honorary member of the Khartoum Lodge in 1927.

Clayton has identified the wrong Bull. Sir John Bull was certainly the Rt. Hon. Sir William Bull, who was the Conservative M.P. for Hammersmith (South), 1918–29, and whose son, Stephen John Bull, was born in 1904 and was later knighted.

11th January—Monday.

[15] Sir 'Abd al-Karim ibn Fadl, 'Abdali Sultan of Lahij.

[16] The Sultan's poet-brother, about whom no further information is avail-

in European style and well cooked. We had some further conversation after lunch and then took our departure, leaving the Lahej station in our motor trolley at 3:10 p.m. and arriving back in Aden at 4:15 p.m. The country en route is bare and unproductive, typical of the Red Sea maritime plain and fit only for habitation by camel and goat-owning tribes. I did a little shopping and then returned to the Residency for tea, devoting the evening to preparations for our departure.

12th January—Tuesday.

Finished my packing after breakfast and then went down to the Resident's office to fix up a few final arrangements and to have a last talk with General Stewart and Major Reilly. Lunched at the Residency and wrote letters afterwards to Enid, Father, John, George Lloyd, the Secretary of the Anglo-Palestine Club and the Director of the American Geographical Society.[17] After tea we drove to the Prince of Wales' jetty, whence we proceeded by launch to the R.I.M.S. *Cornwallis* under Commander Gordon on which we embarked, sailing for Perim at 6:00 p.m. Our mission consists of Sir Gilbert Clayton (Head of the Mission), George Antonius (Secretary), Lieut. Colonel Irani, I.M.S. (Medical Officer), Lieut. Colonel Lake (attached for general duties), Mr. Kaikini (Stenographer), Mohammed Salim (Clerk), Ibn Ruweis (Orderly), a cook, and three servants.[18]

13th January—Wednesday.

Arrived at Perim at 7:00 a.m. after a very smooth and pleasant passage.[19] At 10:00 a.m. we landed and had a walk round the place. It is a lonely, barren spot but better nowadays than formerly as a

---

able, was Ahmed Fadl (2 March). The Amir of Dhala (Ad-Dali') was Nasr ibn Shaif Saif.

12th January—Tuesday.

[17] Enid Clayton; Lieutenant-Colonel William Lewis Nicholl Clayton; John Pilkington Clayton; George Lloyd, Lord Lloyd of Dolobran; Mr. G. Stolar, Secretary of the Anglo Palestine Club (later Secretary of the Palestine Potash Company); and Isaiah Bowman, Director of the American Geographical Society.

considerable number of ships call. Also there is an electric installation for light and fans. I was told that the white population amounts to about thirty men and ten women. The chief recreations are tennis and deep sea fishing. Bathing is also good in a pool carefully protected from sharks which abound. I myself saw three large ones swimming round the ship. We sailed for Kameran at 1:30 p.m. The *Cornwallis* is very comfortable, having been designed and adapted for trooping purposes and for hot weather conditions. She carries six 3-pounders and two 12-pounders.

14th January—Thursday.

At 8:00 a.m. we arrived at Kameran and anchored in the harbour. Kameran is a long, low coral island about 14 miles from North to South and 6 miles from East to West at the widest part. About the centre of the island on the eastern side is a good harbour on which is the little village of Kameran and the large pilgrim quarantine station, capable of accommodating some 5,000 to 6,000 pilgrims in five large compounds. To this station all pilgrims from the East have to come to undergo examination before proceeding to Jeddah and Mecca. The island is low and almost flat with no vegetation whatsoever except a stretch of mangrove swamp at the northern end. It would make an excellent aeroplane base, and the harbour is suitable for submarines. There is water, which is slightly brackish, but the supply for the pilgrims is furnished by two condensers capable of turning out about 80 tons a day. Soon after we arrived the Assistant Resident, Captain Guy Wickham, came on board, and we all went ashore at 10:30 a.m. and had a walk round the quarantine station which is very well equipped and organised. Commander Gordon and I lunched on board H.M.S. *Endeavour* with Commander Geary Hill, R.N., who had come on board the *Cornwallis* to call on me.[20]

---

18 Ibn Ruweis is called Yeslam Ba Ruwais at 1 February.

13th January—Wednesday.

19 Perim (Mayyun) Island is 3½ miles long and about 1,200 yards wide. Perim Port was closed to shipping in 1936 when the Perim Coal Company withdrew from the Island.

14th January—Thursday.

20 H.M.S. *Endeavour* was a survey vessel of 1,280 tons built by Fairfield

The *Endeavour* is a survey ship, which is engaged in surveying and charting the coasts round the island. I decided to remain at Kameran till Saturday, while the *Cornwallis* visits and revictuals the lighthouses at Jabal Teir, Centre Peak, and Abu Ail. She will pick us up again on Saturday afternoon and land us at Hodeida on the morning of Sunday, the 17th, the day on which we told the Imam we would arrive. Wickham has kindly offered to put us up, and I am glad of the chance of a good look at Kameran, which is a place of some strategic importance, and is also always coming to notice in connection with pilgrimage questions. Wickham has a Ford car, and after tea he took us for a drive to the north end of the island, visiting a couple of tiny fishing villages on the coast which are inhabited by pearl fishers. Pearl fishing is a considerable industry all along this coast, but the natives make only a precarious living at it as they are terribly fleeced by the merchants. Dined with Wickham.

15th January—Friday.

Went for a stroll round the harbour before breakfast. Spent the morning writing letters and getting right up to date. In the afternoon played five sets of tennis with Wickham, Paymaster Lieut. Commander Barclay of the *Endeavour*, and Lt. Murcott O.C. Detachment Q.V.O. Corps of Guides. Commander Geary Hill of the *Endeavour* and Murcott of the Guides came to dinner. Wickham had produced a very festive effect with crackers and bon-bons, and we spent a very pleasant evening to the strains of an excellent

---

& Co. and launched in March 1912. She was employed in survey duties in the eastern Mediterranean, West Coast of Africa, Red Sea, Syrian coast, and in 1939 in Australian waters. In 1941 she was converted to a Boom Defense Depot ship at Singapore and in 1943 was an Accommodation Ship at Suez until sold at Port Said in October 1946.

16th January—Saturday.

[21] In March 1513 Alfonso de Albuquerque, the governor of Portuguese settlements and factories in western India, attacked Aden without success and then sailed into the Red Sea and put in at Kameran Island. Here his forces suffered severely from disease, heat, and bad food, and in August he returned to India. The next Portuguese expedition did not arrive at Kameran until 1517, when they found that the island had been occupied by Mam-

gramophone. In the afternoon the two Moslem quarantine doctors, Drs. Shosan and Naqshabandi, came and called on me. They seemed loyal and intelligent men. Both Indian Moslems and both speak good English.

16th January–Saturday.

During the morning Wickham took us round the little town of Kameran. We visited the Court house, the hospital, the prison, the school, the bazaar, and an old ruined Portuguese fort dating from the time of Albuquerque.[21] We also interviewed various refugees from Jizan, from whom we gleaned a certain amount of information as to the progress of hostilities between the Imam and the Idrisi. It appears that Sayed Ali, the young Idrisi, has been deposed and has now fled to the Farsan Islands, and that his uncle, Sayed Hassan el Idrisi, is at the head of affairs and is making some headway against the Imam's forces. Ibn Sa'ud would seem to be supporting the Idrisites.[22] We lunched at Wickham's and embarked on the *Cornwallis* at 3:30 p.m., anchoring for the night in the outer roads.

17th January–Sunday.

We arrived off Hodeida at 7:00 a.m. and shortly afterwards the British political clerk, Hassan Kanjuni, came off in a dhow to receive us.[23] We sent our kit ashore in the dhow, a distance of about two and a half miles, as the ship could not get in any closer and followed ourselves at 8:30 a.m. in the *Cornwallis* motor launch. On the way we

---

lukes from Egypt two years before who had spent eight months constructing a large fortress. Here the Portuguese remained for three months until their losses from disease and the pestilential climate forced them to abandon the island. Although later Portuguese expeditions put in at Kameran, no attempt was made to occupy it.

[22] When Sayyid Muhammad al-Idrisi died in 1922 his son 'Ali, with the encouragement of Imam Yahya, succeeded his father, but he was deposed two years later by his uncle Husayn (not Hassan). Husayn was supported by Ibn Sa'ud, who had agreed to guarantee his position in 'Asir if, on his death, the region would be annexed to Ibn Sa'ud's domains.

17th January–Sunday.

[23] Dhow (Arabic *daw*): an Arab lateen-rigged vessel of the Indian Ocean.

met a launch containing two Imamic notables the head clerk to the Kaid el Am (Commander in Chief), and the nephew of the Amil (Governor) of Hodeida who were coming out to greet us. We stopped and took them on board the launch, all proceeding on to the landing stage, where a large crowd was assembled to greet us, and a guard of honour of Imamic troops was mounted. Hodeida is very similar in appearance to Jeddah but smaller with large, high houses of white stone, looking quite imposing from the sea but proving ruinous and ill-kept on closer acquaintance. On landing we went to the British Agency, an ornate and spacious house, though in bad repair, where we installed ourselves for the time being, realising that our future movements would be vague and dependent on the vagaries of our hosts. We then repaired to the house of the Kaid el Am, who was somewhat indisposed with fever, and paid our first formal visit. The Kaid (Sayed Abdulla ibn el Wazir) is a fine-looking, intelligent man and made a characteristic picture, seated on a divan with flowing robes and lofty turban. He greeted us very cordially and after the usual exchange of compliments and small-talk, we took our leave. The Kaid was attended by the Amil of Hodeida, Sayed Abdel Kadr, and the Mayor of Hodeida a nice-looking, sumptuously-dressed youth, whose father and grandfather had both been Mayors of Hodeida before him. At midday I received a deputation of British subjects of Hodeida, all of whom are Indian merchants from Bombay. They all expressed loyal sentiments and complained of the difficulty of transacting commercial business under the reactionary regulations necessitated by the strict observance of the Sharia Law which is enforced by the Imam.[24] An Italian doctor–Signor Spagelli–who is working here for the local authorities, also called. He talked no politics, being far too busy complaining of his solitary life and regretting his native town of Milan. After lunch the Amil and several other notables arrived to pay the return call and to bring the excuses of the Kaid el Am, who is suffering from fever and therefore confined to the house. We then went for a

[24] Sharia (Arabic *shari'ah*): the canonical law of Islam.

[25] Lieutenant-Colonel Harold F. Jacob, First Assistant Resident at Aden, led a mission that set out from Al-Hudaydah in August 1919 to negotiate an

walk round the town and through the bazaars, taking tea in the houses of two of the leading Indian merchants. In the evening a number of excellent mules arrived, and after much discussion and argument our baggage departed about 9:00 p.m. for Bajil, the first stage on our journey to Sanaa and the place where Col. Jacob's mission was detained by force for four months in 1919.[25] We leave tomorrow in motor cars, a service of which has been started by one Sayed Ali el Yemeni—a very pleasant man who came and paid me a visit here and who is a well-known contractor of labour in Port Sudan.

---

agreement with the Imam Yahya at San'a'. He was detained at Bajil for four months by the Quhra tribe, over whom the Imam Yahya had no control, and finally was forced to return to Al-Hudaydah.

CHAPTER 7

From Hodeida to Sanaa:

18–24 January 1926

18th January—Monday.

Two cars, the only ones available, started for Bajil at 9:00 a.m. with the clerks and servants and with orders to return for us. We spent the morning writing and interviewing various miscellaneous visitors. After an early lunch we waited patiently for the return of the cars, due at 1:00 p.m., realising that we had entered a land where time is no object and fixed programmes an impossibility. Eventually we got off at 3:00 p.m., assisted by a crowd of onlookers. We passed by the house of the Kaid el Am on whom and on the Amil of Hodeida we paid a farewell call. We then started off in our two cars, the inevitable Fords, over a so-called road which is in reality merely a track over sandy, bush-covered desert with occasional stony patches. The going was not too bad and in just under two hours we reached Bajil, a small village standing in a plain about 1240 feet above sea level.

Bajil is the headquarters of the Quhra tribe, and it was here that Colonel Jacob and his mission to the Imam were kept prisoners by the Quhra Shaikhs for four months in 1919. There was no sign of hostility, however, and the guest house, a very dirty and well-populated house of one room, with a small courtyard, had to some extent been garnished for our reception. A meal had also been prepared, mutton, chicken, and rice for us of which we felt bound to partake. The Amil himself, who is an old man nearing 70 years of age, was sick and did not appear. We found our mules and camels all ready for us, and the escort of 4 mounted men and 16 unmounted men was also paraded under an officer. We elected for obvious reasons to sleep in the courtyard and slept well.

19th January—Tuesday.

Rose early but, as usual, much time and discussion was expended on the sorting of loads, tying them up, and getting them onto the camels. We did not therefore get off until 8:00 a.m. Mules had been provided for us to ride, and I had a very comfortable one with pleasant paces. The chief muleteer, one Hussein—a cheery and hard-working rogue—took peculiar care of me and was seldom absent from my stirrup, no matter how rough and steep the road. Our escort, as regards the infantry, were styled "gendarmerie" and wore the blue shirt and drawers which is the usual uniform of the Imam's troops. They were armed with Turkish Mauser magazine rifles and daggers, and each was provided with a well filled bandolier.[1] Our route followed the course of a wide wadi or river bed. We travelled for the first hour or so in a northeasterly direction and then turned west. After two hours and a half we reached a small hamlet, called Buhah where we rested for three hours and had a light lunch, arrangements for our accommodation under a grass shelter being made by a very capable looking lady who appeared to run the village. We then started off again and reached the village of Obal at about 5:00 p.m., having done about twenty-one miles in the day. Here we found a large shelter with a roof of corrugated zinc, a remnant of the Turkish occupation, which made an excellent shelter for the night, being removed from the mosquitoes and other insects which infest the village. After a scratch dinner we turned in and slept well through a cool night.

20th January—Wednesday.

In the morning the confusion of loading and the delay in getting under way were no less, so we did not start until about 8:15 a.m. although we rose well before dawn. The officer in charge of our

---

19th January—Tuesday.

[1] The escort consisted of forty-four N.C.O.'s and men of the Yemen Army under the command of Sayyid Muhammad al-Muta.

escort is not very efficient. His name is Sayed Mohammed, and his fulldress uniform consists of a neat black frock coat, worn over Arab dress. His equipment is completed by a sword which is carried by one of the soldiers and a black umbrella which he carries himself.

We continued up the valley with the hills round Jebel Milhan behind us and on our right a high ridge, Jebel Dhamar, culminating in the massive block of Jebel Bura. After a pleasant ride alternating between valleys and parklike upland rising fairly rapidly all the way, we reached the village of Hajeila in one and a half hours. Here we stopped for midday and were entertained to lunch by the local Amil in the one stone house in the village, a pleasant two-storied building. There was some delay in starting after lunch as some of the soldiers were lazy and reluctant to move. The Amil, however, dealt with the case by consigning two of them forthwith to prison. Their chains were fastened at once, and we could plainly hear the fetters being hammered on from the room in which we were sitting.

We then got on our way, which led us up a steep gorge, rising sharply all the way. The going was exceedingly bad as our way led up the bed of a mountain torrent and the road was conspicuous by its absence.

The scenery made up for it however. Mighty peaks on either side and quite a wealth of shrub vegetation with occasional terraces on the hillside for the cultivation of the famous Yemen coffee. After about one and a half hours' march we reached what is called the Bab el Khud, Gate of the Mountains, a short, low tunnel formed by the fall of a huge block of rock from the mountain side—a very curious phenomenon.[2] Just inside the "Gate" is a well at which we rested for half an hour and from which we could plainly see the village of Wasil, our destination, perched many feet above us. We then went on up the gorge for a couple of miles after which we turned sharply to our right and climbed right up the mountain side by a steep zig-zag path which consisted chiefly of rocks, sliding stones, and boulders. Three-quarters of an hour brought us to Wasil, a tiny hamlet perched on a pinnacle of rock. There was no

---

20th January—Wednesday.

[2] Bab el Khud (Arabic, *Bab al-Khadd*): "Gate of the Ridge."

accommodation in so small a place, so we bivouacked in the open and spent a delightful night well covered in blankets from the cold and with waterproof sheets over ourselves and our clothes to keep off the very heavy dew. The camels were somewhat delayed by the steepness of the stony road, but in due course we arrived safely. Several of our baggage mules have sore backs or are lame, and as no more mules are available on the way, we have had to fall back on camels, which has slowed down the pace of our baggage column. Hajeila is about 2300 feet above sea level and Wasil 4700 feet, so we have had quite a good climb during our afternoon march.

21st January—Thursday.

After an excellent night we started off rather earlier, the camel men having been given some necessary elementary instruction on the previous evening. We got under way punctually at 7:00 a.m. Our road led us right up the huge range which was towering in front of us. A continual climb up a steep zigzag track, covered with rolling stones and large boulders with, every now and then, a stretch of almost precipitous rock up which the mules clambered with wonderful agility and sureness of foot. Round bluffs, across ravines, in and out, but always upwards we went. The view was magnificent—three sides of us mighty peaks, crowned often by minute fortified villages and gashed by deep ravines, while to the west we could look across a maze of valleys and rocky spurs, away to the plain where Hajeila could be seen, a white speck in the distance with the great mass of Jebel Bura and Jebel Dhamar closing in the view beyond. There are many villages to be seen, all of which are perched on apparently inaccessible crags, and the hillsides, wherever the fall is not quite sheer, are covered with terraces on which coffee is grown with occasional patches of barley, wheat, and vegetables. After about two and a half hours' strenuous marching, much of which we did on foot, we reached the small village of Attara (6200 ft.) where we called a halt for rest and consumed a frugal breakfast of hard-boiled eggs, bread, and tea, which was very welcome as we had started our march on a cup of tea and a biscuit. The village turned out in force, and when we started again we were accompanied by the local drummers who headed the column followed by our escort and a throng of local soldiers and villagers, all singing lustily. After about a mile the local people bade us farewell, and we continued our way, still climbing continuously until about 10:50 a.m. we reached the village of Hajjara. Here our party was reinforced by the best part of the village, and about a mile further on we came upon a large assembly headed by the Amil of Menakha who had come to welcome us. The Amil proved to be a very charming old gentleman, rather deaf, but most kind and cordial. From this point we proceeded to Menakha (about half an hour's ride) accompanied by a throng of some 2000 men of whom 600 or 700 were armed soldiers. All were singing lustily. Our escort bugler blew weird fanfares in rivalry with a trumpeter who had come out from Menakha. Rifles were fired at frequent intervals, and altogether we received a very fine and extremely interesting welcome. We were conducted to a beautifully clean and very comfortable house in Menakha, and after a brief reception with coffee and cigarettes by the Amil and some of the local notables, we were served with a very welcome lunch to which we did full justice. In this country it seems that one's hosts do not appear at the meal. It may be that the reason is that we are foreigners and Christians, but, however that may be, the result is that one can enjoy the meal without being forced to overeat by the dictates of courtesy. After lunch and a short rest we went for a walk accompanied by two of our escort and climbed up to the fort which overlooks the town. From the fort, which contains a gun but which we did not enter in case our motives in so doing might be misinterpreted, we obtained the most magnificient view; to the south over Menakha to the lofty peak of Jebel Shibam, which stands over the town like a huge sentry; to the west down the deep ravine of Wadi Siham to the plain below, with the peaks of Jebel Masar rising sharply on the right; to the north towards the mountain tops of the Kawkeban district; and to the east to the towering range beyond which lies Sanaa and over which we have to pass by way of Mefhak, Sug el Khamis, and Bauan. Our escort and a small retinue of men and boys who had appeared from nowhere were much excited at

---

21st January—Thursday.

[3] Manakhah is a fortified town that has figured much in the history of the Yemen. About 100 miles from Al-Hudaydah and over 70 miles from San'a',

being photographed and also at gazing through my field glasses. I am afraid they were somewhat disappointed, however, when they found that the results of the photography could not be produced immediately. Menakha is a town of some size and was an important military centre in the days of the Turkish rule.[3] It possesses some good stone houses, barracks, a small-arms magazine, and a hospital. The staff of the hospital does not appear to be very efficient judging by the number of people who are crowding round Lt. Col. Irani and asking for medical treatment. The Amil again insisted on feeding us and we had quite a nice dinner cooked in Arab style in the house which had been provided for our private accommodation. The Amil paid us another visit in the evening, and we then retired very readily to bed.

22nd January—Friday.

We rose very early but did not succeed in getting on the move until about 7:30 a.m., being seen off by the Amil and a considerable crowd of villagers. For the first hour and a half our way led down the mountain side by a zigzag apology for a road which was almost incredibly rough and boulder-strewn. It was impossible to ride so we all had to walk, but it was a cool morning with quite a nip in the air so walking was very agreeable. When we reached the bottom of the mountain we halted for half an hour or so and had a frugal breakfast of hard-boiled eggs and tea. We then proceeded, always over a rough and stony road, by continual ascents and descents, until we reached a small way-side hut near a hamlet called Idgz. Here we halted for an hour or so and had a picnic lunch. We went on over similar country, up and down, but always rising on the whole, and at one period passing for some three quarters of a mile through a curious rocky gorge about 50 yards wide with high unscalable rocks on either side. About 2:00 p.m. we reached the small hamlet and military post of Mefhak which stands at some distance to the left of the road perched as usual on a lofty pinnacle of rock. We were met by the Amil who had prepared a room for us in a

---

the town had at this time about a population of 7,000, but its importance has since declined now that traffic between Al-Hudaydah and San'a' passes by way of Madinat al-'Abid.

small house, and also a meal to which we did full justice. He is quite a nice man and is the son of one of the Imam's Ministers, El-Kibsi, who is reputed to be very pro-British. After our meal we went for a walk up a neighbouring crag, whence we got a glorious view of the country round, a confused tumble of rocky hills and deep wadis in the foreground backed by towering mountain ranges punctuated by lofty peaks. We remained there watching the sunset and then went back to our camping ground where we found our camels just arrived. We had a simple dinner off some of the contents of our store-boxes and then turned in. We slept in the open, as the one small room available was not particularly inviting and had a lovely night under the stars in the cold, fresh air. The only drawback was the drenching dew which soaked everything through and through. The country has begun to show more signs of cultivation since we left Wasil, and round Menakha especially there is quite a lot of very well executed terracing all over the hillsides. Unfortunately, however, the crops are all under the ground at this time of the year.

23rd January—Saturday.

We left Mefhak shortly after 7:00 a.m. and marched for two and a half hours to the village of Suq el Khamis which is on the side of the main range which we have to cross to reach Sanaa and which lies at a height of about 7750 ft. above sea level. Our march was a steep, steady climb throughout but the going improved somewhat, as the surface of the old Turkish military road over which we passed had still retained some traces of its former state. We halted for one and a half hours at Suq el Khamis and had our usual breakfast of hard-boiled eggs, bread, and tea. Then on we went, always climbing a steep zigzag path up the side of the mountain, sometimes with a sheer precipice yawning on one side, and with a magnificent panorama unfolding itself below us of deep gorges and rocky valleys backed by towering mountain ranges. Behind us across the valley was the great mass of Jebel Shibam with Menakha perched on the pass just below the topmost peak. The hillsides now showed yet increased cultivation, and wherever the surface was not too precipitous, the mountain sides were skillfully terraced and prepared for coffee, barley, wheat, and other crops. Eventually, we reached the top of the pass just before reaching which we passed the village of Salami on the left faced on the right by the Turkish military post which commands the pass [Ri' as-Salami] itself. Here we made our midday halt for lunch at a height of 9400 feet above sea level and feasted our eyes on one of the finest views I have ever seen for rugged grandeur. We then descended for about ten miles along a fairly good road past the village, stream, and bridge of Bauan to Metna, about 9000 feet above sea level, where we stopped for the night.[4] The village is a tiny one, but they had prepared a meal which we ate in a wee room on the third floor of a small square house which had been devoted to our use. We did not care for the appearance of the room which was only about 9 feet square with one minute window, so we elected to spend the night in the open, and after a weary wait for our camels which had been much delayed by the difficulties of the climb up from Mefhak, we set out our camp beds and turned in. It was bitterly cold, and in spite of sleeping in most of our clothes with all available coverings over us, we had a very wretched night.

24th January—Sunday.

We started at 7:00 a.m. on our final day's march into Sanaa. It was bitterly cold in the early morning and we were so cold in bed at 4:30 a.m. that we had to get up and crouch over a wood fire which George Antonius succeeded in getting lighted. Our road lay along a plateau for seven miles or so when it mounted gradually a rocky hill beyond which lies the broad open valley in which Sanaa is situated. As we reached the rising ground we were met by an escort of about 50 men and an officer, mounted on very nice-looking Arab horses. Shortly afterwards a pair-horse carriage sent specially for me by the Imam arrived, and I got into it with George Antonius. Our progress then became somewhat perilous as the road was very far from good. As we topped the rise and started to zigzag down the other side, the whole valley burst into view with the walled city of Sanaa standing up sharp and clear-cut in the plain below us.

23rd January—Saturday.

[4] Metna, today known as Marih.

It was quite a wonderful sight, and we were all quite thrilled at this sudden and dramatic view of the goal towards which we had been travelling for so long. We had a long descent on to the plain and then a drive of about three miles to the city gate. Just before we reached the gate a dense throng of people assembled, and we passed a guard of honour of a whole battalion of infantry who came quite smartly to the salute. On arrival at the gate we found a Ford car waiting into which we were transferred. We passed through the gate of the outer city, Bab el Yahud, and accompanied by a dense crowd and clouds of dust passed through the Jewish quarter into the Bir el Azam or residential quarter. It was quite an experience driving through the motley throng who were all running to keep up and get a good look at the curious creatures who wear hats—ragged beggars, Yemen soldiery, robed merchants and better-class people, Yemen Jews, furiously galloping horsemen, men on donkeys and camels, masses of children of course, but not a woman to be seen. Lying between the residential quarter and the inner city, which is also surrounded by a wall, is an open space used for parades and ceremonies [Burjit Shirara], and just before reaching this space we stopped at a large, well-built house which had been prepared for our accommodation and into which we were ushered. Another guard of honour was formed up at the entrance and presented arms smartly as I entered. A large crowd remained in the street in front of the house for a long time after we had disappeared. Indeed, many stayed till after dark. We found everything quite nicely arranged, and I was very agreeably surprised, although many things are missing which civilization considers essential, the whole place was spotlessly clean and had evidently been whitewashed afresh throughout. We arrived by 11:30 a.m. and our lunch did not appear for a long, weary time, which passed incredibly slowly as I had had nothing but a cup of cocoa and three biscuits at 5:30 a.m. It was eventually announced about 1:00 p.m. precisely at the same instant as were the Imam's Chief Ministers who had come to pay a call of welcome. Of course, the Ministers had to take precedence over lunch, so they were shown in at once. I was very favourably impressed with them and liked their looks. They were Sayed Abdulla ibn Ibrahim, the Imam's Chief friend and adviser; Sayed el Kibsi, the First Secretary; Ragheb Bey (an ex-Turkish officer, formerly Governor of Hodeida), Chamberlain; and Sayed Abdul Kerim, 3rd Secretary.[5] They did not stay long, but after conveying the Imam's welcome to me, indulging in some polite small-talk and taking coffee and cigarettes, they departed. We then had a much needed meal and felt a good deal better. The remainder of the day was spent in unpacking and settling in, our camels, including those which came straight through from Hodeida, having arrived during the course of the afternoon. Ragheb Bey came round again in the evening to arrange for my first meeting with the Imam. They evidently mean to make rather a show of it and want time for preparation; so eventually it was fixed for 9:00 a.m. the day after tomorrow. To bed at 9:00 p.m. and very glad to get there.

24th January—Sunday.

[5] Abdulla ibn Ibrahim appears on 31 January as "Principal of the Theological College."

CHAPTER 8

Negotiations with the Imam: 25 January–20 February 1926

25th January–Monday.

I thought it advisable and more polite not to go out in the town before having made my call on the Imam. I, therefore, stayed in all day but found plenty to do reading up files and refreshing my memory on all the various matters which have to be discussed. The others went out, however, and had a stroll round the bazaars accompanied by a considerable and interested party of spectators. Ragheb Bey came round in the evening to inform me regarding the programme for tomorrow's reception, and I had quite a useful chat with him, making various points which I know will go straight to the Imam. Ragheb told me that the Imam had very much appreciated my action in not going out today, so I evidently did the right thing. We have most of us got incipient colds, due to the night before last, I suppose. Mine is very mild, so I hope to scotch it.

26th January–Tuesday.

This morning I had my first interview with the Imam in order to present to him my credentials in proper form and with due ceremony. At 9:00 a.m. the Ford car arrived, and I set off with

---

26th January–Tuesday.

[1] The Imam's written reply, in brief, was as follows: "We note the contents of His Majesty's letter with extreme satisfaction and are particularly gratified that His Majesty should have seen fit to send so experienced and tried a person as yourself. . . . We believe in the fullest manner in the good will of His Majesty's Government towards us and in their desire to recognize

George Antonius and Mohammed Salim, the interpreter from Aden. I was dressed in Khaki uniform and George was attired in a frock coat and trousers borrowed for the occasion from Ragheb Bey (the general effect being somewhat spoiled by his having nothing but brown shoes to wear on his feet!). We drove across the open square opposite the house and into the gate of the inner city [Bab as-Sabah], where a guard of honour was posted. Then along a street for about a quarter of a mile, lined with troops on either side. As I passed the troops presented arms and the band played, so it was really quite a fine show. The troops are all dressed in dark blue shirt and drawers and dark blue turban, being armed with Mauser magazine rifles and bandoliers with a Yemeni dagger at the waist, worn right in front of the body. On arrival at the Palace, which is quite an imposing building, we were met by the Chamberlain [Ragheb Bey], and ushered into a pleasant, airy room in which we found the Chief Minister, Kadi Abdulla el Amri, and Sayed Abdulla ibn Ibrahim. After a few minutes the Imam Yahya came in and we were duly presented. The Imam said a few words of welcome, and I then read my letter of credentials in English which was repeated in Arabic by Mohammed Salim. The Chamberlain then read a reply which had been composed and written out by the Imam himself.[1] I then communicated to the Imam the greetings of H.M.G. and expressed their desire for a sure and lasting friendship and cooperation. The Imam replied in a similar strain, and after a further interchange of compliments and pious aspirations the Imam retired. We then had coffee, cigarettes, and some conversation with the Ministers, after which I took my leave and returned to our quarters, again passing through the lines of saluting troops.

The Imam impressed me favourably. He is of middle height and rather inclined to stoutness, rather dark in complexion, with a small beard trimmed in the usual Arab style. He speaks a little thickly,

---

the rights and independence of our nation whose existence, for over one thousand years, has spread itself over all those territories which form its inheritance. . . . You have been invested with wide powers enabling you to establish our clear rights, and we confidently hope you will be successful in your mission. We believe that an Agreement between us will pave the way for friendly sentiments in the Yemen towards Great Britain. . . . We extend

as if his tongue was slightly too large for his mouth. His face is rather full, but not fat and he has, as is usual with Arabs, a nice smile which lights up his face and gives it a very pleasant expression. From first impressions I am led to think that our discussions will be friendly and courteous, and that personal relations will always be good, but that I shall have my work cut out to secure what I want. The Imam, in spite of his pleasant manner, gives me the impression of being very obstinate and tenacious.

After our return to the house, Sayed Mohammed and our escort were paraded and each was given a *douceur*, which I accompanied by a few words of thanks and appreciation. After tea George and I went for a stroll, accompanied by a guard of about ten men which made us feel rather like prisoners. We walked out of the gate [Bab ar-Rum] to the north and walked round through the gardens and cultivation. The Imam has begun already to make difficulties. He insists on having my original letter of credentials. I don't know whether I ought to let him have it, but I have said I will on the day when I sign the treaty, if I succeed in concluding one at all.

27th January—Wednesday.

The Imam accepted my proposal in regard to the letter of credentials and has fixed tomorrow at 9:00 a.m. for our first meeting, so we have had a day to ourselves. George Antonius and I went for a walk through the Jewish quarter after breakfast. There are quite a number of Jews here. They do not appear to be persecuted, but they suffer under certain disabilities as compared with the Arabs. They are chiefly small shopkeepers and merchants or artisans, and most

---

to you a more cordial welcome than is dictated by official custom." "Report by Sir Gilbert Clayton, K.C.M.G., K.B.E., C.B. on His Mission to the Imam of San'a'," Annexure 11, p. 44.

27th January—Wednesday.

[2] Hassan Yahya, like his brother, was a labor contractor who had worked for many years at Port Sudan.

28th January—Thursday.

[3] The Imam opened the conversation by emphasizing the independence of Yemen under the present ruling house for the past 1060 years, and that the occupation by the Turks had been only temporary, since they had been

of the menial duties are carried out by Jews. They are a very distinct type to look at, unmistakably Jewish, and they wear a special dress consisting of blue drawers, and short blue shirt and a blue skull cap. All wear side ringlets.

When we got back from our walk I found Ragheb Bey waiting to see me. He obviously wanted to pump me as to the attitude I was going to take up in the negotiations. I saw no reason for being anything but quite frank with him, as I do not mind who knows my attitude. There are evidently two cliques in the Imam's entourage, both of which wish to take the leading part in the discussions, and I suspect Ragheb of wanting to get in first. After tea George and I went for a walk in the inner city through the Arab bazaars and back round the outside of the city walls. We were accompanied by a large escort as usual and as we went on the crowd of sight-seers who joined on, including swarms of small boys, became so dense that in the narrow streets of the bazaar we were hardly able to move. I do not think that I shall visit the bazaars again. In any case they are very poor and to have seen them once is enough. When we got back we found the brother of Ali el Yemeni (of Port Sudan fame) waiting to see me.[2] He expatiated so keenly on the importance of Kadi Abdulla el Amri that I feel sure he must have been sent by him.

28th January—Thursday.

I had today, my first business talk with the Imam. We all went to the Palace at 9:00 a.m., and I introduced Lake and Irani to him. After a few minutes' conversation they took their leave as did also all the Imam's staff, leaving George Antonius and myself with him

---

thrown out with heavy losses on three separate occasions. The Imam only wished recognition of his rights over an independent Yemen, and assurance that the demands of Great Britain would be acceptable not only to him but to his people. Clayton "assured the Imam that there was no question of His Majesty's Government not recognizing him as a fully independent ruler." Indeed the Draft Treaty of August 1924 over which the Imam and the British Resident at Aden had conducted negotiations clearly recognized that independence, and made provisions "towards securing the tangible results of such recognition in regard to postal and telegraphic communication and like matters of international import." The Imam was pleased to hear such assurances and added that acknowledgment of his historic rights over the

alone. We had nearly two hours' talk, and I found the Imam very pleasant to deal with. He came straight to the point and put his case frankly as I did mine in reply.[3] We came to no agreement, of course, but our conversation has cleared the ground and shown that, as I thought would be the case, his evacuation of the protectorate and admission of the frontier is the only really difficult point at issue. After an afternoon of writing, I went for a walk with George Antonius, passing out through the Jewish quarter, skirting the outer walls of the city on the south side, and returning through the Yemen [Bab al Yaman] Gate and the inner city.

29th January–Friday.

Being Friday, the Imam does not carry out official business, so I was not able to have an interview. He proceeds to midday prayer at the principal mosque in state, in the same way as the Sultan used to do in Constantinople.[4] He goes by the route inside the inner city so we were unable to see him then, but as he returns by the Yemen Gate and round the outside of the walls we were then able to get an excellent, though rather distant, view. First came a crowd of people, then three battalions of infantry marching in fours with bands and bugles, then the Imam's special infantry escort and then the Imam riding in a carriage with one of his sons and escorted by a squadron of mounted men. After the carriage rode more of the Imam's sons and some other notables, then came another two companies of infantry, and finally some artillery. I was not near enough to see exactly what kind the guns were, even through my glasses, but I counted

---

protected tribes in the Aden Protectorate would demonstrate the sincerity of these assurances. Clayton countered at once by emphasizing that there were two fundamental principles which the British government could not abandon–the Aden Protectorate Boundary, and the guarantees to the tribes made by Britain in the various Protectorate Treaties. Britain must honor her obligations. The Imam agreed that honoring pledges was a sacred duty and appreciated Britain's obligation to do so despite the fact that she had established Jews in an Arab country contrary to previous pledges to the Arabs. Clayton ignored the reference to Palestine and confined his remarks to Britain's interests in the Red Sea and the advantages of British friendship. The Imam then thanked Sir Gilbert, whom he had continuously flattered

1 Field howitzer
4 Field guns–of the 15 pr [pounder] type
2 " " –probably Krupp old type
2 Machine guns (pack, on mules)
2 Howitzers (pack)
1 Gun (pack)
6 Apparently 7 pr Krupp (old type) with pack equipment.

All were fully equipped with the proper teams of horses and mules respectively. The animals appeared in good condition and the drivers who were all Arabs sat their animals well and seemed to be well-trained.

It was a very interesting sight, and I was struck by the good bearing of the troops and the orderliness of the parade.

After tea George Antonius and I went for a walk round the Jewish quarter and back by the main Hodeida road.

30th January–Saturday.

I had an interview with the Imam at 9:00 a.m. Matters progressed somewhat, and I spoke plainly to him and told him exactly what the situation was. I think it cleared the air and in the end it was suggested that George Antonius should discuss drafts with one of his advisers. Whether it means that he is weakening or not I cannot say, but I hope that in any case it will mean getting a move on, as at present we are progressing very slowly.[5]

After tea I went for a walk with George, through the city, out at the Yemen Gate, round the eastern end of the city by the citadel and back through the northern quarter. My lumbago, which has

---

throughout the meeting, and fixed a time for their next discussion. "Report . . . San'a," pp. 44–46.

29th January–Friday.

[4] The Jami' al-Kabir or Great Mosque incorporates remains of pre-Islamic buildings and is oblong with little external ornamentation, measuring 214 feet by 197 feet with a small domed Ka'ba in the court. The twin white minarets were completed about 1261.

30th January–Saturday.

[5] The third meeting began by the Imam asking Sir Gilbert if he had come to any conclusions after re-examining matters. Clayton replied that it was up

been rather bad today was not improved by the walk as I had hoped and it was all I could do to get home. We ought to get mail from Hodeida tomorrow some time.

31st January—Sunday.

As the Imam had not yet notified me who had been appointed to carry on discussions with George Antonius, nothing could be done all day. In the evening [Ragheb] Bey came round and informed me officially that the Imam had appointed Sayed Abdulla ibn Ibrahim, Principal of the Theological College, and Kadi Abdulla el Amri, 1st Secretary, and that they would come round tomorrow at 9:00 a.m.

I stayed quiet all day and did not go out, in order to give my lumbago, which has been rather tiresome, a chance. Kaikini—our Indian stenographer—has been in bed for a couple of days with an attack of malaria, but is now well on the mend. Dr. Irani thinks he must have caught it at Obal on the march up. It is a very unhealthy

---

to the Imam to take the necessary step (i.e., abandon his claims over the Protectorate Tribes) which would lead to an agreement and friendly relations with Britain. The Draft Treaty of August 1924, continued Clayton, contained principles that the British government could not abandon, and the choice was clear between a continuation of unsatisfactory relations or friendship with Britain. See Appendix III for text of the draft. The Imam replied by a diffuse and flattering discourse that meant he was not yet ready to talk business, so it was arranged that both he and Clayton would appoint a representative to discuss specific points. "Report . . . San'a," pp. 46–47.

1st February—Monday.

6 Sayyid 'Abd Allah ibn Ibrahim opened the discussion by repeating the Imam's historic rights in southwestern Arabia. George Antonius replied that the question before them was whether the Imam was prepared to agree to the principles of the Draft Treaty of August 1924. Although the Draft Treaty had been presented sixteen months ago, the Imam had given no definite expression of opinion. He thus suggested that the Treaty be examined point by point to discover exactly what were the agreements and the differences. The Qadi 'Abd Allah al-'Amri wished however to negotiate without the Draft Treaty so that "we might approach the question with a clear vision. . . . All that he [the Imam] asked for was the due recognition of his ancient rights over the whole of the Yemen, including Aden." Antonius replied that negotiations would be more fruitful if they concentrated on specific facts rather than historical rights or wrongs. These facts, of course, were Britain's

place and Kaikini slept in the village itself, and not outside like we did. Mohammed Salim also has fever.

1st February—Monday.

George Antonius had a long discussion from 9:00 a.m. to 12 noon with Sayed Abdulla ibn Ibrahim and Kadi Abdulla el Amri, with Ragheb Bey. I opened the meeting and then retired. A certain amount of progress was made towards classifying the situation but no definite result was arrived at. It is going to be an exceedingly difficult business.[6] My lumbago being better, I went for a short walk with George after tea. We sent a mail off to Hodeida, in the hopes of catching the *Cornwallis*, due to call there on the 9th. Yeslam Ba Ruwais and the doctor's servant both have fever.

2nd February—Tuesday.

Another long discussion between George and the Imam's representatives. Again no tangible progress, but these apparently point-

---

position at Aden and her obligations to the Protectorate Tribes. He emphasized Britain's friendly intentions toward Yemen and the tangible benefits of her friendship. Sayyid 'Abd Allah agreed to think these matters over and return the following day. Notes by George Antonius, "Report . . . San'a," pp. 47–48.

2nd February—Tuesday.

[7] The Imam had authorized his representatives to devise some formula to reconcile the differences between both parties, but Sayyid 'Abd Allah ibn Ibrahim and the Qadi 'Abd Allah al-'Amri continued to envelop the discussion in "an opaque tissue of polite generalities that lacked any tangible meaning." George Antonius continued to press the Imam's representatives and finally by producing a copy of the Draft Treaty (see Appendix III) managed to get discussion started on Article 3:

> His Excellency the Imam recognizes the Protectorate Treaties made by His Britannic Majesty's Government with the tribes of the Aden Protectorate as shown in the margin. He undertakes not to send any of his armed forces across the frontier demarcated by the Turkish and British Government in 1904 or to interfere in any way with the peoples inhabiting the Aden side of the boundary line.

The Imam's representatives argued that acceptance of this article meant the signing away of the Imam's rights to the southern Yemen in perpetuity. Antonius replied that this article was the minimum the British government

less and circumlocutory discussions are a necessary preliminary in negotiating with Orientals.[7] George and I went for a walk after tea, through the Arab bazaar to the Citadel [Al Qasr] and home by the north city wall.

3rd February—Wednesday.

George Antonius had another talk with the Imam's representatives this morning. They are still extremely obstinate. At last they consented to put forward, informally and subject to the Imam's approval, a counterdraft to Article 3 of the Draft of August 1924 on which my whole attitude is based. Their counterdraft was quite unacceptable, and they were told so at once. They then retired to think matters over and said that they would come back tomorrow. I shall give them one more chance, but it is clear that I must now see the Imam again myself and have some straight talk with him. I fear that I can't do so till Saturday as he doesn't work on Fridays. I went for a walk round the Jewish quarter with Lake after tea.[8]

Kaikini has recovered and the others are mending, but George has now gone down with fever which is most unfortunate. The weather is cloudy and looks like rain.

4th February—Thursday.

Last night after a dinner a long-delayed mail arrived with two delightful letters from Enid, dated December 30th and January 6th. Also a letter from Lenore [Ellinor Clayton] giving Harpenden news. It was a joy to get a breath of home in this place which seems so peculiarly remote and unreal and gives one the impression of living in a rather unpleasant dream. Our negotiations are dragging

---

would accept. The Imam's representatives replied, after considerable evasive talk, that they would consider the wording by themselves and prepare a counterdraft that they would present on the following day. Notes by Antonius, "Report . . . San'a," pp. 48–49.

3rd February—Wednesday.

[8] The Imam's representatives admitted at once that they had failed to find an appropriate formula, and since the British Mission had more experience in such matters, requested it to produce a draft. Regarding this as simply another evasion, for the British already had produced a Draft Treaty, An-

sadly, owing to the extreme difficulty of getting the Imam to move or of pinning him down to anything. His representatives were to have come round this morning, but they sent a note at the last moment to say that they were not yet ready. That means delay till Saturday, as they won't work on Friday. It is perhaps as well, as George is completely *hors de combat* in bed with fever and has been more or less comatose all day. I hope to goodness he will be all right soon, or we shall be delayed here indefinitely. Went for a walk after tea by myself.

5th February–Friday.

Being Friday no progress was possible as regard negotiations. The Imam paid his usual state visit to the mosque at mid-day. I observe one more battalion of infantry on parade than last week, making four in all. I went for a walk with Lake after tea. Ragheb Bey came in the evening, and I had a chat with him. Irani went to the Palace in the afternoon and attended two of the Imam's sons who are suffering from rheumatism. George is still in bed and quite incapable of doing anything. I looked in on him several times as I did yesterday, but I never succeeded in getting even a wink out of him. I have now written the first part of my report, and also the concluding portion, and it only remains to fill in the middle part in accordance with the result of the negotiations. It may seem rather premature, but the general situation is the same in either event.

6th February–Saturday.

George Antonius has no fever today but is still in bed and quite *hors de combat*, so I had to see the Imam's representatives myself,

---

tonius pressed them for a counterdraft. The representatives replied that they would prepare a counterdraft then and there. After a half hour a counterproposal for Article 3 was handed to Antonius (see Appendix IV). Although Antonius had intended to consult with Sir Gilbert before venturing an opinion on the counterdraft, the proposal was so unacceptable that he informed the Imam's representatives he thought it did not even provide a basis for discussion. He urged the representatives to complete a full counterdraft while he consulted with Sir Gilbert Clayton. Notes by Antonius, "Report . . . San'a," pp. 49–50.

which I did at 9:00 a.m., Mohammed Salim acting as interpreter. They talked all round the point and indulged in generalities for a long time and finally produced a complete counterdraft of the agreement. I received it and closed the interview by saying that I would read it, consider it, and then discuss it with the Imam himself.[9] At 3:00 p.m. I went and paid an unofficial visit to the Imam. We talked on various general subjects and I stayed there about an hour and a half. He was extremely cordial and friendly, but we avoided the subject of the negotiations. After tea I went out for a constitutional with Lake. There have been clouds for some days, and this afternoon there was a thunderstorm accompanied by a sharp shower of rain.

7th February—Sunday.

No meeting today, partly because George Antonius has not yet sufficiently recovered and partly because I do not wish the Imam to think that I have not given full consideration to his draft. I went for a walk with Irani after tea. Spent the rest of the day writing and have everything up to date as far as possible. A stormy day with some rain. The spring rains have begun.

8th February—Monday.

I had requested an interview in the afternoon today as George Antonius did not feel up to one in the morning and I did not wish to rely only on Mohammed Salim, but for some reason the Imam

---

6th February—Saturday.

[9] Sir Gilbert opened the discussion by rejecting the counterdraft of Article 3 and hoping that after three days' deliberation they could put forward proposals that could be used as a basis for discussion. Both of the Imam's representatives replied with long, rambling, and evasive speeches that ended with the presentation of a complete counterdraft (see Appendix V). He hoped that the terms of the counterdraft did not violate the principles of the Draft Treaty. "Report . . . San'a," p. 50.

9th February—Tuesday.

[10] Sir Gilbert informed the Imam that his full counterdraft was quite unacceptable and provided no basis for discussion. Moreover, the points of view of both parties appeared so wide apart that if the counterdraft did represent the view of the Imam, the British mission would have to leave. The Imam

could not give one then. Consequently, another day was wasted. I went for my usual walk after tea. The weather is still unsettled and there was rain over the hills.

9th February—Tuesday.

I had an interview of over two hours with the Imam, starting at 9:00 a.m. I informed him that the draft put up by his advisors was quite unacceptable, and I put the whole case before him again—quite clearly and frankly. I told him that he had now got to choose whether he would meet my view or not, but that in any case I must leave in a week. He showed signs of giving way but still held that his claims were such as he could not possibly renounce. I think that I can find a formula which will meet the requirements of H.M.G. without necessitating any formal renouncement of his claims by the Imam. I shall present him with a draft on these lines tomorrow, as my last word, to take or to leave.[10]

Went for a walk with George after tea. I have fixed the 15th as the day of departure of our party, by the land route to which the Imam agreed.

10th February—Wednesday.

Another long interview with the Imam at the conclusion of which I gave him a formula which I told him represented the utmost advance I could make towards meeting his point of view. He must now either take it or leave it. He was, I think, disappointed that I

---

expressed sincere concern and repeated his desires for friendship. He emphasized the power of public opinion in his country and the belief among his subjects that Aden was an integral part of the Yemen. He would go as far as he could but he could not entirely ignore the strong feelings of his subjects. "To sign away the rights of the Yemen to portions which his people looked upon as of their inheritance was a thing he could not and would not do." Since both sides were anxious for a settlement, he hoped Sir Gilbert could find a suitable formula. Clayton replied that the only hope was to use the Draft Agreement as a basis of discussion, but in any case he would review the whole situation and try to find a practical solution within the next twenty-four hours. Sir Gilbert now had the choice between terminating the negotiations or exceeding his instructions and modifying the Draft Treaty of August 1924. He chose the latter course of action since to terminate discussion

had not gone further, but he admitted that I had done something towards reconciling our conflicting points of view. He asked for twenty-four hours in which to think it over, so I left the draft with him on the understanding that he would give me his answer to-morrow.[11] I wonder if we shall get off on the 15th or 16th. I have serious doubts about it, but I must hope for the best. I have already taken the responsibility of going somewhat beyond my instructions, but I feel convinced that the course I am following is right. George and I went for our usual walk.

11th February—Thursday.

I had another interview with the Imam, at which he expressed himself ready in principle to accept my draft. He raised a very difficult point, however, by declaring his complete inability to withdraw from those districts in the Aden Protectorate in which he had for some years established a regular administration. This was entirely contrary to my instructions and I told him that he seemed to have created a deadlock. I am anxious, however, not to lose the ground already gained and to break off negotiations. I therefore said that I would discuss this particular point with him in two or three days' time and suggested in the meanwhile that we should try and reach agreement on all other points and endeavour to produce a final draft of the treaty acceptable to both sides. The point which he had now raised would then be the only one standing in the way of agreement. The Imam agreed to this proposal and expressed the

---

would certainly have produced passive if not active hostility along the Aden frontier. Sir Gilbert was seeking for a formula that would "suit the existing circumstances and deferring the Imam's claims for future discussion and settlement, without prejudice to the standpoint of either party, secure the Imam's signature to an Agreement which would follow, in other respects, the lines of the Draft of August 1924, and would, for the period of that Agreement, secure the interests which His Majesty's Government were determined to maintain." In other words he hoped to secure the Imam's withdrawal from the Aden Protectorate and his acceptance of the terms of the Draft of August 1924 in return for deferring the question of sovereignty over Aden. "Report . . . San'a," pp. 50–51.

10th February—Wednesday.

[11] Sir Gilbert presented his alternative draft that specifically reserved for future settlement the Imam's claims to suzerainty over certain territories

hope that I should be able to find a way out of the *impasse*. He seems to think that I can do whatever I like, in spite of the fact that I keep telling him that I am bound by my instructions.[12] In the afternoon the Imam's representatives came over and had a long and tiring meeting with George with a view to coming to an agreement regarding the various articles of the draft agreement in detail. They were most obstinate and tiresome, but George handled them splendidly and has, I hope, paved the way for some substantial progress tomorrow when they are coming for another meeting. I went for my usual constitutional with George, after tea.

12th February–Friday.

George had another long meeting with the Imam's representatives after breakfast and succeeded by taking up a very firm attitude in making a good deal of progress and securing their agreement, with the exception of a few points on which I shall have to tackle the Imam direct, to the first twelve articles of the draft agreement. They will continue tomorrow morning, and if they can come to general agreement on all the clauses, I shall then discuss the final text with the Imam. If I can get that settled in accordance with my requirements, I must then try and find a solution of the difficult question of the Imam's withdrawal from occupied territories. I think I may be able to do this if all other points are satisfactorily disposed of. Today being Friday, the Imam paid his usual visit to the mosque escorted by a large concourse of people and by all the troops. He

---

without, however, admitting the validity of his claims (see Appendix VI). Clayton emphasized that this was his final offer. "Report . . . San'a," p. 52.

11th February–Thursday.

12 The Imam opened the meeting by announcing that he could accept Clayton's alternative draft in principle but that "he would prefer the clause about evacuation to be removed from the Treaty and to form the subject of a separate understanding. He would ask for this only in case the proposed Treaty were likely to be published; but if it were to remain a secret treaty, then the clause might be retained in its place." He refused, however, to evacuate the Ad-Dali' region but in deference to the British he would restore the Amir of Ad-Dali' to his amirate. Clayton replied that the Imam's first point presented no difficulty, but his refusal to evacuate Ad-Dali' violated the principles fixed by his government and he could not consent to it. It was

very kindly sent us an invitation to come to a room in the Palace precincts where we were able to see the whole ceremony of his return from the mosque. We were situated on the outer wall of the Palace close above the gate at which he enters, and we had a splendid view of his arrival and down the street up which the whole procession came. We had about half an hour to wait, but the time passed quickly in watching the large and motley crowd of Arabs who were assembled in the street below us to watch the show. A body of some 600 schoolboys was also assembled and drawn up in military fashion to take part in the parade. Then we heard the sound of military bands and bugles, and the city gate [Bab Khuzayma] at the bottom of the street down which we were looking was thrown open to admit the procession. First came the Commander-in-Chief of the Army with his staff followed by about 1500 infantry marching in fours by companies and divided into four battalions. They marched very well to military bands and were wonderfully steady on parade. All were armed with Turkish Mauser Magazine rifles, and they marched with fixed bayonets. Then followed the senior year of the Cadets of the military school also with rifles and fixed bayonets and wearing a special uniform of long blue coats and orange turbans. The infantry were followed by a troop of cavalry after whom came the Imam riding in a pair-horse carriage and accompanied by several of his sons and a crowd of notables and high officials on horseback. In front of the carriage was a small special escort of infantry who danced a war dance all along the route, having drawn daggers and rifles and singing war songs and the praises of the Imam. The procession was com-

---

then agreed that the Imam's representatives would meet with the Imam again on Saturday in an attempt to resolve the question of the evacuation of territories in the Aden Protectorate. "Report . . . San'a," pp. 52–55.

13th February–Saturday.

[13] George Antonius met with the Imam's representatives on Thursday afternoon, and Friday and Saturday morning for the purpose of drafting the terms of an agreement. The principal obstacle was the insistence by the Imam's representatives for some kind of acknowledgment of the Imam's suzerainty over the Aden Proctectorate. "They declared that, in their opinion, Aden and its hinterland belonged to the Yemen, and that they could not consent to any treaty that did not contain some more or less explicit recognition of that fact." Antonius patiently pointed out the extrava-

pleted by the Artillery preceded by a magnificent banner, marching in column of route. They were fully horsed and very fairly well turned out, the horses and mules especially being in first-rate condition. There were eight field guns, two pack howitzers, eight mountain guns, and four machine guns on parade, in addition to one machine gun with each infantry battalion. The Imam then ascended to a balcony over the Palace gate and proceedings terminated by a march past of the whole parade, led by the schoolboys. It was an unique and most interesting show which I am extremely glad to have seen.

In the forenoon a mail arrived with most welcome news from home. (Papers up to 21st January.)

13th February—Saturday.

George spent the morning thrashing out the detailed working of the treaty and succeeded in getting the representatives of the Imam to agree on all points, except five or six which I shall take up with the Imam direct.[13] George and I went for a walk through the city after tea. The people seem gradually to be getting used to us, and we are not accompanied by such throngs as formerly. I fear that there is no chance of our getting away from here before the 18th, which means that we shall just miss the P. & O. of the 3rd of March from Aden.

14th February—Sunday.

We had a long interview with the Imam in the morning, and he

---

gance and futility of this claim and sought to undermine their appeals to history by pointing out that although the Yemen had always resented Turkish domination, the inhabitants had accepted it and had even elected deputies to represent them in Constantinople who had not abstained from taking their seats in the Ottoman Chamber on exactly the same footing as the other representatives from the vilayets of the Ottoman Empire. Indeed, the Imam's present negotiator, Sayyid 'Abd Allah ibn Ibrahim, had been one of those delegates. Thus the historic claims could hardly be pressed beyond the practical state of affairs. After three long sittings a draft was prepared with certain reserved points that were to be discussed between the Imam and Sir Gilbert. On the following day, 14 February, this counterdraft was the subject of negotiations between the Imam and Sir Gilbert. That evening the Imam appeared to agree with practically all the drafts of articles discussed by George with the representatives. He was obstinate in maintaining that he could not sign an English version of the Treaty, but that it must be entirely in Arabic. I cannot admit this of course, but the point can probably be got over. He was also rather *difficile* over the question of recognizing the Protectorate Treaties. On the whole, however, things seemed moving satisfactorily towards agreement.[14]

After leaving the Imam we drove in his Ford car, with a very perilous but cheerful chauffeur, to Raudha which is a sort of summer residential town patronized by the wealthier people of Sanaa, situated about five miles to the north. We were rather disappointed in the place as it was bare and ruinous, having in Turkish times frequently been taken and retaken by the Imam and the Turks. Still we lunched there very pleasantly in a small house belonging to the Imam where we reclined in the shade and watched the play of a very attractive fountain. Some of us tried eating Kat, the tender leaves of a certain shrub, which is the universal minor vice throughout the Yemen and Aden.[15] It had no sort of effect on me beyond giving me rather a bad taste in my mouth for the remainder of the day. On our return to our house in Sanaa, I received from the Imam a draft treaty which he intimated to be his final effort as the result of all our discussions. It was entirely unacceptable in almost every way and leaves us further from a settlement than when we began. It is really exceedingly difficult to deal with men who are conceited, obstinate,

---

sent an official counterdraft treaty to Sir Gilbert. Notes by Antonius, "Report . . . San'a," pp. 53–54.

14th February—Sunday.

[14] The Imam refused to recognize the Protectorate Treaties, arguing that they had been made at a time when he was unable to assert his rights. Furthermore, he asserted he could not recognize the frontier fixed in the Anglo-Turkish Boundary Agreement to which he was not a party. Clayton remained adamant on these points, urging the Imam to reconsider his attitude. As to the language of the final version of the treaty, the Imam was vehemently opposed to any but Arabic which he desired to be the official version. Sir Gilbert thought that he could find a compromise solution. The Imam agreed to drop two other articles, a redundant one emphasizing the independence of the Yemen and one which obliged Britain to repair the submarine cable between Shaykh Sa'id and Perim. (For the second counterdraft

ignorant, and disingenuous all at the same time. Well, it has at least brought matters to a climax and I must see him tomorrow and give him a very straight talking to and an ultimatum.

Shaikh Ali el Yemeni, who has just arrived here, came to see me after dinner. He has been in the Sudan for many years.

15th February—Monday.

I decided to give the Imam one more chance by ignoring his latest draft and resuming my conversations with him at the point where they left off yesterday. This succeeded to the extent that I eventually got into the position, which I wanted, where I could send him a final draft, to take or leave without further discussion. This I shall do tomorrow morning and discussions will then be over. I am afraid, though, that we shall not get off on Thursday but shall be delayed for a day or two longer. However, we have still a few days grace as in any case we cannot catch the P. & O. of the 3rd from Aden, but must wait for that of the 10th. We were not able to take our usual walk in the evening, as we were busy preparing our draft for tomorrow. Dear me! What terribly wearisome work it is, to be sure.[16]

16th February—Tuesday.

Today I was told that the Imam was indisposed and regretted that he could not see me. I shrewdly suspect that his illness is a diplomatic one, designed to gain time. It will be a great nuisance if he employs

---

treaty submitted by the Imam on the evening of 14 February, see Appendix VII.) "Report . . . San'a," pp. 54–55.

[15] Qat is the leaf of a bush, *Catha edulis*, cultivated in the Yemen and Aden. Chewing it produces a mildly narcotic effect from an alkaloid in the leaves not unsimilar to caffein. The chewer becomes lively and loquacious. Big plans are made, which are never executed, and if taken with regularity qat permanently yellows the teeth. The drug is supposed not to be habit-forming.

15th February—Monday.

[16] Ignoring the unacceptable draft sent by the Imam the previous evening, Sir Gilbert continued to discuss the question of the Imam's recognition of the Protectorate Treaties. The Imam himself put forward several formulae, and Clayton decided to prepare his own final draft, warning the Imam that the wording must be such as not to cast any doubt on the present position of

such tactics and so delays our departure. However, as I could not see him personally I sent him my final draft with a letter saying that it was my last word which he must either accept or reject. I could not advance any farther, and further discussion could lead to nothing. We shall see what he will do, but I hope he will be quick. Today we went for a trip to a place about five or six miles away called Hadda where we had our lunch. It is quite a nice little place on the side of a hill with a stream running down the hillside through it. There is also some green about, which is comforting to the sight, as the water allows of some cultivation of crops and there are quite a number of fruit orchards—apricots, peaches, walnuts—though, of course, it is not yet the season for fruit. We drove part of the way in a very ramshackle pair-horse carriage and then rode on mules up the hillside to a spot where a tent had been pitched by the running stream. We spent a very pleasant three hours there, which was a nice change after our somewhat prison-like existence in Sanaa and then returned by the way we came. Ragheb Bey, the Imam's Chamberlain, came with us. He is an ex-Turkish official and he never misses a chance of being with us. I fancy he has very few friends here, and our society is a godsend as he is a gregarious and pleasant soul.

17th February—Wednesday.

I could not get an interview with the Imam as he was still by way of being indisposed. Hence, another day was wasted in most annoying fashion and our departure is again delayed. I sincerely hope that he is not going to continue being sick. However, I hear that during the afternoon he held a large meeting of notables to whom he read out the draft treaty. I am informed that the majority were against having any treaty at all, so I foresee another tiresome interview tomorrow. He is mortally afraid of his people though I think sincerely

---

Great Britain in Aden. The Imam then urged that a clause be inserted in which the British government would punish those tribes who committed aggression upon the Yemen. Sir Gilbert considered this a fair request, and then proposed that the Treaty should be drawn up in parallel columns of English and Arabic and that the Imam would sign below the Arabic column. George Antonius would affix a certificate confirming that the two texts were as identical as possible. "Report . . . San'a," pp. 55–56.

anxious himself for a treaty, and consequently they usually persuade him to go back on questions which he has agreed upon with me.

George and I went for our usual walk in the evening. I hope we shall not have many more now.

18th February—Thursday.

I succeeded in getting an interview with the Imam who has apparently recovered. As I feared, it was a very tiresome one and extremely lengthy, lasting from 9:00 a.m. to 1:45 p.m. We discussed my draft and he raised a number of points, some of which had never come up before. Most of them I was unable to agree to, but some of them consisted of requests for the omission of certain articles which the Imam himself had asked for and which I was not sorry to drop out. Eventually I said that I would make such amendments to my draft as I found possible and would send a revised and final copy to him that evening. We also discussed the question of the districts of which he was in actual occupation, within the borders of the Aden Protectorate and from which he had definitely refused to withdraw. He maintained his refusal and I maintained the view of H.M.G. that his withdrawal was a necessary corollary to the conclusion of a treaty. I told him, however, that I would not refuse to sign on account of this conflict of views, provided it was understood that the ratification of the treaty by H.M.G. would depend on their attitude in this question. In the meantime, I asked him to send me a detailed list of the districts from which he refused to withdraw. I think that we shall break on this question, and I shan't be very sorry.[17] We were all invited to lunch with Shaikh Ali el Yemeni, the Sudan contractor, who is up here on a visit to his home. He has a very nice house and garden, and some good horses. He gave us an enormous but quite edible lunch.

18th February—Thursday.

[17] At this long and important meeting Sir Gilbert agreed to alter his draft yet again to meet certain objections that had been raised at the large meeting of notables assembled the previous day by the Imam to discuss Clayton's draft. Despite this conciliatory attitude the Imam refused to evacuate those districts in the Aden where he had established regular administration. Sir Gilbert requested that a list of such districts be submitted to him. (For the

19th February—Friday.

There was no interview with the Imam as it was Friday, and we spent most of the day packing such of our baggage as we do not want on the march which we are sending straight through by camel to Aden. The verandah of the courtyard was full of camel-men in the evening, arranging the tying up of their loads, and by nightfall everything was stacked below in the courtyard ready to start the first thing tomorrow morning.

In the evening Ragheb Bey brought me the Imam's list of the districts within the Protectorate border of which he is in occupation and which he is not prepared to evacuate. I read it through and found that he had included various districts of which he is only in partial occupation, and in which I cannot admit that he has a regular administration. It looks very like a break tomorrow and, on the whole, I shall not be sorry.

20th February—Saturday.

The break came this morning as I had expected. The Imam practically accepted my draft, with the exception of the list of tribes attached to Article 4, in which he would not include the tribes whose districts were in his occupation. I could not give way on this point, as to do so would have been, in a measure, to admit his occupation of those areas. He also insisted on including, in the list of tribes in whose territory he had established a regular administration, certain districts which I could not admit as falling within that category, and from which I insisted that he should withdraw.

I told him, therefore, that there were certain points of vital principle on which it was evident that we could not agree, and that I considered that there was no other course open to me than to return to

---

amended and final draft treaty presented by Clayton to the Imam on 18 February, see Appendix VIII.) "Report . . . San'a," p. 12.

20th February—Saturday.

[18] Sir Gilbert again reiterated the position that the evacuation of territories south of the Aden frontier by the Yemen authorities was a necessary corollary to an agreement. The Imam maintained that he could not evacuate "any portions of those tribal districts of which he was now in occupation. . . .

London and report to my Government. I much regretted that it should be so, but I felt that further discussion was useless. The Imam accepted this decision without demur, which showed plainly that he was of the same opinion, expressing his regret and the hope that even so an agreement in the future would not prove impossible. I thanked the Imam for all his friendship and kindness to me personally and we parted with warm expressions of mutual esteem and protestations of lifelong friendship. Thus ends exactly four weeks of constant thought and discussion. Well, I am not sorry on the whole, as a definite break is better than an unsatisfactory agreement, and in any case much knowledge and experience of the situation has been gained. Thank goodness we are off tomorrow with our faces turned towards Home.[18]

In other words, he endeavored once more to substitute, for the demarcated frontier that he had already implicitly accepted, a tribal boundary." The same clash of concepts that had prevented for so long agreement between Britain and Ibn Sa'ud–the Arab conception of a boundary as an ill-defined zone between tribes versus the European definition of a precisely demarcated line–now dashed any hopes for an agreement between Britain and the Yemen. Clayton had no choice but to break off negotiations and return to London. "Report . . . San'a," pp. 13–14.

CHAPTER 9

From Sanaa to London:

21 February–20 March 1926

21st February–Sunday.

Our heavy baggage on camels left for Mawiya on the Protectorate frontier yesterday and should arrive there on the same day as we do. Lake and Irani with the baggage mules left at 9:00 a.m. for Waalan, leaving George and myself to follow by car after paying a farewell visit to the Imam. We went to the Imam's palace about 10:00 a.m., and I found that he had assembled a large parade of troops, with band, to pay me farewell honours. He was most cordial and friendly and was, I think, full of genuine regret that we had not been able to reach an agreement. I told him that I would explain everything fully to H.M.G., that I could not say what attitude they would take up, but that I should continue to do my best to promote the friendly relations which I was convinced were in the best interests of the two countries. We parted with many expressions of mutual friendship and esteem, and I ended the interview by urging him not to complicate the situation by any further aggression on the Aden Protectorate. After a light lunch we left by car for Waalan, being finally seen off by Ragheb Bey at the village of Hasiaz some five miles out of Sanaa to which he had ridden on horseback. We had an uneventful drive and reached Waalan at 3:30 p.m. after passing our convoy a few miles short of the village. Waalan is quite a small village and accommodation was poor, so we slept in the open through rather a cold night during which I felt rather chilled. Tomorrow we leave the car and continue our journey on horse and mule.

22nd February—Monday.

We left Waalan at 7:30 a.m. We have an escort of 8 mounted men and 25 infantry, the latter being the guard which was with us all the time at Sanaa. They are not very efficient at loading up, and we took a good hour and a half to get on the march. The track led us steadily upwards for a distance of about 6 miles when we reached the top of a pass from which we got a magnificent view across the plain towards Dhamar. Then a steep zigzag descent for an hour or so, down which we had to dismount and walk, and 10 miles along the plain to Mabar a small village where we spent the night. About 3 miles out of Mabar we were met by the Amil with the whole garrison, a posse of drummers, and most of the population who escorted us into the village amidst clouds of stifling dust. I developed a rousing catarrh, which I attributed to the dust, and was glad to find myself at last in quite a clean little room where we were served with quite a passable meal and in which I slept the night. It is still cold at night as we are about 8,000 feet up, but the sun is scorching by day.

23rd February—Tuesday.

Off again at 7:30 a.m. Seen off by the Amil, riding a tear-away Arab horse, and the whole village. An uninteresting and rather tedious march over the plain to Dhamar, the last portion being over undulating basaltic rock which was bad going. We stopped about 10:00 a.m. for some breakfast by a well with rather a nice patch of green grass which was welcome in the midst of the bare surroundings. About 3 miles out of Dhamar we were met by about 600 or 700 troops and a large concourse of some 2,000 people. From there we proceeded at a snail's pace in a cloud of suffocating dust into Dhamar which is a town of fair size but dirty, dilapidated, and unattractive. We were put up in a fairly clean house and lunch was supplied. In the afternoon we went for a stroll and in the evening I went and called on the Amil, one Sayed Mohammed ibn el Wazir, a member of a powerful and very fanatical family. His brother is commanding the Imam's Army at Hodeida and his cousin, Sayed Ali ibn el Wazir, commands at Taiz. He received us courteously in a stifling atmosphere with every window tightly shut, and as my catarrh had turned out to be a bad cold, I got a chill when I went out again into the cold night air.

24th February—Wednesday.

I woke up with a temperature and a sharp pain in my right side when I coughed and took a deep breath. A jolly outlook if I am laid up in this outlandish spot. Irani says it would be most unwise to try and go on today, especially as we have a long march to do to Yarim. Nothing for it but to spend the day in bed and hope for the best tomorrow. Irani gave me medicine and a rousing mustard plaster and by the evening my temperature was down to just over 99°. Irani had a busy day as half the town came round to consult him and to cadge medicine.

25th February—Thursday.

Fever had practically gone when I woke up, and I felt better so decided to push on. We got off about 7:30 a.m. and had rather a long, wearisome march to Yarim. We stopped for some breakfast at a small wayside coffee house about 10:00 a.m. and again by a well for a midday halt and rest at 1:30 p.m. We are still on the plateau at a height varying from 7,500 feet to 8,500 feet, and the track is bad and stony. About 4:00 p.m. we reached a pass at the top of which were waiting a crowd of people who accompanied us into Yarim which we reached about 5:00 p.m. Yarim is rather prettily situated in a fertile valley among the hills but is a miserable, dirty little town, and the best room in the place, which was allotted to us, was in the public prison and dirty to a degree. I was rather tired but a good deal better and free from fever.

26th February—Friday.

I felt a good deal better in the morning. We marched at 7:30 a.m. after the usual hour and a half of wrangling and yelling by the men over loading up. Our first six or seven miles led over a pleasant plain, and we then stopped for a breakfast on a refreshingly green plot of grass by a running stream which appears to be the rendezvous for cattle from some miles around. We then had a very stiff climb up the Samara Pass to a height of 8,500 feet, up a rock-strewn, zigzag track which taxed our animals severely. On reaching the summit we had two or three miles along the top of the pass and then a very sharp zigzag descent down a very attractive gorge clothed with vegetation to Menzil Samara, which we reached at 1:45 p.m. and where we halted for lunch and a midday rest. We were off again at 3:00 p.m. and continued down the gorge which gradually widened out into a fertile, well-cultivated valley. It was a pleasant ride often beside a rushing mountain stream which occasionally leaped over rocky precipices forming a waterfall. We have reached the seaward side of the mountains and the sight of trees and vegetation is very refreshing after the bare, treeless upland plateau. On our way we met a company of Imamic infantry who were marching from Taiz to Sanaa en route to the Tihama where hostilities against the Idrisi are still going on. They struck me as very mobile, their entire transport consisting of four camels and two donkeys. At 5:30 p.m. we reached the pleasant little village of Makhadir, where we were met as usual by the Amil and a large crowd. A nice clean room to sleep in.

27th February—Saturday.

We left Makhadir as usual about 7:30 a.m. and had a very pleasant march of some 16 miles up a wide fertile valley, well cultivated, and watered by a running stream. Vegetation was plentiful and we had our breakfast under a fine, spreading tree beside the brook. A steep climb up a roughly paved causeway brought us to Ibb, a very picturesque walled town perched on a crag which juts out from the flank of lofty Jebel Badan. It rather reminds one of one of the castles on the Rhine and is certainly the most attractive and clean town we have struck so far. The Amil, Sayed Ba Salama, who has a great reputation for hospitality was unfortunately ill with jaundice, but one of his sons met us, with the usual crowd of soldiers, drummers and inhabitants, and conducted us to the pleasantest quarters we have occupied so far at the top of an extremely lofty house which is perched on the top of the city wall overlooking a precipice of some 200 feet. The view is magnificent and the air delightful. After lunch I went and visited the sick Amil, who was much gratified by the attention, and left him in the hands of Irani, who has prescribed for the jaundice from which he is suffering. Poor Irani's mule shied suddenly the other day and, in clutching the pommel of the saddle to save himself, Irani has broken one of the middle bones of his hand. It has set all right, but it is swollen and rather painful and handicaps him considerably in his medical work. I am feeling much better, and we are all enjoying the comparative comfort and cleanliness of our quarters.

28th February—Sunday.

Started at the usual time, being seen off by most of the population and had a long climb for about 3 hours, getting gradually steeper. After 2 hours' march we stopped for our usual breakfast, tea out of a Thermos flask, hard-boiled eggs, and bread, by a well. Shortly afterwards we were intercepted by the Amil, troops, drummers, and population of Jibla, a town some 3 miles off the road, who accompanied us for a couple of miles and greatly retarded our pace. About midday we reached the top of the pass, called Mahras, over 9,000 feet above sea level. We were now at our last peak and it is a continuous descent all the way to Aden. We then had another of those perilous descents, rather like going down the side of a house and in about 2 hours we reached the little village of Sayani where we found an official sent by Sayed Ali ibn el Wazir, the Amil and Military Commander at Taiz, to meet us and see to all our needs. We were expected to stay the night at Sayani, but I decided that we must push on as we had already lost a day at Dhamar and Major Carpendale of the Aden troop was waiting for us with a detachment on the frontier. We, therefore, had lunch at Sayani and then started off again. We marched down a wide wadi and then over very rough country covered with bush and cactus till we reached the little hamlet of Shaikh Salah about 6:00 p.m. We had branched off from the main track to Taiz about 3 miles below Sayani and left it on our right hand. There was no accommodation in the village, so we spent a very pleasant night in the open under a large tree.

1st March—Monday.

We were off again at the usual time and continued our march over rough, stony country, intersected by numerous wadis until we reached Mawiya rather late in the afternoon. There we were met once more by a large concourse who escorted us into the village, where we were accommodated in the only house of any size, which had formerly belonged to rather a well-known Shaikh, Mahmoud Nazir Mukbil, who died not many years ago. Mawiya is a miserable little place, very dirty, and ill-kept, and I was not sorry to think that I should be crossing the frontier into British protected territory on the following day. Irani had a busy time with the sick with whom Mawiya seems to abound.

2nd March—Tuesday.

We spent rather an uncomfortable night as the house was filthy, and I for one felt rather seedy, but we got off at the usual time, and accompanied by large numbers of soldiers and many of the local people, we marched off down a stony but rather attractive wadi towards the frontier. After 2½ hours we came upon Major Carpendale with a very smart escort of the Aden troop, accompanied by Ahmed Fadl, brother of the Sultan of Lahej, who had come up with baggage camels for us. It was a great joy to see an efficient, British-run show again, and we greeted Carpendale with the utmost delight. We had a light breakfast and then came the business of handing over our baggage to the fresh camels and of paying off and bidding farewell to our trusty Imamic escort of whom the infantry had been with us ever since we arrived at Sanaa. George seated himself at a small camp table in the open and proceeded to deal out dollars [Maria Theresa thalers] to all on a scale which we had previously arranged. All seemed very pleased and happy and, at the end, I made them a short speech of thanks and farewell. The whole party then trooped off back to Mawiya.

We now mounted the Aden troop horses which Carpendale had brought for us, and it was a blessed relief to get into a comfortable saddle on a good English horse, after days on mules with their miserably uncomfortable saddles. We did about half the distance, walk and trot, and then had lunch in a shady wadi under the trees where Carpendale had made previous arrangements for a halt.

We reached Musemir, the chief village of the Haushabi tribe, at about 5:00 p.m. where we were met by Mohsin ibn Ali, the Haushabi Sultan. He had paraded all his fighting men who greeted us with a continuous and somewhat perilous, fusillade of ball ammunition. We had tea in the Sultan's house, having to step over two struggling sheep with their throats cut on the threshold, and there we met Lt. Col. Peiniger C.R.A. (Aden) and Major Fowle (Political officer) who had come up to meet us and were staying in the Sultan's so-called palace. We preferred to stay in the camp of the Aden troop where Carpendale provided us with the necessary tents. Our baggage camels turned up all right about 10:00 p.m. I felt pretty tired after a long day and slept well in spite of mosquitoes which are plentiful at Musemir.

3rd March—Wednesday.

We found to our joy that cars had been provided to take us from Musemir into Aden, thereby saving us two wearisome marches of about 20 miles each into Lahej. We started off at 7:30 a.m. and drove down through the foothills of the Aden hinterland to Lahej where we arrived about 11:00 a.m. The Sultan Abdul Kerim of the Abdali [Sultanate] of Lahej had paraded his forces for our reception and we drove through the town between the ranks of his troops all of whom let off their rifles into the air. On arrival at the Palace I was received by a Guard of Honour and a salute of guns, and the Sultan entertained us to an excellent European breakfast. He and the Amir of Dala [Dhala], who has been turned out of his Amirate by the Imam, were naturally very anxious to know the results of my mission, so I gave them a general idea of what had happened. We left Lahej about 12 noon and reached Aden in time for lunch at the Residency where we found the Stewarts kind and hospitable as ever with our rooms swept and garnished for us. I had a chat with General Stewart and walked into the town after tea to get a few necessaries. It is a great relief to feel oneself back again into civilization and, especially, cleanliness. I sent off a cable to Enid to tell her of our safe return.

4th March—Thursday.

Went to the Residency office in the morning. Our heavy baggage

---

4th March—Thursday.

[1] Rear Admiral Angelo Ugo Conz.

arrived all correct in the evening. My cold came on again rather heavily, the result of reaction and fatigue. We had all been asked to dine with the Italian Admiral on board his flagship, but I felt too seedy to go, so I stayed in and went to bed early.[1] We have got passages on the P. & O. *Maloja*, sailing on Wednesday, the 10th March. I shall go straight through via Marseilles.

5th March—Friday.

Felt a bit better, but my cold is still heavy and rather bronchial. The *Calliope* and *Yarmouth* (Captains Brock Birkett and Isaacson) are here again on their way back from China. The two captains lunched at the Residency. I spent a quiet day as I did not feel up to much. A welcome cable from Enid, saying all well.

6th March—Saturday.

Went to the Bank and the Resident's office, on mission business, in the forenoon. The Stewarts and I lunched with Capt. Isaacson on the *Yarmouth*, after which the others went to the races at Khor Muksah, but I came home and spent a quiet afternoon just watching the football after tea. It is very damp and sticky here now, and one feels it after the heights and dry cold of Sanaa. What with my cold, reaction, and fatigue, and the weather, I feel absolutely good for nothing and spend the day perspiring heavily.

7th March—Sunday.

I went to Holy Communion at the Garrison Church at 8:00 a.m. Spent the forenoon writing. The mail from home arrived but there was nothing much for me. I had got Enid's last letters on my way in (Carpendale brought our mails out to the frontier to meet us), and she said she would not write again to Aden. Irani and Kaikini left by the P. & O. for Bombay after cordial farewells. We had some tennis after tea, but it was rather spoilt by a tearing wind. However, I got in four sets, which gave me some exercise. "Padre" Wormald and another man, by name Robinson, came to dinner. Lake came in to tea and to say good-bye. He is staying here till next mail by which he returns to India to rejoin his regiment (The Bombay Grenadiers) in Waziristan.

8th March—Monday.

Went to the P. & O. office in the forenoon and fixed up about our tickets and berths—then to the office of the Resident. Did some packing and writing and, after tea, went for a walk. Dined at the Residency.

9th March—Tuesday.

Went to the Residency office in the forenoon and settled up various matters, also to the Bank to fix up finally the Mission account. In the afternoon went for a stroll and watched a football match.

10th March—Wednesday.

The *Maloja* came in early. After breakfast I went off in a launch with my luggage.[2] I first called on the Italian Admiral in the *San Giorgio* and had a chat with him.[3] I then went on to the *Maloja*, fixed up my cabin and booked a place on the P. & O. special from Marseilles to London, thereby forestalling the Indian passengers from the *China*, who did not arrive from Bombay until the afternoon. I found Major General Sir George Cory on board and brought him ashore with me. Lunched at the Residency—Sir George Cory and the Captain of the *Maloja* (Capt. Warner) came to lunch. Embarked comfortably after tea, about 5:30 p.m., the *China* arrived at 6:00 p.m.[4] General Stewart, the Gobles, Reilly (1st Asst. Resident) and Peiniger (C.R.A.) came on board to see us off. Sailed from Aden about 11:00 p.m.

10th March—Wednesday.

2 The *Maloja* was built at Belfast in 1923 by Harland and Wolff Ltd. for the P. & O., with a displacement of 20,837 tons. She originally had quadruple expansion engines that were later converted to Bauer-Wach. At the outbreak of the Second World War she was converted to a troopship. Afterward she became a tourist-class-only ship and was finally sold for breaking up in 1953.

3 The *San Giorgio* was completed in June 1910 for the Italian Navy with a displacement of 9,332 tons and to carry a crew of 726. Although officially rated as a second-class battleship, she was classified as an Armoured Cruiser, carrying four 10-inch guns and eight 7.5-inch guns. She was later converted into a Cadet Training ship and during the Second World War was employed as a coastal defense ship at Tobruk where she was reduced to a wreck by R.A.F. bombers and naval aircraft, June-December 1940. She was ultimately

11th March—Thursday.

At sea. Passed Perim early in the morning and woke up to find ourselves in the Red Sea with a pleasant breeze meeting us. I am very glad to leave Aden, where it was exceedingly hot and damp which we found trying especially after the dry climate of the Yemen highlands. We were sorry to say good-bye to the Stewarts, though, who have been more than kind. They will be on leave this year and we must try and get hold of them. The *Maloja* is from Sydney via Ceylon, so we have a lot of Australians on board and some people from Colombo, as well as those who came from Bombay in the *China*. I have a good two-berth cabin and a pleasant cabin-mate. George Antonius and I were taken in charge by the Captain and invited to sit at his table for meals.

Beautiful weather and a steady ship.

12th March—Friday.

Captain Creighton R.N. is on board. He took the *Delhi* out to Australia and is now returning.[5] I met him at the Lloyd's in Cairo, where he lunched on his way out. I have also met old Miss Cochrane, who I used to know in Cairo. She has been staying in Ceylon, but failed to meet Muriel though she had introductions to her. Barbara Orr-Ewing is also on board on her way back from New Zealand where she has been staying with Alice and Charlie Fergusson and was a bridesmaid to Helen. She has also been staying on her way back with Muriel and Gilbert, both of whom seem well and flourish-

---

scuttled on 22 January 1941. In 1926 the *San Giorgio* was the flagship of Vice Admiral Angelo Ugo Conz.

[4] The *China* was built for the P. & O. in 1896 at a cost of a quarter million pounds, displacing 8,000 tons. On her way to Australia in 1898 she ran aground off Perim Island and lay there until September when she was eventually refloated, refitted, and, in due course, resumed her normal service to the Far East. In the First World War she served as a hospital ship and was returned to the P. & O. in 1920 where she continued in service until 1928 when she was sold for breaking up.

12th March—Friday.

[5] H.M.S. *Delhi* was a light cruiser of 4,650 tons built by Armstrong-Whitworth and launched on 23 August 1918. She served in the Far East particularly in the China Sea in 1927. During the Second World War she was rearmed with American guns but was scrapped in March 1948.

ing.[6] There was a "cabaret" show and dance in the evening got up by some of the passengers. It was really very good for an impromptu show and was quite amusing.

13th March—Saturday.

At sea. The weather is still lovely. The ship being full, there is the usual bustle of sports, sweepstakes etc. which I have fortunately escaped. There is a Lady Lewis and her daughter on board with whom Creighton and I play cheap and rather frivolous bridge after dinner.

Barbara Orr-Ewing and I had tea with the Captain and he showed us all round the bridge. Humphreys (late Egyptian Surveys) and his niece are on board.[7]

14th March—Sunday.

We arrived at Suez at 7:00 a.m. to find a gale of wind and rain and a dust storm blowing. No ships have been through the Canal for about 3 or 4 days on account of the dust and strong headwind.

George Lloyd had wirelessed to me that he was sending a car to Suez to take me to Cairo to lunch at the Residency, so that I could have a chat with him and leave by the 6:15 p.m. train to Port Said, where I could rejoin the ship. There was great slackness at Suez; the ship had to anchor in the outer roads and no doctor or agent came near her. At 10:30 a.m. a canal pilot came on board with orders to take her straight through the canal, so off we started. As we passed Port Tawfik a launch came alongside containing the British Consul.[8] He was not allowed on board but shouted to me that, as the doctor had not been on board to make a medical inspection, the ship was going through the canal in quarantine and no one could, therefore, be allowed to land. There was nothing for it but to stay on board and give up the trip to Cairo. It is very annoying as I wanted to see

---

[6] Muriel and Gilbert Hunter-Blair.

13th March—Saturday.

[7] Harry A. Humphreys was Deputy Director General of the Egyptian

George Lloyd; also I have some kit at the Sudan Agency which I wanted to pick up and which it is now too late to have sent to Port Said.

We got to Port Said at midnight, and I stayed up till 2:00 a.m. hoping that perhaps my kit might appear with faithful Sayed Effendi, or someone. The Linlithgows came on board, and he brought me a note from George—but no kit. George Antonius disembarked at Port Said, and he will go and see Lloyd and will also do what he can to get the kit home. He may bring it with him if he comes on leave soon. It was sad to part from him after nearly six months together. He has been a valuable helper and a very pleasant travelling companion. I gave him a letter to Lord Plumer.

15 March—Monday.

We left Port Said at daybreak. We are lucky to have missed a heavy gale. The weather has cleared and the sea has gone down though it is still rather dull and cold. There was a selling sweep on the run of tomorrow in the saloon after dinner—£210 in the pool. I did not take part.

The Captain asked me up to the bridge last night, as we came along the canal towards Port Said. It was a very curious and unique sight, looking down on the glare of the headlight from the upper bridge. The canal looks extraordinarily narrow from that height and the ship seems to fill it up completely.

Some of the people in this ship—both male and female—are the limit. Some of the "flappers" especially, fill me with amazement.

16th March—Tuesday.

We passed Crete in the morning. The weather is still lovely and the ship very comfortable. There is quite a drop in the temperature and the snow on the mountains of Crete gives quite a nip to the air. The Marquis and Marchioness of Linlithgow got on at Port Said. They have been staying with the Lloyds at Cairo, on their way back

---

Survey Department until his retirement sometime in 1911.

14th March—Sunday.

[8] Edward Hubert Lascelles Hadwen.

from a visit to Khartoum. He brought me a letter from George Lloyd.

17th March—Wednesday.

We reached the Straits of Messina in the afternoon and passed through them by daylight. I began to feel suspicious aches and pains and towards evening was rather feverish. I am afraid it looks like a go of malaria, probably the result of my nights at Mawiya and Musemir. The cold has doubtless brought it out.

18th March—Thursday.

I woke up feeling a bit better but not right. I got up to breakfast, but felt worse during the morning, so I went and got some medicine from the ship's doctor at noon and went to bed for the rest of the day. I have without doubt got a dose of fever. We passed through the Straits of Bonifaccio in the afternoon.

19th March—Friday.

I woke up feeling very seedy and with a temperature. We reached Marseilles at 8:00 a.m., but I did not get up till 11:00 a.m. when I registered my luggage and fixed up my place on the P. & O. special train which leaves from the docks. I rested in the saloon all day and got on to the train at 3:30 p.m. Sir George Cory was very kind in helping me with my kit and in making arrangements. The train left at 4:00 p.m., and after a very light and early dinner, I turned in, luckily I had a sleeping compartment to myself.

20th March—Saturday.

The train was late so we missed the boat from Boulogne and had to go on to Calais where we arrived soon after noon. I stayed in bed till the last moment and, with Cory's help, got successfully on to the boat. There were no deck cabins available, so I found a place down below where I was able to lie down. We had quite a rough crossing, and on arrival at Dover, we found it very cold, almost snow. I found my seat in the Pullman all right and duly reached Victoria at about 5:30 p.m. where I was gladdened by the sight of dear Enid on the platform.

I still had fever and felt very seedy, so we decided that the best course would be to go to a nursing home. We therefore drove to Sister Agnes' (King Edward VII Hospital) at 17, Grosvenor Crescent. Luckily they were able to take me in, and I tumbled gratefully into a clean, comfortable bed, and very glad I was to get there.

So ends a very interesting and rather arduous trip, which has lasted just three days short of six months.

Epilogue

The mission was over, but the results endured. Clayton's foremost achievement was the climate of confidence in British actions and intentions he created in Sa'udi Arabia and the Yemen where none had existed before. Arabian affairs have traditionally been dominated by personal diplomacy, and Clayton's character and personality produced trust and respect at both Bahra and San'a'. He left Bahra with the friendship of Ibn Sa'ud. He left San'a' having established "personal contact . . . for the first time," having ascertained "the Imam's views and aspirations, which no amount of correspondence could have disclosed," and convinced of the Imam's desire for friendship with Britain.[1] Confidence in British diplomacy was produced by confidence in her diplomat, and subsequent agreements—the Treaty of Jiddah in 1927 regulating Anglo-Sa'udi affairs, and the Treaty of San'a' in 1934 establishing relations between Britain and Yemen—were the direct outgrowth of the new era in Arabian diplomacy begun by the Clayton mission. Although no specific agreement had been signed at San'a' and the terms of the Bahra Agreement were soon to be violated, the dialogue of diplomacy continued after 1925 and was only broken many years later, when the climate of confidence was destroyed by the appearance of lesser men whose character and abilities could no longer control their national interests. But even though the personal factor in Arabian diplomacy has diminished in recent times, Clayton's work has not been entirely undone. Effective diplomacy should withstand the fragility of human existence, and in this sense Clayton's diplomacy was nearly as durable as it was creative. Today the boundary between Sa'udi Arabia and Jordan remains that fixed by the Hadda Agreement and

[1] "Report . . . San'a'," pp. 16–17.

confirmed in an agreement between Jordan and Sa'udi Arabia in August 1965, while the spirit, if not the terms, of the Bahra Agreement were later re-created by the 'Iraqi-Sa'udi Agreement of April 1932.

In addition to the cordial atmosphere and agreements he had fashioned at Bahra and San'a', Clayton had promised Ibn Sa'ud that he would communicate to the British government the Sultan's wish to revise the Anglo-Najdi Treaty of 1915 which governed relations between the two countries. As Ibn Sa'ud's dominions had expanded across the peninsula, this agreement had become an anachronism, and upon his return to London Clayton raised the issue with the British authorities. Throughout the spring and summer of 1926 extended discussions took place in Whitehall concerning revision of the 1915 Treaty, while in Arabia Ibn Sa'ud consolidated his position among the truculent tribesmen of Najd and reorganized the government of the Hijaz.[2] The negotiations were at last begun, entrusted to S. R. Jordan, the British Consul and Agent at Jiddah, who set out on 23 November to confer with Ibn Sa'ud. Clayton himself was soon to take part in the Anglo-Italian discussions at Rome concerning Italian ambitions in the Red Sea area, but in any case the Colonial Office considered Jordan more than capable of conducting the negotiations. This was a mistake. Jordan was a keen and dedicated diplomat, and his superiors had the highest opinion of his abilities, but in the eyes of Ibn Sa'ud he was a minor official who could hardly hope to command the confidence of the Sultan of Najd as had Sir Gilbert Clayton. Thus when Ibn Sa'ud raised more far-reaching questions than the Colonial Office had anticipated, the negotiations soon broke down in mid-December. Jordan returned to London, and the Sultan dashed off to Riyadh in a huff to rally support among his people for his administration in the Hijaz.

Throughout January and February discussions took place in Whitehall, and a revised draft was concluded which sought to overcome Ibn Sa'ud's objections. In March Clayton was asked once again if he would return to Arabia to reopen the discussions. He accepted,

[2] The minutes of Colonial Office Conferences together with the correspondence leading to the sending of a second mission to Ibn Sa'ud are to be found in the Clayton Papers.

and poor Jordan, through no fault of his own, turned over the conduct of the negotiations. Ibn Sa'ud was delighted at Clayton's return, for he trusted Clayton as he trusted no other Englishman since the days of Shakespear. Moreover, during the interval between Clayton's departure in December 1925 and his return in 1927, Ibn Sa'ud had strengthened his position amongst his own people. In January 1927 at a vast tribal gathering at Riyadh he was proclaimed King of Najd and its Dependencies, and he returned to Jiddah in the spring confident of his powers. Clayton, however, did not return to Arabia unprepared. Thanks largely to the work of Jordan and George Antonius, who had accompanied Jordan the previous November, Clayton was thoroughly acquainted with Ibn Sa'ud's objections, many of which the Colonial Office had resolved, while for others it had prepared reasonable alternatives. The combination of Clayton's return with altered instructions quickly transformed the atmosphere from tense suspicion to friendly accommodation, and on 20 May 1927 the Treaty of Jiddah was signed.

Although the negotiations leading to the conclusion of the Treaty cannot compare in diplomatic skill to those which resulted in the Bahra and Hadda Agreements, they were clearly the culmination of Clayton's Arabian diplomacy begun at Bahra a year and a half before. The Treaty was concluded for seven years, renewable by mutual consent. It proved a sound and mutually beneficial arrangement, for the Treaty recognized the independence of Ibn Sa'ud who on his part undertook to facilitate the pilgrimage of British Muslim subjects, to respect Britain's agreements with the Persian Gulf principalities, and to help in the suppression of the slave trade. Clayton's most creative contribution to the negotiations was devising a formula whereby Ibn Sa'ud could accept in practice the status quo of Britain's occupation of the Al-'Aqabah and Ma'an area, even though he could not accept in principle the alienation of that province from his administration in the Hijaz. At a private interview with Clayton, Ibn Sa'ud admitted that he did not wish to press the issue, but the force of public opinion prevented him from abandoning the province outright. Clayton's formula, embodied in an exchange of notes accompanying the Treaty of Jiddah, solved Ibn Sa'ud's dilemma and cleared the way for the conclusion of the agreement.

Within a year Clayton was once again in Arabia. For some years Ibn Sa'ud had had to contend with a growing and powerful opposition to his policies and practices within the Wahhabi community. Led by Faysal ad-Dawish, the Ikhwan leader, the center of resistance lay among the Mutayr, the 'Ajman, and the 'Utaybah. Dawish challenged not only the orthodoxy but the religious efficacy of Ibn Sa'ud's administration. He denounced the laxity of Ibn Sa'ud, judged by Ikhwan standards, and attacked him "for taxing the pilgrims, levying a tax on tobacco—a prohibited article—and fostering the use of telephone, telegraph, radio, and motor car—all instruments of the Devil." Above all, Ibn Sa'ud was criticized for his intercourse "with the 'infidel' British and other foreigners," and Faysal ad-Dawish demanded a jihad against the unbelievers.[3]

The Ikhwan reacted by attacking tribes in 'Iraq, and the British forces responded by sending planes and armored cars to retaliate against the marauding tribesmen. Thus when the 'Iraq Government erected a police post at Busayyah, eighty miles from the 'Iraqi-Najdi frontier, in September 1927, Ibn Sa'ud protested that it violated the first Protocol of Al-'Uqayr in which 'Iraq had pledged not to construct fortifications in the vicinity of the border.[4] Faysal ad-Dawish did more than protest. Busayyah post was overwhelmed by the Ikhwan in November, and a series of larger raids upon 'Iraq tribesmen followed. The R.A.F. pursued the raiders and attacked them, even crossing the border into Najd to do so. For two months an unofficial war raged along the frontier, while Ibn Sa'ud remained passive at Riyadh, reluctant to discipline the raiders who formed the core of those critical to his rule. His solution was characteristic of his good sense and prudence. He proposed to the British government that both sides should meet and try to settle the conflict at

[3] Twitchell, *Saudi Arabia* (Princeton, 1958) p. 160.

[4] At the Bahra negotiations in 1925 Ibn Sa'ud objected to military installations along the 'Iraq frontier on the grounds that he had been denied permission to fortify Kaf. Clayton insisted, however, that certain fortifications in 'Iraq were necessary because "that was a question which affected imperial interests" to protect imperial air and automobile routes. Clayton assured Ibn Sa'ud at the time that the posts would be purely for defensive purposes. Busayyah could hardly be considered in the category of imperial interests however. "Report . . . ," pp. 40–41.

the conference table. His overtures were readily accepted, while the end of the grazing season temporarily halted the raids and counter-raids on the frontier. On 2 May 1928 Sir Gilbert Clayton arrived once again to meet with Ibn Sa'ud.

The discussions did not begin auspiciously. Accompanied by the faithful Antonius, Clayton's arrival coincided with an aerial attack by planes of the R.A.F. on Najd tribesmen. On his part Ibn Sa'ud was threatened with civil war from the frontier tribes of Faysal ad-Dawish whom he could no longer control but for whom he had to accept responsibility. He could not, of course, admit his inability to restore his authority on the frontier, and to cover his embarrassing position, he insisted on the withdrawal of fortifications in 'Iraq rather than precipitate open civil war by marching against Faysal ad-Dawish. When no agreement was reached on the question of fortifications, both parties agreed to adjourn the discussions until after the approaching pilgrimage. Clayton returned to London for consultations with his government, but in August he was once again in Jiddah for a short and fruitless meeting with Ibn Sa'ud who continued to repudiate the right of 'Iraq to construct such fortified police posts in the vicinity of the frontier. Despite assiduous efforts on the part of Clayton to seek a formula suitable to both sides, Ibn Sa'ud remained consistently opposed to the posts and refused to agree to any settlement unless they were demolished.[5] This condition was beyond Clayton's authority to grant, so the mission failed. Sir Gilbert returned to London, while Ibn Sa'ud hurried back to Najd to attempt to restore control over the frontier tribes. The failure of the Ikhwan to raid successfully against 'Iraqi airplanes and armored cars led them eventually to attack other Najd tribes. This was civil war and a direct and open challenge to the authority of Ibn Sa'ud. It was settled on the field of battle. The rebels were totally defeated, and by the autumn of 1929 Ibn Sa'ud was once again master in his own house. The defeat of the Ikhwan fanatics made possible the restoration of the friendly relations between Najd and her neighbors which had existed after the signing of the Bahra Agreement, and in January 1930 Ibn Sa'ud met with King Faysal on board

[5] The details of the 1928 discussions can be found in the Clayton Papers.

H.M.S. *Lupin*, and together the two monarchs agreed to settle the frontier question. A year later the prime minister of 'Iraq, Nuri as-Sa'id, signed a Treaty of Bon Voisinage, Friendship, and Extradition at Mecca. The dispute was settled.

In October 1928 Sir Gilbert Clayton was chosen to succeed Sir Henry Dobbs as High Commissioner of 'Iraq. His appointment was greeted with widespread enthusiasm not only because of his experience and knowledge but his well-known sympathy for the Arabs. Although taken ill on the way to Baghdad, after spending several days snowbound on the Turkish border in the Orient Express, Clayton was delighted to be back again in the Middle East. On a visit to Beirut he spoke of his desire to serve 'Iraq and its people, and on taking leave he paused in the doorway and said, "I love your country: Syria, the Lebanon, Palestine, and 'Iraq: all are my homes and I do not feel a stranger here."[6] Nor was he regarded as one by the Arabs. Faysal greeted him at Baghdad with the personal warmth of an old friend. In response Clayton said that no Arab should ever forget the King's achievements in the cause of freedom, and no Englishman should ever forget his staunch support of the Allies. He added that he felt that the true interests of Britain and 'Iraq were closely tied together, and he hoped that before his period of office expired 'Iraq would take her place in the League of Nations.[7]

Clayton's attitude toward 'Iraqi affairs was much the same as his approach in the past to problems in the Sudan, Egypt, Palestine, and Arabia—sympathetic, liberal, patient. He preferred to advise rather than order, and his tactful regard for 'Iraqi sensibilities soon created a more friendly and cooperative atmosphere that did much to assuage the residual ill-feeling resulting from the imperious Anglo-'Iraqi Treaty of 1927. Until Clayton became High Commissioner, 'Iraq had been administered by men whose experience had been in India and who frequently sought to govern 'Iraq more like an Indian Province than an Arab state. Clayton came from a different imperial tradition, the Egyptian, where the role of British officials had for long been that of advisers rather than masters, and this subtle but

[6] *Al Ahrar*, Beirut, 14 September 1929.
[7] *The Times*, 16 May 1929, p. 15.

vital difference had conditioned his approach to empire which he carried with him out of Egypt and which was in striking contrast to the attitude of former Indian officials in 'Iraq.

During the months following his arrival in Baghdad, Clayton made a careful survey of the country and its people preparatory to making recommendations to the British government about the future relations between Great Britain and 'Iraq. Throughout the summer of 1929 he gathered information in a manner reminiscent of his days in Cairo at the Intelligence Department. Then late in the summer he embodied his proposals in a memorandum in which he outlined the difficulties of the mandatory power in its relations with a proud people, gaining self-confidence, who were increasingly suspicious of British intentions to perpetuate the mandate. Moreover, the mandate had been disliked from the start and had emphasized the contradiction between the national sovereignty of 'Iraq and the limitations imposed on it by the British. He urged the British government to reach an understanding with 'Iraqi leaders on future relations between the two countries and to support 'Iraq's admission to the League of Nations without any of the qualifications contained in the unratified and unpopular Treaty of 1927. While in London the government pondered these views, in 'Iraq Clayton had done much within a few short months to replace doubt and suspicion with understanding and goodwill. As High Commissioner the great task before him was clearly, not only to convince his government of the efficacy of his recommendations, but to carry them out and to bring 'Iraq into the community of nations.

And then suddenly, on the threshold of his greatest opportunity, Sir Gilbert Clayton died. On the afternoon of 11 September 1929 he played polo. While returning to the Residency he suffered a heart attack in the car and collapsed on a couch as he entered the building. He died within the hour at 7:30 P.M. at the age of fifty-four.[8] He was buried with full military honors at the cemetery at Al-Hunaydi in the evening of the following day. A vast assemblage gathered along the route to pay their last respects.

> From four o'clock onwards there was an endless procession of cars, motor-buses, arabanas and cyclists on the road to Hinaidi:

[8] *The Baghdad Times*, 12 September 1929.

> never before had we seen such a general exodus from the city. All transport was at a premium, and hundreds of people walked the fourteen miles to Hinaidi and back. This public demonstration of sympathy was even more impressive than the official ceremony, and it will long be remembered in Baghdad as a remarkable spontaneous tribute to the able British administrator whose life's work was consecrated to his friendship for the Arabs and the amelioration of their lot.[9]

Not only had the Arabs lost a devoted friend but the British government a resourceful public servant. Had he lived he would undoubtedly have had an even greater place among the names of British administrators in the East. Arnold Toynbee expressed the feelings of Clayton's colleagues in England and the East at the time of his death.

> He died . . . at an age at which successful men of action are often just becoming ripe to do their best work. Had he lived, he would assuredly have been remembered as the man who consummated Great Britain's task in 'Iraq. . . . This was the work immediately ahead of him. That work must now be undertaken by other hands; but it will not be easy to find hands so apt as Sir Gilbert Clayton's for carrying it out.[10]

But Clayton's work did not die with him. On the day after his funeral King Faysal was informed that the British government would support 'Iraq's candidacy to the League of Nations without qualifications and two months later the Secretary of State for Colonies announced that the unratified Treaty of 1927 would be abandoned and negotiations would soon begin on a new and more liberal treaty. Clayton's advice had been accepted by his government, which might have conceivably rejected it "on grounds of prudence had it been proffered by a less experienced counsellor."[11] Although his proposals for the future of 'Iraq had been accepted, his character and personality transcended the policies and programs of govern-

[9] *Ibid.*

[10] A. J. Toynbee, "Iraq: 'A Going Concern—with One Proviso'," *Manchester Guardian*, 15 October 1929.

[11] "Britain and Iraq," *The Times*, 21 September 1929, p. 11.

ment, and in the larger sense he remained among the Arabs "a model to be emulated by British statesmen in the East."[12] And the Arabs mourned his loss. Ibn Sa'ud wrote to the Political Agent at Kuwait,

> With great regret and grief I have received the sad news which you have related to us, regarding the death of our dear friend General Sir Gilbert Clayton. Your news was particularly distressing because of what we knew of the deceased's true sayings and faithful actions.
>
> We feel we have lost a very great champion and a faithful worker towards the good relations existing between us and the British Government.[13]

In his dealings with the Arabs he was always frank and sympathetic to their cause, and in matters of general administration he was flexible, courageous, and perceptive. He gained the respect of all with whom he came into contact by his massive store of knowledge and good sense that was contained behind a modest, unassuming manner. He was known throughout the Arab world as "the Friend of the Arabs." Although his name is forgotten today among younger generations, Sir Gilbert Clayton made a lasting impression on the development of British policy in the Middle East where his good judgment reconciled conflicts and settled difficult disputes. He was an exceptional public servant but above all an exceptional person.

> Death has hushed a great and noble heart. With his death the Arabs have lost a sincere and open friend, the like of whom is rarely known. With his death is closed an unsullied page in Arab history inscribed with the deeds of a good man and with efforts to be held in grateful remembrance. Oh. Sir Gilbert Clayton, true you were in your love for the Arabs, noble in your affection for their lands, frank in all your dealings with them. It is for them to recall and extol your greatness of heart.[14]

[12] *Al 'Iraq*, Baghdad, 18 September 1929.

[13] Ibn Sa'ud to Lt. Col. H. R. P. Dickson, Political Agent, Kuwait, 27 September 1929, C.P.

[14] *Al Ahrar*, Beirut, 14 September 1929.

APPENDIX I

The Bahra Agreement

Whereas with a view to securing good relations between the two Governments of 'Iraq and Nejd, a Treaty known as the Muhammara Convention was agreed upon between those two Governments and signed on the 7th Ramadan 1340 (corresponding to the 5th May, 1922), and

Whereas the aforesaid Treaty was supplemented by two Protocols, known respectively as Protocol Number I and Protocol Number II of the Muhammara Convention, which were signed at 'Uqair on the 12th Rabi' Thani 1341 (corresponding to the 2nd December, 1922), and

Whereas the aforesaid Treaty and Protocols have been duly ratified by the two Governments of 'Iraq and Nejd, and

Whereas in Article I of the aforesaid Muhammara Convention the Governments of 'Iraq and of Nejd have guaranteed mutually that they will prevent aggression by their tribes on the tribes of the other and will punish their tribes for any such aggression and, should the circumstances not admit of such punishment, the two Governments will discuss the question of taking combined action according to the good relations prevailing between them, and

Whereas it is considered advisable by His Britannic Majesty's Government and by the two Governments aforementioned, in the interests of friendship and good relations between the two countries of 'Iraq and Nejd to come to an agreement regarding certain matters which are outstanding between these two countries,

We, the undersigned, His Highness 'Abdu' l–'Aziz ibn 'Abdu' l–Rahman, al–Faisal Al Sa'ud, Sultan of Nejd and its Dependencies, and Sir Gilbert Clayton, K.B.E., C.B., C.M.G., the duly accredited Commissioner and Plenipotentiary of His Britannic Majesty's Government, who has been empowered to come to an agreement and sign on behalf of the 'Iraq Government, have agreed upon the following articles:

Article 1.

The State of 'Iraq and Nejd severally recognise that raiding by tribes settled in their territories into the territory of the other State is an aggression which necessitates the severe punishment of the perpetrators by the Government to which they are subject and that the chief of the tribe committing such aggression is to be held responsible.

Article 2.

(a) A special tribunal shall be set up, by agreement between the two Governments of 'Iraq and Nejd, which shall meet from time to time to enquire into the particulars of any aggression committed across the frontier between the two States, to assess the damages and losses and to fix the responsibility. This tribunal shall be composed of an equal number of representatives of the Governments of 'Iraq and Nejd, and its presidency shall be entrusted to an additional person, other than the aforesaid representatives, to be selected by the two Governments in agreement. The decisions of this tribunal shall be final and executory.

(b) When the tribunal has fixed the responsibility, assessed the damages and losses resulting from the raid, and issued its decision in that respect, the Government to whom those found guilty are subject shall execute the aforesaid decision in accordance with tribal customs, and shall punish the guilty party in accordance with Article 1 of the present Agreement.

Article 3.

Tribes subject to one of the two Governments may not cross the frontier into the territory of the other Government except after obtaining a permit from their own Government and after the concurrence of the other Government; it being stipulated, however, in accordance with the principle of the freedom of grazing, that neither Government shall have the right to withhold such permit or concurrence if the migration of the tribe is due to grazing necessities.

Article 4.

The two Governments of 'Iraq and Nejd undertake to stand in the way, by all the means at their disposal other than expulsion and the use of force, of the emigration of any tribe or section of a tribe from one of the two countries into the other unless its emigration takes place with the knowledge and consent of its Government. The two Governments undertake to abstain from offering any present of whatsoever kind to refugees from the territories of the other Government, and to look with disfavor on any of their subjects who may seek to entice tribes belonging to the other Government or to encourage them to emigrate from their country into the other country.

Article 5.

The Governments of 'Iraq and Nejd may not correspond with the Chiefs and Sheikhs of tribes subject to the other State on official or political matters.

Article 6.

The forces of 'Iraq and Nejd may not cross the common frontier in the pursuit of offenders except with the consent of both Governments.

Article 7.

Sheikhs of tribes who hold an official position or who have flags showing that they are the leaders of armed forces may not display their flags in the territory of the other State.

Article 8.

In case one of the two Governments were to call upon tribes residing in the territory of the other State to furnish armed contingents, the said tribes will be free to respond to the call of their Government on condition that they betake themselves with their families and belongings in complete tranquility.

Article 9.

In case a tribe were to emigrate from the territory of one of the two Governments into the territory of the other Government and were subsequently to commit raids into the territory in which it formerly resided, it will be open to the Government into whose territory this tribe has immigrated to take from it adequate guarantees on the understanding that, if a similar aggression were to be repeated by the tribe, those guarantees would be liable to confiscation, without prejudice to the punishment to be inflicted by the Government as provided in Article 1, and without prejudice to whatever impositions may be decreed by the tribunal specified in Article 2 of the present Agreement.

Article 10.

The Governments of 'Iraq and Nejd undertake to initiate friendly discussions with a view to concluding a special agreement in respect of the extradition of criminals in accordance with the usage prevailing among friendly States, within a period not exceeding one year from the date of the ratification of the present Agreement by the Government of 'Iraq.

Article 11.

The Arabic version is the official text to be referred to in the interpretation of the Articles of the present Agreement.

Article 12.

The present Agreement shall be known as "The Bahra Agreement."

Signed at Bahra Camp this fourteenth day of Rabi' Thani 1344, corresponding to the first day of November, 1925.

(Signed) Sir Gilbert Clayton
(Signed and sealed) 'Abdu' l-'Aziz

APPENDIX II

The Hadda Agreement

The High British Government on its own part and His Highness 'Abdu' l-'Aziz ibn 'Abdu' r-Rahman al-Faisal Āl Sa'ud, Sultan of Nejd and its Dependencies on behalf of the Government of Nejd, on his part, in view of the friendly relations which exist between them, being desirous of fixing the frontier between Nejd and Trans-Jordan and of settling certain questions connected therewith, The High British Government have named and appointed Sir Gilbert Clayton, K.B.E., C.B., C.M.G., as their Commissioner and Plenipotentiary, to conclude an Agreement for this purpose with Sultan 'Abdu' l-'Aziz ibn 'Abdu' r-Rahman al Faisal Āl Sa'ud on behalf of Nejd.

In virtue of which the said Sultan 'Abdu' l-'Aziz ibn 'Abdu' r-Rahman al-Faisal Āl Sa'ud and the said Sir Gilbert Clayton, have agreed upon and concluded the following articles:

Article 1.

The frontier between Nejd and Trans-Jordan starts in the northeast from the point of intersection of meridian 39°E and parallel 32°N, which marks the termination of the frontier between Nejd and 'Iraq, and proceeds in a straight line to the point of intersection of meridian 37°E and parallel 31°30'N, and thence along meridian 37°E to the point of its intersection with parallel 31°25'N. From this point, it proceeds in a straight line to the point of intersection of meridian 38°E and parallel 30°N, leaving all projecting edges of the Wadi Sirhan in Nejd territory; and thence proceeds along meridian 38°E to the point of its intersection with parallel 29°35'N.

The Map referred to in this Agreement is that known as the "International" Asia Map, 1:1,000,000.

Article 2.

The Government of Nejd undertake not to establish any fortified post at Kaf or utilize Kaf or the district in its neighborhood as a military centre; and should they at any time consider it necessary to take exceptional measures in the neighborhood of the frontier with a view to the maintenance of order or for any other purpose, involving the concentration of armed forces, they engage to notify His Majesty's Government without delay.

The Government of Nejd undertake to prevent by all the means at their disposal, any incursions by their forces into the territory of Trans-Jordan.

Article 3.

In order to avoid misunderstanding over incidents which may arise in the neighborhood of the frontier, and to promote mutual confidence and full cooperation between His Majesty's Government and the Government of Nejd, the two parties agree to maintain constant communication between the Chief British Representative in Trans-Jordan or his delegate and the Governor of the Wadi Sirhan.

Article 4.

The Government of Nejd undertake to maintain all established rights that may be enjoyed in the Wadi Sirhan by tribes not under their jurisdiction, whether such rights appertain to grazing or to habitation, or to ownership, or the like; it being understood that those tribes, so long as they reside within Nejd territory, will be subject to such internal laws as do not infringe on those rights.

The Government of Trans-Jordan undertake to extend identical treatment to Nejd subjects who may enjoy similar established rights in Trans-Jordan territory.

Article 5.

The Governments of Nejd and Trans-Jordan severally recognise that raiding by tribes settled in their territories into the territory of the other State is an aggression which necessitates the severe punishment of the perpetrators by the Government to which they are subject, and that the chief of the tribe committing such aggression is to be held responsible.

Article 6.

(a) A special tribunal shall be set up, by agreement between the two Governments of Nejd and Trans-Jordan, which shall meet from time to time to enquire into the particulars of any aggression committed across the frontier between the two States, to assess the damages and losses and to fix the responsibility. This tribunal shall be composed of an equal number of representatives of the Governments of Nejd and Trans-

Jordan, and its presidency shall be entrusted to an additional person, other than the aforesaid representatives, to be selected by the two Governments in agreement. The decision of this tribunal shall be final and executory.

(b) When the tribunal has fixed the responsibility, assessed the damages and losses resulting from the raid, and issued its decision in that respect, the Government to whom those found guilty are subject shall execute the aforesaid decision in accordance with tribal customs, and shall punish the guilty party in accordance with Article 5 of the present Agreement.

Article 7.

Tribes subject to one of the two Governments may not cross the frontier into the territory of the other Government except after obtaining a permit from their own Government and after the concurrence of the other Government; it being stipulated, however, in accordance with the principle of the freedom of grazing, that neither Government shall have the right to withhold such permit or concurrence if the migration of the tribe is due to grazing necessities.

Article 8.

The two Governments of Nejd and Trans-Jordan undertake to stand in the way, by all means at their disposal other than expulsion and the use of force, of the emigration of any tribe or section of a tribe from one of the two countries into the other unless its emigration takes place with the knowledge and consent of its Government. The two Governments undertake to abstain from offering any present of whatsoever kind to refugees from the territories of the other Government, and to look with disfavor on any of their subjects who may seek to entice tribes belonging to the other Government or to encourage them to emigrate from their country into the other country.

Article 9.

The Governments of Nejd and Trans-Jordan may not correspond with the Chiefs and Sheikhs of tribes subject to the other State on official or political matters.

Article 10.

The forces of Nejd and Trans-Jordan may not cross the common frontier in the pursuit of offenders, except with the consent of both Governments.

Article 11.

Sheikhs of tribes who hold an official position or who have flags showing that they are the leaders of armed forces may not display their flags in the territory of the other State.

Article 12.

Free passage will be granted by the Governments of Nejd and Trans-Jordan to travellers and pilgrims, provided they conform to those regulations affecting travel and pilgrimage which may be in force in Nejd and Trans-Jordan. Each Government will inform the other of any regulation issued by it in this matter.

Article 13.

His Britannic Majesty's Government undertake to secure freedom of transit at all times to merchants who are subjects of Nejd for the prosecution of their trade between Nejd and Syria in both directions: and to secure exemption from Customs and other duty for all merchandise in transit which may cross the Mandated Territory on its way from Nejd to Syria or from Syria to Nejd, on condition that such merchants and their caravans shall submit to whatever Customs inspection may be necessary, and that they shall be in possession of a document from their Government certifying that they are *bona fide* merchants; and provided that trading caravans carrying merchandise will follow established routes, to be agreed upon hereafter, for their entry into and their exit from the Mandated Territory; it being understood that the above restrictions will not apply to trading caravans whose trade is confined to camels and other animals, or to tribes migrating in accordance with the preceding Articles of the present Agreement.

His Britannic Majesty's Government further undertake to secure such other facilities as may be possible to merchants who are subjects of Nejd and who may cross the area under British Mandate.

Article 14.

This Agreement will remain in force for so long as His Britannic Majesty's Government are entrusted with the Mandate for Trans-Jordan.

Article 15.

The present Agreement has been drawn up in the two languages, English and Arabic, and each of the high contracting parties shall sign two English copies and two Arabic copies. Both texts shall have the same validity, but in case of divergence between the two in the interpretation of one or other of the Articles of the present agreement, the English text shall prevail.

Article 16.

The present Agreement will be known as the HADDA Agreement.

Signed at Bahra Camp on the 2nd of November, 1925 (corresponding to the 15th Rabi' Thani 1344).

(Signed) Gilbert Clayton
'Abdu' l-'Aziz

APPENDIX III

Draft Treaty of August 1924 as Finally Submitted to the Imam by the Resident, Aden

1. His Britannic Majesty's Government acknowledge the absolute independence of His Excellency the Imam in all political and administrative matters internal and external and his authority in the territories which are under His Excellency. Nothing in this clause is to be considered as a contradiction of what is stated in Article 2.

2. His Excellency the Imam shall not correspond with or make any engagement with any Government or with anyone on any matter prejudicial to His Britannic Majesty's Government and similarly His Britannic Majesty's Government shall not correspond with or make any engagement with any Government whatsoever or with anyone on any matter prejudicial to His Excellency the Imam's Government. His Excellency the Imam is at liberty to correspond or enter into engagements with any Government whatever on matters which are not prejudicial to His Britannic Majesty's Government.

3. His Excellency the Imam recognizes the Protectorate Treaties made by His Britannic Majesty's Government with the tribes of the Aden Protectorate as shown in the margin.** He undertakes not to send any of his armed forces across the frontier demarcated by the Turkish and British Governments in 1904 or to interfere in any way with the peoples inhabiting the Aden side of the boundary line.

4. His Excellency the Imam will apply only to His Britannic Majesty's Government for the arms and ammunition, war materials, etc., that he may need for the organization and defence of his country, and His Britannic Majesty's Government will supply him so far as their inter-

national obligations permit at easy and fair rates and as soon as possible with a sufficient quantity of what is mentioned. If for any reason His Britannic Majesty's Government are unable to meet His Excellency the Imam's requirements, they will so inform him without delay, and His Excellency the Imam shall then be free to make other arrangements provided that he gives prior notice to His Britannic Majesty's Government of his intentions and awaits their acknowledgment thereof before doing so.

5. His Britannic Majesty's Government and His Excellency the Imam will jointly prevent the import of arms, ammunition and war material to the territory of His Excellency the Imam apart from those for His Excellency mentioned in the Article 4. His Britannic Majesty's Government will do their best, as far as international law permits, to prevent the import by sea and His Excellency the Imam will prevent the import by land. His Excellency the Imam will confiscate any of them found in his territory to whomsoever they may belong. Both Governments shall act with due regard to any international Convention for the control of the traffic in arms to which they are parties.

6. His Excellency the Imam will apply to His Britannic Majesty's Government for his requirements, such as able instructors, expert engineers, efficient and scientific doctors, medicines, machinery for industrial work, and for telegraph and wireless installations for the purpose of the progress and advancement of his country, and His Britannic Majesty's Government shall grant him his requirements of these at easy and fair rates and as soon as possible. If for any reason His Britannic Majesty's Government are unable to meet His Excellency the Imam's requirements they will so inform him without delay, and His Excellency the Imam shall then be free to make other arrangements provided that he gives prior notice to His Britannic Majesty's Government of his intention and awaits their acknowledgment thereof before doing so.

7. His Excellency the Imam and His Britannic Majesty's Government shall each have an official agent in the other's territory, and the agent of each shall have the same rights and privileges as are accorded to the agent of the other. These rights and privileges shall be agreed upon after the decision as to the places at which the agents of the two Governments shall reside.

8. His Excellency the Imam and His Britannic Majesty's Government will develop the trade and will keep open the trade routes both by land and sea between their respective territories, and His Britannic Majesty's Government will give to the subjects of His Excellency the Imam com-

plete freedom for transacting business both by sea and land. Neither His Britannic Majesty's Government nor His Excellency the Imam shall impose any dues on mercantile goods other than the prescribed transit dues by land and sea known to each of them and when any change in dues is made in either country as provided for in Article 9, it shall be communicated at once by the one to the other.

9. Both His Excellency the Imam and His Britannic Majesty's Government shall have full freedom to impose any tax on goods they wish in their own countries, but each undertake not to impose greater taxes on the subjects of the other than on the subjects of any other Government.

10. His Britannic Majesty's Government declare that they will not interfere in His Excellency the Imam's territory in any way, and likewise His Excellency the Imam declares that he will not either by sale, mortgage or gift, or in any other way, admit interference in his territory by any other foreign Government.

11. For the purpose of the complete achievement of the longed-for peace His Britannic Majesty's Government undertake not to give to any of the neighboring Arab Chiefs who are in treaty relations with them any help, support or supplies in the event of aggression by the said Chiefs against the territories of His Excellency the Imam. In the event of any dispute arising between His Excellency the Imam and any such Arab chief His Excellency the Imam shall inform His Britannic Majesty's Government as soon as possible in order that His Britannic Majesty's Government may advise the Arab Chief concerned to refrain from such aggression. If the Chief does not accept their advice, then His Britannic Majesty's Government undertake to restrain him by all peaceful and practicable means in their power. Similarly, in the event of any aggression by the Imam or by any of his officers or by any of his subordinates against any of the above-mentioned Arab Chiefs, His Britannic Majesty's Government will notify His Excellency the Imam as soon as possible, and His Excellency the Imam undertakes to the best of his ability to stop such aggression.

12. If His Excellency the Imam wishes to inaugurate any scheme in any port or place or to lay any railway line in his country, dig any mines, or undertake anything which would develop the condition of trade in his territory he shall make a request for his requirements to His Britannic Majesty's Government with a view to arrangements being made to carry out any such project or projects; and, if his request is granted, then

preference shall be given to them, but if for any reason His Britannic Majesty's Government are unable to meet His Excellency the Imam's requirements they will so inform him without delay, and His Excellency the Imam shall then be free to make other arrangements provided that he gives prior notice to His Britannic Majesty's Government of his intention and awaits their acknowledgment thereof before doing so.

13. His Excellency the Imam will assist His Britannic Majesty's Government in their efforts to suppress the traffic in African slaves by sea. His Britannic Majesty's Government will, so far as their international obligations permit, do their best to help the Government of His Excellency the Imam in the prevention of the imports of intoxicants, harmful drugs and lewd pastimes and instruments forbidden by the Shari'a into the territories of His Excellency the Imam. His Britannic Majesty's Government will use all efforts to prevent the import of the same by sea and His Excellency the Imam's Government will stop the traffic in such things by land and confiscate the same in his territories to whomsoever they belong.

14. On the conclusion of this Treaty His Excellency the Imam and His Britannic Majesty's Government will mutually agree as to the manner in which the lighthouses on the sea-shores of the Imamic territories are to be lit. His Excellency the Imam will give priority to His Britannic Majesty's Government in this matter and after mutual agreement as to the manner in which the lighting is to be arranged His Excellency the Imam will not enter into any agreement with any other Government in this respect. If no agreement is arrived at His Excellency the Imam will then be free to make other arrangements provided he gives prior notice to His Britannic Majesty's Government of his intention to do so, and provided he grants to no other party more favourable terms than those offered to His Britannic Majesty's Government.

15. His Excellency the Imam shall not be responsible for anyone, whoever he or she may be, or for a subject of any Government who enters Imamic territories without previous formal permission from His Excellency the Imam.

16. Every clause of this Treaty shall be as binding as the whole Treaty and this Treaty of friendship shall be in force and binding upon both parties for a period of ten years, at the end of which time it shall be renewed either in its present form or in such other form as may be agreed upon mutually by His Britannic Majesty's Government and His Excellency the Imam in accordance with the circumstances of the time.

****MARGINAL NOTE*

Tribes of the Aden Protectorate having Treaties with His Britannic Majesty's Government:

The Abdali Sultan, the Fadli Sultan, the Haushabi Sultan; the Amir of Dhala, the Aqrabi Sheikh, the Upper Aulaki Sultan, the Upper Aulaki Sheikh, the Lower Aulaki Sultan, the Sharif of Behan al-Qasab, the Wahidi Sultan of Balahaf, the Wahidi Sultan of Bir 'Ali, the Sheikh of Haura, the Sheikh of Irka, the Kaiti Sultan of Shehr and Mokalla and through him the Kathiri Sultans; the (Mahri) Sultan of Kishn and Socotra; the Upper Yafa Sultan, the Naqibs of Mausatta, the Dhubi Sheikh, the Hadrami Sheikh, the Saqladi Sheikh of Sha'ib, the Lower Yafa Sultan, the Barhimi Sheikh, and the Subeihi Sultan.

APPENDIX IV

The Imam's Counter-draft of Article 3 of the Draft Treaty of August 1924, Submitted 3 February 1926

His Highness the Imam consents to the retention by His Majesty's Government of the town of Aden so long as friendly relations and treaties are maintained between the two parties. His Highness will similarly consent to the continuance of the present administration in those territories in which it is necessary to safeguard the interests of the Aden Government, on condition that the inhabitants of those territories will always act within the bounds of justice and law, and ensure the freedom and security of communications. His Highness will further help by preventing the advance of any armed force to any of those territories (as shown in the list at the end of this article). As for what is actually occupied by the Imam's troops, this shall remain in *status quo* without discussion, but His Highness will have regard for the Chiefs concerned and will compensate them suitably.

Lahej, Abian (i.e. Falli), Haushabi, Subeihi, Bir Ahmad, Bir 'Ali, Balahaf, Yafa—with the exception of Shu'aib and other territories actually under occupation—Hadramaut, Aulaki, Ka'iti, Kathiri.

APPENDIX V

First Counter-draft Treaty Submitted by the Imam on 6 February 1926

Article 1.

His Britannic Majesty's Government recognise the absolute independence of the Imam in all matters political and administrative, internal and external, and his sovereignty in the territories handed down to him (i.e. by inheritance). Nothing in the present Article is to be considered as invalidated by the provisions of Article 2.

Article 2.

His Highness the Imam shall not enter into correspondence or agreement with any Government or individual on any matter prejudicial to His Britannic Majesty's Government. Similarly His Britannic Majesty's Government shall not enter into correspondence or agreement with any Government or individual on any matter prejudicial to the Government of His Highness the Imam. His Highness the Imam will be at liberty to enter into correspondence or agreement with any Government on matters which are not prejudicial to His Britannic Majesty's Government.

Article 3.

(This Article is identical with the Imam's counter-draft forming [Appendix IV], and is not reprinted.)

Article 4.

The fact that the territories referred to in the preceding Article are placed under a particular jurisdiction (such as Aden, which we have allowed to come under the temporary occupation of Great Britain), may not be interpreted as implying any change in their dependence on the Imamate, which remains the original and natural sovereign authority. On the contrary, it will be incumbent on His Britannic Majesty's Government to compel the Rulers and peoples of those territories to establish good relations with the sovereign authority within two years, while His Britannic Majesty's Government undertake to abstain from supplying those territories with any arms or other supplies which may cause controversy. The Rulers and Chiefs of those territories will be required to rule with justice, while the judges, who must belong to the Shafe'ite persuasion, will be men of tried integrity, to be appointed by the Imam. Further, should those Rulers and Chiefs fail in putting an end to dissensions and bloodshed among their tribes, it shall rest with the Imam to take all possible action to restore order and prevent hostilities and destruction.

Article 5.

His Britannic Majesty's Government and His Highness the Imam shall each have an official representative in the territory of the other, and each of the two representatives shall have the same rights and privileges as are accorded to the other, such rights and privileges to be agreed upon when the localities at which each representative is to reside will have been fixed.

Article 6.

His Britannic Majesty's Government and His Highness the Imam will give increased scope to commerce and will keep open the trade routes, both by land and by sea, between the two countries. His Britannic Majesty's Government will give to the subjects of His Highness the Imam complete freedom for the pursuit of trade whether by sea or by land. Neither His Britannic Majesty's Government nor His Highness the Imam shall impose any duty on commercial goods other than the prescribed transit (land and sea) dues which are known to each Government. If any change is made by either Government in the prescribed dues, they will be bound to inform the other Government of such change immediately.

Article 7.

His Britannic Majesty's Government and His Highness the Imam shall each remain absolutely free to impose such duty on goods in their territory as they may wish; but they both undertake not to impose higher duties on the goods of their respective subjects than is imposed on the goods of the subjects of any other Government.

Article 8.

His Britannic Majesty's Government declare that they will not interfere in any way in the dominions of His Highness the Imam; while His Highness the Imam declares that he will not permit the interference of any foreign Government in his dominions whether by sale, or mortgage or gift or any other form of ownership.

Article 9.

In order to achieve the desired peace completely, His Britannic Majesty's Government undertake to refrain from giving neighbouring Arab chiefs who may be in treaty relations with them (with the exception of those mentioned in Article 3) any aid or assistance or reinforcement. In the event of any of those Chiefs attacking His Highness the Imam, or in the event of any difference arising between His Highness the Imam and any of those Arab Chiefs, it will be incumbent upon His Britannic Majesty's Government to advise and oppose the said Arab Chief with a view to checking his aggression.

Article 10.

Should His Highness the Imam desire to construct a railway in his dominions and to entrust its construction to a foreign company, it will be open to His Highness to inform His Britannic Majesty's Government of the offers made by foreign companies, so that, in the event of British companies wishing to undertake the contract on terms more acceptable, cheaper, and more expeditious than those of other foreign companies, preference and priority will be given to them. His Highness the Imam will not place such orders with other than British firms so long as British firms offer the required facilities. But should His Highness the Imam desire to undertake the construction without recourse to a foreign company, he will be free to do so, absolutely and without restriction.

Article 11.

(This Article is identical with Article 13 in the Draft of August, 1924 [Appendix III] and is not reprinted.)

Article 12.

The lighting of lighthouses will be undertaken by His Highness the Imam in agreement with the Central Lighthouse Administration, on the understanding that all officials and servants engaged in this service will be Yamani subjects of His Highness exclusively.

Article 13.

All questions arising within Imamic territory between subjects of His Highness the Imam and recognised subjects of His Britannic Majesty will be settled in Imamic courts and in accordance with Shari'a law. Similarly any claim arising in British territory between subjects of His Britannic Majesty and subjects of His Highness the Imam will be settled in British courts and according to the dictates of justice and of equality before the law.

Article 14.

On the conclusion of the present Treaty, the Government of His Highness the Imam, whose full independence will have been thus recognised, shall have the right to undertake any of the activities which are proper to an independent state, such as the post office, passports, harbours and sea-shores, shipping (including the purchase, sale, hire and construction of vessels) flying the Imamic flag. His Highness the Imam will also be free to purchase whatever he may find necessary in the way of equipment, armaments, supplies and the like, as is the established practice in international commercial usage.

Article 15.

His Britannic Majesty's Government shall supply His Highness the Imam with anything he might require, in the way of weapons of war and medical requirements, on the cheapest and fairest terms. Should His Highness the Imam require the services of a physician or an engineer, His Britannic Majesty's Government will be required to find candidates at cheap and moderate salaries.

Article 16.

Every Article in the present Treaty shall have the same force as the Treaty itself. The present Treaty shall be binding on both parties for ten years, at the end of which period it will be renewed on terms to be agreed upon between His Highness the Imam and His Britannic Majesty's Government.

Article 17.

The Arabic version is the sole authoritative version to which all reference in interpretation is to be made.

APPENDIX VI

Draft Presented to the Imam by Clayton on 10 February 1926

WHEREAS there are certain outstanding matters which require settlement between His Britannic Majesty's Government and the Government of His Highness the Imam of Yemen, and

WHEREAS His Highness the Imam of Yemen advances claims which are held by His Britannic Majesty's Government to be incompatible with their present position and obligations in the Aden Protectorate,

The two High Contracting Parties

Being desirous of establishing friendly relations between the two countries have mutually agreed as follows:

Article 1.

The settlement of the claims advanced by His Highness the Imam with reference to the southern boundary of the Yemen and to rights over certain territories lying within the present boundary of the Aden Protectorate is deferred and shall hereafter form the subject of friendly negotiation between the two parties with a view to arriving at a final settlement before the expiry of the duration of the present Agreement; it being understood that nothing in this Agreement shall be taken as meaning that His Highness the Imam renounces his claims or that His Britannic Majesty's Government admit them.

Article 2.

His Britannic Majesty's Government acknowledge the absolute independence of His Highness the Imam in all matters, political and administrative, external and internal; while His Highness the Imam recognises the Protectorate Treaties between His Britannic Majesty's Government and the Chiefs and tribes of the Aden Protectorate (as shown in the list at the foot of this Article) and undertakes to prevent, by all the means at his disposal, any incursion by armed forces across the frontier which was demarcated in 1903, 1904 and 1905, and ratified in 1914, by the British and Turkish Governments. His Highness the Imam also undertakes to prevent any interference, of whatsoever kind, on the part of his subjects with the peoples inhabiting the Aden side of that frontier.

(The list of Chiefs and tribes is identical with that given in the margin of Article 3 of the Draft of August, 1924 [Appendix III].)

Article 3.

In order to render possible the friendly negotiations envisaged in Article 1 of the present Agreement, His Highness the Imam undertakes, within six months of the date of signature of the present Agreement, to withdraw all his officials and forces of whatsoever kind from those territories lying on the Aden side of the boundary, which are at present in his occupation.

Article 4.

Same as Article 2 of the Draft of August, 1924.

Article 5.

Same as Article 4 of the Draft of August, 1924.

Articles 6–16.

Same as Articles 5–15 of the Draft of August, 1924.

Article 17.

The present Agreement shall be in force for a period of ten years, at the end of which period it shall be renewed in such form as may be agreed upon by the two parties and in such a way as to include a final settlement of the claims advanced by His Highness the Imam.

APPENDIX VII

Second Counter-draft Treaty Presented by the Imam on 14 February 1926

His Britannic Majesty's Government on the one part and His Highness the Imam Yahya of the Yemen on the other part:

Being desirous of settling certain outstanding matters between them and to establish relations between the two countries on a basis of friendship and co-operation for their mutual benefit and with a view to reaching permanent agreement in future:

His Britannic Majesty's Government have named and appointed Sir Gilbert Falkingham Clayton, K.B.E., C.B., C.M.G., as their Representative and Plenipotentiary to conclude a Treaty for this purpose with the Imam Yahya al-Mutawakkil 'ala Allah:

In virtue of which, the said Imam Yahya al-Mutawakkil 'ala Allah on behalf of the Yemen, and the said Sir Gilbert Falkingham Clayton on behalf of His Britannic Majesty's Government, have agreed upon and concluded the following Articles:

Article 1.

His Britannic Majesty's Government recognise the absolute independence of the Imam in all matters political and administrative, internal and external, and his sovereignty in his dominions. Nothing in the present Article is to be considered as invalidating the provisions of Article 2.

Article 2.

(This Article is identical with Article 2 of the first counter-draft forming [Appendix V], and is not reprinted.)

Article 3.

The settlement of the question of the southern frontier referred to in Article 4 is deferred pending the conclusion of the negotiations which shall take place between His Britannic Majesty's Government and His Highness the Imam before the expiry of the present Treaty, it being understood that nothing contained in the Articles of the present Treaty is to be taken as meaning that His Highness the Imam renounces his claims or that His Britannic Majesty's Government recognise any part of his claims.

Article 4.

His Highness the Imam agrees that the territories lying in the southern part should remain as at present in the hands of the Chiefs whose names are enumerated below. His Highness undertakes to prevent by all the means at his disposal any incursion by his armed forces, while Great Britain undertakes to prevent the entry of any of her armed forces into those territories. His Highness the Imam will also prevent any interference on the part of his subjects with the affairs of the inhabitants of those territories on condition that no aggression be committed, whether by His Britannic Majesty's Government or by one of the Chiefs referred to above, on any of the territories which are at present in the hands of His Highness the Imam. Here follows the list of Chiefs: —

(The list is identical with that given in the Imam's first draft, [Appendix VI], save for the addition of The Audali and Jabal Radfan.)

Article 5.

In the event of His Highness the Imam applying to His Britannic Majesty's Government in the first instance for the supply of such arms, ammunition, war material and equipment as he may require, His Britannic Majesty's Government shall supply him with his requirements at fair and moderate rates and with all possible speed. If for any reason His Britannic Majesty's Government are unable to supply His Highness the Imam's requirements within two months, and at a moderate price, His Highness will then be free to apply for his requirements to any Government or Company without restriction.

Article 6.

In the event of His Highness the Imam applying to His Britannic Majesty's Government for the selection of such engineers, doctors and other professional men, and of such medicines, machinery, telegraph and wireless plants as he may require, or should he desire to undertake projects of an economic nature such as the construction of railways, or the exploitation of mines, or similar works, and were to apply to His Britannic Majesty's Government, the latter shall supply him with his requirements at fair and moderate rates and without delay. If, for any reason, His Britannic Majesty's Government are unable to meet His Highness the Imam's requirements, they will so inform him without delay.

Article 7.

(This Article is identical with Article 6 in the first counter-draft forming [Appendix V], and is not reprinted.)

Article 8.

(This Article is identical with Article 7 in the first counter-draft forming [Appendix V], and is not reprinted.)

Article 9.

His Britannic Majesty's Government and His Highness the Imam shall each have an official representative in the territory of the other, and each of the two representatives shall have the same rights and privileges as are accorded to the other, such rights and privileges to be settled by subsequent agreement.

Article 10.

(This Article is identical with Article 8 of the first counter-draft forming [Appendix V], and is not reprinted.)

Article 11.

His Highness the Imam will, by every possible means, assist His Britannic Majesty's Government in their endeavours to prevent the African slave traffic by sea.

Article 12.

After the ratification of this Treaty, His Britannic Majesty's Government and His Highness the Imam will come to an agreement as to the manner in which the lighthouses on the Imamic coast are to be lit. His Highness the Imam will give priority to His Britannic Majesty's Government in this matter; and after agreement as to the manner in which the lighting is to be performed, His Highness the Imam will not conclude any agreement in this matter with any other Government. If no agreement is reached, His Highness the Imam will be free to make other arrangements.

Article 13.

All questions arising within Imamic territory between subjects of His Highness the Imam and recognised subjects of His Britannic Majesty, will be settled in Imamic Courts and in accordance with Shari'a law. Similarly any claim arising in British territory between subjects of His Britannic Majesty and subjects of His Highness the Imam will be settled in British Courts and in accordance with the dictates of justice.

Article 14.

The Government of His Highness the Imam shall have the right to undertake any of the activities which are proper to an independent state, such as the post office, passports, harbours and sea-shores, shipping (including the purchase, sale, hire and construction of vessels) flying the Imamic flag. His Highness the Imam will also be free to purchase whatever he may find necessary in the way of equipment, armaments, supplies, and to restore the submarine cable at Sheikh Sa'id, and deal with similar matters, as is the established practice in international usage. His Britannic Majesty's Government undertake to give their help and guidance towards the achievement of such objects.

Article 15.

The Arabic version is the sole authoritative version to which all reference in interpretation is to be made.

Article 16.

The present Treaty shall remain valid and in force for a period of ten years as from . On the expiry of that period it will be renewed in a form to be agreed upon by both parties and in such a way as to provide a final settlement in regard to the question referred to in Article 3.

APPENDIX VIII

Amended and Final Draft Treaty Presented to the Imam by Clayton on 18 February 1926

His Britannic Majesty's Government on the one part and His Highness the Imam Yahya of the Yemen on the other part:

Being desirous of settling certain outstanding matters between them and to establish relations between the two countries on a basis of friendship and cooperation for their mutual benefit and with a view to reaching permanent agreement in future:

His Britannic Majesty's Government have named and appointed Sir Gilbert Falkingham Clayton, K.B.E., C.B., C.M.G., as their Representative and Plenipotentiary to conclude a Treaty for this purpose with the Imam Yahya al-Mutawakkil 'ala Allah:

In virtue of which, the said Imam Yahya al-Mutawwakil 'ala Allah on behalf of the Yemen, and the said Sir Gilbert Falkingham Clayton on behalf of His Britannic Majesty's Government have agreed upon and concluded the following Articles.

Article 1.

His Britannic Majesty's Government acknowledge the sovereignty and the absolute independence of His Highness the Imam in all matters, political and administrative, internal and external, in his dominions. Nothing in the present Article is to be considered as a contradiction of the contents of Article 2.

Article 2.

His Highness the Imam shall not enter into correspondence or agreement with any Government or individual on any matter prejudicial to

His Britannic Majesty's Government. Similarly His Britannic Majesty's Government shall not enter into correspondence or agreement with any Government or individual on any matter prejudicial to the Government of His Highness the Imam. His Highness the Imam will be at liberty to enter into correspondence or agreement with any Government on matters which are not prejudicial to His Britannic Majesty's Government.

Article 3.

The settlement of the question of the southern frontier referred to in Article 4 is deferred pending the conclusion, in whatever way may be agreed upon by both parties, of the negotiations which shall take place between His Britannic Majesty's Government and His Highness the Imam before the expiry of the present Treaty, it being understood that nothing contained in the Articles of the present Treaty is to be taken as meaning that His Highness the Imam renounces his claims or that His Britannic Majesty's Government recognise any part of his claims.

Article 4.

The territories which are in the hands of the Chiefs and Rulers enumerated at the foot of this Article, and which are bounded by the frontier demarcated in 1903, 1904 and 1905, shall remain under their rule as at present. His Highness the Imam recognises the special relations existing between those Chiefs and Rulers and His Britannic Majesty's Government, it being understood that this recognition does not abrogate the provisions of Article 3. His Highness the Imam undertakes that he will prevent, by all means at his disposal, any aggression by his forces on those territories, and any interference by his subjects with the affairs of the peoples inhabiting the Aden side of that frontier.

In accordance with the provisions of Article 3, nothing in the present Article is to be taken as signifying that His Highness the Imam has recognised the Agreement under which the above frontier was fixed.

[List of Chiefs and Rulers is identical with that found in the Draft of August 1924, Appendix III.]

Article 5.

His Highness the Imam will apply to His Britannic Majesty's Government in the first instance for the selection of such engineers, doctors, and other professional men, and of such medicines, machinery, telegraph and wireless plants as he may require. Likewise, if he should desire to undertake projects of an economic nature such as the construction of railways or harbours, or the exploitation of mines, or similar works, for which he may need foreign assistance, he will apply in the first instance to His Britannic Majesty's Government, who will be expected to supply him with his requirements at fair and moderate rates and with all possible speed. If, for any reason, His Britannic Majesty's Government are not prepared to meet His Highness the Imam's requirements, they will so inform him without delay, and in any case within four months of the receipt of his application. His Highness the Imam will then be free to apply for his requirements wherever else he may choose.

Article 6.

His Britannic Majesty's Government and His Highness the Imam shall each have an agent in the territory of the other, and each of the two agents shall have the same rights and privileges as are accorded to the other.

Article 7.

His Britannic Majesty's Government and His Highness the Imam will give increased scope to commerce and will keep open the trade routes, both by land and by sea, between the two countries. His Britannic Majesty's Government will give to the subjects of His Highness the Imam complete freedom for the pursuit of trade whether by sea or by land. Neither His Britannic Majesty's Government nor His Highness the Imam shall impose any duty on commercial goods other than the prescribed transit (land and sea) dues which are known to each Government. If any change is made by either Government in the prescribed dues, they will be bound to inform the other Government of such change immediately.

Article 8.

His Britannic Majesty's Government and His Highness the Imam shall each remain absolutely free to impose such duty on goods in their territory as they may wish; but each Government undertakes not to impose, on goods belonging to subjects of the other, higher duties than are imposed on goods belonging to subjects of any other Government.

Article 9.

His Britannic Majesty's Government declare that they will not interfere in any way in the dominions of His Highness the Imam; while His Highness the Imam declares that he will not permit the interference of any foreign Government in his dominions whether by sale, or mortgage, or gift or any other form of interference.

Article 10.

His Highness the Imam will, by every possible means, assist His Britannic Majesty's Government in their endeavours to prevent the African slave traffic by sea.

Article 11.

After the ratification of this Treaty, His Britannic Majesty's Government and His Highness the Imam will come to an agreement as to the manner in which the lighthouses on the Imamic coast are to be lit. His Highness the Imam will give priority to His Britannic Majesty's Government in this matter; and after agreement as to the manner in which the lighting is to be performed, His Highness the Imam will not conclude any agreement in this matter with any other Government. If no agreement is reached, His Highness the Imam will be free to make other arrangements on condition that he will not grant, to whomsoever he may conclude an agreement with, more favourable terms than those offered to His Britannic Majesty's Government.

Article 12.

The present Treaty will be known as the Treaty of San'a.

Article 13.

The present Treaty shall remain valid and in force for a period of ten years from the date of its ratification. On the expiry of that period it will be renewed in a form to be agreed upon by both parties and in such a way as to provide a final settlement in regard to the question referred to in Article 3.

Additional Article

Every claim in any matter arising within the Imamic territories between the subjects of His Highness the Imam and the subjects of His Britannic Majesty shall be dealt with in the Imamic courts in accordance with the Islamic Shari'a and the principles of equity; similarly every claim in any matter arising within British territory between the subjects of His Britannic Majesty and the subjects of His Highness the Imam shall be dealt with in British courts in accordance with the principles of equity; it being understood that the subjects of His Britannic Majesty shall not enjoy less favourable rights and privileges than the rights and privileges enjoyed by the subjects of any other Power with whom His Highness the Imam might at any time conclude a Treaty.

APPENDIX IX
Biographies

The following biographical notes have been compiled for British persons largely from published sources, particularly *Who's Who.* The biographical notes for Arabs and non-Westerners, however, have been compiled from mixed sources ranging from well-known journals such as *Oriente Moderno* to hundreds of inquiries by the editor from many of the participants in the *Diary* who are still alive today and whose assistance is gratefully acknowledged in the Preface. Names of Arabs except when obviously anglicized (as in George Antonius), are alphabetized with the *first* of the names given them by Sir Gilbert in the *Diary*, or by the editor if the *Diary* identifies them only by office. Thus, Ibn Sa'ud is placed under the I's rather than under the S's.

Abdel Hamid Pasha Suleiman [Sulayman, Sir 'Abd al-Hamid Pasha] (1882–1945) obtained a B.S. degree in Civil Engineering, and from 1903–07 was employed in the Egyptian Ministry of Public Irrigation in which he became the Technical Secretary to the Minister in 1909. He was appointed Director General of Public Works at Bani Suwayf in 1914, Irrigation Inspector at Suhag 1917, and at Al-Fayyum 1919. In 1921 he was the first Egyptian appointed Under Secretary, Ministry of Public Works for which he received the title of Pasha. In 1923 he was made Minister of Public Works and Dean of the School of Engineering. In 1924 he was appointed Director of Egyptian State Railways, the first Egyptian to hold the post, and was knighted the following year. In 1926 he served as Egyptian delegate to the Water Distribution Committee between Egypt and the Sudan, and in 1928 was the first Egyptian to be Minister of Communications. He became a Senator in 1930 and Minister of Finance in 1940. He was principally responsible for introducing the automatic telephone into Egypt, and for the plans for the Nag' Hamadi dam.

Abdul Kerim, Sayed [Sayyid 'Abd al-Karim] was probably the Qadi 'Abd al-Karim ibn Ahmed Mutahhar, who was Secretary and Chief Clerk to Imam Yahya at the time of Sir Gilbert Clayton's mission in 1926. Yahya relied on him a good deal and consulted him on all official correspondence. He was also editor of *Imam*, the only newspaper allowed in the Yemen at that time. By 1934 he had become the Minister of Justice.

Abdul Mohsin Saadun [Sir 'Abd al-Muhsin as-Sa'dun] (1879–1929) was a Deputy in the 'Iraqi Chamber from Al-Basrah and a member of the famous Sa'dun family. He held moderate views and in 1925 founded the Taqaddum (Progressive) Party. He served as Prime Minister 1922–23; President of the Constituent Assembly 1924; Minister of Interior 1924–25; Prime Minister 1925–26, and again in 1928–29. He committed suicide in 1929.

Abdulla, Amir ['Abd Allah ibn Husayn] (1882–1951), educated privately in Mecca and Istanbul, was the son of Husayn ibn 'Ali, Sharif of Mecca. He served as a member of the Ottoman Parliament for Mecca from 1908 to the outbreak of the First World War. During the Arab Revolt he commanded the Southern Army until the fall of Madina, and afterward moved north to Trans-Jordan as a claimant for the Syrian throne against the French occupation. Unwilling to have him fight the French, Britain offered him the amirate of Trans-Jordan in 1921, which he accepted along with a British subsidy. During World War II he remained a steadfast ally of Britain, and in 1946 Trans-Jordan was declared the independent Kingdom of Jordan and 'Abd Allah was proclaimed its King. In 1948 he sent the Arab Legion to hold a strip of territory on the west bank of the Jordan River which he formally incorporated into the Kingdom of Jordan. He was assassinated on 21 July 1951 by an Arab tailor. 'Abd Allah had a particular fondness for Arabic poetry, chess, and food.

Abdulla el Amri, Kadi [Qadi 'Abd Allah ibn Huhayn al-'Amri] was the Prime Minister to the Imam Yahya at the time of the Clayton Mission. He served as First Secretary to the Imam in 1937.

Abdulla el-Fadl ['Abd Allah al-Fadl] was a prominent merchant of Jiddah born about 1883. He was imprisoned at Mecca in 1917 but was later sent on a delegation to negotiate with Ibn Sa'ud in Mecca. He acted as Ibn Sa'ud's representative at Rabigh for the 1925 pilgrimage and was the delegate from the Hijaz to the Muslim Congress in Mecca in June 1926. He was sent on a mission to Eritrea in 1927 in connection with negotiations for the recognition of Ibn

Sa'ud by Italy and prepared the treaty arrangements. In 1929 he went on a mission to Persia, and in the same year became Assistant to the Viceroy of Mecca and was appointed Vice-President of the Legislative Council, both of which appointments he still held in 1954. He was later the Sa'udi Arabian Ambassador to Egypt.

Abdulla ibn Abdur Rahman Al Sa'ud, Amir ['Abd Allah ibn 'Abd ar-Rahman ibn Faysal ibn Sa'ud] (1900–), youngest brother of King Ibn Sa'ud, commanded the Wahhabi troops before Jiddah and later took an active part in crushing the Dawish rebellion of 1929–30. He has long been prominent in the counsels of Ibn Sa'ud, and since the Second World War has closely concerned himself with the administration of Sa'udi Arabia, being one of the official Advisers to the king and a member of the Privy Council.

Abdulla ibn el Wazir, Sayed [Sayyid 'Abd Allah ibn Ahmed ibn al-Wazir] (? –1948), head of the Waziri family and principal pretender to the Imamate through his relationship to Imam Muhammad al-Wazir, who died in 1888. He served as Governor of Al-Hudaydah but was removed in 1939 and came to San'a' where he was Minister without Portfolio in 1941. He was involved with the "Free Yemeni" revolutionary movement and was proclaimed Imam after the assassination of Imam Yahya in February 1948. He was quickly deposed, however, by the forces of Ahmed ibn Yahya, Yahya's eldest son. He was beheaded in April 1948.

Abdur Rahman el Mahdi, El Sayid ['Abd ar-Rahman al-Mahdi, Sayyid Sir] (1885–1959), the posthumous son of Muhammad Ahmad al-Mahdi who had led the Mahdist uprising against Turko-Egyptian rule in the Sudan, during which Khartoum was captured in 1885 and the British agent General Gordon died. After the death of his father in 1885 and of his father's successor, the Khalifa 'Abd Allahi, in 1899, Sayyid 'Abd ar-Rahman assumed the spiritual leadership of the Ansar (his father's followers), but remained in political eclipse until the First World War when he used his influence on behalf of the Allied cause. Thereafter his power and prestige grew under the aegis of British officials who sought a counterweight to the strength of the other great Sudanese religious leader, Sayyid 'Ali al-Mirghani, and his supporters. As Sudanese nationalism blossomed after the Second World War, Sayyid 'Abd ar-Rahman utilized his position as a religious leader to form the Umma Party, the political purpose of which was to win independence for the Sudan. As the founder and leader of the Umma Party, Sayyid 'Abd ar-Rahman worked assiduously for an independent Sudan, a goal that was achieved in 1956, a few years before his death.

Acland, Alfred Dyke (1858–1937), educated at Temple Grove, East Sheen, and Charterhouse, was a partner in W. H. Smith & Sons. He was an officer in the Devon Yeomanry which he subsequently commanded from 1910–14. During the First World War he served at No. 3 Base Remount Depot, France, and was Assistant Director of Labour, Fourth Army, under Sir William Birdwood, 1917.

Acland, Katharine (1892–   ), educated at home, served in a Voluntary Aid Detachment and was Secretary to the Hertfordshire British Red Cross Society during the First World War. She joined the Auxiliary Territorial Service during the Second World War and afterward became a member of the Chelsea Borough Council in 1949 and was Mayor of Chelsea 1959–61.

Adam, Colin Gurdon Forbes (1889–   ), educated at Eton and King's College, Cambridge, joined the Indian Civil Service in 1913 and served as the Assistant Collector and Magistrate, Ahmednagar, 1913–15, until he was posted to the Mesopotamian Expeditionary Force where he served to the end of the war. He returned to Poona in 1919 but was soon transferred to the post of undersecretary to the government at Bombay, Political and Judicial Department. He was the Private Secretary to the Governor of Bombay, George Lloyd, from 1920 until 1924. In the following year he was posted as Deputy Secretary, Home and Ecclesiastical Departments, 1925–26. He served as a nominated member of the Bombay Legislative Council in 1926 until his retirement the following year. He is the author of *Life of Lord Lloyd*. He married the Hon. Irene Constance Lawley, the only child of the 3rd Baron Wenlock, in 1920.

Ahmed Bey Saddik [Ahmad Sadig Bey] was an Egyptian who was sent to Paris before the First World War to study police methods. Following the war he joined the Egyptian Civil Service, where he held various posts during the 1920's. In the early 1930's, while serving as Head of the Alexandria Municipality, he was connected with a construction scandal involving the "Corniche Road" running to the Muntazah palace.

Ahmed Pasha Sanaa [Ahmad Pasha as-Sani'], the head of one of Al Basrah's leading families, served as Minister without portfolio in the Council of Ministers formed under British guidance in 1920. He later returned to Al Basrah where he served as *mutasarrif* and concerned himself with local politics and his business affairs.

Ali el Yemeni, Sayed [Sayyid 'Ali Yahya] came to Port Sudan in 1905–06 where he engaged in various mercantile enterprises at the new port. In 1920 he left for the Yemen, his home, but returned to the Sudan in 1925 and was a contractor for Yemeni laborers whom he brought from the Yemen to Port Sudan for loading, unloading, and stacking of all cargo. When all Yemeni laborers were replaced by Sudanese in 1937–38, he returned to the Yemen where he constructed the extension of the quays at Al-Hudaydah.

Ali ibn el Wazir, Sayed [Sayyid 'Ali ibn al-Wazir], cousin of 'Abd Allah ibn Ahmed ibn al-Wazir and member of the powerful Waziri family. He served as the 'Amil of Ta'izz until 1939 when he was replaced by a member of the Imam Yahya's own family.

Ali, King ['Ali ibn Husayn, Amir] (1871–1935), eldest son of King Husayn of the Hijaz, played an active role in the Arab Revolt and succeeded to the throne of the Hijaz upon his father's abdication in 1924. He could not halt the inexorable advance of the Wahhabi forces of Ibn Sa'ud, however, and so in December 1925 turned over the Hijaz to Ibn Sa'ud and went into exile in Baghdad where his brother Faysal was King of 'Iraq. He acted occasionally as Regent for 'Iraq but took no further part in Arab politics.

Amery, the Right Honourable Leopold Charles Maurice Stennett (1873–1955), educated at Harrow and Balliol College, Oxford, served on *The Times* before entering Parliament in 1908. He was an assistant secretary to the War Cabinet and in 1919 was the Parliamentary Under-Secretary to Lord Milner at the Colonial Office. In 1922 he was appointed First Lord of the Admiralty and in 1924 became the Secretary of State for the Colonies. He traveled widely in connection with his office and wrote copiously. He later served in Churchill's Cabinet as the Secretary of State for India.

Amos, Sir Maurice Sheldon (1872–1940), educated privately and at Trinity College, Cambridge, was made barrister-at-law, Inner Temple 1897 and went out to Egypt the following year as Inspector of Native Courts. A judge of Cairo Native Court of First Instance, 1903, and of the Native Court of Appeal in 1906, he was seconded as the Director of Khedivial Law School 1913–15. During the First World War he served in the Ministry of Munitions 1915–17, and afterward as the

Acting Judicial Adviser 1917–19, and then the Judicial Adviser 1919–25, to the government of Egypt.

Antonius, George (1891–1942), born of Greek Orthodox parents in the Lebanon and educated at Victoria College, Alexandria, and King's College, Cambridge; was the Deputy Chief Press Censor, Egyptian Expeditionary Force, 1917–21; accompanied Sir Gilbert Clayton on his mission to Arabia and the Yemen, 1925–26; was Chief Inspector of Education, Palestine government, 1925–28; Assistant Secretary to the Palestine Government, 1927–30; Senior Associate for the Near East, Institute of Current World Affairs; Delegate to the London Conferences on Palestine; and Secretary to the Palestine Delegation. He published the influential book, *The Arab Awakening*, in 1938.

Archer, Sir Geoffrey Francis (1882–1964), entered the Colonial Service in the East African Protectorate in 1902 where he served in various offices until sent to Somaliland in 1912 first as Deputy Commissioner, then Commissioner and Commander-in-Chief, then Governor. He directed the campaign against the Mullah in 1920, and in 1922 was appointed Governor of Uganda. He became the Governor-General of the Sudan in 1924, a post which he held less than two years before his retirement in 1926. In 1916 he married Olive Mary Godman, the eldest daughter of Colonel Charles Bulkeley Godman.

Asser Pasha, General Sir Joseph John (1867–1944), entered the Royal Artillery in 1887 and served in the Nile campaign 1897–99, having joined the Egyptian Army in 1892. He commanded the campaigns in southern Kordofan in 1910 and was a member of the Governor-General's Council. In 1901 he married Leila Wotherspoon of New York, whose charm and wit made the Assers one of the most popular couples in the British community at Khartoum. He was promoted to General in 1926.

Awad el-Kerim ['Awad al-Karim as-Sayigh], a gold- and silversmith of Umdurman, was probably of *muwallad* or mixed Egyptian-Sudanese origin. He wrote a three-volume work printed in Cairo entitled *Mukhtarat as-Sayigh*, a work of Oriental sexology, said by the author to be a summary of many books, mainly medical. 'Awad al-Karim was nicknamed al-Hindi, "the Indian" possibly because of the reputed origin of the material in his book. He retired from business in 1953.

Ballereau, Paul-Arthur (1880–   ), educated at the School of Oriental Languages, Paris, served as interpreter at Tangier 1906–1911 when he became Interpreter 3rd class and was attached to the High Commissioner, Morocco, in 1912. In 1913 he was Chief Interpreter at Tangier and in 1919 Interim Chief Interpreter at the French Agency, Cairo, before taking charge of the management of the French consulate, Baghdad. In 1920 he was made Vice-Consul at Mersin and in December he was placed in charge of interpreters at the French Agency, Cairo. In 1921 he was made Chief Interpreter at the French consulate, Jerusalem, where he served until 1926 when he was sent to the French legation, Teheran, as 3rd secretary. Here he managed the legation until 1928 when he was sent to Kabul and in 1930 to Singapore. At Singapore he served as Consul and Consul-General before taking charge of the French legation at Jiddah in 1937 where he served as Consul-General and Minister Plenipotentiary until his retirement in 1940.

Barclay, Lieutenant-Commander John Cedric Hargreave (1895–1937), served as a Clerk and Assistant Paymaster during the First World War. He was commissioned a Lieutenant in 1916 and promoted to Lieutenant-Commander in 1924.

Bell, Gertrude Margaret Lowthian (1868–1926), eldest daughter of Sir Hugh Bell, was educated at Queen's College, London, and Lady Margaret Hall, Oxford. She traveled widely throughout the Middle East for many years before being attached to the Military Intelligence Department, Cairo, in 1915. In the following year she became the Liaison Officer of the Arab Bureau in 'Iraq and in 1917 the Assistant Political Officer, Baghdad, until her appointment as Oriental Secretary, a position she retained until her death.

Bentwich, Norman (1883–), educated at St. Paul's School and Trinity College, Cambridge, and called to the bar in 1908, served at the Ministry of Justice, Cairo, 1912–16. He was the Attorney-General, Government of Palestine, 1920–31; and afterward Professor of International Relations, Jerusalem University, 1932–51. He served on numerous commissions and committees for the relief and restitution of Jews and has published several books on the Palestine problem. In 1915 he married Helen Franklin, who has served as Hon. Secretary, Palestine Council of Women, 1921–30; and as Alderman of London County Council 1937 to 1958, serving as Chairman of the Council, 1956–57.

Birdwood of Anzac and of Totnes, Field Marshal William Riddell Birdwood (1865–1951), educated at Clifton College and the Royal Military College, Sandhurst, entered the army in 1883 and served in India and the South African War after which he returned to service in India as Military Secretary to the Commander-in-Chief, 1905; Brigade Commander 1909; Quartermaster-General in India, 1912; and Secretary to the government of India in the Army Department, 1912–14. He was G.O.C. of the Australian and New Zealand Army Corps, 1914–18, and of the Australian Imperial Force 1915–20, before returning to India as General Officer Commanding-in-Chief, Northern Army in India, 1920–24, and Commander-in-Chief of the Army of India, 1925–30. Upon retirement he became Master of Peterhouse, Cambridge, 1931–38. In 1894 he married Jeannette Hope Gonville, eldest daughter of Colonel, Sir B. P. Bromhead, 4th Bart. of Thurlby Hall, Lincoln.

Birkett, Captain Miles Brock (1882–1948), was commissioned as a Midshipman in the Royal Navy in 1899 and was promoted to Sub-Lieutenant, 1902; Lieutenant, 1905; Lieutenant-Commander, 1913; Commander, 1916; and Captain, 1923.

Bolland, Arthur P. (1877–1959), educated at King's School, Worcester, joined the Secretary's Office of the Great Western Railway in 1894 under the then secretary G. K. Mills. In 1904 he was invited to join the Sudan Civil Service as an extra secretary to the Governor-General, Sir Reginald Wingate. He remained three years in Khartoum and was then transferred to the Sudan Agency in Cairo as the Commercial Secretary under the Sudan Agent, Sir Lee Stack. He continued at the Sudan Agency in Cairo, working under Gilbert Clayton who succeeded Sir Lee Stack as the Sudan Agent, and remained at the Agency until retirement in 1925.

Boulos Pasha [Hanna Bulos Pasha] (1893–   ) received both his primary and secondary education at Victoria College, Alexandria, and then studied Law at Pembroke College, Oxford. He returned to Egypt in 1922 and entered politics, becoming one of the prominent members of the Wafd Party under the presidency of Nahas Pasha. He wrote numerous articles in *Al-Ahram* and *Al-Jihad* condemning government corruption and attacking political figures such as 'Ali Mahir and Isma'il Sidqi. He inherited large land holdings in 1938 upon the death of his father, and in 1940 entered the Stock Exchange where he became an influential figure. He remained in the Stock Exchange until 1958, and in 1962 retired from public affairs to manage his estates near Al Uqsut. He was made Pasha in 1944 and a Senator in 1951. He married Janette Butros Maqar in 1929, and had four daughters and three sons.

Bourdillon, Sir Bernard Henry (1883–1948), educated at Tonbridge and St. John's College, Oxford, joined the Indian Civil Service in 1908 and served in Mesopotamia 1918–19. He was appointed Political Secretary to the High Commissioner of 'Iraq in 1921, Secretary, 1922; Counsellor, 1924–29; and Acting High Commissioner, 1925–26. He later became Colonial and Chief Secretary, Ceylon, 1929–32; Acting Governor, 1930–31; Governor, Uganda, 1932–35; and Governor, Nigeria, 1935–43. In 1909 he married Violet Grace Billinghurst, eldest daughter of the Rev. H. G. Billinghurst of Lynch, Sussex.

Bowman, Humphrey Ernest (1879–1965), educated at Eton and New College, Oxford, entered the Egyptian Civil Service, Ministry of Education, 1903–23, during which time he was an Inspector, Education Department, Sudan, 1911–13; and Director of Education, 'Iraq, 1918–20. He served as Director of Education and Member Advisory Council, Palestine government, from 1920 until retirement in 1936. In 1916 he married Frances Guinevere Armytage who died in 1923. He was remarried in 1925 to Elinor ("Nora") Marion Conybeare, widow of Arthur William Bowman. She died in 1957.

Boyce, Austin Alexander Rodney (1870–1948), born in Tasmania and educated at Toowoomba Grammar School, Queensland, served in Lands and Survey Office, Brisbane, Queensland 1890–1902, when he joined the Gold Coast Survey. In 1906 he was appointed to the Sudan Survey Department, 1906–27, and was awarded the Gill Memorial by the Royal Geographical Society in 1922, for triangulation in the Sudan. In 1923 he served as Chief Commissioner, Anglo-French Sudan Boundary Commission. He retired in 1927 to Queensland.

Bray, Sir Denys de Saumarez (1875–1951), educated at the Realgymnasium, Stuttgart; Blundell's School, Tiverton; and Balliol College, Oxford; entered the Indian Civil Service in 1898 and served in the Punjab, the North West Frontier, and Baluchistan. He was the Deputy Foreign Secretary, 1916; Acting Private Secretary to the Viceroy, 1918; Joint Foreign Secretary, 1919; and Foreign Secretary, 1920–30. He later served on the Indian Delegation to the League of Nations, 1931–37. He was married to Celestina Leigh.

Brocklehurst, Lieutenant-Colonel Henry Courtney (1888–1942) was commissioned in the 11th Hussars in 1908 and served in Palestine, Tanganyika, and North Russia during the First World War. He resigned from the British Army in 1919, and in 1922 was appointed game warden of the Sudan government, a post he held until his retirement in 1931. During the Second World War he returned to active service with the rank of Lieutenant-Colonel and was drowned while leading a commando detachment through the mountains and jungles during the Allied retreat from Burma to India. He is the author of *Game Animals of the Sudan.*

Brooke, Major William Hallily joined the West Yorkshire Regiment, Territorial Army Reserve of Officers, in 1909 as a Second Lieutenant. He was promoted to Lieutenant in 1911 and Captain in 1914. Upon the outbreak of the First World War the Territorial Army was activated, and Brooke served as a Captain until promoted to Major in 1916. After the war he remained on active duty for five years before reentering the Reserves in 1923. When Lord H. C. Plumer was appointed High Commissioner of Palestine in 1925, Major Brooke became his A.D.C. In 1920 he married Marjorie Constance Plumer, daughter of Lord Plumer.

Bull, the Rt. Hon. Sir William (1863–1932), was a prominent solicitor and politician, elected as a Conservative M.P. in 1900 representing Hammersmith, and from 1918–29 representing Hammersmith South. He was the Chairman of London Unionist M.P.'s, 1910–29, and served on a host of civic organizations including the Royal Humane Society, the Royal Life Saving Society, and the boards of several hospitals and such government commissions as the Land Tax Commission for Kensington and the Speakers Conference on Electoral Reform. His son, Stephen John Bull, was born in 1904.

Bury, Lindsay Edward (1882–1952), educated at Eton and Trinity College, Cambridge, joined the Egyptian Irrigation Service in 1904 and served as Inspector and later Assistant Inspector-General of Irrigation, Egypt, 1919–25. During the First World War he was a Major in the Royal Engineers, Suez Canal Defences, 1915–16. In 1925 he was appointed Director of Irrigation and Adviser to the Ministry of Communications and Works, 'Iraq, and later Adviser to the Ministry of Irrigation and Agriculture, 'Iraq, until his retirement in 1928. His first wife, Frances Beckwith, whom he married in 1909, died in 1932.

Byrne, Brigadier-General Sir Joseph Aloysius (1874–1942), educated at St. George's College, Weybridge, and Maison de Melle, Belgium, entered the Royal Inniskilling Fusiliers in 1893 and served in the South African War and later as the Assistant Adjutant-General at the War Office. During the First World War he was the D.A.G., Irish

Command, and later Inspector-General of the Royal Irish Constabulary. In 1922 he was appointed Governor of the Seychelles Islands, and in 1927 Governor of Sierra Leone where he served until 1931 when he became Governor, Kenya, a post he held until retirement in 1937. In 1908 he married Marjorie Joseph, daughter of Allan F. Joseph of Cairo.

Cadell, Sir Patrick Robert (1871–1961), educated at Edinburgh Academy, Haileybury, and Balliol College, Oxford, joined the Indian Civil Service in 1891 and served until his retirement in 1927 in Bombay, Calcutta, and as A.D.C. to the Viceroy. He was the Commissioner in Sind, 1925–26; and after retirement President of the Council, Junagadh State, 1932–35, and President of the Council, Sangli State, 1937. In 1920 he married Agnes Aimée Kemp of London.

Carpendale, Major Frederic Maxwell (1887–1958), educated at Malvern College and the Royal Military College, Sandhurst, served in the First World War, 1914–19; he was the Assistant Military Secretary, General Headquarters, Mesopotamia, 1919–1920; and later in the Indian Army in the Aden Protectorate. He was the D.A.A.G., Aldershot Command, 1939–41.

Carter, Howard (1873–1939), educated privately, went to Egypt in 1890 on the staff of the Egyptian Exploration Fund's Archaeological Survey where in 1892 he took part in the excavations under the direction of Flinders Petrie. In 1899 he joined the Egyptian Antiquities Department and made several notable discoveries, including the tombs of Tuthmosis IV and Hatshepsut, before resigning in 1903. In 1907 he began to direct the excavations of the Earl of Carnarvon, with whose support he achieved his most remarkable find in 1922, the tomb of Tutankhamen.

Cecil, Lord Edward Herbert Gascoyne (1867–1918), soldier and civil servant, was the fourth son of the third Marquess of Salisbury. Educated at Eton, he entered the Grenadier Guards in 1887. He served in the Sudan campaigns and the Boer War. He joined the Egyptian Army and was appointed Sudan Government Agent and Director of Military Intelligence at Cairo in 1903. He later became the Undersecretary of State in the Egyptian Ministry of Finance and the Financial Adviser in 1912. During the First World War he continued as the chief British adviser in Egypt after Kitchener's departure and played a leading role during the high commissionership of Sir Henry McMahon. He died at Leysin, Switzerland, on 14 December 1918 shortly after his return to England.

Cherei Pasha at the time of Sir Gilbert Clayton's visit in 1925 was Undersecretary in the Ministry of Interior. He later served as Governor of Cairo.

Chilcott, Lieutenant-Commander Sir Warden Stanley (1871–1942), served with the Royal Naval Air Service in France during the First World War and afterward was the Conservative M.P. for Walton Division of Liverpool from 1918 to 1929.

Clayton, Ellinor Maria (1878–), the eldest daughter of Lieutenant-Colonel William Lewis Nicholl Clayton, was educated at a private school in England and in Italy and Belgium and qualified in physiotherapy, which she practiced during and after the First World War.

Clayton, Lady Enid Caroline (née Thorowgood) was born in Madras, India, on 8 September 1886, the third child of Frank Napier Thorowgood and his wife, the former Elizabeth Montgomery Hunter-Blair. Frank Napier Thorowgood came from a professional family of East Anglia. One brother was a doctor, another a lawyer, and he himself a civil engineer who worked on the design and construction of Madras harbor as well as other construction projects in India. In 1888 the family returned to England, living in Wimbledon until 1894 when they moved to Montreux, Switzerland. Here Enid and her two sisters were educated by private governesses, learning to speak French and German fluently. Returning to Wimbledon in 1901, she began to study art seriously in Paris and later under Alexander Jamieson in London where she exhibited her paintings. In 1911 she met Gilbert Clayton at Kelburn, the family home of the Earl of Glasgow whose wife was a Hunter-Blair and cousin of Elizabeth Thorowgood. Gilbert and Enid Thorowgood met again at Kelburn the following year, became engaged, and were married in London in September 1912. From then until her husband's death in 1929 she was mother and consort in Khartoum, Cairo, Jerusalem, and Baghdad. She concerned herself with her five children, two of whom died in infancy, and charitable organizations, particularly the Y.W.C.A. and the Girl Guides which she represented at an International Conference in the United States in 1926. Upon Sir Gilbert's death she retired to their home on the Isle of Wight and devoted herself to her family. In 1937 she moved to Hampton Court Palace where she lives today, providing a gracious home for her children and grandchildren and occupying herself with painting.

Clayton, Brigadier-General Sir Gilbert Falkingham (1875–1929), educated at Isle of Wight College and the Royal Military Academy,

Woolwich, entered the army in 1895 and served in the Nile campaign 1898. He joined the Egyptian Army in 1900–10 and served with the Sudan Government 1910–19. He was Director of Intelligence, Egypt, 1914–17; B.G.G.S. Hijaz Operations, 1916–17; and Chief Political Officer, Egyptian Expeditionary Force, 1917–19. After the war he served as Adviser to the Ministry of Interior, Egypt, 1919–22; Chief Secretary, government of Palestine, 1922–25; and Special Envoy to Ibn Sa'ud in 1925 and 1927, in which office he negotiated the Bahra and Hadda Agreements and the Treaty of Jiddah. In 1928 he again was sent on a mission to Ibn Sa'ud, and in the following year was appointed High Commissioner for 'Iraq, a post he held but a few months before his untimely death.

Clayton, Brigadier Sir Iltyd Nicholl (1886–1955), brother of Sir Gilbert, educated at Lancing College and Royal Military Academy, Woolwich, served with the Royal Artillery in Europe 1914–19 before being sent to 'Iraq in 1920, where he was attached to the 'Iraq Army until 1928. During the Second World War he was stationed in the Middle East, first in Military Intelligence, 1940–43; then Adviser on Arab Affairs, Minister of State, 1943–45; and Head of British Middle East Office, 1945–48, the last year of which he was attached to the British Embassy, Cairo, as Minister.

Clayton, John Pilkington (1921–), educated at Copthorne Preparatory School; Wellington College; Gomville and Caius College, Cambridge; and King's College Hospital, London. During 1949–1950 he served in the Royal Air Force, Medical Branch, in Malaya with the rank of Squadron Leader. Since 1953 he has served in hospital appointments at Windsor and Eton, including Medical Officer to Eton College.

Clayton, Patience Elizabeth: see Marshall, Patience Elizabeth (née Clayton).

Clayton, Samuel Wittewronge (1918–), educated at Copthorne Preparatory School, Winchester College, and Pembroke College, Cambridge; joined the Colonial Administrative Service, Malaya, 1939; and at the outbreak of war enlisted in the Federated Malay States Volunteer Light Battery of Artillery and was taken prisoner at the fall of Singapore. Since the war he has worked in the chemical industry, traveling extensively in Western Europe. He married Mary Cecilia Leveson-Gower in 1956.

Clayton, Lieutenant-Colonel William Lewis Nicholl (1945–1927), the father of Sir Gilbert Falkingham Clayton, joined the Hampshire and

Isle of Wight Royal Artillery Militia in 1867, rose to Lieutenant-Colonel in 1887, and retired in 1900. As the only island-born officer he always played a principal role in the preparations for the annual four-week training period in May of the Isle of Wight Royal Artillery Militia held at Carisbrooke Castle until the early 1880's and thereafter at Sandown Bay, Isle of Wight. He married Maria Martha Pilkington, daughter of Captain Edward Williams Pilkington, R.N.

Collins, Major-General Robert John (1880–1950), educated at Marlborough College, joined the army in 1897 and served through the South African War. He joined the Egyptian Army in 1904 in which he remained until 1911 during which time he was the A.D.C. to the Sirdar, Sir Reginald Wingate, 1905–06. He was the Private Secretary to G.O.C. in Somaliland in 1910 and was then stationed at the Staff College 1912–13. He served in numerous posts during the First World War after which he was an Instructor at the Staff College, Camberley, 1919–23; Director of Military Training, India, 1924–26; Commandant 9th Infantry Brigade, 1926–27; Commandant Experimental Armoured Force, 1927–28; and Commandant Small Arms School, 1929–32. He was G.O.C. 3rd Indian Division from 1924 until his retirement in 1938. During the Second World War he served as the Commandant, Staff College, Camberley, 1939–41. He married Violet Monro, widow of Captain S. Hill, in 1922.

Conz, Fleet Admiral Angelo Ugo was born in Ancona, 6 February 1871 and entered the Italian Naval Academy at Leghorn on 1 November 1885 as a cadet of the General Staff Corps. He graduated in 1890 with the rank of Midshipman. He took part in the Italo-Turkish War 1911–12 and in the First World War, 1915–18. He served on official missions to London, Paris, and Madrid in 1918 and attended the Paris Peace Conference 1919 as a naval expert to the Italian delegation. Following the war he served as Naval Commander of the La Spezia region 1923–24 and in 1925 assumed command of the Far East Naval Division. He left Shanghai on the *San Giorgio* in October 1925 and from November 1925 to April 1926 was in command of the Second Naval Division of the Red Sea and Indian Ocean. On his return to Italy he took command of the Naval District of Jonio and the Lower Adriatic, 1926–28; commanded the First and Second Naval Squadron, 1928–29; and was President of the High Naval Council and President of the Council of Admirals, 1933–34. He was promoted to Fleet Admiral in 1932, and made Senator of Italy in 1933. He retired at the legal age limit in 1934.

Cornwallis, Sir Kinahan (1883–1959), educated at Haileybury and University College, Oxford, joined the Sudan Political Service in 1906 and served in the Civil Secretary's Office, 1907; Kassala, 1908–11; was Assistant Private Secretary to the Governor-General in 1912–13, and then transferred to the Ministry of Finance, Egyptian government, 1914–24. He was seconded to the army in 1915; was Director of the Arab Bureau, 1918; and Assistant Chief Political Officer, Egyptian Expeditionary Force, 1918–19. Following the war he accompanied the Amir Faysal to 'Iraq in 1921 and was seconded to the 'Iraq government as Adviser, Ministry of Interior from 1921 until his retirement in 1935. He was later attached to the Foreign Office 1939–41, and served as the British Ambassador in Baghdad 1941–45. He was a close personal associate of Clayton, serving under him when Clayton was the Private Secretary to the Governor-General, and later at the Arab Bureau and with the Egyptian Expeditionary Force.

Cory, Lieutenant-General Sir George Norton (1874–), entered the army in 1895 and served in South Africa 1899–1902, the Aden Hinterland 1903, and in the First World War, after which he was the D.A.G. and Director Personal Services, Indian Army, 1921–22; and Deputy C.G.S., India, 1922–26. He retired in 1931 but served as Chief Liaison Officer, Allied Contingents, 1940–43.

Cox, Lieutenant-Colonel Sir Charles Henry Fortnom (1880-1953), educated at Rugby and the Royal Military Academy, Woolwich, served in the South African War 1901–02, the Sudan 1913–15, and in Europe 1915–18. After the war he served in Palestine from 1919 to 1924 when he was appointed British Resident, Trans-Jordan, a post he held until 1939. In 1919 he married Edith Fortescue Blair, youngest daughter of Roland L. N. Mitchell.

Cox, Major General Sir Percy Zachariah (1864–1937), educated at Harrow and Sandhurst, entered the army in 1884. He served with the Second Battalion Cameronians until 1889, when he joined the Indian Staff Corps. The following year he entered the Indian Political Department. From 1890 until the outbreak of the war he served as Vice-Consul at Zaila, Somali Coast, 1893, and at Berbera 1894–95; Consul and Political Agent at Muscat, Arabia, 1899–1904; Consul-General at Bushire, Persian Gulf, 1904; Political Resident, Persian Gulf, 1909; and Secretary of the Foreign Department, Government of India, 1914. During the war he was the Chief Political Officer, Indian Expeditionary Force "D," 1915–18. In 1918 he became Acting British Minister to Persia until his appointment as High Commissioner to Mesopotamia in 1920. He was replaced in this position in 1923, and in subsequent years served on various diplomatic missions for the British government.

Creighton, Rear-Admiral Kenelam Everard Lane (1883–1963), educated at Fermoy College, Ireland, joined the Royal Navy as a Midshipman in 1898. He took part in the actions of Heligoland Bight, Dogger Bank, and Jutland during the First World War and in 1918 was Navigator and Master of the Fleet. Promoted to Captain in 1921, he was Captain of the Royal Naval College, Greenwich 1928–29; Director of Navigation, Admiralty, 1929–31; and Captain of H.M.S. *Royal Sovereign* 1932–33. He was A.D.C. to the King 1933–34 and retired as Rear Admiral in 1934. He later served as Director-General of Ports and Lights Administration, Egypt, 1943–46.

Crowfoot, John Winter (1873–1959), educated at Marlborough and Brasenose College, Oxford, went to Egypt in 1901 as the Assistant Master, Ministry of Education, and in 1903 was appointed the Assistant Director of Education in the Sudan. In 1908 he returned to Cairo as the Inspector, Ministry of Education, only to return to the Sudan in 1914 as the Director of Education and the Principal of Gordon College, Khartoum, a post he held until 1926. Upon retirement from the Sudan service he directed the British School of Archaeology at Jerusalem until 1935.

Crump, Leslie Maurice (1875–1929), educated at Merchant Taylors' School, Crosby, and Merton College, Oxford, joined the Indian Civil Service in 1898 and entered the Political Department in 1900, serving in Hyderabad, North West Frontier, Central India Phulkian States, and Baroda. He was appointed Resident, Gwalior in April 1925 where he served until his death.

Curzon of Kedleston, George Nathaniel Curzon (1859–1925), educated at Eton and Balliol College, Oxford, served as Private Secretary to the Marquess of Salisbury in 1885, and became M.P. for Southport Division of S.W. Lancashire from 1886 until 1898. While a Member of Parliament he was the Undersecretary of State for India, 1891–92, and Undersecretary of State for Foreign Affairs, 1895–98. He was then appointed Viceroy and Governor-General of India, 1899–1905. He traveled extensively in Central Asia, Persia, and Afghanistan before becoming Lord Privy Seal, 1915–16; Lord President of the Council, 1916–19; Leader of the House of Lords, 1916–24; and Secretary of

State for Foreign Affairs, 1919–24. He took special interest in the restoration of Delhi during his tenure as Viceroy of India.

Cust, Colonel Sir Lionel George Archer (1896–1962), educated at Eton, served in the First World War and afterward joined the Palestine Civil Service in 1920 and was employed in various positions, including A.D.C. to the High Commissioner, 1921–23, and Private Secretary, 1928–31. He was seconded as Private Secretary to the Governor of Northern Rhodesia 1932–34, and during the Second World War served in Military Intelligence and Psychological Warfare. He married Margaret Violet Louisa Clowes in 1925.

D'Albiac, Air Vice-Marshal John Henry (1894–1963), educated at Seabrook Lodge, Hythe, Kent, and Framlingham College, was commissioned in the Royal Marine Artillery in 1914 and served in France. Commissioned in the Royal Air Force in April 1918, he served in Egypt and Trans-Jordan, 1920–26, before entering the Royal Air Force Staff College in 1929. Thereafter he served in India and at South Farnborough. During the Second World War he commanded the British Air Forces in Greece and Ceylon, and in 1943–44 commanded the Tactical Air Force. He retired in 1946.

Daly, Major-General Arthur Crawford (1871–1936), educated at Winchester, joined the West Yorkshire Regiment in 1890, served in the South African War and the European War in which he commanded the 24th Division, 1917–19. He was the Inspector-General and Military Adviser, Ministry of Defense, 'Iraq from 1925 until his retirement in 1928. In 1897 he married Grace Wilkinson, the third daughter of Major H. C. Wilkinson and the elder sister of Eva Wilkinson, who married Richard Graves (q.v.).

Davies, Reginald (1887–1958), educated at Hymers College and St. Catharine's College, Cambridge, joined the Sudan Political Service in 1911 and served in Khartoum, Kordofan, 1912–20; Darfur, 1920–24; Intelligence Department, 1924–28; Assistant Civil Secretary, 1929; Assistant Financial Secretary, 1930–31; Secretary for Economic Development, 1931–32; Deputy Financial Secretary, 1932–33; and Chairman of the Board of Economics and Trade until his retirement in 1935.

Davis, Sir Steuart Spencer (1875–1950), educated at Dean Close School and called to the bar, Gray's Inn, 1915; served in Customs and Treasury, St. Kitts, West Indies, 1893–1901; and then became Assistant Treasurer, Gold Coast, 1901, and Chief Assistant Treasurer in 1908.

He served as Treasurer, Tanganyika Territory, 1916; Acting Chief Secretary, 1919; and Administrator's Deputy the following year. In 1922 he was appointed Treasurer, Palestine government, and remained in that post until 1932, during which time he served on numerous commissions for the government of Palestine.

Dent, Major-General Wilkinson (1883–1934), educated at Sedbergh and the Royal Military College, Sandhurst, entered the Indian Army in 1904, and served in Mesopotamia during the First World War as a G.S.O. Following the war he remained in Mesopotamia, first as G.S.O. at General Headquarters, 1919–21, and from 1922–28 as G.S.O. Intelligence, Air Headquarters, 'Iraq. From 1929 until his retirement in 1932 he was a Brigade Commander in India.

Dobbs, Sir Henry Robert Conway (1871–1934), educated at Winchester College and Brasenose College, Oxford, entered the Indian Civil Service in 1892 and served in the North West Frontier Province, Mysore, and Baluchistan. He was Consul for Seistan and Kain, 1903; explored between Herat and Kabul, 1904; and returned to Kabul as Secretary to Kabul Mission, 1904. He continued to serve in various positions in Baluchistan and in the North West Frontier Province until the outbreak of war when he was appointed Political Officer with the Mesopotamian Expeditionary Force, supervising the civil administration of British-occupied areas. He became Foreign Secretary to the government of India in 1919; Head of British Mission of Kabul, 1920–21; and High Commissioner and Consul-General for 'Iraq from 1923 until his retirement in 1929.

Dowson, Sir Ernest MacLeod (1876–1950), educated at Isle of Wight College and the Central Technical College, London, before joining the Egyptian Delta Light Railways as Assistant Engineer in 1898. Appointed to the Survey of Egypt in 1900, he became its Director-General in 1909. In 1919 he was made the Undersecretary of State for Finance, Egypt, and then served as the Financial Adviser to the Egyptian government, 1920–23. After retiring from the Egyptian service, he advised at various times between 1923–40 the governments of Palestine, Trans-Jordan, 'Iraq, Zanzibar, and Kenya on questions of land surveying, registration, and ownership.

Dun, Robert Hay (1870–1947), educated at Loretto School, Musselburgh, and Brasenose College, Oxford, was called to the bar (Inner Temple) 1895 and practiced before the bar on the Northern Circuit, Liverpool. He went out to the Sudan as Advocate-General in 1905 and was made Chief Justice of the Sudan in 1917, a post which he held until his retirement in 1926. He was an avid golfer, playing on the Oxford University team and later as Captain of the Chislehurst Golf Club. He continued his passion for golf in the Sudan on the sandy course laid out south of the city and served as Honourable Secretary of the Khartoum Golf Club, founded by another enthusiastic player, Sir Reginald Wingate.

Ellington, Air Marshal Sir Edward Leonard (1877–1967), educated at Clifton and the Royal Military Academy, Woolwich, served in the First World War, 1914–18 with distinction and afterward became Director-General of Supply and Research, Air Ministry, 1919–21; commanded R.A.F. in Middle East, 1922–23; in India, 1923–26; and in 'Iraq, 1926–28. He was made Air Officer Commanding-in-Chief, Air Defense of Great Britain, 1929–31; Chief of the Air Staff, 1933–37; and Inspector-General of the Royal Air Force, 1937–40.

Ewart, Sir John Murray (1884–1939), educated at Malvern College, joined the Indian Police Service in 1905 and served as a District Officer, Frontier Constabulary, 1919. In 1924 he was seconded to the Sudan government for one year to reorganize the Intelligence Department. He returned to India in 1926 as the Deputy-Inspector-General of Police and was promoted in 1932 to Inspector-General of Police and Undersecretary Home (Police) Department, Punjab. In 1936 he was appointed Director, Intelligence Bureau, government of India. He married Evelyn Florence Pott in 1920. There is no evidence that Sir John was ever a Colonel though his father was the Temporary Colonel of the 191st Seaforth's and Cameron's Territorial Brigade.

Faisal, King [Faysal ibn Husayn] (1883–1933), son of Husayn ibn 'Ali, was born in At-Ta'if and when about six years old accompanied his father to Constantinople. Here he was educated in private schools and acquired a decided dislike of the Turks. In 1908 when his father was proclaimed Sharif of Mecca, Faysal was sent into the steppes to be hardened by a bedouin's life. At the outbreak of the First World War he returned to Mecca from Constantinople and on 1 June 1916 led his bedouin forces in revolt against the Turks. With British support and the advice of Captain T. E. Lawrence, Faysal led his Arab army northward up the Red Sea coast to effect a juncture with General Allenby's Egyptian Expeditionary Force advancing into Palestine. Taking Damascus, Faysal seemed near his goal of an independent

Arab state and in 1920 he assumed the title of King of Syria. His position in Syria, however, conflicted with the French mandate and he was deposed from office. When 'Iraq was officially established as a British mandate, Faysal was enthroned after a plebiscite in 1921. He continued to work for an independent Arab kingdom and after prolonged negotiations with Britain 'Iraq was admitted to the League of Nations as an independent kingdom. King Faysal had at last achieved his goal of an independent Arab state less than a year before his sudden and unexpected death in September 1933.

Fergusson, General Sir Charles (1865–1951), educated at Eton and the Royal Military College, Sandhurst, joined the Grenadier Guards in 1883 and the Egyptian Army in 1895. He served with the 10th Sudanese Battalion throughout the campaigns of 1896–98, commanded the 15th Sudanese in 1899, and was Commandant of the Garrison at Umdurman, 1900. He was the Adjutant General of the Egyptian Army, 1901–03, and commanded the 3rd Battalion Grenadier Guards, 1904–07. He served in the First World War in command of the 5th Division and subsequently of the 2nd and 17th Army Corps. He was the military governor of occupied German Territory, 1918–19. He retired in 1922 but later served as Governor-General and Commander-in-Chief of New Zealand, 1924–30. He married Lady Alice Mary Boyle, second daughter of the seventh Earl of Glasgow.

Firuz, Prince [Muhammad Husayn Mirza] (1899–), the son of Prince Husayn Mirza Farman-Farma Kajar, was educated at the École St. Michel, Brussels, the Lycée Jannson De Sailly, Paris, and in the Corps de Page, Petrograd. He served in the Emperor's own Hussar Regiment, Russia, during the First World War and from 1918–19 was A.D.C. to His Imperial Majesty, Ahmad Shah Kajar. In 1921 he was appointed Chief, Topographical Section, General Staff and Commander of the Expeditionary Forces in Guilan. In 1922 he was made Chief of Operational Section, General Staff, Chief of Staff, Azarbaijan Forces, and Chief of Staff, Southern Division, Ispahan, Iran. From 1923–27 he was Brigade Commander, first at Ispahan and later Shiraz. During the Second World War he was Governor-General of Fars and Commander of Southern Division, 1942–44; and after the war Minister of Roads and Communications, 1945–46; Inspector-General of the Army, 1946; and Inspector-General of the Air Force, 1947 when he was Head of Mission to the Civil Aviation Conference in Montreal. He married Safiyeh Nemazee (1908–) in October 1925 and has two sons, Eskandar and Narcy. Princess Firuz has devoted herself to philanthropic and charitable work both in Iran and with many international organizations. Prince and Princess Firuz visited India in November-December 1925 during which they met Sir Gilbert Clayton at Bombay. Prince Firuz was the head of an Iranian Military Mission sent to attend military maneuvers on the North-West Frontier.

Fleming, Maxwell (1871–1935), educated at Edinburgh Academy; Balliol College, Oxford; and Edinburgh University, called to Scots bar in 1897 and was appointed civil judge in the Sudan in 1904. He rose to judge of the High Court in the Sudan. He was married to Elsa Blackwood and together they were one of the most popular couples in the British community in Khartoum. He retired from the Sudan service in 1924.

Fouracres, Charles Edward (1897–), educated at Woodbridge and the Royal Military Academy, Woolwich, was commissioned as a 2nd Lieutenant in the Royal Field Artillery in 1916 and served in France until wounded in 1917 when he returned to England and studied at the London School of Oriental Studies, 1918–19. In 1919 he was posted to General Staff Intelligence in Palestine and the following year to Cairo. In 1922 he was seconded to the Sudan government where he held various posts, including Assistant Private Secretary to the Governor-General; Assistant Controller, Public Security Intelligence; and Assistant Sudan Agent, Cairo, from 1939 until his retirement in 1949. He later served as Information Officer at the British embassies in 'Amman and in Libya, 1952–58.

Fowle, Sir Trenchard Craven William (1884–1940), educated at Clifton College, joined the Royal Munster Fusiliers in 1904, and three years later transferred to the Indian Army. He traveled in Arabia and Syria in 1910 and in Persia in 1912–13, before transferring to the Indian Political Department in 1914. He was the Vice-Consul, Kerman, 1914; and served as Political Officer with the Mesopotamian Expeditionary Force, 1915–18. After the war he became the Consul-General, Meshed, 1918–20; Consul, Seistan, 1921; and Baluchistan, 1921–24. He served as the Assistant Resident, Aden, 1925–28; British Consul at Bushire, 1929; and the Political Agent, Muscat, 1930.

Fuad el-Khatib [Shaykh Fu'ad Hasan al-Khatib] (1882–1957) was born in Shuhaym, Lebanon and educated at Shimlan and at the American University at Beirut. He served as an Inspector of Education in the Sudan before joining the Arab Revolt in 1916. He was appointed

Minister of Foreign Affairs for the Hijaz in 1917. He retired to Jordan at the collapse of King 'Ali's rule in the Hijaz where he remained until 1940, when he returned to Lebanon. In 1944 Ibn Sa'ud called him as an adviser and then as Ambassador to Afghanistan. He died of a heart attack in Kabul in 1957. He has published an anthology of poems; a play, *Fath al-Andalus* ("The Conquest of Spain"); *Jughrafiyat Bilad al 'Arab* ("Geography of the Arab Land"); and has written an unpublished work entitled *Nazarat fi Tarikh al-Jahiliyah* ("Views on Pre-Islamic History").

Fuad, King [Fu'ad I] (1868–1936), the youngest son of the Khedive Isma'il, lived quietly in Egypt occupying himself with charitable activities. On the death of his brother in 1917, he became Sultan of Egypt under the British Protectorate; and when the Protectorate was abolished in 1922, Fu'ad was proclaimed King of Egypt. He was a great patron of learning and liberally subsidized Egyptian and Sudanese studies. He was succeeded by his eldest son, King Faruq.

Furness, Sir Robert Allason (1883–1955), educated at Rugby and King's College, Cambridge, entered the Egyptian Service in 1906, was seconded to the staff of the High Commissioner for Egypt in 1917, and appointed Oriental Secretary to the High Commissioner, 1923–26. He later served as Deputy Director-General, Egyptian State Broadcasting, 1933–34; Press Officer for the government of Palestine, 1934–36; and Professor of English at the University of Cairo until his retirement in 1944.

Garstang, John (1876–1956), educated at Blackburn Grammar School and Jesus College, Oxford, was appointed Hon. Reader in Egyptian Archaeology at the University of Liverpool in 1902, and was Professor of Archaeology from 1907–41. During that time he engaged in archaeological research in Britain, Egypt, Nubia, Sudan, Palestine, and Turkey. He served in France as Red Cross Delegate, 1915–19; and was the Director of the British School of Archaeology in Jerusalem, 1919–26; Adviser on Antiquities to the Military Administration, Palestine, 1919–20; and Director of Department of Antiquities of Palestine government, 1920–26, during which time he became a close friend of Sir Gilbert Clayton. In 1907 he married Marie L. Bergès of Toulouse.

Gerrard, Phyllis Louisa Ball (1888–), daughter of Edward Stone, was educated at Wycombe Abbey School, Buckinghamshire, and in 1922 married Eugene Louis Gerrard. Air Commodore Gerrard (1881–

1963) was Commanding Forces in Palestine, 1924–27. He retired in 1929.

Goble, Donald Christopher (1900–), educated at Christ's Hospital, West Horsham, King's School, Canterbury, and Wellington College, was commissioned a 2nd Lieutenant in 1920 in the 39th Royal Garhwal Rifles and was promoted to Lieutenant in 1923. In 1925 he was appointed A.D.C. to the Political Resident at Aden for three years, and then was a Senior Staff Officer in Meerut District, 1931–34. Throughout the Second World War he served with the Royal Garhwal Rifles and was made Lieutenant Colonel in 1946. He retired in 1949.

Godeleine, the Reverend Marie, had been the superior of the convent of Notre Dame de Sion in North Africa where she helped organize hospital services during the First World War. In 1921 she was appointed the assistant superior of the Ecce Homo convent, Jerusalem, and served as the superior from 1927 to 1950. Under the direction of the Dominican archaeologist, Père Vincent, she carried out numerous excavations at the Basilica of the Ecce Homo, including the finding of the Lithostrotos. She died in 1960.

Godwin, Lieutenant-General Sir Charles Alexander Campbell (1873–1951), educated in the United States and at Sandhurst, entered the army in 1895 and served in India. During the First World War he commanded the 6th Yeomanry Brigade, France, and later took part in the advance on Jerusalem. He was B.G.G.S., Desert Mounted Troops in the advance on Damascus and afterward with North Force, Syria. He returned to the War Office in 1920 but the following year went out to India where he commanded the 5th Indian Cavalry Brigade, 1921–23; served as Major-General Cavalry, A.H.Q., 1923–27; and was the G.O.C., the Peshawar District, 1927–30. He retired in 1932.

Gordon, Commander Bryan, of the Royal Indian Marine was commissioned a Sub-Lieutenant in 1907, Lieutenant in 1911, Lieutenant-Commander in 1919 and a Commander in 1922.

Goschen, Sir Edward Henry (1876–1933), educated at Eton, was the Hon. Attaché at Petrograd 1897, Tangier 1901, and later Controller of the Secretariat in the Egyptian Ministry of Finance and, from 1916 until his death, a partner of Joseph Sebag & Co.

Grafftey-Smith, Sir Laurence Barton (1892–), educated at Repton and Pembroke College, Cambridge, began his career in the Middle

East as a Student Interpreter, Levant Consular Service in 1914. He became a Vice-Consul in 1920, serving at Alexandria, Cairo, Jiddah, and Constantinople. He was the Assistant Oriental Secretary at the Residency, Cairo, 1925–35 and later served in various diplomatic posts. He was the Minister to Sa'udi Arabia, 1945–47; and the High Commissioner in Pakistan, 1947–51, after which he retired from government service.

Graves, Richard Massie (1880–1960), educated at Haileybury, Magdalen College, Oxford, and King's College, Cambridge, entered the Levant Consular Service in 1903 and served at several stations as Acting Vice-Consul, 1906–07, before becoming Vice-Consul at Alexandria, 1909, and at Cairo the following year. He entered the Egyptian Civil Service in 1910 and served as Inspector of Interior, 1910–22; Assistant Director-General, European Department, Ministry of Interior, 1924; and Director, Labour Department of the Egyptian Ministry of Commerce and Industry, 1930–39. At the outbreak of the Second World War he served in the Intelligence Service with the rank of Major but in 1940 became first the Labour Adviser and in 1942 the Director of the Labour Department of the Palestine Government until 1946. He was the Adviser on Social Affairs, International Administration, Tangier from 1949–51. In 1912 he married Eva Wilkinson, fourth daughter of Major H. C. Wilkinson, 82nd Regiment; her sister Grace was married to Major-General A. C. Daly (q.v.).

Greenhouse, Major Frank Stewart (1885–   ), educated at Liverpool College and the Royal Military College, Sandhurst, entered the Indian Army in 1905 and served in India, Persia, 'Iraq, and Kurdistan during the First World War. In 1916 he transferred to the Political Department and served as Political Officer at al-Basrah, an-Najaf, and Sulaymaniyah, and was on the High Commissioner's Staff in Baghdad, 1921. He joined the Anglo-Persian Oil Company in 1923 at Abadan, and retired in 1935 as Manager in Teheran. In 1925 his services were loaned to the Turkish Petroleum Company for one year as its Manager in Baghdad.

Gwynne, the Right Reverend Llewellyn Henry (1863–1957), educated at Swansea Grammar School and St. John's Hall, Highbury, received ordination in 1886 and held a curacy at St. Chad's, Derby. During this period he was an outstanding player for the Derby County Association football team that met Crewe Alexander in the semifinal of the

Football Association Cup. He went to the Sudan in 1899 as a missionary for the Church Missionary Society and in 1908 was consecrated as Suffragan Bishop of Khartoum. During the First World War he was appointed Deputy Chaplain-General in France, a post in which he served with great devotion and distinction. In 1919 Gwynne returned to Khartoum, and the following year he was appointed Bishop of the new diocese of Egypt and the Sudan. He remained in charge of his diocese for the next twenty-five years until he was eighty years of age.

Hadwen, Edward Hubert Lascelles, was the acting Vice-Consul at Port Tawfiq (Suez) in March 1926 and in the following year was appointed Vice-Consul in the Levant Consular service and continued to serve at Suez. In 1929 he was transferred to Sofia and subsequently served at Durazzo and Tangier before he retired in 1934. He died on 28 March 1947.

Hafez Wahbeh, Shaikh [Hafiz Wahba, Shaykh] (1889–1968), educated at Al-Azhar University and the Muslim Jurisprudence College, Cairo, practiced journalism before being exiled from Egypt to India at the beginning of the First World War. He was later expelled by the Indian government to the Persian Gulf where he engaged in the pearl business until 1920, after which he became Counsellor to Ibn Sa'ud, and later Governor of Mecca, 1924–27; Minister of Education and Assistant to the Viceroy of Hijaz, 1927–29; Minister to Great Britain and the Netherlands, 1930–48; and Ambassador from 1948–1956, when diplomatic recognition between Sa'udi Arabia and Great Britain was broken. In 1959 he was made a Director of the Arabian American Oil Company, and in 1963 negotiated the resumption of diplomatic representation with Great Britain.

Haking, General Sir Richard Cyril Byrne (1862–1945), entered the army in 1881 and was promoted to General, 1925. He served in the South African War with the rank of Major and lectured at the Staff College 1901–04. During the First World War he commanded the 5th Infantry Brigade, the 1st Division, and the XI Corps. He commanded the British Military Mission in Russia and the Baltic Provinces in 1919, and served as the G.O.C. British troops in Egypt until retirement in 1927. In 1891 he married Rachel Violette Burford-Hancock, daughter of Sir Henry Burford-Hancock, Chief Justice of Gibraltar.

Harari, Sir Victor Pasha (1857–1945), educated in Paris and London, became Director-General of Accounts, Egyptian Ministry of Finance;

Chairman, Mortgage Company of Egypt; Director, Agricultural Bank of Egypt and the National Bank of Egypt. He married Emma Aghion of Alexandria in 1887.

Harvey, E. C., was a clerk in the Treasury Department of the Palestine government. He was later transferred to the Department of Education as Chief Clerk. In 1925 he was seconded for special service with Sir Gilbert Clayton as clerk and stenographer of the mission to Ibn Sa'ud. He was known among his superiors as completely reliable and trustworthy. He also gained a reputation as a master of conjuring tricks.

Hassan el Idrisi [Husayn al-Idrisi] was the brother of Sayyid Muhammad al-Idrisi, Ruler of 'Asir until 1922. In 1925 he became Ruler of 'Asir after deposing his nephew 'Ali with the support of Ibn Sa'ud. In 1932 he attempted to foment a tribal revolt in 'Asir against Sa'udi domination, but he was forced to flee to the Yemen when Sa'udi forces suppressed the rising.

Hassan Khaled Pasha [Hasan Khalid Abu 'l-Huda as-Sayyid Pasha] (1871–1936) was born in a village near Aleppo. His father, the famous Tawfiq Pasha, was professor and friend of 'Abd al-Hamid II. He was educated at the Imperial School at Constantinople and was received at Court. He later became director of the Turkish Office at the Khedive's palace in Cairo where he remained until 1914. Through the acquaintance with the Amir 'Abd Allah, whom he met at Vienna in 1922, he was later named Special Councillor in Trans-Jordan; and on the resignation of the Prime Minister Mazhar Arslan Pasha in 1923, he succeeded him with the title of Pasha. In 1924 he was appointed Minister of Finance upon the return of Rikabi Pasha from Damascus. He was again Prime Minister of Trans-Jordan in 1929 but resigned. In 1931 he resigned as President of the Council of Ministers but assumed the post again the following year. In 1933 he accompanied 'Ali, former King of the Hijaz, to Rome. He died on 22 December 1936 in Jerusalem.

Haycraft, Sir Thomas Wagstaffe (1859–1936), educated at St. John's College, Oxford and called to the bar, Inner Temple, 1885, practiced on the Southeast circuit and was Examiner of the High Court 1889–99; President of District Court of Larnaca in Cyprus, 1899–1911; Police Magistrate of Gibraltar, 1911–13; Puisne Judge, Mauritius, 1913–16; Chief Justice of Grenada, 1916–21; and Chief Justice of Palestine, 1921–27. In 1891 he married Pauline Richard, daughter of Captain Paul Richard of the Imperial Guard of France.

Headlam, Brigadier-General Hugh Roger (1877–1955), educated at Wellington College and the Royal Military College, Sandhurst, entered the army in 1897 and served in South Africa before being seconded to the Egyptian Army 1903–13. He served with distinction in France during the First World War and afterward was in command of 1st Battalion The King's Own Royal Regiment, 1920–24; Commandant British Troops in the Sudan, 1924–26; and Brigadier, 12th Infantry Brigade, 1926, until his retirement in 1930 when he became Inspector, Staff School, 'Iraq Army, 1931–34.

Henderson, Sir Nevile Meyrick (1882–1942), educated at Eton and abroad, entered the diplomatic service in 1905 and served in the Foreign Office, St. Petersburg, Tokyo, Rome, Paris, and Constantinople. In 1924 he was transferred to Cairo as Minister Plenipotentiary. He served under Lord Allenby and Lord Lloyd with whose views he disagreed. In 1928 he left Cairo to become the Counsellor-Minister at Paris. He later served with distinction in Belgrade and in 1937 began his historic but futile mission in Berlin. He retired at the outbreak of war and died in London in 1942.

Henley, Sylvia Laura was the third daughter of the 4th Baron Sheffield. In 1906 she married the Hon. Anthony Morton Henley, third son of the 3rd Baron Henley who was educated at Eton and Balliol College, Oxford, enlisted in the army in 1899, served with distinction in the First World War, and rose to the rank of Brigadier-General before his death in 1925. After her husband's sudden death Sylvia Henley traveled with her cousin, Gertrude Bell, from London to Baghdad in October 1925.

Higgins, Air Marshal Sir John Frederick Andrew (1875–1948), entered the army in 1895 and served with distinction in the South African War and the First World War. In 1924 he was appointed Air Officer Commanding Forces in 'Iraq, and in 1926 was made Air Member for Supply and Research of the Air Council. Although retired in 1930, he served as Air Officer, Commander-in-Chief, India, 1939–40.

Hikmat Sulayman (1889–1964), educated at Istanbul University, filled several appointments during the Ottoman regime. He returned to 'Iraq after the First World War and was Director-General of Posts in 1922, and Director-General of Posts and Telegraphs, 1923–25. Elected a Deputy in 1925, he was successively Minister of Education, Minister of the Interior, President of the Chamber of Deputies, and Minister of Justice. He served as Minister of the Interior in the two

Gaylani Ministries of 1933. He later served as Prime Minister 1936–37, but was convicted of conspiring to overthrow the government of Nuri as-Sa'id in 1939. He also published *Al-Bayan* newspaper.

Hill, Commander Sidney Arthur Geary, was educated at South Lodge School, Lowestoft, and was commissioned a midshipman in 1898. He served on the China Station and in the Boxer Rebellion, 1900. He was promoted to Lieutenant, 1903; Lieutenant-Commander, 1911; and Commander, 1917. He was mentioned in despatches in the First World War after which he commanded *H.M.S. Endeavour*.

Holt, Sir Vyvyan (1896–1960), educated privately, served with the Indian Signals and the North West Frontier Intelligence Corps, 1914–18. He joined the 'Iraq Political Service, 1919, served as the A.D.C., 1922–24; Private Secretary, 1924–26, to the High Commissioner. He succeeded Gertrude Bell as the Oriental Secretary in 1926. He later served as the Oriental Counsellor, British Embassy, Teheran, 1946; Minister to Korea, 1949; and Minister at San Salvador, 1954; until his retirement from the Foreign Service in 1956.

Hotson, Sir John Ernest Buttery (1877–1944), educated at Edinburgh Academy and Magdalen College, Oxford, entered the Indian Civil Service in 1900 and served as the Assistant Collector in Kathiawar, the Under and Deputy Secretary, Bombay, and Private Secretary to the Governor of Bombay. During the First World War he was Commandant, Mekran Levy Corps, and afterward Consul at Shiraz, Secretary and Chief Secretary, Bombay, and in 1931 acting Governor of Bombay. In 1924 he married Mildred Alice Steward whose father had served in the Indian Civil Service.

Huddleston, Sir Arthur (1880–1948), educated at Eton and King's College, Cambridge, joined the Sudan Political Service in 1905 and served at Barbar until 1910; the Upper Nile, 1911; Blue Nile, 1912; Barbar, 1913–19; Governor, Khartoum, 1920–22; Governor, Blue Nile, 1922–27; Financial Secretary, 1928–31; and Economic Adviser until retirement in 1932.

Hunter, C. J. H. (1888–), educated at Marlborough and in Switzerland, was employed by the Great Northern Railway from 1906 to 1911 before taking a position with the Traffic Department of the Buenos Aires Western Railway until 1913 when he was appointed District Traffic Manager of Sudan Railways. He was promoted in 1923 to Commercial Manager, Sudan Railways, a post he held until 1927 when he joined the Board of Peter Jones, Ltd., Chelsea. He returned to Sudan Railways in 1930 as Deputy General Manager and retired in May 1938. During the Second World War he served, first as Major then Colonel, in Movements and Transportation G.H.Q., Middle East, and in 1950 joined Civil Defence, Somerset.

Hunter-Blair, Gilbert Wauchope, was a well-known tea planter in Ceylon who retired in 1926 and died in 1939. He was married to Muriel Frances Thorowgood, the sister of Lady Clayton.

Hussein, King [Husayn ibn 'Ali] (1856–1931), born in Constantinople, member of the Hashemite family of the Hijaz. He received his education and early training in Constantinople and Mecca, and soon after was appointed assistant to his uncle, Amir 'Abd Allah, the Grand Sharif of Mecca, by the Ottoman government. He served in this position until 1895, when he was ordered back to Constantinople. He remained in the Ottoman capital and served as a member of the Council of State until 1908, when he was appointed Sharif of Mecca and returned to the Hijaz. From 1908–1914 he spread his authority throughout the Hijaz, while opposing the Ottomanization of the province. After the outbreak of the war he refused to obey his Ottoman superiors and declared the Arab Revolt on 5 June 1916. He proclaimed himself King of the Arabs in June 1917, but he was recognized by the Allied Powers only as King of the Hijaz and limited to this position at the Peace Settlement of 1919. During the postwar years he continued to attempt to expand his authority, and in March 1924 he caused himself to be proclaimed Caliph. This stirred up a violent reaction, however, and in September his kingdom was overrun by the Wahhabi forces of 'Abd al-'Aziz ibn Sa'ud. He abdicated his throne in favor of his eldest son 'Ali on 3 October 1924, and retired on his yacht to 'Aqabah. In June 1925 he was removed by British warship to Cyprus. He resided in Nicosia until 1930, when he moved to Trans-Jordan to live with his son 'Abd Allah until his death.

Ibn Rashid [Amir 'Abd al-'Aziz ibn Muhammad ibn Rashid] (ruled 1897–1906), the nephew and successor to Muhammad ibn Rashid as the Amir of Ha'il, was the strongest ruler in Arabia at the opening of the twentieth century. In 1901 he defeated the combined forces of Shaykh Mubarak of Kuwait and his Sa'udi supporters and sought to repress the Sa'udi faction in Najd. The following year his control of Najd was again challenged when 'Abd al-'Aziz ibn Sa'ud captured Riyadh. Ibn Rashid clearly underestimated the Sa'udi danger and allowed Ibn Sa'ud to consolidate his position. For several years active warfare raged between the two rivals until 1906 when Ibn Rashid was killed in battle.

Ibn Sa'ud ['Abd al-'Aziz ibn 'Abd ar-Rahman ibn Faysal ibn Sa'ud] (1880–1953), while in exile at Kuwait, recaptured Riyadh in 1902 and reclaimed the family title of Amir of Najd which in 1921 he changed to Sultan of Najd. In 1925 he conquered the Hijaz and the following year assumed the title of King of the Hijaz, Najd and its Dependencies. In 1932 he once again changed his title to King of Sa'udi Arabia over which he ruled until his death.

Ibrahim ibn Jumas'a [Jumai'ah] was the Captain of the Guard and Master of Ceremonies to Ibn Sa'ud. He was designated by Ibn Sa'ud to accompany H. St. John Philby during his Arabian travels. Upon his arrival at Riyadh, Philby had taken an instant dislike to Ibrahim and, not surprisingly, the two men quarreled constantly. Although Philby intimates that Ibrahim later lost his position at court to Rushaid, Clayton does not confirm that he had in fact lost any status.

Ingpen, Wing Commander Donald Lane (1884–1953), educated at Wellington College, Trinity Hall, Cambridge, and barrister-at-law, Middle Temple, 1909, entered the West Yorkshire Regiment as a 2nd Lieutenant in 1914 and served until 1918 when he was transferred to the R.A.F. as Acting Major. He was granted a permanent commission as a Flight Lieutenant Legal Officer, R.A.F. in 1923–27; Squadron Leader, Legal Branch, 1927–30; Wing Commander, 1930–33, when he retired on account of ill health. He was the Deputy Judge Advocate General, H.Q. 'Iraq Command, 1923–24; and at H.Q. Middle East, 1924–27, when he transferred to the Home Establishment.

Irani, Merwan Sorab (1878–   ), educated at Edinburgh and Glasgow and a Fellow of the Royal College of Surgeons, joined the Indian Medical Service in 1904 and served in the Military Department until 1909 and was appointed Civil Surgeon 1913. He was posted to military duty in Mesopotamia during the First World War from 1914 until 1922, and in the following year was promoted to the rank of Lieutenant-Colonel. He served as the Civil Surgeon, Aden, 1924–26; and retired from the Indian Medical Service in November 1933.

Mother Irene was born in New York and traveled widely in her youth. In 1918 she was called to Jerusalem to organize the teaching of English at the convent school, where she was frequently asked to escort English-speaking visitors, like the Claytons. She worked closely with the Reverend Marie Godeleine from 1920 to 1926 when she went to Kansas City, Missouri, U.S.A.

Isaacson, Captain Egerton Wotton (1882–1929), entered the Royal Navy in 1896 and went to sea as a Midshipman in 1898, serving in the *Royal Sovereign* and *Ramillies*. In 1901 he joined the sloop *Beagle* in the South Atlantic as a Sub-Lieutenant and in 1904 qualified as a torpedo officer and Lieutenant on H.M.S. *Vernon*. From May 1910 he was torpedo Lieutenant of the *Bacchante* and from February 1912 torpedo Lieutenant-Commander of the *Good Hope*, flagship of Admiral Sir Berkeley Milne. During the First World War he served in the North Sea and the Dardanelles and was promoted to Commander and made Chevalier of the Legion of Honour. From January 1917 he was commander of the battleship *Agamemnon* and later the *Conqueror*. He was promoted to Captain in 1924 and the following November took command of the *Yarmouth* signal school ship and in December 1926 of the cruiser *Concord* in the Mediterranean. He was killed in an automobile accident on 30 August 1929.

Ismail Husseini Bey [Isma'il Bey al-Husayni] served as Director of Education in Palestine for the Ottoman government prior to the First World War. At the time of Sir Gilbert Clayton's visit to Jerusalem in November 1925 he was a member of the Advisory Council of Education.

Jackson, Sir Frederick John (1860–1929), educated at Shrewsbury and Jesus College, Cambridge, commanded an expedition to Uganda sent by the Imperial British East Africa Company in 1889. He was British Vice-Consul, Uganda, 1895; Deputy Commissioner, Uganda Protectorate, 1896; Acting Commissioner, 1897–98 and 1901–02; and Chief Political Officer for the Nandi Patrol, 1900. He later served as Lieutenant-Governor for the East Africa Protectorate, 1907–11; and Governor and Commander-in-Chief, Uganda, 1911–17. In 1904 he married Aline Cooper, daughter of William Wallace Cooper of Dublin.

Jacob, Lieutenant-Colonel Harold Fenton (1866–1936), educated at Malvern College, Highgate School, and the Royal Military College, Sandhurst, entered the army in 1887 and served as the Political Agent, ad-Dali', 1904-07; First Assistant Resident and Acting Resident, Aden, 1910–17; Chief Political Officer, Aden Field Force, 1914–17; Adviser on Southwest Arabia to High Commissioner, Egypt, 1917–20. In 1919 he led a mission to the Imam Yahya which had to return after nearly four months' arbitrary detention at Bajil. He retired in 1921. He is the author of *Kings of Arabia* (London, 1923) and *Perfumes of Araby: silhouettes of Al Yemen* (London, 1915).

Jordan, Stanley Rupert (1894–), served as an Assistant in the Levant Consular Service, 1919. In 1925 he was appointed Diplomatic Agent at Jiddah, a post that he held during the period of the Clayton mission and later, until 1927. In 1930 he was appointed Trade Commissioner at Durban but returned to the Middle East in 1934 as the Commercial Secretary at Cairo. In 1936 he was transferred to Athens and two years later became the Commercial Secretary at Angora and in 1940 the Commercial Counsellor. He was Envoy Extraordinary and the Minister Plenipotentiary at Jiddah, 1943–45.

Joseph, Dr. Allan F., was a chemist who joined the Irrigation Department of the Egyptian government in 1919 and retired in 1929.

Joyce, Lieutenant-Colonel Pierce Charles, was educated at Beaumont College, and joined the Connaught Rangers in 1900 and served in the South African War. Attached to the Egyptian Army in 1907, he served at Gallipoli and with the Egyptian Expeditionary Force. Following the war he served as Military Adviser to the 'Iraqi government until retirement in 1932. In 1921 he married Colin Murray, the only daughter of Major General R. H. Murray.

Kamel [Effendi] Fahmy was a Copt employed by the Egyptian State Railways service. In 1922 he escorted Rosita Forbes across the Red Sea and to 'Asir, at the time when she and H. St. John Philby planned to cross the Empty Quarter from 'Asir, but they had to abandon the venture.

Kenny, Lieutenant-Colonel William David (1884–1963), educated at Sandhurst, joined the Irish Inniskilling Fusiliers during the Boer War. He was seconded to the Egyptian Army in 1900 and appointed Staff Officer to Sir Reginald Wingate in Khartoum. During the First World War he served on Sir Ian Hamilton's staff at the Dardanelles and afterward was appointed military governor at Jaffa and Nablus. He was then in succession Military Secretary to Sir Lee Stack and to Sir Geoffrey Archer, when they held the position of Governor-General of the Sudan. During the Second World War he served in the War Office, was demobilised in 1947, and went to Ireland where he became President of the British Legion of Kingstown, and Chairman of the British Red Cross of Dublin for eight years. In 1913 he married Alexandra Mouravieff, daughter of Nicholas Mouravieff, Russian Ambassador in Rome.

Keown-Boyd, Sir Alexander William "K. B." (1884–1954), educated at Merchant Taylors' School and St. John's College, Oxford, joined the Sudan Political Service in 1907 and served in various posts in the Sudan until 1917 when he became the Private Secretary to the High Commissioner for Egypt, 1917–19, and Oriental Secretary, 1919–22. In 1922 he became the Director-General, European Department of the Egyptian Ministry of the Interior, a post which he held until retirement in 1937. In 1921 he married his second wife, Joan Mary Partridge, daughter of John Croker Partridge.

Kfouri was the son of Aziz Kfouri, a Syrian businessman and farmer; he came to the Sudan in 1899 and, making his home in Khartoum, contributed to the rebuilding of the city. He was a pioneer of pump irrigation, owner of a model farm in Khartoum North, and president of the Sudan Chamber of Commerce in 1929.

Lake, Lieutenant-Colonel Morice Challoner (1885–1943), educated at Wellington College and the Royal Military College, Sandhurst, served in the Indian Army from 1905 to 1937; raised and commanded 1st Yemen Infantry in Aden, 1918–25; raised and commanded the Aden Protectorate Levies, 1928; and was the Political Officer, Aden, 1928–34, and Political Secretary, Aden, from 1934 until his retirement in 1940.

Leach, Thomas Archibald (1882–1964), educated at Winchester and Brasenose College, Oxford, joined the Sudan Political Service in 1906 and served in the Legal Department, 1907–10; Wadi Halfa', 1911; Blue Nile, 1912–15; Khartoum, 1916; Kassala, 1916–18; Kordofan, 1918–21; and Red Sea, 1921. He later served as Governor consecutively at Barbar, 1921–24; Khartoum, 1924–25; and Wadi Halfa' from 1925 until his retirement in 1927.

Linlithgow, 2nd Marquess of, Victor Alexander John Hope (1887–1952), educated at Eton, served in the First World War and commanded the 1st Lothians and Border Armoured Car Company, 1920–26; Civil Lord of the Admiralty, 1922–24; Deputy Chairman, Unionist Party Organization, 1924–26; President of Navy League, 1924–31; Chairman, Royal Commission on Indian Agriculture, 1926–28; Chairman, Joint Select Committee on Indian Constitutional Reform, 1933; Viceroy and Governor-General of India, 1936–43. He also served on numerous other commissions and on the Board of Midland Bank Ltd. He married Doreen Maud Milner in 1911.

Lion ("Old Lion") was an Austrian by birth who had been employed by Thomas Cook & Sons at Tagg Island, Molesey, Surrey. When an Egyptian company was formed and managed by Cook's for trips on the Nile, Lion was sent to manage the Nile Steamers. At the time the Steamers and Boats Department of the Sudan government took over the firm in 1902, Lion continued as the Catering Manager of the Nile Steamers, traveling between Ash-Shallal and Wadi Halfa'. Fluent in many languages, "Old Lion" was a great character, known with warm affection by the numerous British officials who traveled the Halfa' Reach.

Lloyd, 1st Baron of Dolobran, George Ambrose Lloyd (1879–1941), educated at Eton and at Trinity College, Cambridge, traveled extensively in the East until appointed Hon. Attaché to H.M. Embassy at Constantinople. He served in Egypt, Gallipoli, Mesopotamia, and the Hijaz during the First World War. He was the Governor of Bombay, 1918–23; M.P. for Eastbourne, 1924–25; High Commissioner for Egypt and the Sudan, 1925–29; and afterward president and chairman of numerous societies. He married the Hon. Blanche Lascelles in 1911.

Lord, Lieutenant-Colonel Peter C. (1880–1960), educated at Rossell School, Blackpool and the Royal Military Academy, Woolwich, was commissioned into the Royal Engineers in 1896. He joined the Egyptian Army in 1901 and was posted to the Sudan Government Railways. He was the Acting Chief Engineer of Sudan Railways when he was sent to direct an Egyptian Works Battalion at Gallipoli in 1915. Following the war, he returned to Sudan Government Railways as Chief Engineer, a post he held until his retirement in 1926. He later returned to Egypt in 1936 as Transportation Officer in Egypt but did not join the Egyptian State Railways.

Lord, G. Wilfrid (1875–1947), joined Sudan Government Railways as an architect in 1913 after being employed in the Lands Department, Port Sudan from 1906. He remained Sudan Government Railways Architect from 1913 until he retired in 1926. He was the brother of Lieutenant-Colonel P. C. Lord.

MacDonald, the Right Honourable James Ramsay (1866–1937), educated at a Board School, was the Secretary of the Labour Party, 1900–12; Treasurer, 1912–24; and Leader of the Labour Party, 1911–14.

He was a member of the Royal Commission on Indian Public Services, 1912–14; Member of the London County Council, 1901-04; and M.P. for Leicester 1906–18. He became Prime Minister, First Lord of the Treasury, and Secretary of State for Foreign Affairs from January to November 1924, and again Prime Minister and First Lord of the Treasury 1929–35. He served as Lord President of the Council, 1935–37.

MacEwen, Air Vice-Marshal Sir Norman Duckworth Kerr (1881–1953), educated at Charterhouse and the Royal Military College, Sandhurst, served in the South African War, 1901–02; the First World War, 1914–18; and the Afghan War, 1919. In 1922 he was appointed Group Captain in charge of the R.A.F. at 'Amman until 1926, when he became Deputy Director of Training, Air Ministry. He commanded No. 22 Group, R.A.F., 1929–31, and was Air Officer Commanding, R.A.F., Halton, 1931–34. He was made Air Vice-Marshal in 1932 and retired in 1935.

MacInnes, the Right Reverend Rennie, Bishop of Jerusalem (1870–1931), educated at Windlesham House, Brighton; Harrow; and Trinity College, Cambridge; ordained in 1896 and served as curate, St. Matthew's Bayswater, 1896–99. He went to Cairo under the auspices of the Church Missionary Society in 1899. In 1896 he married Janet Waldegrave Carr, youngest daughter of the Rev. Canon Carr of Holbrook Hall, Derby.

MacMichael, Sir Harold (1882–), educated at King's Lynn, Bedford, and Magdalene College, Cambridge, joined the Sudan Political Service in 1905 and served in Kordofan, 1905–12; Blue Nile, 1912–13; Khartoum, 1913–15; Political Officer, Red Sea Patrol, 1915; Political Officer, Darfur Expeditionary Force, 1916; Sub-Governor, Darfur, 1917–18; attached to Foreign Office for Paris Peace Conference; Assistant Civil Secretary, 1919–25; Civil Secretary, 1926 until his retirement from the Sudan service in 1934. He later served as the Governor of Tanganyika, 1934–38; High Commissioner for Palestine and High Commissioner for Trans-Jordan, 1938–44. He was also the Special Representative of the British government in Malaya, 1945; and a Constitutional Commissioner, Malta, 1946.

Madden, Doctor Frank Cole (1873–1929), educated at Soctoch College, Melbourne, the University of Melbourne, and St. Mary's Hospital, London; served as House Surgeon and Resident Medical Officer, Melbourne Hospital, 1894; Fellow of the Royal College of Surgeons, 1896; and Resident Medical Officer, Hospital for Sick Children, London,

1896–98. In 1898 he was appointed Professor of Surgery and Senior Surgeon at Kasr-al-Ainy Hospital, Cairo, a post that he held until 1925. He was the Civil Surgeon attached to the Egyptian Expeditionary Force, 1915–18. He had an extensive private practice, and in 1927 was appointed Dean of the Faculty of Medicine at the University of Egypt. In 1929 he became Vice-Rector of the University, dying the same year of overwork and nervous exhaustion in that position.

Madden, John Franklin (1901–   ), educated at Rugby and Magdalen College, Oxford, joined the Sudan Political Service in 1925 and served in the Red Sea, 1925–28; Deputy Assistant Civil Secretary, 1929–32; Darfur, 1932–37; Equatoria, 1937–42; Civil Secretary's Office, 1942–44; Deputy Governor, Darfur, 1944–46; Deputy Governor, Northern Province, 1946–48; and Governor, Northern Province until his retirement in 1951.

Mahmud Hamuda [Mahmud Hamdi Hamudah], Doctor of Medicine, was a Syrian of Damascus born about 1882. He studied medicine at Beirut and Constantinople and served in the Turkish Army during and up to the end of the First World War, after which he settled in Syria. He was appointed the Professor of Rhino-laryngology at Damascus until 1925, when he left to join Ibn Sa'ud. He was appointed Director-General of Public Health for Sa'udi Arabia in January 1926, and represented Ibn Sa'ud at the International Sanitary Conference of that same year. In 1932 he was the Sa'udi representative at a meeting of the International Health Office following the accession of Sa'udi Arabia to the Rome Convention. He died sometime between July 1939 and June 1943.

Marshall, Patience Elizabeth (née Clayton) (1913–   ) educated at St. Mary's Anglican Convent School, Hastings; Harones School, Bedfordshire; Perse High School, Cambridge; and at Newnham College, Cambridge; and went on to take a Diploma in Social Science at the London School of Economics. She was appointed Probation Officer in the London Metropolitan Area. In 1940 she married Dr. Alfred Gordon Marshall and had two sons and two daughters. In 1951 she was appointed Justice of the Peace in the County Borough of Wolverhampton, and in 1952 was selected and trained as a Marriage Guidance Counsellor.

Matthew, John Godfrey (1881–1947), educated at Charterhouse and Wadham College, Oxford, joined the Sudan Political Service in 1905 and served at Sannar until 1909; Red Sea, 1909–15; Sannar again, 1915–17; and Acting Governor, Red Sea, 1917–20. He was made the Assistant Financial Secretary in 1921 and served at that post until becoming Secretary for Education and Health in 1927 up to his retirement in 1932.

Maude, Lieutenant General Sir Frederick Stanley (1864–1917), educated at Eton and the Royal Military College, Sandhurst, entered the army in 1884 and served in the Sudan, 1884–85; the South African War and the European War, 1914–15. He was given command of the Tigris Army Corps in July 1916 and made Commander-in-Chief in Mesopotamia in August. He died in November 1917.

Maugras, François-Gustave-Gaston (1884–), licencié ès lettres et en droit, political and commercial attaché to the French Ambassador in Berlin, 1908; secretary 3rd class at Washington, 1911; and at Tokyo, 1912, where he was promoted to secretary 2nd class in 1916. In 1918 he was chargé d'affaires at Bangkok and at Peking the following year. He served as first secretary at Berlin in 1920 and chargé d'affaires in 1921. In 1924 he was promoted as Consul-General at Jerusalem, and in 1926 was attached to the French legation at Teheran. In 1927 he was attached to the French High Commissioner in Syria but returned to Teheran in 1929 as Resident Minister, and Minister Plenipotentiary, 1930. In 1934 he was Envoy Extraordinary and Minister Plenipotentiary at Budapest and in 1938 at Athens. He was retired in 1943 by the Vichy government but in 1944 was sent as Ambassador to Turkey. He retired from the diplomatic service in 1948.

Meade, Major [Mead, Major Roger], was the Inspecting Officer of Police at ar-Ramadi at the time of Sir Gilbert Clayton's visit. He had previously been an Assistant Political Officer before transferring to the police. He served in various stations and finally joined the Iraq Petroleum Company. During the Second World War he returned to government service as Political Adviser to the British forces in al-Basra.

Midwinter Pasha, Sir Edward Colpoys (1872–1947), entered the Royal Engineers in 1892 and was transferred to the Egyptian Army in 1897. Working under Lieutenant E. P. C. Girouard, who was in charge of Kitchener's military railway in the Sudan, Midwinter was stationed at Wadi Halfa', Abu Hamad, and 'Atbara as and he followed the advancing Anglo-Egyptian Army up the Nile. He remained in the Sudan service after the capture of Umdurman, and in 1906 succeeded C. B. Macauley as Director of the Sudan Government Railways, a post he retained until 1925 when he became the controller of the Sudan Government Office in London up to his retirement in 1932.

Miller, Sir Ernest (1879–1939), educated privately, entered the firm of Arbuthnot Ewart & Co. in 1900, went to India in 1902 and was stationed at Bombay and Karachi until 1914. At the outbreak of the First World War he joined the Scots Guards in September 1914 and rose to the rank of Acting Captain after serving in France, in the War Office, 1917, and with the British War Commission to U.S.A., 1918. After the war he returned to India in 1919 as Manager of Ewart Ryrie & Co., Karachi. He joined the Asiatic Petroleum Company, India in 1921 and was posted to Calcutta but was transferred to Bombay in 1925. He joined Burmah-Shell upon its formation in 1928 and became General Manager for Burmah Shell Oil Storage & Distributing Co. India. He retired in 1935. He was a Member of Committee, Bombay Chamber of Commerce 1926 and 1928 and its Vice-President 1929. He was also a Member, Bombay Legislative Council Committee, was attached to the Simon Commission, and was Member of Indian Franchise Committee 1932, as well as President, Indian Road and Transport Development Association 1930–35. He was also a Director of Associated Tin Mines of Nigeria Ltd., London Nigerian Tin Mines Ltd., Southern Kinta Tin Dredging Co. Ltd., and Talering Tin Dredging Co. Ltd.

Miller, Ernest Combe (1872–194?), was born in London and joined H.M.S. *Worcester* as a Cadet in 1885. In 1888 he left the Royal Navy to take service on the S.S. *Hurunui* as an Apprentice; and except for two years between 1892–94 as Acting Sub-Lieutenant on the H.M.S. *Sovereign*, he remained in the merchant service and was employed on 13 ships between 1888 and 1924, advancing from Apprentice to 2nd Officer. He was made Master of the S.S. *Morea* in 1924 and the following year Master of the S.S. *Razmak*, a post he held until 1927.

Mills, Eric (1892–1961), educated at Cambridge, was one of the first Military officers appointed to administer the Occupied Territory of Southern Palestine in December 1917. He remained in the Palestine Civil Service until 1948, serving as Assistant Secretary, Deputy Chief Secretary, Director of Immigration and Labour, Controller of the Census, and planner of the liquidation of British administration in the Mandate. After retirement in 1948 he served on special missions to Jamaica 1949, Fiji 1950, the Sudan 1950–51, British Guiana 1952–54, and Nigeria, 1956.

Mirza 'Ali Akbar Khan Bahman (1893–) joined the Iranian Ministry of Foreign Affairs in 1918 after completing studies at the College of Political Science, Beirut. His first position was First Vice Consul to

Istanbul, after which he was Head of the Department of Accounts, Foreign Ministry; Head of the Department of Non-neighboring Countries; and Minister to the Balkans. He was Minister to Egypt when on 28 September 1925 he was appointed to the commission to enquire into the possible damages to Mecca by the Wahhabi troops. He later served as Superintendent of Iranian Students in Europe, Minister to Brussels, Chief of Protocol at the Ministry of Court, Ambassador to Egypt, and Ambassador to Sa'udi Arabia until his retirement in 1950.

Mirza Habibolah Khan Hoveyda (1885–1945), was born in Iran. He began work in government service in 1907 in the Department of Finance, where he served as a Member of the Department of Government-Owned Lands, Head of the Department of Accounts, and Vice-Governor of Lahijan, Northern Iran. In 1920 he transferred to the Ministry of Foreign Affairs, serving as a Member of the Department of Translation, Assistant to the Department of Nationality, and Consul General to Palestine when in September 1925 he was appointed to serve on the commission to enquire into possible Wahhabi damages to Mecca. After 1925 he was the Envoy to the government of Sa'udi Arabia to establish diplomatic relations with that country, Consul to the Yemen, Minister to the Balkans, and Minister to Sa'udi Arabia until his death in 1945.

Mohammed ibn Abdur Rahman ibn Faisal Al Sa'ud, Amir [Muhammad ibn 'Abd ar-Rahman ibn Faysal ibn Sa'ud] (1880–1943) was the fourth son of 'Abd ar-Rahman and took part in the expedition to recover Riyadh in 1902 and in the subsequent military operations commanded his brother's cavalry. Beside these military interests, however, he took little part in Arabian politics, preferring the life and activities of a large landholder.

Mohammed ibn el Wazir, Sayed [Sayyid Muhammad ibn al-Wazir] ? –1944), brother of 'Abd Allah ibn al-Wazir and member of the powerful Al-Wazir family. He was for some years the 'Amil of Dhamar. He died of typhus in 1944 and his amirate was abolished.

Mohammed Sagaf [Sayyid Ahmad 'Alawi as-Saqqaf] (1880–1959) was born in Mecca of a prominent family from Hadramaut with a high religious standing. He was tutored privately by learned men in Mecca on Islamic Jurisprudence, Logic, and Arabic Studies. He was Secretary to Husayn ibn 'Ali and one of his distinguished men during the Arab Revolt. He remained with 'Ali in Jiddah during the struggle with Ibn Sa'ud and stayed behind when granted asylum by Ibn Sa'ud to liquidate his assets. He was later expelled from the Hijaz and went to Lahij where he resided until 1937, when he was called by 'Abd Allah to assume the position of Chief Justice and Minister of Justice. His last assignment was Chief of the Royal Cabinet, a position he held until his retirement.

Monson, Edmund St. John Debonnaire John (1883–), son of Sir Edmund Monson the former British Ambassador in Vienna and Paris, entered the diplomatic service in 1906 and served at Constantinople, Tokyo, Paris, and Teheran. He was the British Minister to Columbia 1926–29, to Mexico 1929–34, to the Baltic States 1935–37, and to Sweden 1938–39.

More, Richard Edwardes (1879–1936), educated at Westminster and Christ Church, Oxford, joined the Sudan Civil Service in 1902 and served in the Red Sea Province, 1902–03; Kordofan, 1904; White Nile, 1905; Khartoum, 1906–19, during which time he was Governor of Khartoum, 1914–19. He became Sudan Agent, Cairo in 1920, a post he held until his retirement in 1931. He married Ethel Alice Bodkin in 1905.

Morhig, George N. (1879–1962), was born on 15 November 1879 in Shwayr, Lebanon and educated in a local village school and at the Syrian Protestant College, Beirut, where he took a degree in pharmacy. He joined the Medical Corps of the Sudan Expeditionary Force and afterward served in the Sudan from 1900 to 1906 when he resigned at the rank of lieutenant and opened his own business in Khartoum. As the principal supplier of European goods to the expanding British community in Khartoum, his business prospered. Well-known, respected, and popular, he was at varying times President of the Syrian and Lebanese communities in the Sudan. He married in 1913 and upon his death had three surviving children.

Muhammad Amin al-Husayni, Hajj (1900–) had served as an officer in the Turkish Army during the First World War and was suspected of instigating the anti-Jewish riots in Jerusalem in April 1920. Pardoned by Lord Samuel, he was appointed Mufti and elected President of the Supreme Muslim Council in 1922 where he led the Arab opposition to the Jews. He was instrumental in calling the World Islamic Congress held in Jerusalem in December 1931 which enhanced his own prestige as well as that of the office of Mufti. He was elected President of the Congress and traveled widely, organizing branches in India and 'Iraq. In 1934 he led a delegation that arranged a peace treaty between Ibn Sa'ud and Imam Yahya of the Yemen. In 1936 he was elected President of the Arab Higher Committee for Palestine and was the chief Arab witness before the Royal Commission in Palestine, before his removal from the presidency of the Supreme Muslim Council by the British authorities for seditious activities. In disagreement over the British policy of establishing a Jewish National home in Palestine, he fled to Syria where he openly supported Germany. At the outbreak of World War II he fled from French-controlled Lebanon to 'Iraq and later, with the triumph of British arms in the Middle East, to Germany itself. On his return from Europe in 1946 he resided in Egypt and was reelected President of the Arab Higher Committee for Palestine and in 1948 President of the Assembly and Supreme Council of All-Palestine government. He was later President of the World Muslim Conference held in Karachi in 1951 and Chairman of the Palestine Arab Delegation to the Bandung Conference in 1955.

Muhammad Amin Zaki (1880–1948), a Kurd educated at the Military and Staff Colleges, Istanbul, graduated a Captain in 1902 and was attached to the Sixth Army stationed in Baghdad. In 1903 he was seconded as an engineer, Saniyah Department but returned to the army in 1908 as a Topographic Officer. He participated in the Bulgaro-Turkish Frontiers Demarcation Commission in 1910 and the Russo-Turkish Frontiers Demarcation Committee. He served in the Balkan war as a Staff Officer and was sent on a military mission to France in 1913. During the First World War he was promoted to Major and transferred to the General Staff where he took part in the battles on the Iraqi front. In 1917 he was made the Assistant Chief of Staff of the Seventh Army under the command of Mustafa Kamal Pasha in Palestine, and later served with the Third Army in the Caucasus. After the war he transferred to the History of War Section and wrote several books on the war in 'Iraq. He returned to 'Iraq in 1924 as Commandant of the Baghdad Military College. The following year he served as Deputy for Sulaymanya and was Minister of Communications and Works 1925–27, Minister of Education 1927 and 1929, Minister of Defence 1929, Minister of Communications and Economics 1931–32 and 1935–36, Member of Parliament 1937–39, Minister of Communications and Works 1940, Minister of Economics 1941, and Member of the Senate 1944.

Murcott, Lieutenant-Colonel Andrew Karslake (1903–1945), educated at the Rossall School, was commissioned a 2nd Lieutenant in the Essex Regiment in 1924 and joined the 12th Frontier Force Regiment, Q.V.O. Corps of Guides in 1925. From 1929 to 1944 he then served in numerous positions in India, including Instructor in the Small Arms Schools 1932–35 and Deputy Assistant Quarter Master General for Madras and Southern Indian Command 1940–42. He was promoted to Temporary Lieutenant-Colonel in 1943.

Musa Kazim Pasha [al-Husayni] was a former official in the Ottoman government in Palestine and a prominent member of the family of Husayni. He was appointed mayor of Jerusalem at the beginning of the British occupation in 1917 until March 1920, when he was dismissed from office for his part in the demonstrations following the proclamation of Faysal as King in Damascus. He led the opposition to Zionism at the Third Palestine Arab Congress which met under his chairmanship in December 1920 and was thereafter active in the Executive Committee of the Congress. He led delegations to London in autumn 1921 and May 1930 on behalf of the Arab cause. He died in March 1934, and with him passed away his unifying influence on the Arab executive.

Mustafa al-Idrisi, brother of a Ruler of the Idrisi family of 'Asir, lived in Luxor. He often visited the Residency at Luxor to appeal for British aid for the Idrisi against the Yemeni forces of Imam Yahya and the Wahhabi troops of Ibn Sa'ud.

Nalder, Leonard Fielding (1888–1958), educated at Rugby and Corpus Christi College, Oxford, joined the Sudan Political Service and served at Khartoum 1912, Red Sea 1913–17, and was then seconded for service in Mesopotamia and 'Iraq until 1922 where he met Sir Gilbert's brother, Iltyd. He returned to the Sudan in 1922, serving consecutively in Kordofan and Khartoum 1923–26. He was a member of the Turko-'Iraq Frontier Delimitation Commission in 1927, and then returned to the Sudan first as Governor, Fung, 1927–30, and then Governor, Mongalla, 1930–36, at which time he retired. While in Mongalla he edited *A Tribal Survey of Mongalla Province* (London, 1937). He married Veronica Entwisle Martindale in 1924.

Nuri Pasha Es Said [Nuri Pasha as-Sa'id] (1888–1958), educated at Istanbul Military and Staff College, Commander-in-Chief 'Iraq Army, Minister of Defence 1922–24, 1926–28, and 1933–34. He served as Prime Minister 1930–32, Minister of Foreign Affairs 1933–34 and 1934–36. He was exiled after the coup d'état of October 1936 but returned to be Prime Minister and Minister of the Interior 1939–40, Minister of Foreign Affairs 1940–41, and Prime Minister and Acting Minister of Defence 1941–47. After the war he served as President of the 'Iraqi Senate 1946, Prime Minister and Minister of the Interior in 1949 and again 1950–52, and Prime Minister and Minister of Defence 1954 until the revolution of 1958 during which he was killed.

Orr-Ewing, Barbara Dorothea (1902–), the daughter of Charles Orr-Ewing and Lady Augusta Boyle, married Lieutenant-Commander William Edmund Halsey, R.N., in 1931. He was the second son of Sir Walter Johnston Halsey.

Osborne, Francis Paget (1882–), educated at Monmouth and Lincoln College, joined the Sudan Political Service in 1905 and served at Khartoum; Sannar, 1906–07; Legal Department, 1908–18; Judge of the High Court, 1918–26; and Director of Lands from 1926 until his retirement in 1928.

Palmer, Clarence Edward Stanhope (1883–1936), educated at St. Paul's School and Trinity College, Cambridge, was appointed a Student Interpreter in the Levant in 1906 and promoted to an Assistant Interpreter in 1908. He was made the Acting Vice-Consul at Salonica in 1909 and at the Dardanelles in 1910, where the following year he was advanced to H.M. Vice-Consul, a post which he held until the outbreak of the First World War. During the war he served as Temporary Lieutenant R.N.V.R. when he was captured by the Turks on H.M. Submarine E 15 on 17 April 1915 and held a prisoner until the Armistice. After the war he held a variety of positions including a Special Mission to Asia Minor, 1919, and service in the Department of Overseas Trade. He was appointed Consul at Damascus in 1920 and transferred to Port Said in July 1924 until 1926 when he left to take up successive Consularships at Benghazi, Tripoli, Tabriz, and Sarajevo, where he died on 16 May 1936.

Palmer, the Right Reverend Edwin James (1869–1954), educated at Winchester and Balliol College, Oxford; Fellow, Tutor, Chaplain of the College, ordained in 1896, appointed Bishop of Bombay in 1908, a post he held until 1929 when he became the Assistant Bishop of Gloucester. He married Hazel Hanning-Lee in 1912.

Park, James Loder (1895–), educated in the grade and high schools of Indiana and Pennsylvania and at Pennsylvania State College, attended Harvard Medical School 1916–19, and was employed at various capacities with the Near East Relief Committee at Aleppo. He served as a clerk in the American consulate at Smyrna in 1921 and later at Constantinople, Aden, and Addis Ababa. He resigned from the United States Foreign Service in 1940.

Parker, Arthur Claude (1880–1960), educated at Stafford House, City of London College, joined the Sudan Government Railways in 1904 and later served as the General Manager from 1925–1932.

Patterson, Sir Reginald Stewart (1878–1930), educated at Marlborough and Trinity College, Oxford, entered the Egyptian service in the Ministry of Education in 1901 and transferred to the Ministry of Finance 1905. He was Director General of Accounts 1915, Adviser to the Ministry of Education 1919, and Financial Adviser 1923–27.

Peake, Frederick Gerard Sandhurst (1886–), educated at Stubbington House, Fareham, and the Royal Military College, was commissioned in the Duke of Wellington's Regiment in 1906 and served in India until 1913 when he was seconded to the Egyptian Army and posted to the Camel Corps in the Sudan. He took part in the Darfur Expedition 1916 and the E.E.F. In 1921 he was appointed Inspector-General of Gendarmerie, Trans-Jordan, and in 1922 raised and organized the Arab Legion.

Pearson Pasha, Hugh Drummond (1873–1922), was born in London and commissioned into the R.E. in 1892. In 1904 he was seconded to the Egyptian Army and joined the Sudan Government Survey Department. The following year he was appointed Director of Surveys, a post that he held until his death. He served in the Palestine campaign in 1917–19. While serving as British Commissioner on the Anglo-French Boundary Commission demarcating the Darfur-Wada'i frontier, he fell ill and died at Umm Dafug.

Peiniger, Lieutenant-Colonel Robert Francis (1877–1952), was commissioned a 2nd Lieutenant in the Royal Artillery 1898 and served at Fort St. George, India, 1914; and as D.A.A.G. to G.O.C., R.A. Mesopotamia Expeditionary Force, in 1918. He was the G.S.O., 2nd Royal Artillery, Mesopotamia Expeditionary Force, 1919–20; and Deputy Assistant Quarter Master General, Mesopotamia Expeditionary Force, 1920–21. He commanded the Royal Artillery at Aden 1925–26 and retired in 1927.

Percival, Sir John Hope (1870–1954), educated at Charterhouse and Trinity Hall, Cambridge, was barrister of the Inner Temple 1894, Judge of Native Courts of First Instance, Egypt 1903, Judge of Native Court of Appeal 1909, and Vice-President thereof 1919. He was Legal

Adviser to the G.O.C., Egypt, 1919, and later Judicial Adviser to the government of Egypt and Legal Adviser to the High Commissioner, 1925–28. He served as Alderman, Gloucestershire County Council from 1937 to 1949.

Percival, Philip Edward (1872–1939), the brother of Sir John Percival (q.v.), educated at Charterhouse and Balliol College, Oxford, barrister at law 1895, entered the Indian Civil Service, Bombay Establishment in 1895 and served for 35 years in the Bombay Presidency, chiefly in the Judicial Department. He married Sylvia Baines in 1901, the only daughter of Sir J. A. Baines.

Philby, Harry St. John Bridger (1885–1960), educated at Westminster and Trinity College, Cambridge, joined the Indian Civil Service in 1908 where he served in various positions until 1915 when he went to Mesopotamia as the Political Officer to the Mesopotamian Expeditionary Force. In 1917–18 he was in charge of the British Political Mission to Central Arabia during which he crossed the Arabian Peninsula and carried out explorations in South Central Arabia. He was the Adviser to the Ministry of the Interior, Mesopotamia, 1920–21; and the Chief British Representative, Trans-Jordan, 1921–24. He retired from the Indian Civil Service in 1925 and became Director in Jiddah, first of Sharqieh Ltd., and later of Mitchell Cotts until 1955, during which time he carried out extensive explorations in Arabia. He has written numerous books about Arabia.

Plumer, of Messines and of Bilton, Yorkshire, 1st Baron, Herbert Charles Onslow Plumer (1857–1932), educated at Eton, entered the York and Lancaster Regiment in 1876 and served in the Sudan in 1884, the South African War, and during the First World War commanded the 5th Army Corps, the 2nd Army of the British Expeditionary Force, and the Italian Expeditionary Force. Following the War he was Governor of Malta 1919–24 and High Commissioner of Palestine 1925–28. In 1884 he married Annie Constance Goss, youngest daughter of George Goss.

Power, Sir John Cecil (? –1960), founder of the Institute for Historical Research, Founder of the Institute of International Affairs and its Hon. Treasurer 1920–43, Conservative M.P. for Wimbledon 1924–31. He has also served as the Hon. Treasurer of the British Council; a Director of the Royal Insurance Company, 1934–39; Member of Committee, Royal Humane Society; and Member of the Travel and Industrial Development Association of Great Britain and Ireland.

Prideaux, Lieutenant-Colonel Francis Beville (1871–1938), entered the army in 1890 and served in India before joining the Indian Political Department in 1895. In 1897 he was appointed First Assistant Resident, Persian Gulf, and was made the Political Agent in Bahrain in 1904, in the Southern Rajputana States in 1911, and in the Eastern Rajputana States in 1912. He served as Consul in Seistan and Kain, 1912–18; Consul-General at Mashhad, 1920–24; and as the Political Resident, Persian Gulf, from 1924 until his retirement in 1927.

Ragheb Bey [Qadi Muhammad Raghib ibn Rafiq Bey], Chamberlain and Foreign Minister to the Imam Yahya at the time of the Clayton Mission. He had served previously in the Yemen as a Turkish official during the First World War only to return after the Kemalist revolution of 1924. Beginning his career in the Ottoman service at Constantsa on the Black Sea and then at Cetinje, he was posted to St. Petersburg in 1900 and then to Paris, Brussels, and Vienna. He was appointed Mutasarrif at Al-Hudaydah in 1913, returning to Constantinople in 1918 after the Ottoman defeat. Upon his return to the Yemen in 1924 Imam Yahya gladly accepted his services. His daughter ʻAziza married the sixth son of the Imam Yahya, the Minister of Health. Another daughter, Wahabia, was married to the Crown Prince Ahmad, eldest son of the Imam. In 1935 Raghib was appointed Minister of State.

Rashwan Pasha Mahfouz [Mahfuz Pasha] (1881–), born in Asyut where he received his primary education before attending the Tawfiqiyah Secondary School of Cairo, took his B.A. degree in Law in 1903 after which he served as a Muʻawin in the governorate of Giza. He was soon promoted to Ma'mur in Daqahliyah and then at Mit Ghamr. He then was promoted to *wakil* at Al Fayyum, Al Gharbiyah, Al Buhayrah, and Aswan. He subsequently served as *mudir* at Bani Suwayf and Qina during which he founded numerous schools and hospitals. In 1921 he transferred to Al Minufiyah with the title of Pasha where he continued to devote his energies to school construction. During the ministry of Saʻd Zaghlul he was placed on pension but upon the fall of the Zaghlul government he was appointed *mudir* of Al Gharbiyah and later *wakil* of the Ministry of Agriculture. He was a leading member of the Constitutional Liberal party and served as Minister of Agriculture in more than one cabinet.

Raymond, Lieutenant-Colonel Maurice Claud (1884–1959), educated at the Isle of Wight College, 2nd Lieutenant in the Northamptonshire

Regiment in 1904 and served in the First World War as A.D.C. to Brigade Commander 1914–15, Staff Captain 1915–17, and D.A.A. 1917–18. Following the war he was appointed Officer Commandant, Military Police, Pyawbwe, Burma, in 1921 and was promoted to Assistant Commandant, Military Police, Burma in 1923 and Commandant 1932. The following year he was made Deputy Inspector General at Rangoon. He retired in 1934 and was employed in censorship duties during the Second World War.

Redhead, Captain Charles Mahon (1871–1940), educated at Bedford School, joined the Peninsular and Oriental Steam Navigation Company in 1894 while continuing to serve in the Royal Navy Reserve in which he reached the rank of Captain in 1921. During the First World War he had fought at the Battle of Falkland and in 1925 was appointed Captain of the P. & O. R.M.S. *Rawalpindi*.

Reilly, Lieutenant-Colonel Sir Bernard Rawdon (1882–1968), educated at Bedford and entered the Indian Army in 1902, serving in India and Aden. He was appointed H.M.'s Commissioner and Plenipotentiary to H.M. the King of Yemen in 1933. He served as the Resident and Commander-in-Chief at Aden, 1931–37; Chief Commissioner, Aden, 1932–37; Governor and Commander-in-Chief, Aden, 1937–40; and Member of British Delegation to Ethiopia which concluded the Anglo-Ethiopian Agreement of 1944. He has also served on numerous commissions and special assignments, including the Commission of Inquiry into the importation and possession of qat in Aden, 1958.

Rikabi Pasha ['Ali Rida ar-Rikabi Pasha] was born in Damascus and received a military education, rising to the rank of General. In 1918 he was appointed military governor of Damascus after the British occupation. He was later President of the Council of Faysal in Damascus and a member of the Council of the Amir 'Abd Allah. In 1922 he was appointed Prime Minister of Trans-Jordan. He returned to Damascus in 1924 to replace Hasan Khalid as Prime Minister. In 1932 he was instrumental in organizing the moderate nationalist elements to form the Arab Syrian Youth Association.

Ryder, Charles Frederick (1879–1960), was educated at Charterhouse and Magdalen College, Oxford. An enthusiastic cricketer and sportsman, he joined the Survey Department of the Sudan government in 1905 and transferred to the Legal Department two years later where he served as a Province Judge. At the outbreak of the First World War he joined the Special Intelligence Duties, H.Q., E.E.F., 1915–18, and was promoted to Lt.-Col. G.S.O. 1 in charge of Intelligence Service, Egypt, and Lines of Communications. He transferred to the Egyptian government, Public Security, in 1920 from which he retired in 1924 to become the Assistant Sudan Agent, Cairo. In 1931 he assumed the duties of Sudan Agent and retired in 1935.

Safwat Pasha al-Awa (1866–1956) was born in Damascus into a commercial family, and after elementary education in a Turkish school was sent to Istanbul at the age of 14 to prepare for entrance into the military academy. He graduated a Second Lieutenant from the academy in 1887 and continued his military career until he reached the rank of Miralai (Colonel) and a Pasha at the age of 52. During his years in Istanbul he became closely associated with the Hashemite family, and Husayn requested the Turkish government to appoint him tutor to his three sons 'Ali, 'Abd Allah, and Faysal. When Faysal proclaimed himself King of Syria he called Safwat al-Awa to Damascus as Personal Advisor and Keeper of the Royal Privy Purse. After the fall of Syria he accompanied Faysal to Baghdad where he became Chancellor of the Privy Seal and Keeper of the Privy Purse, a post he held until his retirement.

Said Shoucair [Shuqayr, Sir Sa'id Pasha] (1868–1938), born at Shwayfat in the Lebanon of a distinguished Protestant family, was educated at the Syrian Protestant College in Beirut. After graduation he taught Arabic at the college from 1886–89 when he emigrated to Egypt, where he worked as a journalist before joining Egyptian government service. He was employed in the Ministry of Finance but was later transferred to the Intelligence Department in Cairo. In 1900 he was placed in charge of the accounts of the newly formed Sudan government, and from 1907 to 1921 was Director-General of Accounts. From 1921 until his death he was the Financial Adviser to the Sudan government where he played a decisive part in the organization of Sudanese finances. He and his wife were devoted and loyal friends of the Claytons.

Saleh Gabril [Salih Jabril] was born in the Sudan before the turn of the century. His family were prominent camel breeders, probably of the 'Ababda tribe. He served in the Sudan Frontier Force and died about 1940.

Sarruf, Dr. Ya'qub (1852–1927), educated at 'Abayh Academy and the Syrian Protestant College (later the American University of Beirut), where he was one of the first sixteen students to be enrolled in 1866 and from where he obtained a B.A. degree in 1870, being one of the first five to be graduated from the college. After graduation he was first a teacher in Sidon and then in Tripoli. In 1873 he joined the teaching staff of the Syrian Protestant College where he remained until the summer of 1884. While a teacher he and Faris Nimr, the father-in-law of George Antonius, founded *Al-Muqtataf*, a monthly, and continued to edit it first in Beirut and then, after 1885, in Cairo. When in 1888 Nimr started the political daily *Al-Muqattam*, Ya'qub Sarruf continued to devote his time to the monthly *Al-Muqtataf* which, from its beginning, had played an increasingly important role in the Arab intellectual and scientific renaissance. He was granted an honorary degree from the University of the State of New York in 1890. In addition to his work as editor of *Al-Muqtataf*, he was author of several books, three of them novels, and translator of others.

Sayed [Sa'id] Effendi was an Egyptian soldier in charge of all the orderlies at the Sudan Agency in Cairo. He was a much respected and beloved man and a faithful and loyal friend to Sir Gilbert.

Schuster, Sir George Ernest (1881–), educated at Charterhouse and New College, Oxford, became barrister-at-law 1905 and partner in Schuster Son & Co. 1906–14. During the First World War he served in France and in 1919 with the Murmansk Force in North Russia. After the war he held numerous positions, including Chief Assistant to Organizer of International Credits under the League of Nations 1921, and Member of Advisory Committee to the Treasury 1921–22. He served as Financial Secretary of the Sudan government 1922–27, and Economic and Financial Adviser to the Colonial Office 1927–28, before becoming Finance Member of the Executive Council of the Viceroy of India 1928–34. Thereafter he served on numerous government financial and economic commissions and as director of various corporations. He married the Hon. Gwendolen, daughter of Lord Parker of Waddington in 1908.

Scindia, Lieutenant-General His Highness Jiwajirao (1916–1961), Maharajah of Gwalior, was privately educated under distinguished tutors. After passing the matriculation examination in the second division of the Ajmer Board, he attended Victoria College, Gwalior. He received settlement and revenue training at Lyallpur, Punjab, administrative training at Bangalore, and military training at Poona and Bombay. He was Raj Pramukh of Madya Bharat until its merger into Madya Pradesh in November 1956, and he served as Chancellor of Banareo

Hindu University. He also became an avid sportsman and was a member of many Indian sporting clubs.

Shute, Florence Eugenie (née Lord), was the daughter of Francis Aylmer Lord. In 1913 she married Cyril Aveling Shute (1886–1950), who served in the First World War and later with the Trans-Jordan Frontier Force of which he was the Officer Commanding 1928–33. He retired in 1933 with the rank of Lieutenant-Colonel, and during the Second World War served with the R.A.F. Volunteer Reserve with the rank of Wing Commander.

Skeen, General Sir Andrew (1873–1935), served on the North West Frontier, India, 1897–98; in China, 1900; East Africa, 1902–04; and in the European War, 1914–17. He fought in the Third Afghan War, 1919; commanded the Peshawar District, 1922–23; and was G.O.C.-in-Chief, Southern Army, India, 1923–24. He was appointed C.G.S., Indian Army, 1924–28; and A.D.C. General to the King from 1928 until his retirement in 1929.

Sparkes Pasha, William Spottiswode (1862–1906), entered the British Army in 1881 and was promoted to Captain in 1888. In 1894 he was seconded to the Egyptian Army and fought in the Dunqula and Umdurman campaigns. In 1899 he was governor of Fashoda, and between 1901 and 1903 opened up the Bahr al Ghazal to British administration. He established British posts at Wau, Tonj, Rumbek, and Shambe during which time he was assisted in 1902–03 at Wau by Gilbert Clayton. In 1904 he reverted to the British Army, having been frequently and seriously ill with malaria during his tour of duty in the Southern Sudan, and died two years later.

Stack, Sir Lee Oliver Fitzmaurice (1865–1924), educated at Clifton College and Royal Military College, Sandhurst, served in India and Crete before joining the Egyptian Army in 1899. He commanded the Shambe Field Force in the Bahr al Ghazal in 1902, and in 1904 was appointed private secretary to the Governor-General of the Sudan, Sir Reginald Wingate. In 1908 he was made the Sudan Agent and Director of Military Intelligence in Cairo. In 1914 Stack became Civil Secretary of the Sudan government and in 1917 became Sirdar of the Egyptian Army and Governor-General of the Sudan. On 19 November 1924 Stack was shot and wounded in three places while driving home from the Ministry of War in Cairo. He died the following day. Clayton was a close personal friend of Stack, having succeeded him as Wingate's personal secretary in 1908 and as Sudan Agent and Director of Military Intelligence in 1914. Sir Gilbert and Lady Clayton were lunching with Allenby and Mr. Asquith when the news was brought of Stack's assassination.

Sterry, Sir Wasey (1866–1955), educated at Eton and Merton College, Oxford, and barrister of Lincoln's Inn, 1892, was appointed Civil Judge in the Sudan in 1901 and Chief Judge in 1903. From 1917–26 he served as the Legal Secretary of the Sudan government and afterward Judge of H. B. M.'s Supreme Court for Egypt, 1928–38. In 1919 he married Renée Bonfils, the eldest daughter of M. Adrien Bonfils of Nice.

Stewart, Major-General Sir John Henry (1872–1955), educated at Repton and the Royal Military College, Sandhurst, entered the army in 1892 and served on the Tirah Expedition 1897–98 and in the First World War 1914–18, after which he was stationed in 'Iraq 1918–22. He commanded the 19th Indian Brigade 1922–23 and the Delhi Independent Brigade Area 1924–25. He was the G.O.C. and Political Resident, Aden, from 1925 until his retirement in 1929. In 1898 he married Frances Jane Hampden, the second daughter of the Hon. G. A. Hobart Hampden of the Indian Civil Service.

Stiven, Doctor Harold Edward Sutherland (1884–1956), educated at Harrow and Trinity College, Cambridge, and qualified for medicine at the London Hospital, first as House Surgeon and later as Resident. He joined the Egyptian Public Health Department as the Director of Medical Stores, but in his passion to practice he joined the Red Crescent and served in the Balkan War of 1912. He returned to Egypt and during the First World War served in the British Royal Army Medical Corps and was placed in charge of the Prisoner of War Camps in the British Middle East with the rank of Lieutenant-Colonel. He returned to civilian life in 1919 as Director of the Egyptian Government Hospital at Port Said, where he remained until 1930, when he became Director of a private hospital in Cairo. He retired from that position and a large private practice in 1937. During the Second World War he served as a Colonel in the Royal Army Medical Corps at Al 'Alamayn. He married a daughter of Faris Nimr Pasha in 1917.

Storrs, Sir Ronald (1881–1955), educated at Temple Grove, Charterhouse, and Pembroke College, Cambridge, joined the Egyptian government, Ministry of Finance, in 1904 and later served in several branches of the Egyptian administration. He became Oriental Secretary to the British Agency, Egypt, and Assistant Political Officer to the Anglo-French Political Mission of the E.E.F., 1917. He served in the Secretariat of the War Cabinet 1917 and was then appointed Military Governor of Jerusalem 1917–20 and Civil Governor 1920–26. He was the Governor and Commander-in-Chief of Cyprus 1926–32 and of Northern Rhodesia from 1932 until invalided from tropical service in 1934. Storrs and Clayton were old friends since before the war and worked together in the Arab Bureau during the war and again afterward in Palestine. In 1923 Storrs married Mrs. Louisa Lucy Clowes, widow of Lt.-Col. H. Clowes and daughter of Rear-Admiral Hon. Algernon Littleton.

Strathearn, Sir John Calderwood (1878–1950), educated at the High School, Glasgow, and the Universities of Glasgow and Edinburgh, served as the House Surgeon, Glasgow Royal Infirmary; House Physician, Glasgow Western Infirmary; House Surgeon, Hospital for Skin Diseases; and Ophthalmic Surgeon to the Dundee School Board and to the Educational Authority, County of Fife. He became Assistant Surgeon and later Warden and Chief Surgeon at the British Ophthalmic Hospital, Jerusalem.

Swann, Air Vice-Marshal Sir Oliver (1878–1948), educated at Elstree, entered the Royal Navy in 1892 and commanded H.M.S. *Campania*, Fleet aircraft carrier 1915–17, before transferring to the R.A.F. in 1919. He served as Air Officer Commanding, Middle East 1924–26, and retired in 1929. During the Second World War he served as Air Liaison Officer, North Midland Region 1940–43. He married Elizabeth Laidlaw-Purves in 1913.

Symes, Lieutenant-Colonel Sir George Stewart (1882–1962), entered the army in 1900, earning the rank of Captain in 1907, Major in 1915, and Lieutenant-Colonel in 1917. In early years he served in South Africa, the Aden Hinterland, and on the Blue Nile Expedition, Sudan, 1908. After participating in the European war he served in the positions of A.D.C. to the Sirdar, Assistant Director of Intelligence, Sudan government; Private Secretary of the Sirdar and Governor-General of the Sudan; G.S.O. attached to the staff of the High Commissioner in Egypt; Governor of the Northern District in Palestine, 1920–1925; Chief Secretary to the Government of Palestine, 1925–1928; Resident and Commander-in-Chief at Aden, 1928–1933; Governor and Commander-in-Chief of the Tanganyika Territory, 1931–1933. In 1934 he returned to the Sudan to serve as Governor-General until his retirement in 1940.

Tahsin al-Qadri (1894–), was born in Baalbek and educated at the

Military College, Istanbul. He graduated as a Second Lieutenant of Cavalry in 1914 and saw action in the First World War on the Caucasian and Hijazi fronts. At the outbreak of the Arab Revolt he joined King Faysal's army and was appointed Military A.D.C. to Faysal on the occupation of Syria. He accompanied Faysal in his travels to Europe and came with him to Baghdad where he served as A.D.C. from 1921–1931. He was Master of Ceremonies at the Royal Palace 1931 and after the death of the King served in the 'Iraqi Legation in Teheran. He retired to Lausanne, Switzerland.

Tannahill, John, was a prosperous merchant of Calcutta and a prominent member of the Calcutta Chamber of Commerce.

Taufik Bey Suaidi [Tawfiq Bey as-Suwaydi] (1891–), educated at Istanbul University and the Sorbonne, Paris, was a veteran nationalist who was the 'Iraqi representative at the Arab Conference in Paris 1913; President of the 'Iraqi Conference, Damascus, 1920; Assistant Government Counsellor in the Ministry of Justice and Dean of the Baghdad Law College; and in 1923 'Iraqi Representative at the Lausanne Conference. In 1925 he was appointed Director General of Justice and from 1928–29 was Minister of Education. He later served as Prime Minister of 'Iraq and Minister of Foreign Affairs, 1929; President of the Chamber of Deputies, and Minister to Persia, 1931; Permanent Delegate at the League of Nations, 1934; Minister of Foreign Affairs in 1934 and later in 1937–40. At the close of the Second World War he was the Deputy Prime Minister, 1944, and once again Prime Minister, 1946 and 1950.

Thorowgood, Elizabeth Montgomery (née Hunter-Blair) (1855–1936), was the daughter of John Hunter-Blair, son of Sir David Hunter-Blair, Baronet, of Blair Quhan in Ayrshire. She married Frank Napier Thorowgood in 1881 and had one son, Arthur, who became an officer in the Royal Navy and three daughters, Muriel, Enid, and Maud. She was a lady of great charm and beauty, intolerant in some ways, but lively and receptive of new ideas and customs up to the time of her death.

Tippetts, Sydney Atterbury (1878–1946), educated at St. Paul's and Merton College, joined the Sudan Political Service in 1902 and served in the Upper Nile, 1902–03; Red Sea and Kordofan, 1904; Sannar, 1905; Legal Department, 1906–07; Kordofan, 1908–11; Sannar, 1912–14; Red Sea, 1915–16; Governor, Halfa', 1917–22; Governor, Red Sea, until his retirement in 1927.

Townshend, Major-General Sir Charles Vere Ferrers (1861–1924); entered the Royal Marines in 1881 and served in the Sudan 1884–85, the Nile Campaign 1898, the South African War, and commanded the Mesopotamian Expeditionary Force, 1914–16, until his surrender at Al-Kut. He resigned in 1920.

Turki [Turki ibn 'Abd al-'Aziz ibn Sa'ud] (1900–1919), the eldest son of Ibn Sa'ud, was born at Kuwait during his father's exile. He participated in military expeditions when he was sixteen and was in command of the Wahhabi troops during the operations against Ibn Rashid in 1918. He died the following year during the great influenza epidemic.

Turner, Norah Beryl (née Clayton), (1895–), youngest sister of Sir Gilbert Clayton, educated at Roper House, Canterbury, in 1926 married James Reginald Bingham Turner, Captain Royal Artillery, who retired following the Second World War as Brigadier-General and died in 1963.

Udal, Nicholas Robin (1883–1964), educated at Winchester and New College, Oxford, entered the Sudan Civil Service in 1906 and was appointed Chief Inspector of Education, Sudan government, in 1915. From 1918–30 he was the Assistant Director of Education for the Sudan government and Warden of Gordon College from 1927–1930. He served as the Secretary and Bursar, Clifton College, 1930–36 and was the long-time Secretary of the Athenaeum, 1936–51.

Vernon, Roland Venables (1877–1942), educated at Clifton and Balliol College, Oxford, joined the Colonial Office in 1900 and served in numerous capacities in the West Indies, South Africa, and the South Pacific. He transferred to the Treasury in 1914 but returned to the Colonial Office in 1921, serving in Egypt, Palestine, and in 1925–28 as the Financial Adviser to the government of 'Iraq. In September 1925 Vernon had composed for the Colonial Office the instructions for Sir Gilbert Clayton's forthcoming negotiations with Ibn Sa'ud. Vernon married Marjorie Leon, daughter of A. L. Leon, in 1913 and retired from the Colonial Office in 1937.

Vester, Frederick Emil (1869–1942), the son of Ferdinand Vester, a German-Swiss Lutheran missionary who came to Jerusalem in 1853, was born outside the city walls in a house that is today the Consulate of the United States. Educated in Jerusalem and Switzerland, Frederick Vester assisted his father in the management of several workshops manufacturing olivewood articles. About 1894 he joined the

American Colony, founded in 1881 by H. C. Spafford, a Chicago lawyer and businessman, and upon the retirement of Ferdinand Vester from the business, his son went into financial partnership with the American Colony under the name of Vester and Company, American Colony Stores. The business flourished and diversified under the combination of his business acumen and the energy of his future wife, Bertha Spafford, daughter of the founder of the American Colony, whom he married in 1904. The Vesters were good friends of the Claytons and purchased some of their furniture when they left Palestine. Bertha Spafford Vester died in 1968.

Warburton, Mabel Clarisse (1879–1961), educated at Cheltenham Ladies College, first went out to Egypt as a missionary and later became head of the British Syrian School in Beirut. Near the end of the First World War she went out to do refugee work in Jerusalem under the Bishop of Palestine, the Rt. Rev. Rennie MacInnes. At the close of the war she took over a German orphanage and from it built the British High School that later became the Jerusalem Girls College. She left the school in the late twenties but returned to Palestine as an educational adviser to the Palestine government, in which capacity she accomplished numerous tasks for the government and missionary societies as well. During and after the Second World War she continued her social and missionary work in the East End of London.

Warner, Shipley Charles (1868–193?), was born in Agra, India, and joined the S.S. *Tweed* as an apprentice in 1885. He thereafter served on some nineteen ships between 1885 and 1902, advancing from apprentice to First Mate on the S.S. *Ceylon.* He was employed as First Mate, Chief Mate, and Super First Mate on ten ships between 1902–16 when he was made Master of the S.S. *Candia* in December 1916. He was Master of seven ships between 1916–23 when he took command of the S.S. *Maloja* in October 1923 and made fifteen voyages as her captain until his retirement in February 1928.

Waterfield, Ernest Weatherall (1882–), educated at Plymouth College, Devon, joined the Eastern Telegraph Company in 1899 and was appointed to the Established Staff while at the Porthcurno Training School. He subsequently served at Gibraltar, Aden, Rodrigues, Mauritius, Suez, Sawakin, Carcavelos, and Fayal. He was Officer-in-Charge at Lisbon and Luanda and served as Assistant Superintendent at Port Sudan 1923–26, and later at Capetown, Mossamedes, and Cairo, where he was the Assistant Manager. He returned to England in 1931 as the

Assistant Traffic Manager at the Head Office in London and retired in 1937.

Waterfield, Dr. Noel Everard (1879–1959), educated at Plymouth College, Devon, and St. Bartholomew's Hospital, London, where he served as House Surgeon and Ophthalmic House Surgeon and became a Fellow of the Royal College of Surgeons. He joined the Sudan Medical Service in 1905 and was at first stationed in Khartoum but later moved to Port Sudan. He also served as the personal physician to the Maharajah of Nepal for one year. Upon retiring from the Sudan Medical Service in 1930 he was a private practitioner at Banbury, Oxfordshire, and later at Bookham, Surrey. He also served for many years as Chairman of the Ethical Committee of the British Medical Association and was a representative member of the General Medical Council. He also held posts with the British Red Cross and was Chairman of the Surrey Medical Committee.

Watson, Sir Frank Pears (1878–1941), educated at Winchester, entered the Egyptian Ministry of Public Works 1899, and served as Financial Secretary to the Ministry of Public Works from 1920. He succeeded Sir Reginald Patterson as Financial Adviser to the Egyptian government in 1927, a post that he held until his retirement in 1937. He married Audrey Florence Reid in 1913.

Wickham, Captain Guy Vivian (1890–1963), was attached to the Department of Health and Education of the Bombay Presidency and on 14 February 1924 was appointed Civil Administrator for Kamaran Island and Director of the Kamaran Lazaretto, a position he held until his retirement in 1935.

Wiggin, Arthur Francis Holme (1892–1935), educated at Felsted and Oriel College, Oxford, served in the Rifle Brigade and on various intelligence staffs during the First World War. He joined the diplomatic service in 1919 and was appointed 2nd Secretary, Cairo, in 1920 and 1st Secretary in 1925. He was transferred to Rome in 1927 and subsequently served in the Foreign Office, Washington, and Tokyo.

Williams, Elsie Noel Sims (1897–1966?), educated at Frances Holland Church of England School and North Foreland Lodge, journeyed to Palestine as a tourist in 1923 and was drawn into teaching at the Jerusalem Girls College. She remained on the staff until 1939 when she returned to England.

Wilson, Colonel the Right Honourable Sir Leslie Orme (1876–1955), educated at St. Michael's, Westgate, and St. Paul's School, served in the South African War, Gallipoli 1914–15, and in France 1915–16 until severely wounded. He was M.P. for Reading, 1913–22; Parliamentary Assistant Secretary to the War Cabinet, 1918; Chairman, National Maritime Board, 1919; Parliamentary Secretary to the Treasury and Chief Unionist Whip, 1921–23. He was the Governor of Bombay, 1923–28; and the Governor of Queensland from 1932 until his retirement in 1946.

Wilson, Thomas Murray (1881–), educated in a military school, business college, and at a summer artillery school in France, employed in the cotton business, in a bank, and in farming, 1899–1916. He served in the U. S. Army in 1917–19 and was appointed as the American Consul at Hankow, China, and thereafter served in various posts in China and India. In 1925 he was detailed as a Foreign Service Inspector. He later served as Chief, Division of Foreign Service Personnel, and Consul-General at Sydney, 1937–40; Calcutta, 1940–41; and Commissioner of the United States to India with the rank of Minister, 1941. He was the Minister and Consul-General at Baghdad in 1942, and retired from the Foreign Service in 1944.

Wingate, General Sir Francis Reginald (1861–1953), attended the Royal Military Academy, Woolwich, entering the Royal Army as a Lieutenant in 1880. Early duty (1881–83) took him to India and Aden. He joined the Egyptian Army in 1883, serving in various positions until promoted to Captain and Baronet-Major in 1889. From 1889–99 he gained distinction in numerous campaigns, including the Nile Campaign against the Mahdist forces in the Sudan. In 1899 he was promoted to Colonel and Sirdar of the Egyptian Army and Governor-General of the Anglo-Egyptian Sudan (1899–1916). It was during this time that he made the acquaintance of Gilbert Clayton, who became his private secretary in 1908. In 1903 he was promoted to Major-General, 1908 to Lieutenant-General, and 1913 to General. During the war years he was High Commissioner in Egypt (1917–19), while serving as G.O.C. Hijaz Operations (1916–19). He retired from the army in 1922, entering private business. He served as the Director of Tanganyika Concessions Limited, and associated companies, until April 1945. He also became the author of various books on the Sudan. In 1888 he married Catherine Leslie Rundle, daughter of Captain Joseph Sparkhall Rundle, R.N.

Winter, Reginald Keble (1883–1955), educated at King's Lynn, Felsted, St. Andrews, and Oriel College, Oxford, joined the Sudan Political

Service in 1908 and served in Khartoum; Halfa', 1909–1910; Red Sea, 1910–12; Legal Department, 1913–16; Assistant Civil Secretary, 1917–20; Deputy Governor, Red Sea, 1921; Bahr al-Ghazal, 1921–25; Red Sea, 1925–26; Assistant Civil Secretary, 1926–32; and Secretary for Education until his retirement in 1937.

Woodward, Captain Hugh Joseph (1886–1943), served in the First World War (despatches, D.S.O. and Bar), and as Commander was Senior Naval Officer, Red Sea, until placed on the retired list in 1926. He was promoted to Captain, retired, in 1931.

Woolley, Sir Charles Leonard (1880–1960), educated at St. John's, Leatherhead, and New College Oxford, became the Assistant Keeper, Ashmolean Museum, Oxford, 1905–07; excavated at Corbridge, 1906–07; Nubia, 1907–12; Carchemish, 1912–14. During the First World War he worked in intelligence in Egypt and was a prisoner in Turkey 1916–18. After the war he excavated in Egypt, 1921–22; and then began his greatest excavations at Ur which extended from 1922 to 1934. He also excavated at Al-Mina in Syria 1936–37 and at Atchana, Hatay, 1937–39.

Wormald, the Reverend Robert Leonard (1882–1960), was Probationary Chaplain, Colaba 1914–16 and in the following year was temporarily placed under the Army Department. He then served as Assistant Army Chaplain, Deolali, 1919; Chaplain, Ghorpuri, 1923; Aden, 1925–26; Bombay, 1927; Senior Army Chaplain, Belgaum, 1928–29; Colaba, 1930–32. He retired in 1935.

Worthington, Colonel Sir Edward Scott (1876–1953), educated privately and at Trinity University, Toronto, entered the Royal Army Medical Corps in 1900 and served in the South African war and the European war. He was Medical Officer on the staff of the Duke of Connaught for opening of the Union of South Africa Parliament; and when Governor-General of Canada, 1911–14; and at the opening of the Princes Council, India, 1920–21. He retired from the Corps in 1926. He was not in fact an M.P.

Yahya ibn Muhammad Hamid ad-Din, Imam (ruled 1904–48), succeeded to the Imamate on the death of his father, the Imam Muhammad Al Mansur. Yahya took the title Al Mutawakkil 'ala Allah, "the Relier on God," and had two ambitions, to consolidate his rule throughout the Yemen and to drive out the Turkish invaders. He continued the revolt against the Turks but was compelled to come to terms in 1913. The First World War accomplished what Yahya could not do, and following the Armistice of Mudros the Turks departed. In subsequent years Yahya consolidated his control in the highlands and in 1925 extended his rule to the Tihama which he captured from the Idrisi. Since the departure of the Turks, he had also occupied areas in the Aden Protectorate from which he eventually withdrew in 1928 after the conclusion of the Anglo-Yemeni Agreement in 1934. In 1933 he attempted to extend his northern frontier but was opposed by Ibn Sa'ud. The boundary was fixed in the Treaty of Taif, 1934. Thereafter he confined his activities to the Yemen and continued to rule until, over eighty years old, he was assassinated in January 1948 by a rival party wishing to forestall the succession of Imam Yahya's son, Ahmad.

Yousef Pasha Suleiman [Yusuf Sulayman Pasha] (1862– ?) was educated at the Coptic School in Clot Bey Street (Madrasat al-'Aqbat al Kubra), Cairo, where he received his primary and secondary education. In 1878 he was admitted to the School of Administration, later known as the School of Law, from which he graduated in 1881 with a B.A. degree. He then worked as a clerk in the Mixed Courts and in 1883 transferred to the National Courts. In 1884 he was appointed assistant to the prosecution of the Egyptian Court and became Chief Prosecutor in 1890. In 1902 he was appointed Chief of the Prosecution of the Appellate Court and in 1906 judge of the Mixed Court of Mansurah. In 1909 he transferred to Cairo as judge at the Mixed Court. In 1916 he was promoted to Counsellor in the National Appellate Court. He served as Minister of Agriculture and Minister of Finance in the cabinets of Muhammad Tawfiq Nasim Pasha, 1920–23. He was a Member of the official delegation sent to London in 1919. He and his relatives erected the Greek Church in Sandabis and founded two schools affiliated with it.

Yusuf Yasin, Shaykh (c. 1890–1962), a Syrian from Latakiya, was formerly a schoolmaster in Jerusalem before joining Faysal at 'Aqabah and accompanying him to Damascus. He was expelled from Damascus by the French, served King Husayn at Mecca, and later the Amir 'Abd Allah at 'Amman. He arrived in Arabia about 1923 where he joined the Wahhabi cause and gained the confidence of Ibn Sa'ud who appointed him Political Secretary. He started *Umm al Qura*, the official gazette of the Sa'udi Arabian government, and remained its editor for some years. He took part in the negotiations with Sir Gilbert Clayton in 1925, 1927, and 1928. He was the delegate from Najd at the

Muslim Congress of 1926, and acted as Deputy Minister of Foreign Affairs from 1926 onward. In 1935 he went to Baghdad to negotiate the Sa'udi-'Iraqi Treaty of Brotherhood and Alliance, and in 1942 negotiated the Sa'udi-Kuwaiti Agreement. He was the Sa'udi delegate at the Preparatory Committee meeting of the Arab Conference at Alexandria in October 1944, and signed the Covenant of the Arab League on behalf of Sa'udi Arabia in March 1945. He accompanied Ibn Sa'ud to Egypt in 1945 for his meeting with President Roosevelt and Mr. Churchill and returned again to Egypt with Ibn Sa'ud later in the year for a state visit. In 1946 he was appointed Minister of State. He was the Sa'udi delegate at the Damascus Conference in 1952. Thereafter he played an active role in public life until his death in 1962.

Zaid, Amir [Zayd ibn Husayn, Amir] (1898–), the son of Husayn ibn 'Ali, was educated at Balliol College, Oxford, and in 1922 went to Mosul to strengthen the position of his half brother King Faysal in that area. He accompanied his father into exile on Cyprus after Ibn Sa'ud had forced Husayn to flee from the Hijaz. In 1932 he was appointed 'Iraqi Minister to Turkey and in 1935 was made 'Iraqi Minister in Berlin. He was the 'Iraqi Ambassador to Great Britain from 1946 until the revolution of 1958, after which he lived in retirement in England.

Ziwer Pasha [Ziwar Pasha Ahmad] (1864–1945), educated at the College of Lazarists, Alexandria, the Université St.-Joseph, Beirut, and the Faculty of Law at Aix-en-Provence, held numerous positions in the Native Courts of Justice, Egypt, before he became Governor of Alexandria in 1913. From 1918 to 1924 he served in numerous government positions, including Minister at Rome, President of the Senate, and several ministerial posts in Egyptian governments. In 1924 he became Prime Minister after the resignation of Zaghlul Pasha over the crisis following upon the assassination of Sir Lee Stack. His moderate ministry, however, could not find sufficient support in parliament, and rather than turn the government over to the radical opposition, he convinced King Fu'ad to dissolve parliament. Although the Ittihad, a palace party, attempted to take advantage of this, Ziwar was able to retain his power until the elections of May 1926, when the opposition Wafd Party was returned in such overwhelming numbers that Ziwar resigned and thereafter played no major role in Egyptian politics.

Bibliography

In 1963 the papers of Sir Gilbert Clayton were deposited by his family in the Sudan Archive, Durham University, where they are available for use by acknowledged scholars. The collection includes letters to his parents from the Sudan between 1896 and 1902, and a very full and detailed correspondence with Sir Reginald Wingate, Governor-General of the Sudan, covering the years 1910–16 which complements Wingate's very full and detailed correspondence with Clayton also on deposit in the Sudan Archive. There is a full correspondence with Sir Lee Stack 1915–17, press clippings, and the important correspondence concerning Egyptian affairs 1921–22. There is then, of course, correspondence and reports concerning his first mission to Ibn Sa'ud and the Imam of the Yemen described in the Diary. There is also correspondence about his second and third missions to Ibn Sa'ud. During my researches I have examined the material listed above with great care. I have not, however, seen Sir Gilbert's correspondence regarding Palestine which, I believe, has subsequently been placed with the rest of his papers.

The intention of this bibliography is to provide the reader with a selected list of published sources in which the activities of Sir Gilbert Clayton are recorded or the events in which he took part are described.

Antonius, George. *The Arab Awakening*. New York, 1939.

Aldington, Richard. *Lawrence of Arabia: A Biographical Enquiry*. Chicago, 1955.

Armstrong, H. C. *Lord of Arabia: A Biography of Abdul Aziz Ibn Saud*. Beirut.

Bell, Lady Florence, ed. *The Letters of Gertrude Bell*. New York, 1927.

Bénoist-Méchin, Jacques G. P. M. *Ibn Séoud ou la naissance d'un royaume*. Paris, 1955.

——. *Le loup et le leopard*. Paris, 1954. (English translation, by Denis Weaver, as *Arabian Destiny*. London, 1957.)

Béraud-Villars, Jean M. E. *T. E. Lawrence or Search for the Absolute.* London, 1958.

Bowman, Humphrey. *Middle East Window.* London, 1942.

Brémond, Général Édouard. *Le Hedjaz dans la Guerre Mondiale.* Paris, 1931.

Bullard, Sir Reader. *Britain and the Middle East.* London, 1951.

———. *The Camels Must Go: An Autobiography.* London, 1961.

Burgoyne, Elizabeth, ed. *Gertrude Bell from her Personal Papers, 1914–1926.* 2d vol. London, 1961.

Cumming, Henry H. *Franco-British Rivalry in the Post-War Near East.* London, 1938.

Dickson, H. R. P. *Kuwait and Her Neighbors.* London, 1956.

Glubb, Sir John Bagot. *Britain and the Arabs.* London, 1959.

———. *War in the Desert: An R.A.F. Frontier Campaign.* London, 1960.

Graves, Philip P., ed. *The Memoirs of King Abdullah of Trans-jordan.* London, 1950.

———. *The Life of Sir Percy Cox.* London, 1941.

Hanna, Paul L. *British Policy in Palestine.* Washington, 1942.

Hickinbotham, Sir Tom. *Aden.* London, 1958.

Hurewitz, J. C. *Diplomacy in the Near East. A Documentary Record.* 2 vols. Princeton, 1956.

Ingrams, William Harold. *The Yemen, Imams, Rulers, and Revolutions.* London, 1963.

Ireland, P. W. *Iraq, A Study in Political Development.* London, 1937.

Kheirallah, George. *Arabia Reborn.* Albuquerque, 1952.

Kohn, Hans. *A History of Nationalism in the East.* New York, 1929.

———. *Nationalism and Imperialism in the Hither East.* London, 1932.

Lawrence, Thomas Edward. *Revolt in the Desert.* New York, 1927.

———. *Seven Pillars of Wisdom.* Garden City, 1936.

Lenczowski, George. *The Middle East in World Affairs.* Ithaca, 1956.

———. *Oil and State in the Middle East.* Ithaca, 1960.

Liddell Hart, Basil H. *Colonel Lawrence.* New York, 1934.

Lloyd, Lord (George). *Egypt Since Cromer.* 2 vols. London, 1933.

Longrigg, Stephen H. *'Iraq, 1900 to 1950.* London, 1953.

———. *Oil in the Middle East.* London, 1960.

McMunn, Sir George Fletcher. *Military Operations, Egypt and Palestine from June 1917 to the End of the War.* Vol. 1. "History of the Great War." London, 1930.

Marlowe, John. *Arab Nationalism and British Imperialism.* New York, 1961.

Memorial of the Government of Saudi Arabia. Vol. 1. 1955.

Nutting, Anthony. *Lawrence of Arabia.* New York, 1961.

Philby, H. St. John B. *Arabian Days, An Autobiography.* London, 1948.

———. *Arabian Jubilee.* London, 1952.

———. *The Heart of Arabia.* 2 vols. New York, 1922.

———. *Sa'udi Arabia.* New York. 1955.

Rendel, Sir George. *The Sword and the Olive. Recollections of Diplomacy and the Foreign Service, 1913–1954.* London, 1957.

Great Britain. Colonial Office. *Report by His Britannic Majesty's Government to the Council of the League of Nations on the Administration of Iraq for the Year 1925.* Colonial, no. 21. London, 1926.

———. ———. *Report by His Britannic Majesty's Government to the Council of the League of Nations on the Administration of Iraq for the Year 1926.* Colonial, no. 29. London, 1927.

———. ———. *Report by His Majesty's Government in the United Kingdom and Northern Ireland to the Council of the League of Nations on the Administration of Iraq for the Year 1928.* Colonial, no. 44. London, 1929.

———. Royal Institute of International Affairs. *British Security.* London, 1946.

———. ———. *Great Britain and Egypt, 1914–1951.* Information Papers No. 19. London, 1952.

———. ———. *Great Britain and Palestine, 1915–45.* Information Papers No. 20. London, 1946.

Sanger, Richard H. *The Arabian Peninsula.* Ithaca, 1954.

Seton-Watson, M. V. *Britain and the Arab States.* London, 1948.

Storrs, Sir Ronald. *The Memoirs of Sir Ronald Storrs.* New York, 1937.

Toynbee, Arnold J. "The Islamic World Since the Peace Settlement," in *Survey of International Affairs,* 1925. Vol. 1, Oxford, 1927.

Twitchell, K. S. *Saudi Arabia.* Princeton, 1958.

Williams, Kenneth. *Ibn Sa'ud, The Puritan King of Arabia.* London, 1933.

Wilson, Arnold T. *Loyalties, Mesopotamia 1914–1917.* London, 1930.

———.*Mesopotamia 1917–1920, A Clash of Loyalties.* Oxford, 1931.

Wingate, Sir Ronald. *Wingate of the Sudan.* London, 1955.

Young, Sir Hubert. *The Independent Arab.* London, 1933.

Zeine, Zeine N. *The Struggle for Arab Independence.* Beirut, 1960.

Index